SCRIBAL TOOLS IN ANCIENT ISRAEL

HISTORY, ARCHAEOLOGY, AND CULTURE OF THE LEVANT

Edited by

JEFFREY A. BLAKELY, *University of Wisconsin, Madison*

K. LAWSON YOUNGER, *Trinity Evangelical Divinity School*

1. *The Horsemen of Israel: Horses and Chariotry in Monarchic Israel (Ninth–Eighth Centuries B.C.E.)*, by Deborah O'Daniel Cantrell
2. *Donkeys in the Biblical World: Ceremony and Symbol*, by Kenneth C. Way
3. *The Wilderness Itineraries: Genre, Geography, and the Growth of Torah*, by Angela R. Roskop
4. *Temples and Sanctuaries from the Early Iron Age Levant: Recovery after Collapse*, by William E. Mierse
5. *Poetic Astronomy in the Ancient Near East: The Reflexes of Celestial Science in the Literature of Ancient Mesopotamia, Ugarit, and Israel*, by Jeffrey L. Cooley
6. *A Monetary and Political History of the Phoenician City of Byblos in the Fifth and Fourth Centuries B.C.E.*, by J. Elayi and A. G. Elayi
7. *The Land before the Kingdom of Israel: A History of the Southern Levant and the People Who Populated It*, by Brendon C. Benz
8. *Baal, St. George, and Khidr*, by Robert D. Miller II
9. *Scribal Tools in Ancient Israel: A Study of Biblical Hebrew Terms for Writing Materials and Implements*, by Philip Zhakevich

Scribal Tools in Ancient Israel

A Study of Biblical Hebrew Terms for Writing Materials and Implements

PHILIP ZHAKEVICH

EISENBRAUNS | University Park, Pennsylvania

Library of Congress Cataloging-in-Publication Data

Names: Zhakevich, Philip, date– author.
Title: Scribal tools in ancient Israel : a study of biblical Hebrew terms for writing materials and implements / Philip Zhakevich.
Other titles: History, archaeology, and culture of the Levant.
Description: University Park, Pennsylvania : Eisenbrauns, [2020] | Series: History, archaeology, and culture of the Levant | Includes bibliographical references and index.
Summary: "Examines the technology of writing as it existed in ancient Israel. Utilizes the Hebrew Bible as its corpus and focuses on a set of Hebrew terms that designated writing surfaces and writing instruments"—Provided by publisher.
Identifiers: LCCN 2020029081 | ISBN 9781646020621 (hardback)
Subjects: LCSH: Writing materials and instruments—History—To 1500. | Hebrew language—Writing—History—To 1500. | Writing—Israel—History—To 1500.
Classification: LCC Z45.Z425 2020 | DDC 681/.609334—dc23
LC record available at https://lccn.loc.gov/2020029081

Printed in the United States of America
Published by The Pennsylvania State University Press
University Park, PA 16802-1003

Eisenbrauns is an imprint of The Pennsylvania State University Press.

The Pennsylvania State University Press is a member of the Association of University Presses.

It is the policy of The Pennsylvania State University Press to use acid-free paper. Publications on uncoated stock satisfy the minimum requirements of American National Standard for Information Sciences—Permanence of Paper for Printed Library Material, ANSI Z39.48–1992.

CONTENTS

List of Figures and Tables ix
Acknowledgments xi
List of Abbreviations xiii

CHAPTER 1. Introduction 1
1.1. Summary of Previous Research 2
1.2. Methodology 5

CHAPTER 2. Papyrus 8
2.1. Reeds, Marshes, and Papyrus in the Ancient World 8
2.2. The Terms *ʾāḥû*, *biṣṣā*, *ʾēbe*, *ʿārôt*, and *gebeʾ* 13
2.3. The Term *ḥāṣîr* 20
2.4. The Terms *ʾăgam* and *ʾagmôn*/*ʾagmōn* 22
2.5. The Term *qāne* 27
2.6. The Term *sûp* 30
2.7. The Term *gōmeʾ* 36
2.8. Definitions of Terms Designating Reeds, Marshes, and Papyrus 43

CHAPTER 3. Stone and Plaster 45
3.1. Stone 45
3.1.1. Writing on Stone in the Ancient World 45
3.1.2. Geological Properties of Limestone and Basalt 48
3.1.3. The Terms *ʾeben*, *maṣṣēbā*/*maṣṣebet*, and *gāzît* 49
3.1.4. The Terms *selaʿ* and *ṣûr* 53
3.1.5. Definitions of Terms Designating Stone Surfaces 56
3.2. Mud, Clay, Plaster, and Whitewash 57
3.2.1. Mud, Clay, Plaster, and Whitewash in the Ancient World 57
3.2.2. The Terms *bōṣ* (and *biṣṣā*), *repeš*, and *yāwēn* 60
3.2.3. The Term *ʿāpār* 63

3.2.4. The Terms *ṭîṭ* and *ḥōmer* 65
3.2.5. The Terms *ṭîaḥ* (and *ṭ-w-ḥ*) and *tāpēl* (and *ṭ-p-l*) 71
3.2.6. The Term *śîd* (and *ś-y-d*) 78
3.2.7. Definitions of Terms Designating Mud, Clay, Plaster, and Whitewash 83

CHAPTER 4. Skins, Scrolls, Tablets, Ostraca, and Uncommon Writing Surfaces 85
4.1. Animal Skins (*ʿôr*) 85
4.1.1. Use of Leather in the Ancient World 85
4.1.2. The Term *ʿôr* 86
4.1.3. Archeological Evidence for Writing on Animal Skins 87
4.2. Scrolls, Tablets, and Ostraca 89
4.2.1. The Term *məgillā* (and *məgillat sēper*) 89
4.2.2. The Term *delet* 94
4.2.3. The Term *gillāyôn* 97
4.2.4. The Term *lûaḥ* 102
4.2.5. The Term *ḥereś* 110
4.2.6. Definitions of Terms Designating Scrolls, Tablets, and Ostraca 115
4.3. Uncommon Writing Surfaces 115
4.3.1. Writing on a Staff, *maṭṭe* (Numbers 17:16–26) 116
4.3.2. Writing on a Wooden Stick, *ʿēṣ* (Ezekiel 37:15–20) 118
4.3.3. Writing on a Rosette of Pure Gold, *ṣîṣ zāhāb ṭāhôr* (Exodus 28:36–38; 39:30–31) 122

CHAPTER 5. Scribal Instruments and Glyptics 124
5.1. Writing Instruments 124
5.1.1. The Term *ʿēṭ* (*ʿēṭ barzel*, *ʿēṭ sōpēr/sōpərîm*) 124
5.1.2. The Phrase *ṣippōren šāmîr* 129
5.1.3. The Term *ḥereṭ* 133
5.1.4. The Term *śered* 135
5.2. Accessories of the Scribal Kit 136
5.2.1. The Term *dəyô* 136
5.2.2. The Phrase *qeset hassōpēr* 139
5.2.3. The Phrase *taʿar hassōpēr* 143
5.2.4. Definitions of Terms Designating Writing Instruments and Accessories of the Scribal Kit 145
5.2.5. Note on Scribal Training in Ancient Israel and the Scribal Tool Set 146
5.2.6. Production of Monumental Inscriptions and the Tools Involved 147

5.3. Glyptics 148
5.3.1. Seals in the Ancient World and Ancient Israel 149
5.3.2. Engraved Precious Stones and Weights 152
5.3.3. The Terms *ḥôtām*/*ḥōtām* and *ḥōtemet* 155
5.3.4. The Term *ṭabbaʿat* 157
5.3.5. Bullas and Jar Handles 158
5.3.6. Definitions of Terms Designating Seals 159

CHAPTER 6. Egypt's Influence on Canaan and Ancient Israel. 160
6.1. Egypt's Contact with Canaan and Ancient Israel 160
6.2. The Influence of Egypt and Mesopotamia on Writing Technology in Canaan and Ancient Israel 163

CHAPTER 7. Conclusion 169

Works Cited. 171
Ancient Sources Index 195
Subject Index 207

FIGURES AND TABLES

Figures

2.1. Ink-on-papyrus document from Elephantine 12
3.1. Code of Hammurabi 46
3.2. Tel Dan stele 46
3.3. Mesha stele 47
3.4. Siloam tunnel inscription 47
3.5. Beer-Sheba horned altar 55
3.6. Balaam son of Beor inscription from Deir ʿAlla 82
4.1. Great Isaiah Scroll 88
4.2. Gezer calendar 104
4.3. Amman citadel inscription 105
4.4. Assyrian ivory writing boards 108
4.5. Egyptian wooden writing board 108
4.6. Arad letter 24 112
4.7. Minaic inscription on palm-leaf stalk 121
5.1. Egyptian palette and pens 141
5.2. Egyptian scribal knife 145
5.3. Seals from Iron Age II Israel 150
5.4. Seal impressions from Jerusalem 151
5.5. LMLK jar handle impression 152
5.6. Engraved weights from Syria-Palestine 154

Tables

3.1. The Root *ḥ-m-r* in Biblical Hebrew 69
3.2. The Roots *t-p-l* and *ṭ-p-l* in Biblical Hebrew 73
5.1. Seals from Iron Age II Israel 132
5.2. Precious Stones of Exodus 28:17–21; 39:6, 10–14 153

ACKNOWLEDGMENTS

This book is a revision of my dissertation, which I completed at the University of Texas at Austin in August 2015. It is a joy, now, for me to thank the people who played a key role in the development of this project from its inception as a dissertation topic to its production as a book. First of all, I thank my teachers John Huehnergard and Jo Ann Hackett, who served as my supervisor and co-supervisor, respectively. John taught me comparative Semitics and a historical perspective on the Hebrew language, both of which have served as the foundation for all of my scholarly research. Likewise, I thank Jo Ann, who taught me ancient Hebrew epigraphy and trained me in the scholarly study of the Hebrew Bible. I am also grateful to Naʿama Pat-El and Jonathan Kaplan for their instructive comments on the project. Finally, I thank Christopher Rollston, who offered so much pertinent advice on how to refine this study.

I thank Eisenbrauns-Penn State University Press for accepting the manuscript for publication. It has been wonderful to work with Jim Eisenbraun and the representatives at Eisenbrauns, all of whom have provided helpful guidance throughout the publication process. I also thank the two external reviewers of the initial manuscript, whose judicious remarks have strengthened the argumentation of this work. Additionally, my good friend Ben Kantor deserves my thanks for providing assistance regarding various aspects of this book.

Much of the revision process of the manuscript took place at the library of the Institute of Archaeology at the Hebrew University of Jerusalem during the summer of 2016. I am grateful to the Hebrew University for giving me the opportunity to use its resources to revise this project. Columbia University provided me with the funding to travel to Israel in 2016, for which I am thankful. I am also grateful to my home department at Princeton University, the Department of Near Eastern Studies, for supporting this book project. While I began revising the manuscript at the Hebrew University of Jerusalem, the final revisions took place in the Firestone Library of Princeton University and in the Princeton

Theological Seminary library. I am indebted to both institutions for providing me with the academic resources needed for the completion of this book. I am also very grateful to Todd Bolen at BiblePlaces.com, who very graciously provided many images included in this book.

Most of all, I thank my family. My siblings Elizabeth and her husband Alex, Mark, Iosif, and Anya were a continual source of strength while I worked on this book. Likewise, my mother Natalya has supported this work from start to finish, and she deserves my highest thanks for teaching my siblings and me how to persevere despite seemingly insurmountable difficulties. This book is dedicated to her.

ABBREVIATIONS

Bibliographical

AB	Anchor Bible
AeL	Ägypten und Levante
AHw	Wolfram von Soden. *Akkadisches Handwörterbuch.* 3 vols. Wiesbaden, Harrossowitz, 1965–81
AnSt	*Anatolian Studies*
BA	*Biblical Archaeologist*
BASOR	*Bulletin of the American Schools of Oriental Research*
BDB	Francis Brown, S. R. Driver, and Charles A. Briggs. *A Hebrew and English Lexicon of the Old Testament*. Boston: Houghton, Mifflin and Company, 1906. Repr., Peabody, MA: Hendrickson, 2003
BHS	*Biblia Hebraica Stuttgartensia*. Edited by Karl Elliger and Wilhelm Rudolph. 4th ed. Stuttgart: Deutsche Bibelgesellschaft, 1990
CAD	*The Assyrian Dictionary of the Oriental Institute of the University of Chicago*. Edited by A. Leo Oppenheim, Erica Reiner, and Martha T. Roth. 21 vols. Chicago: The Oriental Institute of the University of Chicago, 1956–2010
CAL	*Comprehensive Aramaic Lexicon Project*. Edited by Stephen A. Kaufman. Cincinnati, OH: Hebrew Union College, 1986–. http://cal.huc.edu/
CDG	Wolf Leslau. *Comparative Dictionary of Geʿez (Classical Ethiopic): Geʿez-English, English-Geʿez with an index of the Semitic Roots*. Wiesbaden: Harrassowitz, 1987, 1991
CHANE	Culture and History of the Ancient Near East

DCH	*Dictionary of Classical Hebrew*. Edited by David J. A. Clines. 9 vols. Sheffield: Sheffield Phoenix Press, 1993–2014
DCH 2018	*Dictionary of Classical Hebrew Revised.* Edited by David J. A. Clines. Volume 1. Sheffield: Sheffield Phoenix Press, 2018
DLE	*A Dictionary of Late Egyptian.* Edited by Leonard H. Lesko and Barbara S. Lesko. 4 vols. Berkeley: B. C. Scribe, 1982–1989
DNWSI	Jacob Hoftijzer and Karel Jongeling. *Dictionary of the North-West Semitic Inscriptions*. 2 vols. Leiden: Brill, 1995
DSSC	Martin G. Abegg, James E. Bowley, and Edward M. Cook. *The Dead Sea Scrolls Concordance*. 3 vols. Leiden: Brill, 2003–2016
DSSR	Donald W. Parry, Emanuel Tov, and Geraldine I. Clements. *The Dead Sea Scrolls Reader*. 2 vols. 2nd ed. Leiden: Brill, 2014
DSSSMM	Millar Burrows. *The Dead Sea Scrolls of St. Mark's Monastery*. 2 vols. New Haven, CT: American Schools of Oriental Research, 1951
DULAT	Gregorio del Olmo Lete and Joaquín Sanmartín. *A Dictionary of the Ugaritic Language in the Alphabetic Tradition.* Translated and edited by Wilfred G. E. Watson. 2 volumes. 3rd ed. Leiden: Brill, 2015
GAG	Wolfram von Soden. *Grundriss der akkadischen Grammatik.* 3rd ed. Analecta Orientalia 33. Rome: Pontifical Biblical Institute, 1995
GHL	Harry A. Hoffner Jr. and H. Craig Melchert. *A Grammar of the Hittite Language*. 2 vols. Winona Lake, IN: Eisenbrauns, 2008
GMD	Wilhelm Gesenius, Rudolf Meyer, and Herbert Donner. *Hebräisches und Aramäisches Handworterbuch über das Alte Testament*. 18th ed. Edited by Rudolf Meyer and Herbert Donner. Berlin: Springer, 2013
HALOT	Ludwig Koehler, Walter Baumgartner, and Johann J. Stamm. *The Hebrew and Aramaic Lexicon of the Old Testament*. 2 vols. Leiden: Brill, 2001
HSS	Harvard Semitic Studies
IEJ	*Israel Exploration Journal*
JAOS	*Journal of the American Oriental Society*

JJS	*Journal of Jewish Studies*
J-M	Paul Joüon. *A Grammar of Biblical Hebrew*. Translated and revised by Takamitsu Muraoka. 2nd ed. Rome: Gregorian and Biblical Press, 2006. Repr. with corrections, 2011
KAI	Herbert Donner and Wolfgang Röllig. *Kanaanäische und aramäische Inschriften*. 3 vols. 3rd ed. Wiesbaden: Harrassowitz, 1971–1976
LSJ	Henry George Liddell, Robert Scott, and Henry Stuart Jones. *A Greek-English Lexicon*. 9th ed. with revised supplement. Oxford: Clarendon, 1996
OBO	Orbis Biblicus et Orientalis
SMNIA	Tel Aviv University Sonia and Marco Nadler Institute of Archaeology Monograph Series
TA	*Tel Aviv*
TDOT	Gerhard J. Botterweck and Helmer Ringren, eds. *Theological Dictionary of the Old Testament*. Translated by John T. Willis. 16 vols. Grand Rapids, MI: Eerdmans. 1976–2006
VT	*Vetus Testamentum*
WÄS	Adolph Erman and Hermann Grapow. *Wörterbuch der ägyptischen Sprache*. 5 vols. Leipzig: Hinrichs; Berlin: Akademie, 1926–1931. Repr., 1963

Other

PN	personal name
X > Y	X developed into Y
X < Y	X derives from Y
*	precedes reconstructed or unattested form
**	precedes an impossible form
/ /	enclose phonemic normalizations of words or individual phonemes
<Hebrew script>	enclose a letter omitted by a scribe but reconstructed by a modern scholar
[roman]	enclose phonetic pronunciations
[*italic*]	enclose damaged sign(s)

D. Dead Sea Scroll Documents

1QH^{a}	1QHodayot^{a}
1QpHab	1QPesher to Habakkuk
1Q28b	1QRule of Benedictions (1QSb)

1Q33	1QWar Scroll (1QM)
4Q69	4QIsaiah[p] (pap4QIsa[p])
4Q120	4QSeptuagint Leviticus[b] (4QpapLXXLev[b])
4Q121	4QSeptuagint Numbers (4QLXXNum)
4Q158	4QReworked Pentateuch[a] (4QBibPar = 4QRP[a])
4Q160	4QVision of Samuel (4QVisSam)
4Q162	4QIsaiah Pesher[b] (4QpIsa[b])
4Q169	4QNahum Pesher (4QpNah)
4Q171	4QPsalms Pesher[a] (4QpPs[a])
4Q177	Catena A (4QCatena A = 4QMidrEschat[b]?)
4Q185	4QSapiental Work
4Q264a	4QHalakhah B
4Q266	4QDamascus Document[a] (4QD[a])
4Q270	4QDamascus Document[e] (4QD[e])
4Q271	4QDamascus Document[f] (4QD[f])
4Q274	4QPurification Rules A (4QTohorot A)
4Q276	4QPurification Rules B[a] (Tohorot B[a])
4Q299	4QMysteries[a] (4QMyst[a])
4Q300	4QMysteries[b] (4QMyst[b])
4Q364	4QReworked Pentateuch[b] (4QRP[b])
4Q365	4QReworked Pentateuch[c] (4QRP[c])
4Q368	4Qapocryphon Pentateuch A (4QapocrPent A)
4Q372	4Qapocryphon Joseph[b] (4QapocrJoseph[b])
4Q377	4Qapocryphon Pentateuch B (4QapocrPent B)
4Q381	4QNon-Canonical Psalms B
4Q382	4QParaphrase of Kings (4Qpap paraKings et al.)
4Q411	4QSapiental Hymn
4Q421	4QWays of Righteousness[b]
4Q424	4QSapiental Text (Instruction-like Composition B)
4Q491	4QWar Scroll[a] (4QM[a])
4Q509	4QFestivals Prayer[c] (4QpapPrFêtes[c])
5Q20	Unclassified Fragments
6Q4	6QKings (6QpapKgs)
6Q7	6QDaniel (6QpapDan)
7Q1	4QSeptuagint Exodus (7QLXXExod)
11Q19	Temple Scroll[a] (11QT[a])
11Q21	Temple Scroll[c]? (11QT[c]?)
CD	Damascus Document (Cairo Geniza)
PAM	Unclassified Fragment

CHAPTER I

Introduction

WRITING IN THE SOUTHERN LEVANT has existed since the second millennium BCE. Already in the Middle and Late Bronze Ages, two distinct writing technologies are evident in Canaan: cuneiform and alphabetic. Artifacts inscribed with cuneiform, primarily in Akkadian, have been uncovered at sites such as Hazor, Taanach, Megiddo, and Aphek. And, while the corpus of such finds is not extensive—almost seventy diverse objects (e.g., tablets, seals) from Canaan and about one hundred tablets from Amarna that originated in Canaan—the existence of such a corpus suggests that cuneiform was actively studied and utilized on an administrative level in the southern Levant (Horowitz, Oshima, and Sanders 2018, 4–7; Cohen 2019, 248–252, 254). Besides cuneiform finds, fragmentary artifacts with alphabetic writing from the Middle Bronze Age through Iron Age I have been unearthed in various Canaanite locations, including Lachish, Shechem, Gezer, and Beth Shemesh. Such artifacts, inscribed with Canaanite dialect(s), demonstrate that an alphabetic writing system existed in the southern Levant, a system that has its origin in Egypt. Although alphabetic writing is attested in Canaan since the nineteenth century BCE, the number of finds inscribed with alphabetic writing is not extensive, with only around forty extant artifacts (Sass 1988, 51–52, 174–79; Finkelstein and Sass 2013). Despite the paucity of alphabetic finds from the second millennium BCE, almost all finds from ancient Israel beginning with Iron Age II are alphabetic in nature. In essence, during the last two centuries of the second millennium BCE, a transition took place in which cuneiform writing was displaced by an alphabetic writing system, which would be inherited by ancient Israel.

The writing practices of the southern Levant after the alphabetic writing system had fully taken root in the region comprise the focus of this study. Specifically, the study concerns ancient Israel's technology of writing during Iron Age II. Utilizing the Hebrew Bible as its corpus and focusing on a set of Hebrew terms that designated writing surfaces and writing instruments, this examination synthesizes the semantic data of the Bible with the archeological and art historical evidence for writing in ancient Israel. The aim of this work is twofold: to present a lexicographical analysis of Biblical Hebrew terms related to Israel's technology of writing, and to draw conclusions on the origin of ancient Israel's writing practices. The bulk of this work (chapters 2–5) relates to the first goal; namely, to present a thorough evaluation of relevant Hebrew terms. In order to address the second goal, chapter 6 evaluates the findings of chapters 2–5 in light of ancient writing practices, especially focusing on the ties that Canaan and Israel had with ancient Egypt over the centuries. The argument ultimately put forth in chapter 6 is that Israel's most common form of writing—writing with ink on ostraca and papyrus—is Egyptian in nature and was introduced into Canaan by Egypt during the New Kingdom (1549–1069 BCE), a period when Egypt exercised political domination over the Levant.

1.1. Summary of Previous Research

When one considers the existing scholarship concerning issues of writing in ancient Israel, it quickly becomes apparent that much has been written on education, literacy, and scribes.[1] These topics have also been researched in regard to Mesopotamia, Egypt, and the Greco-Roman world.[2] While there is an abundance of works on literacy and related topics, there are few works that contain discussions of the mechanics of writing in ancient Israel. The current study seeks to fill this lacuna in research by examining Biblical Hebrew terms that designate writing surfaces and instruments in light of the archeological and art historical evidence available for the relevant lexemes. While works on Israel's writing technology seldom synthesize the semantic data of the Bible with the archeological and art historical evidence, it is worth noting those that have done this in the past as well as other works particularly relevant for this study.

Although few in number, there are some works that consider the technology of writing as it existed in ancient Israel. Driver's *Semitic Writing* (1976)

1. Scholars writing on such topics include Carr 2005; Crenshaw 1998; Byrne 2007; G. I. Davies 1995; P. R. Davies 1998; P. R. Davies and Römer 2013; Demsky 2012; Demsky and Bar-Ilan 2004; Hess 2002, 2006; Hezser 2001; Jamieson-Drake 1991; Lemaire 1981, 1984, 1992, 2001, 2015; Na'aman 2015; Niditch 1996; Richelle 2016; Rollston 2006, 2010, 2015; Sanders 2009; Schmidt 2015; Schniedewind 2004, 2013, 2014, 2017, 2019; van der Toorn 2007; Whisenant 2015. See Quick (2014) for a summary and a critique of the main works. Work has also been done on the origin of the alphabet and the development of the Hebrew script; e.g., Cross 1989, 2003a; Driver 1976; Finkelstein and Sass 2013; Goldwasser 1991, 2016; Hackett and Aufrecht 2014; Hamilton 2006; Lemaire 2017; Naveh 1987, 2009; Rico and Attucci 2015; Sass 1988, 2005; Vanderhooft 2017.

2. Scholars evaluating these questions include Baines 2007; Bowman and Woolf 1994; Brunner 1991; Carr 2005; Cohen 2009; Hagen 2006, 2007, 2011, 2013; Harris 1991; J. J. Janssen 1992; R. M. Janssen and J. J. Janssen 1990; Johnson and Parker 2009; McDowell 1996; 1999, 127–64; 2000; Morgan 1998; Piacentini 2002; Thomas 1992; van Egmond and van Soldt 2012; van Heel and Haring 2003; Veldhuis 1997; Visicato 2000.

discusses the various tools and writing materials of the ancient Near East and connects the textual data of the Bible with archeological and art historical evidence from the ancient Near East. King and Stager's *Life in Biblical Israel* (2001) has a succinct and helpful description of certain tools of writing in ancient Israel. Galling's "Tafel, Buch und Blatt" looks at the main terms for writing within the Bible (1971). Tov's *Scribal Practices and Approaches Reflected in the Texts Found in the Judean Desert* (2004) discusses the technology of writing in the Qumran community. Rollston's *Writing and Literacy in the World of Ancient Israel* (2010) has a section on the attested forms of writing material (e.g., stone, ostraca, papyrus). The 1986 dissertation by van der Kooij, "Early Northwest Semitic Script Traditions," closely analyzes alphabetic inscriptions in an effort to understand how the shapes of the letters were affected by the tools used to write each inscription (1986), while the collection of articles in Hoftijzer and van der Kooij's *Aramaic Texts from Deir ʿAlla* (1976) contains an analysis of the plaster of the Deir ʿAlla inscription as well as a discussion of the ink and pens used to produce the inscription. These last two works provide useful information regarding the mechanics of ancient Israel's writing technology, although they do not limit their discussion to ancient Israel.

Various works discuss individual words or a small group of words related to writing in ancient Israel. *TDOT* (1974–2006) includes semantic studies of various terms (e.g., *lûaḥ*, *ʿēṭ*, *qāne*). Noonan (2019), Muchiki (1999), and Lambdin (1953) discuss the Egyptian origins of certain writing-related Hebrew terms (e.g., *dəyô*, *qeset*, *gōmeʾ*). Hurvitz (1997; 1996) has contributed diachronic studies of terms such as *ʾiggeret*, *sēper*, and *məgillat sēper*. The commentary on Jeremiah by Lundbom (1999, 514, 776) has helpful comments on terms such as *ʿēṭ*, *ḥereṭ*, and *ṣippōren*. Hicks (1983) traces the concept of the term *delet* back to the Akkadian terms *daltu* and *lēʾu*, arguing that a scroll (*məgillā*) resembled in appearance the ancient polyptych writing boards. A brief article by Hyatt (1943) considers a number of the terms from an archeological perspective. Koller's *The Semantic Field of Cutting Tools in Biblical Hebrew* (2012) includes a section on the scribal knife (*taʿar hassōpēr*), while Millard (1997) collects and glosses many of the biblical terms related to writing. There are also websites that contain information on biblical terms related to writing. For instance, the Semantic Dictionary of Biblical Hebrew website (http://www.sdbh.org/) gathers and glosses most of the writing-related terminology. The כלי Database: Utensils in the Hebrew Bible website (http://www.otw-site.eu/en/kli-database/) also has brief articles on various terms connected to writing. Although they lack a discussion of the archeological and art historical evidence, they are helpful because they attempt to map out the meanings of terms related to writing.

Certain works discuss both general and specific aspects of the technology of writing in the ancient world. Diringer's *The Book Before Printing: Ancient,*

Medieval, and Oriental (1953) has a discussion of the technology of writing in the ancient Near East as well as in ancient Greece and Rome; McLean's *An Introduction to Greek Epigraphy of the Hellenistic and Roman Periods from Alexander the Great down to the Reign of Constantine (323 B.C.–A.D. 337)* has a helpful synopsis of the production of lapidary inscriptions in ancient Greece (2002, 1–23). Avrin's *Scribes, Script, and Books* (1991) presents a nice survey of the writing materials and tools used by various cultures in the ancient world. Ellison's 2002 dissertation, "A Paleographic Study of the Alphabetic Cuneiform Texts from Ras Shamra/Ugarit," contains helpful information on the metal styli of Ugarit. Various articles discuss the writing instruments of the ancient Near East (Taylor 2011; Bülow-Jacobsen 2009; Vernus 2002; Black and Tait 2000; Gunter 2000; Pearce 2000; Wente 2000; Whitt 2000; Breasted 1905). Dougherty (1928) considers the use of parchment and papyrus in Mesopotamia, while other articles focus on ancient writing boards (Warnock and Pendleton 1991; Payton 1991; Wiseman 1955). Moore's master's thesis, entitled "Writing Religion: A Study on the Scribes, Materials and Methods Used in the Writing of the Hebrew Prophecies," contains a helpful chapter that collects writing-related lexemes of the Bible and focuses on the use of writing boards in the ancient Near East (Moore 2011, 32–66). Pritchard's *The Ancient Near East in Pictures Relating to the Old Testament* (1974) contains many pictures of actual finds from the ancient Near East. Ashton's *Scribal Habits in the Ancient Near East* (2008) is focused on the technical side of writing in the ancient world. It covers practically all issues concerning the mechanics of writing, including details of layout conventions of inscriptions as well as dimensions of pens, scrolls, and tablets.

Several works focus on the utilization of papyrus in the ancient Near East. Černý's very brief book, *Paper and Books in Ancient Egypt* (1952), discusses the technology of making and using papyrus as a writing material; the book also presents information about writing tools. Bierbrier's edited volume, *Papyrus: Structure and Usage* (1986), consists of studies devoted to close analysis of the papyrus used during different periods in Egyptian history. Lewis's *Papyrus in Classical Antiquity* (1974) focuses on two main topics—the preparation of papyrus and its widespread use in the ancient world. Various scholars have addressed the question of whether biblical texts were written on leather or papyrus. Some scholars have argued that leather was used as early as the First Temple period (Demsky 2007, 238; Hicks 1983, 60–61). Other scholars, however, hold that biblical texts were initially written on papyrus and then on leather during and after the Persian Period (Haran 1982, 1983; Lemaire 1992, 1003; Whitt 2000, 2393).

Other works discuss the artifacts related to the technology of writing. For instance, Nicholson and Shaw's *Ancient Egyptian Materials and Technology* (2000) and Moorey's *Ancient Mesopotamian Materials and Industries: The Archeological Evidence* (1999) contain discussions of Egyptian and

Mesopotamian artifacts used to produce writing implements. Also, one must not forget to mention the collections of the actual inscriptions from the land of Israel and Transjordan; Aḥituv (2008), Dobbs-Allsopp et al. (2005), and Cross (2003b) provide such collections, while shorter works also collect the inscriptions (Finkelstein and Sass 2013; Lemaire 2015). All these works have contributed to examining the Biblical Hebrew terms belonging to the semantic field of writing tools and materials.

1.2. Methodology

The methodology utilized in this study resembles that of Koller (2012); it employs comparative Semitics, archaeology, and lexical semantics. While the former two tools are used to arrive at specific information such as definitions of words and actual finds, the latter tool provides a theoretical framework for the interpretation of the data gathered.

The discussion of each Hebrew term consists of several components. First, the etymological origin of each term is discussed. Each term's Semitic cognates or possible loan vectors are considered, and new suggestions are made wherever necessary. In discussing loanwords, an attempt is made to determine when such words were borrowed into Canaanite or Hebrew. After looking at questions of etymology, the study moves on to analyze the biblical texts containing each term. These biblical texts are closely studied in order to glean information on the meaning of each lexeme. The appearance of the relevant terms in the Dead Sea Scrolls and in Ben Sira is also considered in this study in order to trace the continued use of the terms from Iron Age II to the Hellenistic Period and to acquire any additional semantic information regarding each term. Additionally, in discussing the terms that are actually loanwords, the use of such words in the original language is evaluated in order to supplement the biblical data.

Besides examining the etymology of the relevant words as well as their use in the Bible and extrabiblical texts, the current study also considers the pertinent data available in the early translations of the Bible. The Old Greek translation is examined in order to see how each relevant Hebrew term was translated into Greek; the Targums and the Peshitta are also consulted for a number of infrequently occurring lexemes whose meanings are difficult to ascertain from relevant etymological data and from the translation of these lexemes in the Septuagint.[3] In discussing the Greek translation of relevant Hebrew lexemes,

3. Data regarding the translation of Hebrew terms in the Targums and the Peshitta are taken from the *Comprehensive Aramaic Lexicon* website (*CAL*) and from Sokoloff's *A Syriac Lexicon* (2009). For citations from the Targums, I use the three-volume set *The Bible in Aramaic Based on*

I will use the designations "Septuagint" and "Old Greek translation" to refer to the original Greek translation of the Hebrew Bible.

In gathering the linguistic data available in the Greek translation of the Hebrew Bible, I utilized several resources to check how the Septuagint renders the writing-related terms in Greek. Specifically, I made use of Accordance Bible Software, the Rahlfs and Hanhart abridged critical edition of the Septuagint (2006), the Göttingen Septuagint (1926–), the Cambridge Septuagint (1906–1940), Holmes and Parsons Septuagint (1798–1827), and Field's edition of the Hexapla (1875). Every occurrence of each term was initially checked in Rahlfs and Hanhart 2006, and I used Accordance Bible Software to assist me in checking the translation of every lexeme. These two resources are the basis for the statistical data that I provide regarding the Greek translation of the relevant words. I understand, however, that the different manuscripts of the Septuagint have variant readings. For this reason, although the statistical data is based on one edition (Rahlfs and Hanhart 2006), I have also incorporated into this discussion all relevant data available in the main critical editions of the Septuagint. Accordingly, with the exception of a few high-frequency terms (e.g., *ʾeben*, *maṭṭe*, *ʿēṣ*), all occurrences of the relevant words were also checked in the Göttingen Septuagint series (1926–); in cases where the Göttingen Septuagint lacked a corresponding volume, the Cambridge Septuagint (1906–1940) and the Holmes and Parsons edition (1798–1827) were utilized. In my discussion of the Greek data, I note every time there is a variant reading for a particular lexeme, and I also refer to the hexaplaric versions and other Greek recensions of the pertinent passages. All references to variant readings are taken from the aforementioned resources, while references to hexaplaric versions or other Greek recensions are taken from the Göttingen Septuagint series (1926–) and, in a few cases, from Field's edition of the Hexapla (1875). Whenever material relating to hexaplaric versions or Greek recensions is relevant, I cite individual volumes in the discussions of the terms.

While I have sought to present a comprehensive picture regarding the translation of the relevant Hebrew terms into Greek, I understand that the Old Greek translation has a complex transmission history that includes various revisions of the Greek text to make it more like the Hebrew text (Tov 2012, 127–47). Nevertheless, it is fruitful to utilize the data available in the Old Greek translation, as well as its revisions, because these sources reveal how the Hebrew words were understood by the Greek translators of the biblical text. Even those revisions that corrected the Greek text according to their Hebrew source disclose how

Old Manuscripts and Printed Texts by Sperber (2004), *Targum de Salmos* by Merino (1982), and *The Text of the Targum of Job* by Stec (1994); for citations from the Peshitta, I use the *The Old Testament in Syriac According to the Peshiṭta Version* by ter Haar Romeny and van Peursen (1972–2019).

the Greek translators understood the Hebrew text. For this reason, it is worthwhile to examine how Hebrew writing-related lexemes were translated into Greek. I am aware, however, that using the Septuagint to determine meanings of Hebrew words (especially those that occur infrequently) may be problematic. First of all, the *Vorlage* of the Septuagint cannot be checked to confirm that a particular Hebrew term stands behind a particular Greek term. When the Greek translation differs slightly from the Masoretic Text, the difference may be the result of a paraphrastic translation on the part of the Greek translator, or it may reflect a difference in the Hebrew *Vorlage* that lies behind the Greek translation. Secondly, it is also possible that the translator's choice to use a particular Greek word stems not from accurate knowledge of the word, but from inference regarding the word's meaning in view of the surrounding context. Suffice it to say that the Septuagint should be used with caution in determining meanings of Hebrew terms. For this reason, the evidence from the Septuagint is utilized in this study as supporting evidence, not as the main argument.

In addition to evaluating the relevant lexemes in regard to their etymology, their biblical and extrabiblical usage, and their rendering in ancient Bible translations, I also make an attempt in the examination of each term to link the textual data of the Bible with archeological and art historical evidence. The discussion of this evidence is not restricted to the finds of ancient Israel. The finds of the ancient Near East from Mesopotamia to Egypt—as well as those of the ancient Mediterranean world—are also utilized to arrive at a better understanding of the terms related to writing in the Bible.

Because this work focuses specifically on lexemes designating writing surfaces and the instruments utilized to produce writing, many writing-related terms are not examined in the study. For instance, Hebrew verbs for writing as well as terms denoting scribes and various types of documents are not considered. While chapters 2–5 comprise the bulk of the discussion regarding the meanings of the relevant writing-related lexemes, concise definitions of the terms discussed can be found at the end of chapter 2 (2.8) and at the end of the main sections of chapter 3 (3.1.5, 3.2.7), chapter 4 (4.2.6), and chapter 5 (5.2.4, 5.3.6).

CHAPTER 2

Papyrus

THE BIBLE CONTAINS a number of terms that carry the meaning 'reed, marsh'. I will argue, however, that only the word *gōme'* specifically refers to the manufacturable papyrus material that was used for writing purposes in ancient Israel. Prior to evaluating the terms designating reeds and their habitats, I will present a historical sketch of the actual technology that was involved in the utilization of papyrus as a writing material in the ancient world. Understanding the historical context surrounding the use of papyrus will shed light on the meanings of the relevant Hebrew terms.

2.1. Reeds, Marshes, and Papyrus in the Ancient World

2.1.1. Manufacturing Papyrus in Egypt

The ancient Egyptians first used papyrus as a writing material shortly after the invention of the Egyptian writing system which emerged in the late fourth millennium BCE (Baines 2007, 117, 128).[1] While stone was the most visible writing surface in ancient Egypt, papyrus was the most commonly used writing surface. Workable papyrus material was designated by the term *šfdw*, and, beginning in the New Kingdom (1549–1069 BCE), it was called *ḏmʿ*; a sheet of papyrus was called *q3ḥt*, while a roll was called *ʿr.t* (Gestermann 1984, 702).[2] During the Ptolemaic Period (332–30 BCE), papyrus was a royal monopoly and was therefore called **p3-(n)-pr-ʿ3* 'of the king' (Wente 2000, 2212; Gestermann 1984, 702).

As I discuss Hebrew words designating the papyrus plant and other types of reeds, I will classify these plants according to their taxonomy.[3] The plants dis-

1. Allen (2013, 1) states that the earliest Egyptian writing dates to 3250 BCE.
2. All references to ancient Egypt's chronology are taken from Ikram (2010, xiii–xxiii).
3. Information regarding taxonomical classification of various reed plants is taken from two online resources: United States Department of Agriculture (www.plants.usda.gov) and Global Biodiversity Information Facility (www.gbif.org).

cussed here all belong to the subclass *Commelinidae*, a grouping within the class *Liliopida* which consists of plants containing one seed leaf (monocotyledons) as opposed to plants that contain two seed leaves (dicotyledons). Within the subclass of *Commelinidae*, we will focus on two orders: *Cyperales* and *Typhales*. In looking at the *Cyperales* order, we will consider two families: the sedge family *Cyperaceae* and the grass family *Poaceae*. Within the *Typhales* order, we will study the cattail family *Typhaceae*. Taxonomy designates papyrus with the species name *Cyperus papyrus* L., which is in the sedge family *Cyperaceae*.

Papyrus is a freshwater plant that grows well in marshes and swamps. In appearance, the plant consists of a stem that is tall, green, and leafless; standing at a usual height of fifteen feet, the stem is topped with an umbel. Today, the plant is common in the swamplands of central and east Africa, as well as parts of west Africa, but, surprisingly, not along the Egyptian Nile. Nevertheless, reports of early travelers from medieval times as well as depictions of papyrus in Egyptian temples confirm that papyrus was indeed indigenous to and widespread in the Nile valley and the Delta region. Papyrus was gathered from the Nile region mainly between March and August, because the Nile flooded during September–March. Although wild papyrus was plentiful in Egypt, it is possible that the plant was also cultivated specifically to be used as a writing material; however, the exact subspecies of the plant that was utilized for writing purposes cannot be known with certainty (Leach and Tait 2000, 227–29, 234; Lewis 1974, 4–5).

We have no extant description written by the ancient Egyptians of how papyrus was converted into writing material. Pliny the Elder, however, a Roman from the first century CE, does describe the process of preparing papyrus to be used for writing material (Lewis 1974, 34–69; Niditch 1996, 73; Leach and Tait 2000, 231–36). First, papyrus reeds were removed from their habitat, and the rind was peeled away from the stem. The soft pith was cut into long strips, about half an inch to an inch in thickness. Perhaps a dozen strips were laid down flat, side by side, to form the initial layer. Another dozen strips were placed on top of the first layer so that the second layer was perpendicular to the first. The two layers were then hammered together with mallets and left to dry under pressure. The natural gums in the cell sap of papyrus produced an adhesive that bonded the strips of pith. After drying, the final sheet may have been polished.

Papyrus paper was always manufactured as a roll and usually used as such. Rarely was it used as individual sheets. Papyrus rolls were typically eight inches in height and seldom exceeded a height of sixteen inches (Black and Tait 2000, 2200–2204). In general, a role consisted of twenty joined sheets of papyrus, which were often between 6 and 16 inches in width (Černý 1952, 5–6, 9; Avrin 1991, 82–87; Ashton 2008, 32–33); this means a scroll could be 6.5–8.5 yards long, although the longest Egyptian scroll we have is about 43 yards long (Bülow-Jacobsen 2009, 21). Rolls of papyrus were produced by overlapping a sheet over another sheet by approximately 0.3–0.8 inches and then joining the overlapped portion with an adhesive (Leach and Tait 2000, 236). One would seal a papyrus roll by placing a small amount of mud on a thong of loosened papyrus fibers (Wente 2000, 2211–14).

The utilization of papyrus as a writing material was just one of the many uses of papyrus in ancient Egypt. The plant was employed for producing items such as "matting, ropes, boats, sandals, and numerous kinds of everyday objects"; it was also used for decorative purposes and as food (Leach and Tait 2000, 228). Wendrich (2000, 255) adds that papyrus was utilized in making "baskets, boxes, coffins, simple furniture."[4] Leach and Tait (2000, 228) suggest that the wild papyrus plant was used for the purposes listed above, while the cultivated plant was used specifically for writing material.

2.1.2. Papyrus in the Ancient World

Although papyrus paper is the invention of ancient Egypt, it was used throughout the ancient world. The Report of Wenamun confirms that papyrus was used as a writing material outside of Egypt already in the eleventh century BCE. The report, which dates to the Twenty-First Dynasty (1064–940 BCE), recounts the mishaps encountered by Wenamun on his journey from Thebes to Byblos (Redford 2000, 2228). This account records that five hundred rolls of papyrus were delivered to Byblos along with an array of other gifts in exchange for cedar wood that would be used for the construction of a temple for Amon (Breasted 1905). It is not unreasonable to suggest that papyrus was known throughout the Mediterranean world by the end of the second millennium BCE, when the West Semitic alphabet was probably adopted by the Greeks (Naveh 2009, 110*, 114*; Waal 2018); in adopting the alphabetic writing system from the Levant, the Greeks probably also inherited the use of papyrus paper for writing purposes (Lewis 1974, 85–87). Greek art and literature confirm that papyrus paper was used by the Greeks by the sixth century BCE (Lewis 1974, 87). Art historical evidence may show that papyrus was also employed for writing purposes in Assyria as early as the eighth century BCE (Lewis 1974, 85; Pearce 2000, 2267).

While it is certain that papyrus was exported from Egypt to the Levant and all over the ancient world, it is not entirely clear whether papyrus paper was produced outside of Egypt (Lewis 1974, 4, 116). Reeds grew in ancient Israel near the Sea of Galilee and near Lake Huleh, and they were plentiful in the southern marshlands of ancient Mesopotamia (Gilbert 2000, 157; Lewis 1974, 6, 10). Reeds and papyrus also grew in the southern marshes of Italy (Lewis 1974,

4. Other reeds and sedges, although less well known than *Cyperus papyrus* L., were also used for such purposes (Leach and Tait 2000, 228; Wendrich 2000, 255).

14–16). In Mesopotamia, reeds were used for making doors, fences, and screens as well as for construction purposes such as roofing and matting; they were also utilized in the production of mats, beds, baskets, chairs, tables, ropes, and boats, as well as reed pens and styli.[5] Texts from the Garshana archives detail the use of reeds in various construction projects (Heimpel 2009, 173–76, 178–82, 210–20, 258–68). In the Levant, evidence exists for the use of reeds for construction purposes such as flooring at Jericho, matting at Lachish, and roofing and vaulting at Byblos (Wright 1985, 1:29, 413, 436, 456–57). Still, while papyrus grew in various places throughout the ancient world—and while reeds were used for a variety of purposes throughout the ancient Near East—we have no evidence that papyrus *paper* was manufactured outside of Egypt.

2.1.3. Archeological and Art Historical Evidence for the Use of Papyrus in the Ancient World

Because papyrus deteriorates over time, it is no surprise that the examples of preserved papyrus scrolls come primarily from Egyptian tombs, where the stable temperature allowed for their preservation (Leach and Tait 2000, 241; Diringer 1953, 113–69).[6] An uninscribed papyrus roll from the First Dynasty (3050–2813 BCE) was found at Saqqara in the tomb of a high official (Baines 2007, 128), and the earliest inscribed roll dates to the Fourth Dynasty (2597–2471 BCE) from Gebelein in southern Upper Egypt (Baines 2007, 128). However, the earliest substantial group of inscribed Egyptian papyri are the Abusir Papyri from a temple near Abusir. They date to the Fifth Dynasty (2471–2355 BCE) (Black and Tait 2000, 2204). Other texts preserved on papyrus include the Dialogue of a Man with His Ba from the Twelfth Dynasty (1994–1781 BCE), the Prophecy of Neferti also from the Twelfth Dynasty but preserved on manuscripts dating to the fifteenth–thirteenth centuries BCE, the Story of Two Brothers from the Nineteenth Dynasty (1298–1187 BCE), and the Report of Wenamun from the Twenty-First Dynasty (1064–940 BCE) (Redford 2000, 2226–29).

Papyrus documents dating to a much later time than the aforementioned examples have been discovered in Egypt as well as the Levant. Ten hieratic documents dating from the Old Kingdom (2663–2160 BCE), Middle Kingdom (2066–1650 BCE), New Kingdom (1549–1069 BCE), and the Ptolemaic Period (332–30 BCE) (Porten et al. 2011, 31), as well as thirty-seven demotic texts from

5. For use of reeds in Mesopotamia, see Moorey 1999, 361–62; van de Mieroop 1987, 37, 39, 41; Postgate 1980, 101–9; and Driver (1944) 1976, 18–19.

6. Leach and Tait (2000, 239–43, 245) discuss the various causes of papyrus deterioration. Among other causes, papyrus deteriorates due to microorganismal fungi, insect attack, and the natural breakdown of cellulose that makes up papyrus; a modern cause of papyrus deterioration is overexposure to light.

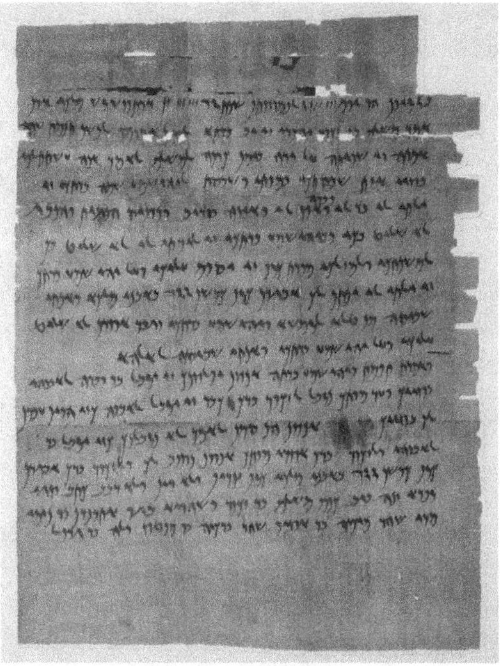

FIGURE 2.1. Ink-on-papyrus document from Elephantine, 427 BCE. Brooklyn Museum. Photo: Wikimedia Commons.

the mid-sixth century BCE to the early first century CE (Porten et al. 2011, 276), were discovered on the island of Elephantine in Egypt. Fifty-two Aramaic letters and legal documents on papyri, most of which come from a Jewish military colony and date to the fifth century BCE, were also discovered at Elephantine (Porten et al. 2011, 75, 82–83) (See figure 2.1). Egypt, however, is not the only region where papyrus documents have been discovered. A Hebrew papyrus palimpsest dating to the seventh century BCE was found in a cave in Wadi Murabbaʿat, near the Dead Sea (Aḥituv 2008, 213). About twenty Aramaic papyri (and many fragments) dating to the fourth century BCE were found in a cave in Wadi ed-Daliyeh (Dušek 2007, 65–66). Furthermore, extant ancient Israelite bullae indirectly confirm that papyrus was used as writing material in preexilic Israel. Fifty-one bullae dating to the eighth and seventh centuries and fragments of 170 bullae dating to the ninth and eighth centuries were discovered in the City of David (Avigad 1997, 167; Reich, Shukron, and Lernau 2007, 156–7). Such bullae—which would have been attached to papyrus rolls—bear markings of papyrus fibers, thereby attesting to the utilization of papyrus for documents in ancient Israel. Finally, 131 texts in the corpus of the Dead Sea Scrolls (ca. 250 BCE–68 CE) were written on papyrus (Tov 2004, 31; 2012, 99).

The use of papyrus in the ancient world is confirmed not only by actual papyrus finds but also by art historical evidence; that is, papyrus seems to be depicted on various reliefs in Egyptian tombs and in Assyrian palaces. The Egyptian tomb of Ti at Saqqara from the Fifth Dynasty (2471–2355 BCE) depicts Egyptian scribes working with papyrus. One scribe unrolls a piece of papyrus and shows it to another scribe, while a different scribe arranges rolls on a short table-like stand. Other scribes are represented as simply writing on papyrus scrolls (Black and Tait 2000, 2205). Similar depictions of scribes working with papyrus also appear in tombs from the Eighteenth Dynasty (1549–1069 BCE) (Diringer 1953, 114). Additionally, art historical evidence of the use of papyrus in Mesopotamia may survive in an Assyrian relief from the Southwest Palace of Nineveh. The relief shows scribes recording booty: one records the plunder on a wooden diptych while another scribe writes on a role of papyrus or perhaps leather (Pearce 2000, 2267).

Having surveyed the process of manufacturing papyrus and its use in the ancient world, we will now consider Biblical Hebrew terms with the meaning 'reed, marsh, papyrus'.

2.2. The Terms *ʾāḥû, biṣṣā, ʾēbe, ʿārôt,* and *gebeʾ*

2.2.1. The Term ʾāḥû

2.2.1.1. Etymology and Biblical Usage

The word *ʾāḥû*, which occurs three times in the Bible (Gen 41:2, 18; Job 8:11), derives from Egyptian *3ḫ(y)* 'plants' (*WÄS* 1:18; Lambdin 1953, 146; Muchiki 1999, 238). In the Bible, *ʾāḥû* refers to pastureland and perhaps also to sedges and reeds (*HALOT* 1:30–31). Because *ʾāḥû* in the Bible refers to the vegetation growing near the Nile (GMD 34; Löw 1967, 1:571–72), it is possible that the word designates the pond sedge *Carex vesicaria* Leers, also known as *Carex riparia.*[7] In Egyptian texts, *3ḫ(y)* first appears during the New Kingdom (1549–1069 BCE) (Muchiki 1999, 238; *WÄS* 1:18). Lambdin (1953, 146) points out that *3ḫ(y)* initially referred to the land that was inundated by the Nile river and later acquired the meanings 'grass, reeds' and 'pastureland'.[8] Besides being loaned into Hebrew, *3ḫ(y)* was also loaned into Aramaic (*ʾaḥwā* 'meadow grass, reeds'; Jastrow 1926, 1:39) and Greek (ἄχει 'reed grass'; LSJ 295).[9]

7. *Carex vesicaria* Leers (*Carex riparia*) belongs to the *Cyperaceae* sedge family.

8. Clines connects *ʾāḥû* with the papyrus plant (*Cyperus papyrus*) (*DCH* 1:246). This is certainly possible, but because the Egyptian term refers to vegetation in general it is likely that the Hebrew word refers more generally to vegetation or sedges along the Nile.

9. The Aramaic term *ʾaḥwā* is attested already in Old Aramaic, in lines 29 and 32 of the Aramaic stele Sefire I, which dates to the eighth century BCE (*KAI* 1:41; Dušek 2019, 2–3, 57). It is also attested in Targumic Aramaic (e.g., in Gen 41:2 of Targum Onkelos) (*CAL*; Jastrow 1926, 1:39).

The word *ʾāḥû* was probably borrowed into Canaanite quite early. Lambdin (1953, 146) argues that the preservation of the final *w* of *ʾāḥû* in Biblical Hebrew points to a borrowing that occurred perhaps in the Old Kingdom (2663–2160 BCE), when the final *w* of the Egyptian word was still pronounced.[10]

The three passages containing *ʾāḥû* use this lexeme to signify plants growing around bodies of water. In two almost identical passages in Genesis (41:2, 18), the term refers to plants within or near the Nile. For instance, Gen 41:2 reads: וְהִנֵּה מִן־הַיְאֹר עֹלֹת שֶׁבַע פָּרוֹת יְפוֹת מַרְאֶה וּבְרִיאֹת בָּשָׂר וַתִּרְעֶינָה **בָּאָחוּ** ‘From the Nile there came up seven cows attractive and corpulent, and they grazed in the ***ʾāḥû***’.[11] According to this verse, cows graze in the *ʾāḥû*, which may refer to the pastureland near the Nile river. Alternatively, it may designate the sedges or reeds which grew plentifully near the Nile (Gilbert 2000, 157). That *ʾāḥû* may denote sedges and reeds is especially implied by Job 8:11: הֲיִגְאֶה־גֹּמֶא בְּלֹא בִצָּה יִשְׂגֶּה־**אָחוּ** בְלִי־מָיִם ‘Will papyrus [*gōmeʾ*] grow without a swamp [*biṣṣā*]? Will ***ʾāḥû*** increase without water?’. The comparison of *ʾāḥû* with papyrus (*gōmeʾ*) suggests that the former, like the latter, is a type of sedge or reed. While *ʾāḥû* occurs only three times in the biblical text, in each case the term refers to plants growing along bodies of water, such as the Nile river in Egypt.

2.2.1.2. Translation of ʾāḥû *in the Septuagint*

In the Septuagint, *ʾāḥû* is translated twice as ἄχει ‘reed grass’ (Gen 41:2, 18), which is itself an Egyptian loanword within Greek (LSJ 295; Muraoka 2009, 109). Once, *ʾāḥû* is rendered as βούτομον ‘sedge; *Carex riparia*’ (Job 8:11) (LSJ 326–27; Muraoka 2009, 122). Both Greek terms seem to designate wild sedges growing along water. There are also variant readings of *ʾāḥû* in these verses (Wevers 1974, 381, 385; Ziegler 1982, 246); for instance, λῑβάδιον ‘small stream, wet place’ (Gen 41:2; LSJ 1047), ὄχθη ‘bank of river’ (Gen 41:18; LSJ 1281), and ἕλος ‘marshy meadow, marshy ground’ (Gen 41:2, 18; LSJ 537;

10. Lambdin (1953, 146 n. 12) also views Ugaritic *ʾḫ* (‘meadow’ [?], shore’ [?]) as a loanword deriving from Egyptian *3ḫ(y)* (see also Muchiki 1999, 280; *DULAT* 1:36). He argues that the lack of a final *w* in Ugaritic points to a later borrowing of *3ḫ(y)* into Ugaritic than into Canaanite; Lambdin thus implies that Ugaritic would have borrowed the term when final *w* was no longer pronounced in Egyptian. Indeed, it is possible that *3ḫ(y)* was first loaned into Canaanite and later into Ugaritic. On the other hand, perhaps Ugaritic *ʾḫ* is related to Akkadian *aḫu* ‘bank, shore, side’, which is unrelated to Egyptian *3ḫ(y)* (*CAD* 1/1:205–8). If this is correct, we would not expect Ugaritic to display a final vowel because it would be a case vowel, which is expected only in Akkadian orthography. The presence of final *w* in Hebrew *ʾāḥû*, however, would indeed reflect an early borrowing of Egyptian *3ḫ(y)*.

11. All quotations from the Hebrew Bible are taken from *BHS*, while the English translations are my own.

Muraoka 2009, 224). According to the Hexapla, Aquila and Symmachus render *ʾāḥû* as ἕλος in the three passages (LSJ 537; Muraoka 2009, 224), while Theodotion has ἄχι (Gen 41:18; LSJ 295; Muraoka 2009, 109), a variant spelling of ἄχει (Wevers 1974, 381, 385; Ziegler 1982, 246). Based on the Greek translations of *ʾāḥû*, it seems reasonable to suggest that the translators understood the term as referring to a sedge plant and to the area where it grew. It should be noted, however, that in the case of *ʾāḥû* and other infrequently occurring terms, it is difficult to know whether the Greek translators inferred the meaning of the words from the surrounding context or whether they were actually aware of the correct meaning of the lexemes.

The term *ʾāḥû* was an Egyptian loanword that had entered Canaanite probably quite early. The term referred to pastureland and probably also sedges and reeds but not manufacturable papyrus material.

2.2.2. The Term **biṣṣā**

2.2.2.1. Etymology and Biblical Usage

The term *biṣṣā*, which occurs three times in the Bible (Ezek 47:11; Job 8:11; 40:21), carries the meaning 'swamp, marsh' (GMD 166; *DCH* 2:244) and probably derives from Proto-Semitic **biśś-at-*.[12] The term may also appear once in 4QSapiental Hymn (4Q411 1ii8), but the reading of *bet* is uncertain (*DSSR* 2:250; *DSSC* 1:156). The root from which *biṣṣā* derives is also attested in Akkadian (*baṣṣum*/*bāṣum* 'sand' and *b-ṣ-ṣ* 'to trickle'; *CAD* 2:134–35) and Arabic (*baḍḍat* 'soft, tender, plump' and *b-ḍ-ḍ* 'to trickle, to ooze'; Lane 1968, 1:213). The clear relation between the words *biṣṣā* and *bōṣ* 'mud' suggests that *biṣṣā* initially carried a meaning such as 'mud' or 'mire' and later came to mean 'swamp, marsh'.[13]

In the Bible, *biṣṣā* is clearly associated with reeds and marshes. Job 8:11 implies that the papyrus plant (*gōmeʾ*) cannot grow without *biṣṣā*, while Job 40:21 speaks of reeds (*qāne*) in parallel with *biṣṣā*. Job 8:11 reads: הֲיִגְאֶה־גֹּמֶא בְּלֹא **בִצָּה** יִשְׂגֶּה־אָחוּ בְלִי־מָיִם 'Will papyrus [*gōmeʾ*] grow without ***biṣṣā***? Will sedges [*ʾāḥû*] increase without water?'. And Job 40:21 reads: תַּחַת־צֶאֱלִים יִשְׁכָּב בְּסֵתֶר קָנֶה **וּבִצָּה** 'Under the lotus it [Behemoth] lies, in the shelter of reeds [*qāne*] and ***biṣṣā***'. While both passages display a clear relationship between *biṣṣā* and reeds, the former passage distinguishes *biṣṣā* from reeds; that is, according to Job 8:11,

12. According to *HALOT* (1:147), *biṣṣā* refers to "waterlogged ground." The biblical text suggests, however, that *biṣṣā* was not only associated with water but also with reeds.

13. For discussion of the lexeme *bōṣ* and its relation to *biṣṣā* see 3.2.2.1.

biṣṣā is the habitat of reeds, so we may conclude that *biṣṣā* refers to the marshy swamp as a whole, not specifically to the reeds themselves.

2.2.2.2. *Translation of* biṣṣā *in the Septuagint*

In the Septuagint, *biṣṣā* seems to be translated with three distinct words. Twice the term is rendered with words that have to do with water, once as διεκβολή 'outlet, estuary' (Ezek 47:11; LSJ 423; Muraoka 2009, 167) and once as ὕδωρ 'water' (Job 8:11; LSJ 1845–46; Muraoka 2009, 693). Another time, *biṣṣā* is rendered with the term βούτομον 'sedge, *Carex riparia*' (Job 40:21; LSJ 326–27; Muraoka 2009, 122). In translating *biṣṣā* in Job 40:21, Aquila, Symmachus, and Theodotion have κάθυγρος 'very wet' (LSJ 856; Ziegler 1982, 400) in place of βούτομον, which of course seems to point to the wet nature of *biṣṣā*. Based on the Septuagint's translation of *biṣṣā* in these passages, it seems that the term was understood as referring to reed plants or bodies of water in which such plants grow.

We may conclude that the primary meaning of *biṣṣā* is 'swamp, marsh'. Since reeds grew in a marsh, it is natural that the term could also be used as a collective signifying the reeds and sedges of a marsh, which seems to be how the Septuagint understood it. The term, however, does not designate the manufacturable papyrus used to make writing material.

2.2.3. *The Term* **ʾēbe**

2.2.3.1. *Etymology and Biblical Usage*

The term *ʾēbe*, which occurs once in the Bible (Job 9:26), designates a type of reed, perhaps even the papyrus plant (Löw 1967, 1:565, 572; *HALOT* 1:3–4; *DCH* 2018, 1:99). The Arabic term *ʾabāʾ* 'reed' seems to be etymologically connected, but the noun pattern is different (GMD 4). Akkadian *ap/bu* 'reed thicket' (*a-pa-a-am*, *a-pi-i-im*, *a-pi*; but also, *a-bi*) may also be connected (*CAD* 1/2:199–200). In Akkadian, *ap/bu* is used to refer to wild plants and also reeds used for construction purposes (*CAD* 1/2:199–200).

Job 9:25–26, wherein *ʾēbe* appears, compares Job's fleeting days with ships passing by. The passage reads: וְיָמַ֣י קַ֭לּוּ מִנִּי־רָ֑ץ בָּ֝רְח֗וּ לֹא־רָ֥אוּ טוֹבָֽה׃ חָ֭לְפוּ עִם־אֳנִיּ֣וֹת **אֵבֶ֑ה** כְּ֝נֶ֗שֶׁר יָט֥וּשׂ עֲלֵי־אֹֽכֶל 'My days are swifter than a runner; they have fled away, they have seen no good. They have passed by with ships of ***ʾēbe***, as an eagle swoops upon prey'. The passage speaks of ships of *ʾēbe* (*ʾŏniyyôt ʾēbe*), and presumably, *ʾēbe* designates the material of which the ships are made. Indeed, boats and especially rafts were made of reeds in the ancient Near East (Moorey 1999, 10; Casson 1986, 11–13; Postgate 1980, 102).

2.2.3.2. *Translation of* ʾēbe *in Ancient Versions*

In Targum Job, *ʾēbe* is rendered as *mgd* ‘gift, precious goods’ and in another translation of the same passage as *qlyl* ‘quick’ (*CAL*; Stec 1994, 67*), while in the Peshitta, the word is translated as *bʿldbbʾ* ‘enemy’ (Sokoloff 2009, 171; *CAL*). The Septuagint’s rendering of this passage is not helpful in establishing the exact meaning of *ʾēbe* inasmuch as there is not a corresponding term in the Greek (Ziegler 1982, 252).

Based on the use of the word in the biblical text—and in view of the comparative Semitic evidence—*ʾēbe* can apparently be used to designate the reed material used to manufacture goods, namely, boats. However, since *ʾēbe* is a hapax legomenon, it is difficult to know more about this lexeme.

2.2.4. *The Term* ʿārôt

2.2.4.1. *Etymology and Biblical Usage*

The noun *ʿārôt*, which occurs only once in the Bible (Isa 19:7), probably carries the meaning ‘wild papyrus plant’.[14] The word probably derives from the Egyptian term *ʿr* ‘reed plant’, which is attested as early as the Old Kingdom (2663–2160 BCE) (*WÄS* 1:208; Muchiki 1999, 252; GMD 1012). In Egyptian, *ʿr* refers either to reed plants or reed pens (*WÄS* 1:208). The feminine form of the word (*ʿr.t*) designates papyrus rolls (Gestermann 1984, 701). It is clear, then, that the terms *ʿr* and *ʿr.t* in Egyptian refer to the papyrus plant and items made of the plant. Consequently, it seems reasonable to surmise that the Hebrew term *ʿārôt*, like the Egyptian terms *ʿr* and *ʿr.t*, also refers specifically to the papyrus plant. Indeed, Löw (1967, 1:572, 577) identifies Hebrew *ʿārôt* as the papyrus plant. While it is difficult to date when the word *ʿārôt* entered the Hebrew language, the lexeme was perhaps borrowed along with other Egyptian terms (e.g., *gōmeʾ*, *sûp*), as discussed in chapter 6.

In the single occurrence of *ʿārôt* (Isa 19:7), the term is used to designate plants that grow by the Nile (*HALOT* 1:882). Additionally, *ʿārôt* is very clearly associated in this passage with other water plants that grow near the Nile (*qāne* ‘reed’; *sûp* ‘wild reed, marsh’; *wekōl mizraʿ yəʾôr* ‘and every sown thing of the Nile’). This suggests that *ʿārôt* probably designates the reeds that grew along the Nile. Isaiah 19:6–7 reads: וְהֶאֶזְנִיחוּ נְהָרוֹת דָּלֲלוּ וְחָרְבוּ יְאֹרֵי מָצוֹר קָנֶה וָסוּף קָמֵלוּ׃ **עָרוֹת** עַל־יְאוֹר עַל־פִּי יְאוֹר וְכֹל מִזְרַע יְאוֹר יִיבַשׁ נִדַּף וְאֵינֶנּוּ ‘The rivers will stink, the rivers of Egypt will decrease and will dry up, reeds [*qāne*] and marshes of reeds [*sûp*]

14. The lexeme *ʿārôt* also occurs in Hab 3:13, but it does not refer to reeds or marshes in this verse. Rather, it seems to be the *piel* infinitive absolute form of the root *ʿ-r-y*.

will decay; ***ʿārôt*** on the Nile, on the edge of the Nile, and every sown thing of the Nile [*wekōl mizraʿ yəʾôr*] will dry up, will be driven away, and will be no more'.

2.2.4.2. Translation of ʿārôt *in Ancient Versions*

We cannot know whether the ancient translators inferred the meaning of *ʿārôt* or whether they had an accurate understanding of the term. In the Septuagint, the word is translated with the term ἄχι 'reed grass' (LSJ 295–96; Muraoka 2009, 109; Ziegler 1939, 189). Also, the word is translated as *rwb* 'riverside plant growth' in Targum Jonathan and as *lwʿʾ* 'name of water plant' in the Peshitta (Sokoloff 2009, 680; *CAL*). These translations suggest that *ʿārôt* was understood as referring to a plant that grew in or along rivers. While it is possible that *ʿārôt* refers to the wild papyrus plant, the term is not used in the Bible to refer to the manufacturable papyrus material.

***2.2.5. The Term* gebeʾ**

2.2.5.1. Etymology and Usage in the Bible and the Dead Sea Scrolls

The term *gebeʾ*, which appears twice in the Bible (Isa 30:14; Ezek 47:11), carries the meaning 'pool of water, pond' (GMD 191).[15] In the Damascus Document (CD X, 12; 4Q270 6iv21; *DSSR* 1:98, 188; *DSSC* 1:156), the word occurs once to designate pools of water in rocky areas. The term probably derives from the root *g-b-ʾ*, which appears as a verbal root in some West Semitic languages (e.g., Arabic *jabaʾa* 'to turn back, to remain behind', Lane 1968, 2:372; Geʿez *gabʾa* 'to return' and, in noun form, *məgbāʾ* 'gathering place', *CDG* 177). Huehnergard (personal communication) suggests that the root carries the meaning 'to return, to collect'.

While *gebeʾ* probably derives from the root *g-b-ʾ*, the semantics of *gebeʾ* may have been influenced by other superficially similar lexemes that are, however, etymologically unrelated. Such lexemes resemble *gebeʾ* in that they, too, have a *g* and *b* as their first and second radicals. Examples of such lexemes can be seen in Hebrew *gēb* 'pit' (2 Kgs 3:16; Jer 14:3), Geʿez *gəbb* 'pit, ditch', and Arabic *jubb* 'well, pit' (Lane 1968, 2:371; *CDG* 176–77; *HALOT* 1:170). These words, however, probably derive from the Semitic reduplicated root *g-b-b* 'to gather'. As a verbal root, *g-b-b* is attested in Ethiopic (*gabbaba* 'to gather'; *CDG* 177)

15. The term *gebeʾ* is also usually glossed as 'cistern' (*HALOT* 1:170; *DCH* 2:297; Jastrow 1926, 1:202). In the Bible and the Dead Sea Scrolls, however, it is not clear that the term refers to a man-made cistern. Rather, it seems to refer to natural pools or cavities with water.

and Aramaic (*gabbeb* 'to collect'; Jastrow 1926, 1:203). In addition to the unclear connection of the aforementioned lexemes with the term *gebe'*, the relation between *gebe'* and the root *g-b-y* 'to collect', which is attested in Arabic and Aramaic, is also not entirely transparent (Lane 1968, 2:378; *CAL*).

That the word *gebe'* refers to a pool of water is apparent in Isa 30:14. The passage reads: וּשְׁבָרָהּ כְּשֵׁבֶר נֵבֶל יוֹצְרִים כָּתוּת לֹא יַחְמֹל וְלֹא־יִמָּצֵא בִמְכִתָּתוֹ חֶרֶשׂ לַחְתּוֹת אֵשׁ מִיָּקוּד וְלַחְשֹׂף מַיִם **מִגֶּבֶא** 'He shall break it like the breaking of a smashed potter's vessel without mercy, and among its fragments there will not be found a potsherd to snatch fire from a hearth and to scoop water from a ***gebe'***'. In the Damascus Document, *gebe'* occurs in a context that describes ritual bathing and purification of vessels in pools of water located in rocky areas. The passage reads: על הטהר במים אל ירחץ איש במים צואים ומעוטים מדי ... אל יטהר במ כלי וכל **גבא** בסלע אשר אין בו די 'Concerning purification with water, one should not wash in dirty water and (in) too little water ... one should not wash in it a vessel, and every ***gebe'*** in a rock in which there is not enough' (CD X, 10–12; *DSSR* 1:98). Also, Ezek 47:11 reads: בצאתו בְּצֹאתָיו **וּגְבָאָיו** וְלֹא יֵרָפְאוּ לְמֶלַח נִתָּנוּ 'Its swamps [*biṣṣō(')tā(y)w*] and its ***gəbā'ā(y)w*** shall not be healed; they shall be left for salt'. The meaning of Ezekiel's oracle is clear: the swampy areas in the land of Israel will increase in their salinity and will no longer produce vegetation as a result. While *gebe'* in Isa 30:14 denotes a pool of water, in Ezek 47:11, the lexeme probably refers to the pools of water that were specifically located within marshes because, in this passage, *gəbā'ā(y)w* is used in connection with *biṣṣō(')tā(y)w* 'swamps, marshes'.

2.2.5.2. Translation of gebe' *in the Septuagint*

In translating Ezek 47:11, the Septuagint seems to render *gəbā'ā(y)w* as ὑπέραρσις 'exaltation, high water mark' (LSJ 1859; Muraoka 2009, 697; Ziegler 1952, 322), although the Hebrew *Vorlage* of this passage perhaps contained a term other than *gəbā'ā(y)w*. If ὑπέραρσις is indeed a translation of *gəbā'ā(y)w*, it seems that the Hebrew term was understood as being connected to the root *g-b-h* 'to be high, exalted' (*HALOT* 1:170–71) and used apparently in reference to rising waters in a body of water. While the Septuagint's rendering of Isa 30:14 does not have a Greek equivalent for *gebe'*, Aquila renders it with the term βόθυνος, which, like βόθρος, carries the meaning 'pit dug in ground' (LSJ 320; Muraoka 2009, 120; Ziegler 1939, 228–29). The evidence from the Greek translations thus connects *gebe'* with water, and, in one case (Isa 30:14), with pits of water.

In sum, the term *gebe'* seems to derive from the root *g-b-'*, which in West Semitic probably means 'to return, to collect'. The primary meaning of *gebe'* is 'pool of water, pond' (i.e., 'that which is collected').

2.3. The Term *ḥāṣîr*

2.3.1. Etymology and Biblical Usage

The word *ḥāṣîr* 'grass, vegetation' occurs twenty-two times in the Hebrew Bible.[16] The term also occurs once in 4QSapiental Work (4Q185 1–2i10; *DSSR* 2:242; *DSSC* 1:274), where it refers to effervescent grass. It also probably occurs in a version of Ben Sira found in the Masada Scroll, although the *yod* is restored in this instance (40, 16); in this passage, the term apparently refers to withering grass. Hebrew *ḥāṣîr* derives from Proto-Semitic **ḫaṣ̂īr*-, having cognates in Arabic (*ḫaḍīr* 'green'; Lane 1968, 2:755) and Syriac (*ḥē⁽ʾ⁾rē* 'reed'; Sokoloff 2009, 424).

In most cases, the term simply refers to grass (e.g., Isa 15:6; Ps 37:2; Prov 27:25). In one case, the word may have meant 'leeks' (Num 11:15; GMD 385). It has also been suggested that there are three passages where *ḥāṣîr* may have meant 'reeds' (Isa 35:7; 44:4; Job 8:12) (*DCH* 3:295–6; *HALOT* 1:344; Löw 1967, 1:581).[17] The Syriac cognate *ḥē⁽ʾ⁾rē* does mean 'reeds', so it is possible that the Hebrew term also meant this. Nevertheless, in the three verses where *ḥāṣîr* may mean 'reeds', it is just as reasonable to understand it as designating grass (GMD 385).[18]

Isaiah 35:7 reads: וְהָיָה הַשָּׁרָב לַאֲגַם וְצִמָּאוֹן לְמַבּוּעֵי מָיִם בִּנְוֵה תַנִּים רִבְצָהּ **חָצִיר** לְקָנֶה וָגֹמֶא 'The parched ground shall turn into a pool of water [*ʾăgam*] and the thirsty ground into streams of water [*mabbûʿê māyim*]; in the pasture of jackals, which is their dwelling place, ***ḥāṣîr*** (will turn) into reeds [*qāne*] and papyrus [*gōmeʾ*]'. The syntax of the latter half of this verse is somewhat difficult to understand. Nevertheless, it is clear that this verse, as well as the verses preceding it, describes various transformations of certain realities of lack and deficiency into realities of fullness and abundance. Thus, according to verses 5 and 6, the blind shall see, the deaf shall hear, the lame shall leap, and the dumb shall sing.

Verses 6 and 7 continue the theme of transformation by stating that water will emerge in the wilderness, desert, and dry ground. Syntactically, this transformation of sorts is signaled in verse 7 by the use of the verb *hāyā* and the preposition *lə*-. Accordingly, just as the *šārāb* 'parched ground' will become an *ʾăgam* 'pool of water', so will the *ṣimmāʾôn* 'thirsty ground' become *mabbûʿê*

16. The lexeme *ḥāṣîr* (22x) occurs in Num 11:5; 1 Kgs 18:5; 2 Kgs 19:26; Isa 15:6; 34:13; 35:7; 37:27; 40:6–8 (4x); 44:4; 51:12; Pss 37:2; 90:5; 103:15; 104:14; 129:6; 147:8; Job 8:12; 40:15; Prov 27:25.

17. According to *HALOT* 1:344, the term *ḥăṣērîm* in Ps 10:8 should be vocalized as *ḥăṣīrîm*, which also supposedly means 'reeds'. There is, however, no persuasive reason to repoint this word or to understand the word as referring to reeds.

18. The meaning of Syriac *ḥē⁽ʾ⁾rē* as 'reed' can be explained as a semantic shift from the general meaning 'grass, vegetation' to the more specific meaning 'reed'.

māyim 'streams of water'; both *ʾăgam* and *mabbûʿê māyim* are preceded by the preposition *lə*-. At the end of the verse, the noun phrase *qāne wāgōmeʾ* 'reed and papyrus' is also preceded by *lə*-, so it stands to reason that the noun that precedes *qāne wāgōmeʾ* (i.e., *ḥāṣîr*) is that which will be transformed into *qāne wāgōmeʾ*. The message seems to be that mere grass (*ḥāṣîr*)—which is depicted in several passages as being ephemeral (e.g., Isa 15:6; 40:8; Ps 37:2)—will become a river plant such as reed or papyrus, which are continually nourished by water.

Isaiah 44:4 reads: וְצָמְח֖וּ בְּבֵ֣ין **חָצִ֑יר** כַּעֲרָבִ֖ים עַל־יִבְלֵי־מָֽיִם 'They shall sprout forth among ***ḥāṣîr*** like willows by streams of water'. According to this verse, the descendants of Jacob will spring forth like some sort of plant or vegetation, comparable to willows growing by waterways. It is possible that this verse is comparing the Israelites with reeds growing along the river, but the verse is more likely stating that the Israelites will sprout up like willows from the short-lived grass (*ḥāṣîr*) that springs forth quickly and dries up thereafter. There is then no compelling reason to view *ḥāṣîr* in this passage as referring to reeds rather than grass.

Job 8:11–12 reads: הֲיִגְאֶה־גֹּ֭מֶא בְּלֹ֣א בִצָּ֑ה יִשְׂגֶּה־אָ֥חוּ בְלִי־מָֽיִם׃ עֹדֶ֣נּוּ בְ֭אִבּוֹ לֹ֣א יִקָּטֵ֑ף וְלִפְנֵ֖י כָל־**חָצִ֣יר** יִיבָֽשׁ 'Will papyrus [*gōmeʾ*] grow without a swamp [*biṣṣā*]? Will sedges [*ʾāhû*] increase without water? While it is still in flower and not having been cut down, it already dries up before any ***ḥāṣîr***'. If in this passage *ḥāṣîr* means 'reeds', it is difficult to see the point of these two verses. The passage would be saying that *gōmeʾ* and *ʾāhû* wither before any other reeds. However, since both *gōmeʾ* and *ʾāhû* already refer to reeds, it seems more likely that they are being compared to something other than reeds. Therefore, *ḥāṣîr* in this passage probably refers to grass or vegetation in general. The verse would then be stating that when reeds do not have water, they dry up just as quickly as grass or other vegetation.

2.3.2. Translation of ḥāṣîr *in the Septuagint*

In the Septuagint, *ḥāṣîr* is primarily understood as designating grass. Even in two of the three passages (Isa 44:4; Job 8:12) where *ḥāṣîr* supposedly refers to reeds, the lexeme is rendered with Greek terms that denote grass, not reeds; in one passage (Isa 35:7), *ḥāṣîr* appears to have been understood as *ḥāṣēr* because the Septuagint has a Greek term that corresponds semantically to *ḥāṣēr* rather than to *ḥāṣîr*.[19] Twelve times *ḥāṣîr* is rendered with the term χόρτος 'pasture, grass' (e.g., Isa 15:6; 40:6–7; Ps 37:2 [36:2 LXX]; LSJ 2000; Muraoka 2009,

19. In two passages (Isa 34:13; 35:7), the translators of the Septuagint apparently read *ḥāṣîr* as *ḥāṣēr* and therefore rendered the Hebrew word with the Greek terms αὐλή 'courtyard, enclosure in building' and ἔπαυλις 'country house, temporary living quarters' (LSJ 276, 611; Muraoka 2009, 102, 260).

734), including Isa 44:4 (LSJ 1994; Muraoka 2009, 734–35).[20] Twice *ḥāṣîr* is translated as βοτάνη 'pasture, herbage', including Job 8:12 (see also 2 Kgs 19:26; LSJ 323; Muraoka 2009, 120).[21] Another two times *ḥāṣîr* is translated as χλόη 'grass' (2 Kgs 19:26; Ps 90:5 [89:5 LXX]; LSJ 1994; Muraoka 2009, 733); χλόη is also used to render *ḥāṣîr* in Symmachus's revision of Isa 37:27, although the Septuagint's rendering of the verse does not have a Greek word corresponding to *ḥāṣîr* (Ziegler 1939, 258).[22] In Prov 27:25, *ḥāṣîr* is translated as πόα 'plant, grass' (LSJ 1425; Muraoka 2009, 568), whereas *ḥāṣîr* is rendered in Num 11:15 as πράσον 'leek' (LSJ 1994; Muraoka 2009, 581).[23] In sum, the Septuagint and its revisions appear to understand *ḥāṣîr* as designating 'grass'.

We may conclude that the term *ḥāṣîr* carried the meaning 'grass, vegetation', but there is no compelling reason to hold that the lexeme also refers to reeds.

2.4. The Terms *ʾăgam* and *ʾagmôn*/*ʾagmōn*

2.4.1. Etymology

While the word *ʾăgam* carries the meaning 'swamp, reed marsh' (*DCH* 2018, 1:132; *HALOT* 1:11), the term *ʾagmôn*/*ʾagmōn* refers to the reed plants that grew along swamps and other bodies of water (*HALOT* 1:11; *DCH* 2018, 1:133). Some take *ʾagmôn*/*ʾagmōn* as a designation of the common reed *Phragmites communis* Trin., also known as *Phragmites australis* (Cav.) Trin. Ex Steud. (GMD 12; Löw 1967, 1:667). Zohary (1982, 135), however, understands the term as designating the lake bulrush *Scirpus lacustris* L., also known as *Schoenoplectus lacustris* (L.) Palla.[24]

20. According to the Syro-Hexapla, the lexeme χόρτος 'pasture, grass' is also used to render *ḥāṣîr* in Symmachus's revision of Ps 90:5 (89:5 LXX) (Field 1875, 2:246). The same Greek word is also used to render an occurrence of *ḥāṣîr* in Isa 40:7 in the revisions of the verse by Aquila, Symmachus, and Theodotion (Ziegler 1939, 267). In the Masoretic Text, *ḥāṣîr* occurs four times in Isa 40:6–8, but the Greek translation and its revisions seem to render it only three times, all with χόρτος, perhaps because the Hebrew *Vorlage* differed from the Masoretic Text.

21. According to the Syro-Hexapla, the lexeme βοτάνη 'pasture, herbage' is also used to render *ḥāṣîr* in Aquila's revision of Ps 147:8 (146:8 LXX) (Field 1875, 2:303).

22. According to Eusebius, the lexeme χλόη 'grass' is also used to render *ḥāṣîr* in the revisions of Isa 44:4 by Symmachus and Theodotion (Ziegler 1939, 285).

23. It is noteworthy that the lexeme πράσον 'leek' is also used to render *ḥāṣîr* in Aquila's revision of Isa 40:6–7 (Ziegler 1939, 267). Perhaps a more general sense of the word, such as 'herbage', is meant in this passage.

24. *Phragmites communis* Trin. (i.e., *Phragmites australis* (Cav.) Trin. ex Steud.) is a species that belongs to the *Cyperaceae* sedge family, and *Scirpus lacustris* L. (i.e., *Schoenoplectus lacustris* (L.) Palla) is a species of the *Poaceae* grass family.

The etymology of *ʾăgam*—and that of *ʾagmôn*/*ʾagmōn*, which is derived from *ʾăgam*—can be traced back to Sumerian agam (A×BAD, A.BAD) ‘swamp, reed lagoon’ (*CAD* 1/1:142). From Sumerian, the word entered Akkadian as *agammu*, and from Akkadian it entered Aramaic as *ʾăgam*/*ʾagmā*. From Aramaic, the term was finally loaned into Hebrew as *ʾăgam* (Mankowski 2000, 20).[25] The word *ʾagmôn*/*ʾagmōn* consists of the base *ʾăgam* with the sufformative *-ôn*/*-ōn*. The lexeme seems to be an adjectival form that became nominalized; the word’s meaning would thus have shifted from ‘of the pond’ to ‘reed’. Similar adjectival forms are *ʾaḥărôn* ‘last’ and *ḥîṣôn* ‘outer’; according to J-M (241), both are used adjectivally (Exod 4:8; 2 Chr 33:14) and nominally (1 Kgs 6:29; Eccl 1:11).[26]

In Akkadian, *agammu* refers to any marsh and specifically to the marshland in southern Babylonia. Two examples of the use of *agammu* in Akkadian should suffice to show its meaning. One text reads: *qanī apparāti ša qereb* ÍD *agammi akšiṭma* ‘I cut the reeds which were in that swamp’ (*CAD* 1/1:142). Another reads: *ultu Bīt-Jakin qereb* ÍD *agammē u apparāte ušēṣâm-ma* ‘I brought (booty) out from Bīt-Jakin which is amidst the marshes and swamps’ (*CAD* 1/1:142). In these passages, *agammu* clearly refers to the habitat of reeds, not the reeds themselves. In Aramaic, *ʾagmā* appears with meanings similar to those of Akkadian. The word refers to marshes and swamps, as well as meadows (Jastrow 1926, 1:13; Sokoloff 2003, 79; 2002, 34).

2.4.2. *Biblical Usage of* ʾăgam

Within the Bible, *ʾăgam* appears a total of nine times. In eight cases, the word is used to signify a body of water (Exod 7:19; 8:1; Isa 14:23; 35:7; 41:18; 42:15; Pss 107:35; 114:8). It also occurs once in 4Qnon-Canonical Psalms B where it refers to a body of water as well (4Q381 1, 4; *DSSR* 2:420; *DSSC* 1:7). That *ʾăgam* refers to a body of water is especially apparent in Exod 7:19: וַיֹּאמֶר יְהוָה אֶל־מֹשֶׁה אֱמֹר

25. That Hebrew borrowed the word from Aramaic rather than from Akkadian is confirmed by the vocalization of the term; that is, the Semitic noun pattern of *ʾăgam* is *qatall*. This pattern should become *qāṭāl* in Hebrew but *qtal* in Aramaic dialects (J. Fox 2003, 284–85). Because the term appears in Hebrew as *ʾăgam*, which reflects an underlying Aramaic *qtal* pattern, we must conclude that the word entered Hebrew via Aramaic (J. Fox 2003, 284). Had the word entered Hebrew directly from Akkadian, it would have been vocalized as ***ʾāgām*. J. Fox (2003, 284) points out that the Hebrew nouns *məʿaṭ* ‘little, few’, *hădas* ‘myrtle’, and *zəman* ‘time’—all nouns that reflect an Aramaic *qtal* pattern—were borrowed, like *ʾăgam*, from Aramaic.

26. While Hebrew borrowed *ʾăgam* from Aramaic, Aramaic borrowed *ʾagmôn*/*ʾagmōn* from Hebrew; *ʾagmōn*/*ʾagmōnā* is attested in Targum Jonathan (Jastrow 1926, 1:13). It is clear that Aramaic *ʾagmōn*/*ʾagmōnā* is a loan of Hebrew *ʾagmôn*/*ʾagmōn* because the Aramaic form, like the Hebrew form, has an *ō* vowel in the suffix *-ōn*/*-ôn*; if the word were native to Aramaic, the suffix would have remained an *ā* vowel (i.e., ***ʾagmān*/*ʾagmānā*). In Hebrew, on the other hand, the *ō* vowel of the suffix is expected.

אֱל־אַהֲרֹ֗ן קַ֣ח מַטְּךָ֣ וּנְטֵה־יָדְךָ֩ עַל־מֵימֵ֨י מִצְרַ֜יִם עַֽל־נַהֲרֹתָ֣ם ׀ עַל־יְאֹרֵיהֶ֣ם וְעַל־**אַגְמֵיהֶ֗ם** וְעַ֛ל כָּל־מִקְוֵ֥ה מֵימֵיהֶ֖ם וְיִֽהְיוּ־דָ֑ם וְהָ֤יָה דָם֙ בְּכָל־אֶ֣רֶץ מִצְרַ֔יִם וּבָעֵצִ֖ים וּבָאֲבָנִֽים 'YHWH said to Moses: "Say to Aaron, 'Take your staff and stretch out your hand against the waters of Egypt, against their rivers, against their streams, and against *ʾ**agmêhem*** ['their swamps'] and against all their pools of water, and they shall become blood. There will be blood in all the land of Egypt, and in (the vessels of) wood and stone'"'.

While the eight examples listed above clearly imply that *ʾăgam* denotes a body of water, the meaning of *ʾăgam* in Jer 51:32 seems to imply the presence of water plants. This verse is part of an oracle of doom against Babylon (Jer 51:1–58); according to the oracle, Babylon will be utterly destroyed for its razing of the temple in Jerusalem (Jer 51:11). Speaking of the capture and destruction of Babylon's waterways, Jer 51:32 reads: וְהַמַּעְבָּר֣וֹת נִתְפָּ֔שׂוּ וְאֶת־**הָאֲגַמִּ֖ים** שָׂרְפ֣וּ בָאֵ֑שׁ וְאַנְשֵׁ֥י הַמִּלְחָמָ֖ה נִבְהָֽלוּ 'The fords have been captured, and they burned the ***ʾăgammîm*** with fire, and the warriors are terrified'. Because the text speaks of burning the *ʾăgammîm*, we may conclude that the word in this verse refers not just to a body of water, but a body of water abundant in water plants; accordingly, the term probably signifies a marsh of reeds.[27]

2.4.3. Translation of ʾ**ăgam** *in the Septuagint*

Of the nine passages that contain *ʾăgam*, the Septuagint translates seven with corresponding Greek terms that designate marshes or bodies of water. In five instances, the word ἕλος 'marshy meadow, marshy ground' is used to render *ʾăgam* (Exod 7:19; 8:1; Isa 35:7; 41:18; 42:15; LSJ 537; Muraoka 2009, 224). Twice *ʾăgam* is translated as λίμνη 'pool of standing water, marshy lake' (Pss 107:35 [106:35 LXX]; 114:8 [113:8 LXX]; LSJ 1050; Muraoka 2009, 432). The lexeme ἕλος is also used to render *ʾăgam* in the revision of Isa 14:23 by Symmachus and Theodotion (Ziegler 1939, 177), and λίμνη is used in Aquila's revision of the same verse (Ziegler 1939, 177), although the Septuagint does not have a corresponding Greek word for *ʾăgam* in this verse inasmuch as the Hebrew *Vorlage* of the passage perhaps did not contain it.[28] Finally, in translating Jer 51:32 (28:32

27. The medieval commentator Ibn Janah compared *ʾăgammîm* of Jer 51:32 with Arabic *ʾujum* 'fortress' (Lane 1968, 1:26; Wehr 1976, 6), arguing that *ʾăgammîm* in this passage should be understood as referring to fortresses (Lundbom 2004b, 467). Some, indeed, follow this interpretation (*DCH* 1:132; *HALOT* 1:11). There is, however, no support for this view in the Septuagint, which renders *ʾăgammîm* as συστέματα 'gatherings, communities, pool of water' (LSJ 1735; Muraoka 2009, 664). Moreover, while Arabic *ʾujum* does indeed mean 'fortress', Arabic also has *ʾajama*, which refers to reeds and thickets. The similarity between the vowels in Hebrew *ʾăgam*/*ʾăgammîm* and Arabic *ʾajama* suggests a connection between these two lexemes rather than between *ʾăgam*/*ʾăgammîm* and *ʾujum*.

28. According to the Syro-Hexapla, the lexeme ἕλος 'marshy meadow, marshy ground' is also used to render *ʾăgam* in Symmachus's revision of Ps 114:8 (Field 1875, 2:268). The same Greek word

LXX), the Septuagint renders *ʾăgammîm* with the term συστέματα 'gatherings, communities, pool of water' (LSJ 1735; Muraoka 2009, 664), which seems to refer to reservoirs or pools of water.[29] The Septuagint's rendering of *ʾăgam* as συστέματα and λίμνη suggests that *ʾăgam* refers to a body of water; the rendering of *ʾăgam* as ἕλος, on the other hand, suggests that *ʾăgam* was understood as designating a body of water that was characterized by the presence of reeds in it.

2.4.4. Biblical Usage of ʾagmôn/ʾagmōn

The word *ʾagmôn/ʾagmōn* occurs five times in the Bible (Isa 9:13; 19:15; 58:5; Job 40:26; 41:12). The context of the passages containing *ʾagmôn/ʾagmōn* hints at the meaning of this term. In a couple passages, *ʾagmôn/ʾagmōn* stands in parallel with a lexeme designating a branch (*kippā*; Isa 9:13; 19:15), which implies that *ʾagmôn/ʾagmōn* is perhaps also a plant of an elongated shape. For instance, Isaiah 9:13 reads: וַיַּכְרֵת יְהוָה מִיִּשְׂרָאֵל רֹאשׁ וְזָנָב כִּפָּה **וְאַגְמוֹן** יוֹם אֶחָד 'YHWH cut off from Israel head and tail, branch and ***ʾagmôn*** in one day'. Additionally, we learn from Isa 58:5 that an *ʾagmôn/ʾagmōn* bends and bows. The verse criticizes the fasting of Israelites who bow their heads like an *ʾagmôn/ʾagmōn*. Isaiah 58:5 reads: הֲכָזֶה יִהְיֶה צוֹם אֶבְחָרֵהוּ יוֹם עַנּוֹת אָדָם נַפְשׁוֹ הֲלָכֹף **כְּאַגְמֹן** רֹאשׁוֹ וְשַׂק וָאֵפֶר יַצִּיעַ הֲלָזֶה תִּקְרָא־צוֹם וְיוֹם רָצוֹן לַיהוָה 'Will such a fast be the one that I choose—a day of a person's humbling his soul? Is it to bow his head like an ***ʾagmōn*** and to spread sackcloth and ashes? Will you call this a fast and an acceptable day to YHWH?'. We may deduce from these passages that an *ʾagmôn/ʾagmōn* is a thin plant prone to bending, presumably because of the wind blowing at it. Moreover, since *ʾagmôn/ʾagmōn* is derived from *ʾăgam* ('swamp; reed marsh'), we can safely infer that the term *ʾagmôn/ʾagmōn* designates the reed plant that grew along marshy bodies of water.

Of the five occurrences of *ʾagmôn/ʾagmōn*, four use the term with the meaning 'reed' (Isa 9:13; 19:15; 58:5; 41:12). In one instance (Job 40:26), the meaning of *ʾagmôn/ʾagmōn* is not clear. Because in this verse *ʾagmôn/ʾagmōn* stands in parallel to *ḥôaḥ* 'thorn, hook' (GMD 329), the term may refer to a reed hook;

---

is used in the revision of Jer 51:32 by Aquila and Symmachus (Ziegler 1957, 298). On the other hand, the lexeme λίμνη 'pool of standing water, marshy lake' is also utilized to render *ʾăgam* in Aquila's revision of Isa 35:7 and 41:18 (Ziegler 1939, 248, 274), and it is used in the revision of Isa 42:15 by Aquila and Symmachus (Ziegler 1939, 279). Also, the same term is used to render *ʾăgam* in variant readings of Exod 7:19 and 8:1 (Wevers and Quast 1991, 124, 126).

29. The word σύστεμα (pl. συστέματα) carries the meaning 'a whole compounded of several parts, pool of water'. It can refer to organized government, a flock or herd, machine apparatuses, and other entities that consist of multiple elements (LSJ 1735; Muraoka 2009, 664). That it can refer to bodies of water is made clear by the fact that it is used in the Septuagint to render *miqwē hammāyîm* 'pools of water' of Gen 1:10.

alternatively, it may denote a rope made of reeds (GMD 12).[30] The verse rhetorically asks if one would be able to put an *ʾagmôn/ʾagmōn* into the nose of Leviathan, presumably to pull the creature out of the water. Job 40:26 reads: הֲתָשִׂים **אַגְמֹון** בְּאַפּוֹ וּבְחוֹחַ תִּקּוֹב לֶחֱיוֹ ‘Will you place an ***ʾagmôn*** into its nose? Will you pierce its cheek with a hook?’. Admittedly, the passage is a bit difficult to understand, so the meaning of *ʾagmôn/ʾagmōn* in this verse remains elusive.

2.4.5. Translation of ʾagmôn/ʾagmōn *in the Septuagint*

The translation of *ʾagmôn/ʾagmōn* in the Septuagint is not particularly helpful because there is not a one-to-one match between *ʾagmôn/ʾagmōn* and a corresponding Greek term with the meaning ‘reed’, either because the Hebrew *Vorlage* did not contain *ʾagmôn/ʾagmōn* or because the Greek translation is paraphrastic in nature. Twice it seems to be translated as κρίκος ‘ring on a horse’s breastband’ (Isa 58:5; Job 40:26; LSJ 995; Muraoka 2009, 412); in these two cases, it may be that the Greek text is comparing the shape of a bent reed to the oval shape of a ring. The word appears to be rendered once as μικρός ‘small’ (Isa 9:13; LSJ 1133; Muraoka 2009, 462–63) and once as τέλος ‘end’ (Isa 19:15; LSJ 1773; Muraoka 2009, 675–76).[31] In the Hebrew text of both of these passages, *ʾagmôn/ʾagmōn* is used in a merism that speaks of tree branches growing high above the ground and of reeds growing down below near rivers (i.e., *kippā wəʾagmôn* ‘branch and reed’); in colloquial English, this merism can be rendered as ‘high and low’. In the Greek text, however, the Hebrew merism is paraphrased in two different ways, once as the phrase μέγαν καὶ μικρόν ‘great and small’ (Isa 9:13; LSJ 1088–89, 1133; Muraoka 2009, 462–63, 445–46) and another time as the phrase ἀρχὴν καὶ τέλος ‘beginning and end’ (Isa 19:15; LSJ 252, 1773; Muraoka 2009, 94–95, 675–76). In another verse, the Septuagint seems to render *ʾagmôn/ʾagmōn* as ἄνθραξ ‘charcoal’ (Job 41:12; LSJ 141; Muraoka 2009, 52). Unfortunately, the Septuagint’s translation of *ʾagmôn/ʾagmōn* does not elucidate the word’s meaning.

All in all, neither *ʾăgam* nor *ʾagmôn/ʾagmōn* refer to the cultivated papyrus plant out of which writing material was manufactured. The former term refers to the location of the reeds (marshy swamps), while the latter term refers to the reeds themselves that grew near bodies of water. Without a certain case in which *ʾăgam* or *ʾagmôn/ʾagmōn* is used in connection with the production of goods,

30. Ropes were indeed made of reeds (Leach and Tait 2000, 228), so it is possible that *ʾagmôn/ʾagmōn* is used with that meaning in this passage.

31. According to Jerome, Theodotion’s revision of Isa 19:15 merely transliterates *ʾagmôn/ʾagmōn* into Greek as ἀγμόν (Ziegler 1939, 190; Field 1875, 2:463).

we may safely conclude that these two lexemes were not the ancient Hebrew terms that designated the manufacturable papyrus used as writing material.

2.5. The Term *qāne*

2.5.1. Etymology and Biblical Usage

The Hebrew term *qāne* 'wild reed plant; tubular rod, stick' is inherited from Proto-Semitic **qanaw*- and has cognates in Akkadian (*qanû* 'reed'; *CAD* 13:85), Arabic (*qanāt* 'spear'; Lane 1968, 8:2994), Syriac (*qanyā* 'reed'; Sokoloff 2009, 383–84; *CAL*), and Ugaritic (*qn* 'reed'; *DULAT* 2:704–5). It appears that **qanaw*- would have been the Proto-Semitic term designating the reeds that grew in the reed marshes of southern Mesopotamia. Today, two species are most commonly used there: *Phragmites australis* (Cav.) Trin. Ex Steud. and *Arundo donax* L. (Moorey 1999, 361; Postgate 1980, 102).[32] Indeed, scholars have identified Hebrew *qāne* and Akkadian *qanûm* as designating these two species (GMD 1175; *HALOT* 2:1113; Zohary 1982, 134; Löw 1967, 1:664). In the cases where *qāne* refers to reeds used to produce spices (e.g., Exod 30:23; Isa 43:24), it has been suggested that the term designated the plant *Cymbopogon Martinii* (Roxb.) J.F. Watson, which is also known as *Andropogon aromaticus*, a type of lemon grass used to produce aromatic oil (GMD 1176).[33]

The word *qāne* occurs sixty-two times in the Bible. It also occurs at least five times in the Dead Sea Scrolls, excluding cases with restored letters (*DSSC* 2:656). In only nine cases in the Bible does the word refer to the wild reed plant or a type of staff made of reed (1 Kgs 14:15; 2 Kgs 18:21; Isa 19:6; 35:7; 36:6; 42:3; Ezek 29:6; Ps 68:31; Job 40:21). In a few passages, *qāne* refers to the wild reed plant that grows in bodies of water. For instance, in 1 Kgs 14:15, *qāne* is depicted as swaying to and fro in water. The passage reads: וְהִכָּה יְהוָה אֶת־יִשְׂרָאֵל כַּאֲשֶׁר יָנוּד **הַקָּנֶה** בַּמַּיִם וְנָתַשׁ אֶת־יִשְׂרָאֵל מֵעַל הָאֲדָמָה הַטּוֹבָה הַזֹּאת 'Yʜᴡʜ will strike Israel just as the ***qāne*** sways in water, and He will uproot Israel from this good land'. Similarly, Isa 19:6 mentions *qāne* in connection with rivers. In this passage, *qāne* stands in parallel with *sûp* 'wild reed plant, papyrus (?), marsh of reeds'. The verse reads: וְהֶאֶזְנִיחוּ נְהָרוֹת דָּלְלוּ וְחָרְבוּ יְאֹרֵי מָצוֹר **קָנֶה** וָסוּף קָמֵלוּ 'The rivers will stink, the rivers of Egypt will decrease and will dry up, ***qāne*** and marshes of reeds [*sûp*] will decay'. It seems that *qāne* designates the reed plant in Isa 35:7 as

32. While *Phragmites australis* (Cav.) Trin. ex Steud. is a species belonging to the *Cyperaceae* sedge family, *Arundo donax* L. is a species in the *Poaceae* grass family.

33. *Cymbopogon martinii* (Roxb.) J.F. Watson (i.e., *Andropogon aromaticus*) is a species within the *Poaceae* grass family.

well, because in this passage it stands in parallel with *gōme*ʾ 'papyrus', which suggests that the two words carry a similar meaning. In Ps 68:31, we learn that *qāne* is a habitat for animals; and in Job 40:21, *qāne* stands in parallel with *biṣṣā* 'swamp, marsh', which again implies that *qāne* refers to wild reeds growing in swamps and marshes.

In another five cases, the word refers to a specific reed plant that was used to produce spices (Exod 30:23; Isa 43:24; Jer 6:20; Ezek 27:19; Song 4:14), and twice the word refers to the stalk of grain (Gen 41:5, 22). The remaining forty-six occurrences are those in which *qāne* refers to something other than a plant but that has a tubular shape. Accordingly, in twenty cases, *qāne* refers to a measuring reed;[34] in twenty-four cases, it refers to a golden rod or branch of a menorah;[35] once it refers to the beam of a balance (Isa 46:6); and once it refers to an arm bone (Job 31:22). In the Dead Sea Scrolls, twice it refers to an arm bone (1QHᵃ XV, 5; XVI, 34; *DSSR* 2:308, 314; *DSSC* 2:656) and three times perhaps to a rod or branch (4Q266 16a, 3; 11Q19 IX, 9; 11Q21 2, 2; *DSSR* 1:149, 638, 732; *DSSC* 2:656).

As all of these passages demonstrate, *qāne* can refer to the wild reed plant, a reed marsh, or an object made of reed. The term *qāne* can also refer to a variety of objects that have a tubular shape, regardless of whether these objects are made of reed (e.g., golden menorah branches, arm bone) (*DCH* 7:269). The term probably initially meant 'reed stalk' and over time developed the general meaning 'tubular, rod, stick'. It seems probable that certain objects designated by the term *qāne* were in fact made of reed (e.g., measuring reed, beam of balance),[36] but the biblical text does not explicitly use *qāne* to refer to manufacturable papyrus utilized for the production of papyrus paper.

2.5.2. *Translation of* qāne *in the Septuagint*

When looking at the Septuagint's translation of passages containing *qāne*, it is clear that *qāne* is translated in the majority of cases with a word related to κάλαμος 'reed' (LSJ 865–66). When the Hebrew text refers to the reed plant, κάλαμος or καλάμινος 'made of reed' is used (LSJ 865–66; Muraoka 2009, 358); κάλαμος is also used in verses where a measuring rod is mentioned (e.g., Ezek 40:3). In total, κάλαμος appears to be used twenty times (e.g., Isa 19:6), while καλάμινος is used four times (e.g., 2 Kgs 18:21). When *qāne* refers to a menorah

34. The term *qāne* means 'measuring reed' in the following passages: Ezek 40:3, 5–8; 41:8; 42:16–19.

35. The term *qāne* refers to a golden rod or branch of a menorah in the following passages: Exod 25:31–33, 35–36; 37:17–19, 21–22.

36. Measuring rods in Mesopotamia (i.e., *qan mindati*; *CAD* 13:89) were indeed made of reeds (Driver 1976, 32).

handle (e.g., Exod 25:31), the Septuagint has καλαμίσκος 'branch of candlestick', a diminutive form of κάλαμος (LSJ 865–66; Muraoka 2009, 358). The Septuagint has a few other translations of *qāne* that are unrelated to κάλαμος, particularly the cases in which *qāne* pertains to spices (Isa 43:24; Jer 6:20), the beam of a balance (Isa 46:6), stalks of grain (Gen 41:5, 22), and an arm bone (Job 31:22).[37] There are also cases in which the Septuagint does not include a corresponding word for *qāne*, although, according to the Syro-Hexapla, *qāne* is rendered in one case (1 Kgs 14:15) as κάλαμος (Brooke, McLean, and Thackeray 1906–40, 2:264).

The lexeme κάλαμος was used in most cases to translate *qāne* because κάλαμος carried the same range of meanings as *qāne*. In addition to designating the reed plant, both terms carry the general meaning 'tubular, rod, stick'. Thus, as mentioned above, *qāne* can refer to tubular objects such as a reed, a stalk of grain, a golden menorah branch, a measuring reed, or an arm bone. In similar fashion, κάλαμος in Greek texts can refer to a reed, an arrow, or a fishing rod (LSJ 865–6; Muraoka 2009, 358); it can also refer to a writing instrument made of reed (e.g., 3 Macc 4:20 and Ps 45:2 [44:2 LXX]).

To sum up, we can say that the Hebrew term *qāne* had a variety of meanings. Nevertheless, the primary meaning, which probably derived from Proto-Semitic, was 'wild reed'. Although the term can refer to reeds as a wild plant, it is most often used to speak of objects of a tubular shape—that is, a shape that would resemble a wild reed. Furthermore, while *qāne* does not designate manufacturable papyrus material, I would suggest that it is the particular lexeme that refers to the material utilized to make reed pens. While no biblical passage explicitly refers to reed pens, we know that pens were made of reeds in the ancient world (*CAD* 13:89; Driver 1976, 32). Moreover, translations in the Septuagint and Peshitta of Ps 45:2 [44:2 LXX], which speaks of a 'pen of a skilled scribe' (*ʿēṭ sōpēr māhîr*), support the idea that *qāne* designates the reed material used to produce pens in ancient Israel. The Septuagint renders the lexeme *ʿēṭ* 'pen' as κάλαμος; as mentioned above, κάλαμος is also used in the Septuagint to translate *qāne* when it refers to wild reeds (e.g., 2 Kgs 18:21). In the Peshitta's translation of Ps 45:2, the term *ʿēṭ* is rendered as *qnē*/*qanyā* 'reed'; as expected, the Peshitta also uses the term *qnē*/*qanyā* to translate occurrences of the word

37. When *qāne* refers to spices, it is translated once as θυμίαμα 'incense' (Isa 43:24) and once as κιννάμωμον 'cinnamon' (Jer 6:20) (LSJ 809, 953; Muraoka 2009, 333, 398). In Isa 43:24, however, Aquila, Symmachus, and Theodotion have κάλαμος 'reed' (Ziegler 1939, 284), and Aquila and Josephus also have κάλαμος in Jer 6:20 (Ziegler 1957, 181). When referring to stalks of grain, *qāne* is rendered as πυθμήν 'stem' (Gen 41:5, 22) (LSJ 1551; Muraoka 2009, 607), although the versions by Aquila and Symmachus render these cases as κάλαμος (Wevers 1974, 382, 386); the case in Gen 41:22 is also rendered as κάλαμος by Origen (Wevers 1974, 386). When *qāne* refers to the beam of a balance, it is rendered as ζυγός 'weight' (Isa 46:6) (LSJ 1633; Muraoka 2009, 632); when designating an arm bone, *qāne* is translated as ἀγκών 'elbow' (Job 31:22) (LSJ 10; Muraoka 2009, 6).

qāne when it refers to wild reeds, as in Isa 19:6 (Sokoloff 2009, 1383–84; *CAL*). We may thus surmise that, just as Greek κάλαμος and Syriac *qnē*/*qanyā* refer to the reed plant as well as a reed pen, Hebrew *qāne* may refer to the reed plant and perhaps also the material of which pens were made in ancient Israel.[38]

2.6. The Term *sûp*

2.6.1. Etymology

The term *sûp*, which occurs twenty-nine times in the Bible, carries the meaning 'wild reed plant, papyrus (?), marsh of reeds' (*DCH* 6:134). It also probably occurs three times in the Dead Sea Scrolls, once referring to the geographical location Suph (4Q364 20a–c, 2; *DSSR* 1:752; *DSSC* 2:530), and once referring to the Sea of Reeds, although in this instance the *pe* is restored (1Q33 XI, 10; *DSSR* 1:260; *DSSC* 2:529); in another fragmentary text, the consonants *swp* follow a *mem* letter, which suggests that the reference is also to the Sea of Reeds (4Q491 18, 5; *DSSR* 1:292; *DSSC* 2:529). Zohary (1982, 136) holds that *sûp* designates the cattail plant, specifically *Typha australis* Schum and Thonn., also known as *Typha domingensis* Pers.[39] Others take it to be the papyrus plant (GMD 878; Löw 1967, 1:572, 575).

Traditionally, *sûp* has been viewed as a loanword from Egyptian, deriving from *ṯwfy* 'marsh plant, papyrus' (*WÄS* 5:359).[40] Albright (1934, 65), and later Lambdin (1953, 153), suggested that *ṯwfy* should be vocalized as *ṯăwfĕy*. There are difficulties, however, with accepting the view that Hebrew *sûp* derives from Egyptian *ṯwfy*. Lambdin himself points out that the expected Hebrew derivation from Egyptian *ṯăwfĕy* should be *sôp*, not *sûp*. Moreover, because *ṯwfy* is first attested only in the New Kingdom (1549–1069 BCE; *WÄS* 5:359), Muchiki (1999, 251–52) suggests that *ṯwfy* may be a syllabic spelling and therefore a loanword within Egyptian. Lambdin (1953, 153), however, points out that *ṯwfy* appears in Coptic as *ǧouf*, which suggests that the *w* of *ṯwfy* was probably consonantal;[41] a consonantal *w* rules out the possibility that *ṯwfy* was written syllabically.

38. See 5.1.1.3–5.1.1.5 for further discussion of reed and rush pens.

39. *Typha australis* Schum and Thonn. (i.e., *Typha domingensis* Pers.) is a species belonging to the *Typhaceae* cattail family.

40. In transcriptions of Egyptian words, *ṯ* designates a palatalized unvoiced apical stop (IPA *c*) (Allen 2013, xii), not Semitic *ṯ* (= *θ*).

41. In Late Egyptian, a stressed *a* vowel becomes a stressed *o* vowel; this sound shift is inherited by Coptic (Loprieno 1995, 46). Lambdin is thus right in arguing that the Coptic word *ǧouf* suggests that the vocalization of *ṯwfy* was perhaps **ṯăwfĕy*.

In support of Muchiki's claim that *ṯwfy* is a Semitic loanword in Egyptian, we may mention that, in the twelve cases of Semitic words with *s* that entered Egyptian, Semitic *s* is always written as Egyptian *ṯ* (Hoch 1994, 432).[42] These data fit Muchiki's suggestion nicely. Nevertheless, here I will argue in support of the traditional view, focusing primarily on the question of whether Egyptian *ṯ* could have entered Hebrew as *s*. By considering Egyptian loanwords within Northwest Semitic languages and Semitic loanwords within Egyptian, I will attempt to show that the loan vector of Egyptian *ṯ* entering Canaanite/Hebrew as *s* was plausible, although it is supported by indirect evidence.

***2.6.2. Phonology of Egyptian* ṯwfy *and Hebrew* sûp**

In his collection of Egyptian loanwords in Northwest Semitic languages, Muchiki does not offer any concrete examples of Egyptian *ṯ* entering Northwest Semitic languages as *s*. Nevertheless, the examples given in his work do provide a context in which the correspondence Egyptian *ṯ* > Canaanite/Hebrew *s* may have occurred. Muchiki lists only two possible cases of Egyptian words with *ṯ* entering Canaanite/Hebrew. First, he evaluates the geographical name *ṯkw* 'Tell el-Maskuta' and rightly concludes that this instance is actually a borrowing into Egyptian of Canaanite Sukkôt (Muchiki 1999, 233). Indeed, the loan vector of Semitic *s* > Egyptian *ṯ*, as reflected in the case of *Sukkôt* > *ṯkw*, is also apparent in twelve other examples mentioned below. Secondly, Muchiki (1999, 251) discusses the Egyptian term *nṯr(ỉ)* 'natron', which appears in Hebrew as *neter* 'lye'. In this instance, Egyptian *ṯ* was clearly realized as [t] at the time this word was loaned into Canaanite/Hebrew. These two examples offer little support for the claim that Egyptian *ṯ* could have entered Canaanite/Hebrew as *s*. Nevertheless, the penetration of Egyptian words containing *ṯ* into other Northwest Semitic languages does provide some indirect evidence that Egyptian *ṯ* could have entered Canaanite/Hebrew as *s*.

Muchiki examines Egyptian words containing *ṯ* that entered into Amarna Canaanite, Aramaic, and Phoenician. Of the three Egyptian words loaned into Amarna Canaanite, Egyptian *ṯ* is rendered as *t* in one word (*Paḫa(m)nata/e* < *p(3)-ḥm-nṯ(r)* 'Servant of god', see Muchiki 1999, 294), but as *z/s* in two other words. The two words in which Egyptian *ṯ* is rendered as Amarna Canaanite *z/s* are normalized by Muchiki as *pazite* < *p(3)-ṯ(3)t(y)* 'vizier' (1999, 300) and *zabnakû* < *ṯ(3)b-n-k(3)* 'ka-vessel' (1999, 303). While Muchiki transcribes both words with a *z*, it is just as reasonable to transcribe them with *s*, or with *ṣ* for

42. See the end of 2.6.2 for the twelve words in which Semitic *s* entered Egyptian as *ṯ*.

that matter; *CAD* normalizes the former term as *pasite/pazite* < *pa-sí-t[e]* (*CAD* 12:221), but the latter word as *zabnakû* < *za-ab-na-ku-u* (*CAD* 21:9).[43]

In regard to Aramaic, a total of fourteen words derive from Egyptian terms that contain *ṯ*. Of the fourteen, eight appear in Aramaic with *t*, according to Muchiki 1999:

pṭnty < *p(3)-d(ỉ)-nṯ(r)* 'He whom the god has given' (117)
pṭntr < *p(3)-d(ỉ)-nṯr(.w)* 'He whom gods have given' (118)
pqṭnwty < *p(3)-qd-nṯ(r)* 'The builder of god' (130)
ptyrwt < *p(3)-ṯ(3w)-rwḏ(.w)* 'The strong wind' (137)
ptnwṭ' < *p(3)-(n-)ṯn(ỉ)-wḏ3(.w)* 'The Thinite is prosperous' (137)
psḥmṣnwty < *p(3)-sḥ-mḏ(3.t)-nṯ(r)* 'The scribe of the god's book(s)' (170)
qnḥnty < *qnḥ(.t)-nṯr* 'the chapel of god' (172)
tmw'nty < *t(3)-mỉ(.t)-nṯ(r)* 'the way of god' (174)

Six appear with *š*:

smšk < *s-n-mṯk* 'Man of mixed drink' (99)
psmšk < *psmṯk* 'Psammetich' (128)
psmškmr < *psmṯk-mr(y)* 'Psammetich, the beloved of' (128)
psmškḥsy < *psmṯk-ḥsy* 'Psammetich is favored' (128)
šḥpymw < *ṯ(3y)-ḥp-ỉm.w* 'Apis can seize them' (143)
šmw < *ṯ(3y)-ỉm.w* 'he (a god) can seize them' (143)

Only three Egyptian words with *ṯ* entered into Phoenician. In these three Phoenician words, Egyptian *ṯ* appears twice as *ṣ* (*ṣḥpmw* < *ṯ(3y)-ḥp-(ỉ)m.w* 'Apis can seize them' and *ṣknsmw* < *ṯ(3y)-ḫns(.w)-(ỉ)m.w* 'Khons can seize them', see Muchiki 1999:41) and once as *š* (*šmw* < *ṯ(3y)-(ỉ)m.w* 'he (a god) can seize them', see Muchiki 1999:42). Thus, while in most cases Egyptian *ṯ* came into Northwest Semitic languages as *t*, the cases of Egyptian *ṯ* entering Northwest Semitic languages as *ṣ*, *z/s*, and *š* demonstrate that Egyptian *ṯ* was perceived by Semites not only as [t], but also as other phones, two of which (*ṣ* and *z/s*) resemble in part Hebrew *s* (=[ts]). Accordingly, because Northwest Semitic consonants *ṣ* and *z/s* can derive from Egyptian *ṯ*—and because Hebrew *s* and Northwest Semitic *ṣ*

43. Ward (1974, 347 n. 1) gathers a few other examples supposedly demonstrating that Egyptian *ṯ* entered other languages as *z* or *t* but not as *s*; for instance, in the Akkadian place name *Zabnūti* (< *ṯb-nṯr*), Egyptian *ṯ* entered as *z* and *t*. Also, in the Hittite place names *Zinapa* (< *ṯ3-nfr*) and *Perizzi* (< *prṯ*), Egyptian *ṯ* entered as *z*. In all these cases, however, the transcription of Egyptian *ṯ* as *z* is a matter of writing convention. We can just as easily transcribe the Akkadian cases with *s* or *ṣ* (*GAG* 35–36), and the *z* of the Hittite examples could have been realized as [ts] rather than [z] (*GHL* 37–38).

and *z/s* share similar acoustic features—perhaps it is not unreasonable to consider the *s* of *sûp* as deriving from Egyptian *ṯ* of *ṯwfy*.

The study of Semitic loanwords within Egyptian by Hoch (1994) offers more indirect support for such a claim. Hoch examines Semitic loanwords within Egyptian in the time period between the New Kingdom (1549–1069 BCE) and the Third Intermediate Period (1064–656 BCE). This coincides with Late Middle Egyptian (1650–1350 BCE) and Late Egyptian (1350–650 BCE) (Allen 2013, 3). In discussing the correspondences of Semitic *s* and Egyptian *ṯ*, Hoch points to twelve fairly certain cases of Semitic words containing *s* that were rendered in Egyptian with *ṯ* (1994, 432). Hoch provides the following examples:

> *ʾa*$_2$*=ṯi*$_2$*=ra* < **ʾa*^{t}*sīr-* 'captive' (45)
> *ḫa=ra=ṯi=ta* <**ḫar*^{t}*sit-* 'sun' (251)
> *ku=ṯi*$_2$ < **kō*^{t}*s-* 'cup, goblet' (339)
> *ku=ṯi*$_2$*=ta* < **ku*^{t}*sīt-* 'garment, covering' (341)
> *na*$_2$*=wa=ṯi*$_2$*; nu=ṯi*$_2$ < **nawa*^{t}*sa; nū*^{t}*sa* 'to tremble' (184)
> *ṯ=r=r=ya* < ***^{t}*sōlilā* 'siege-mound' (368)
> *ṯu=ru*$_2$*=ta; ṯu*$_2$*=ru*$_2$*=ta; ṯi*$_2$*=—r=ta* < ***^{t}*sult-* 'finely ground wheat flour' (369)
> *ṯi*$_2$*=pa=ra* < ***^{t}*sipl-* 'large drinking bowl' (364)
> *ṯu=pi*$_3$*=—r* < ***^{t}*sōpir-* 'scribe' (364)
> *ṯu=pi=ra=ta*$_5$ < ***^{t}*saparr-; **^{t}*siparr-* 'bronze covered chariot' (365)
> *ṯi*$_2$*=ra=ya=na; ṯi*$_2$*=ru*$_2$*=yu=na* < ***^{t}*siryān-* 'body armour' (367)
> *k=ṯi*$_2$*=ma*$_4$ < **qi*^{t}*sm-* 'divination' (339)

Posener (1940, 68) offers an even earlier example from the Middle Kingdom. He suggests that *ʾa=ṯ=p H=d=du* contains the Semitic root *ʾ-s-p/y-s-p*. However, Egyptian *ṯ* was also used five times to render Semitic *t*, twice to render Semitic *ḏ*, and once to render Semitic *θ* (Hoch 1994, 436). Hoch (1994, 408, 429) argues that Egyptian *ṯ* was initially a palatalized *t* ([t^j] = IPA *c*) but was pronounced as the affricate [ts] by the New Kingdom (1549–1069 BCE). If Hoch is right that *ṯ* was realized as an affricate in the New Kingdom, it is not surprising that Egyptian *ṯ* was used to render the *s* of Canaanite loanwords within Egyptian; after all, Canaanite *s* derives from the Proto-Semitic affricate ***^{t}*s* and was probably pronounced as such at the time that the aforementioned Semitic words were loaned into Egyptian (Huehnergard 2002, 13). Conversely, if Egyptian *ṯ* was indeed realized as the affricate [ts], it is quite possible that Egyptian *ṯ* could have entered Canaanite/Hebrew as *s*.[44]

44. Allen (2013, 54) holds that Egyptian *ṯ* was realized not as affricate [ts], but as [t/t^h] and [ṯ/$ṯ^h$]; in Allen's peculiar transliteration system, *t/*$ṯ^h$ is equivalent to IPA *c/*c^h. Contrary to Hoch (1994, 408, 429), who holds that Egyptian *ṯ* was realized as affricate [ts], Allen (2013, 48, 210 n. 60) argues that

To recap, in a number of Egyptian words that entered Canaanite, Egyptian *ṯ* is rendered as Semitic *s/ṣ/z* (e.g., *piz/satu*, *zabnakû*). Semitic *s* was also rendered as Egyptian *ṯ* in Semitic words that entered Egyptian. These data suggest that Egyptian *ṯ* and Semitic *s* were pronounced in a similar manner, perhaps as the affricate [ts]. Accordingly, it is not unreasonable to view the *s* of Hebrew *sûp* as deriving from the *ṯ* of Egyptian *ṯwfy*. Nevertheless, it is difficult to explain how the diphthong *aw* of Egyptian *ṯăwfĕy* could have become *û* of Hebrew *sûp*.

2.6.3. Usage of ṯwfy *in Egyptian*

Within Egyptian texts, *ṯwfy* is used as a collective term to speak of marsh plants in general, and at times it may refer specifically to the papyrus plant (Ward 1974, 339–43). Ward (1974, 340–41) discusses an insightful example in which various marsh plants are referred to as *ṯwfy*. In this example, rushes (*ỉsr*), sedges (*šmʿ.t*), and papyrus (*w3ḏ*) are listed under the title '*ṯwfy*-work' (*b3k.w nw ṯwf*). Ward also suggests that in some texts *ṯwfy* should be understood as referring specifically to papyrus. One passage, for instance, mentions that *ṯwfy* is situated in a garden. Ward (1974, 341) argues that, because Egyptian gardens were lined with papyrus, we must understand *ṯwfy* in this case as referring to papyrus. It seems, then, that the Egyptian term *ṯwfy* has a general meaning of 'marsh plant' and can also specifically denote the papyrus plant. As will be shown shortly, the semantics of *sûp* correspond nicely to the semantics of *ṯwfy*.

Assuming Egyptian *ṯwfy* is the source of Hebrew *sûp*, the term was probably loaned during the New Kingdom (1549–1069 BCE) when other Egyptian writing-related terms entered Canaanite/Hebrew, as discussed in chapter 6.

2.6.4. Biblical Usage of sûp

The term *sûp* appears twenty-nine times in the Hebrew Bible. In four cases the word is used to refer to some type of water plant or to the area where the water plant grows (Exod 2:3, 5; Isa 19:6; Jonah 2:6). In Exodus, Moses is placed into the *sûp* of the Nile after being placed in a basket made of papyrus (*gōmeʾ*; Exod 2:3); he is later discovered by Pharaoh's daughter among the *sûp* (Exod 2:5). In these two passages, *sûp* is used to refer to an area abundant with reeds. Exodus 2:3 reads: וְלֹא־יָכְלָה עוֹד הַצְּפִינוֹ וַתִּקַּח־לוֹ תֵּבַת גֹּמֶא וַתַּחְמְרָה בַחֵמָר וּבַזָּפֶת וַתָּשֶׂם בָּהּ

Semitic *s* was rendered as Egyptian *ṯ* due to approximation. Even if Allen is correct that Egyptian *ṯ* was only realized as [t/t^h] and [ṯ/ṯ^h], my argument remains intact. After all, my claim is not that Egyptian *ṯ* was in fact realized as the affricate [ts], but that Egyptian *ṯ* could have been perceived as such by Semites. In view of the examples of Egyptian *ṯ* entering Northwest Semitic languages as *ṣ* and *z/s*, both of which resemble the affricate [ts], it seems plausible to me that Egyptian *ṯ* could have been perceived by Semites also as [ts].

אֶת־הַיֶּלֶד וַתָּשֶׂם **בַּסּוּף** עַל־שְׂפַת הַיְאֹר ‘She could no longer hide him, so she took for him a basket of papyrus [*gōme*ʾ] and daubed it with bitumen and pitch, and she put the child into it, and put (it) in the ***sûp*** on the bank of the Nile river’. Isaiah 19:6 also refers to the *sûp* of the Nile. In this verse, *sûp* stands in parallel with *qāne* ‘wild reed plant’, and *sûp* seems to be referring to the wild reed plant as a collective. The passage reads: וְהֶאֶזְנִיחוּ נְהָרוֹת דָּלְלוּ וְחָרְבוּ יְאֹרֵי מָצוֹר קָנֶה **וָסוּף** קָמֵלוּ ‘The rivers will stink, the rivers of Egypt will decrease and will dry up, reeds and ***sûp*** will decay’. Finally, in Jonah 2:6, *sûp* refers to the seaweed attached to Jonah’s head.

The term *sûp* is also used once to designate the geographical location Suph (Deut 1:1). Another twenty-four times it is used in the phrase *yam sûp*—that is, the ‘Sea of Reeds’ (Exod 10:19; 13:18; 15:4, 22; 23:31; Num 14:25; 21:4; 33:10, 11; Deut 1:40; 2:1; 11:4; Josh 2:10; 4:23; 24:6; Judg 11:16; 1 Kgs 9:26; Jer 49:21; Pss 106:7, 9, 22; 136:13, 15; Neh 9:9). For instance, Exod 15:3–4 reads: יְהוָה אִישׁ מִלְחָמָה יְהוָה שְׁמוֹ׃ מַרְכְּבֹת פַּרְעֹה וְחֵילוֹ יָרָה בַיָּם וּמִבְחַר שָׁלִשָׁיו טֻבְּעוּ **בְיַם־סוּף** ‘YHWH is a warrior, YHWH is His name. The chariots of Pharaoh and his army He cast into the sea, and his choice officers were sunk in ***yam sûp***’. In four passages (Exod 2:3, 5; Isa 19:6; Jonah 2:6), *sûp* unambiguously connotes a water plant or its habitat. In the twenty-four occurrences of the phrase *yam sûp*, the lexeme *sûp* also probably refers to wild reeds or marshes of reeds. In Deut 1:1, it is not clear how the geographical location *sûp* ‘Suph’ should be understood. Perhaps it denotes a place of marshes, but this is difficult to prove. In about half of all occurrences of *sûp*, the term appears in connection with the Nile Delta (Roskop 2011, 196; Exod 2:3, 5; 15:4, 22; Deut 11:4; Josh 2:10; 4:23; 24:6; Judg 11:6; Pss 106:7, 9, 22; 136:13, 15; Isa 19:6; Neh 9:9). This association of *sûp* with Egypt does not prove that *sûp* is Egyptian in origin, but it suggests that this may indeed be the case.

2.6.5. Translation of* sûp *in the Septuagint

The Septuagint’s rendering of *sûp* suggests that the word refers to the habitat of reeds as well as the reeds themselves. In translating Exod 2:3 and 2:5, the Septuagint renders *sûp* as ἕλος ‘marsh meadow, marshy ground’ (LSJ 537; Muraoka 2009, 224), although *sûp* is also rendered as πάπυρος ‘papyrus’ (LSJ 1302; Muraoka 2009, 522) once in Aquila’s revision of Exod 2:3 and another time in a variant reading of Exod 2:5 (Wevers and Quast 1991, 72).[45] Similarly, *sûp* is rendered as πάπυρος in Isa 19:6, although it appears to be rendered as

45. The Greek word πάπυρος ‘papyrus’ (LSJ 1302; Muraoka 2009, 522) generally refers to the wild reed plant, not to manufacturable papyrus material. It is usually the Greek term βύβλος ‘Egyptian papyrus’ (LSJ 333; Muraoka 2009, 117, 124) that refers to manufacturable papyrus material (Lewis 1974, 14–15). See also the discussion below on the term *gōme*ʾ, which outlines the semantics of the two Greek terms in more detail.

ἕλος in a variant reading of the same verse (Ziegler 1939, 189). In Jonah 2:6, the translators of the Septuagint apparently read *sôp*, not *sûp*, because the Greek has ἔσχατος 'farthest' (LSJ 699; Muraoka 2009, 294; Harl et al. 1999, 150);[46] however, a variant reading of the verse has ἕλος (Ziegler 1943, 248). Almost all cases in which *sûp* appears as part of the phrase *yam sûp*, the Septuagint renders *sûp* as ἐρυθρός 'red', interpreting *yam sûp* as referring to the Red Sea (LSJ 693; Muraoka 2009, 292). In one case (Jer 49:21 [30:15 LXX]), there is not a corresponding Greek word for *sûp*, although it is rendered as ἐρυθρός in the revisions of Aquila, Symmachus, and Theodotion and in the Hexapla's fifth column; it is also rendered as such in variant readings of the passage, one of which includes a Lucianic recension (Ziegler 1957, 310). While the Septuagint's translation of the phrase *yam sûp* does not help us in understanding the meaning of *sûp*, the rendering of *sûp* as ἕλος and πάπυρος in the Exodus, Isaiah, and Jonah passages by the Septuagint and its revisions suggests that the term was understood as identifying the reed plant as well as the area where reeds grew.

In sum, the term *sûp* was used in Biblical Hebrew to refer to marshes of reeds or to the reeds themselves. Furthermore, because *ṯwfy* in Egyptian can refer to a marsh of reeds as well as the papyrus plant—and because the Septuagint and its revisions render *sûp* in three cases as πάπυρος—it is possible that *sûp* also designated both a marsh of reeds and the wild papyrus plant. Nowhere in the Bible is the term *sûp* used to refer to the material utilized to manufacture papyrus paper.

2.7. The Term *gōme'*

2.7.1. Etymology

The Hebrew term *gōme'* carries the meaning 'wild papyrus plant, manufacturable papyrus'. Several scholars have connected this lexeme with the papyrus plant *Cyperus papyrus* L. (GMD 221; *HALOT* 1:196; *DCH* 2:362; Zohary 1982, 137; Löw 1967, 1:564, 570). The word seems to have its origin in the Egyptian language; Lambdin (1953, 149; see also *WÄS* 5:37) suggested that it derived from Egyptian *qmꜣ* 'reed'. He presented the development of Egyptian *qmꜣ* into Hebrew *gōme'* in the following steps: **qĭmꜣĕw* > **q/gĭm'u* > **gŭm'u* > *gōme'*.

In Egyptian, *qmꜣ* designates the reed material that was used, in addition to its other purposes, in the production of matting and baskets (*WÄS* 5:37). The word

46. Similarly, Symmachus's revision of the verse has ἀπέραντος 'boundless, infinite' (LSJ 185–86; Muraoka 2009, 67; Ziegler 1943, 248), whereas Aquila has ἐρυθρός 'red' (LSJ 693; Muraoka 2009, 292; Ziegler 1943, 248).

is first attested in Late Egyptian during the Twentieth and Twenty-First Dynasties (1197–940 BCE) (*WÄS* 5:37; *DLE* 2:151). Similarly, the word *gmy* refers to vegetable plants as well as reeds that were used in basketry (*WÄS* 5:170; Keimer 1927, 147, 153). It is also first attested in Late Egyptian, during the Nineteenth and Twentieth Dynasties (1298–1069 BCE) (Keimer 1927, 146; Caminos 1954, 167; Hagen 2006, 85).

2.7.2. Phonology of Egyptian **qmꜣ, gmy,** *and Hebrew* **gōmeʾ**

The main difficulty in deriving *gōmeʾ* from *qmꜣ* is the lack of strong evidence confirming that Hebrew *g* can indeed be derived from Egyptian *q*. Muchiki (1999) lists only four Hebrew words that derive from Egyptian terms with *q*. The words listed are:

qab < *qb(.y)* ‘kab, a measure of capacity’ (254)
qallaḥat < *qrḥ.t* ‘pot, caldron’ (1999, 254)
Šîšaq, *Šāšāq* < *šš(n)q* ‘Shishaq, Shashaq’ (227–28)
Tirhāqā < *thrq* ‘Tirhaqah’ (229)

In these examples, Egyptian *q* remains *q* in Hebrew, so these examples do not support the claim that Hebrew *g* can derive from Egyptian *q*. Noonan (2012, 234–35; see also *WÄS* 5:27), however, argues for one case in which Egyptian *q* entered Hebrew as *g*—namely, *gābiaʿ* ‘cup, cup-shaped candleholder’ < *qbḥw*. If this example is valid, it would be the only one in which Egyptian *q* entered Hebrew as *g*.

Muchiki (1999) also lists Egyptian terms with *q* that were loaned into Northwest Semitic languages other than Hebrew. A total of nine Egyptian terms with *q* seem to have penetrated into Northwest Semitic languages, including six in Aramaic:

pqṭnwny < *p(ꜣ)-qd-nṯ(r)* ‘His breath is in the hand of Keith’ (30)
qb < *qb(.y)* ‘a kind of jar as measure of capacity’ (171)
qlby < *qlby* ‘a kind of wine’ (172)
qnḥnty < *qnḥ(.t)-nṯr* ‘the chapel of god’ (172)
thrqʾ < *thrq*, PN (146)
ʾskšyt/*ʾskyšw* < *(n)s-q(ꜣy)-š(w.)t(y)*/*ns-qꜣy-šw.ty* ‘He belongs to *qꜣy-šw.ty*’ (69)

We also find one each in Phoenician (*ʿbdkrr* < *ʿbd-qrr* ‘Servant of the Frog’ (30)), Ugaritic (*qlḥt* < *qrḥ.t* ‘vessel’ (282)), and Amarna (*qapqapu* < *qfqf*, cult utensil (301)). In general, when these nine loans took place, Egyptian *q* was rendered as *q* in Northwest Semitic languages. Phoenician deviates from this pattern because it uses the grapheme *k* to transcribe the *q* of one Egyptian word; there is also one Aramaic word that renders Egyptian *q* as *k*. Thus, with one possible exception (*gābiaʿ* < *qbḥw*), the written evidence, although not extensive, suggests that Egyptian *q* usually remained *q* when it was loaned into Northwest Semitic languages.

In order to explain the presence of *g* in Hebrew *gōmeʾ*, Muchiki (1999, 241–42) argues that *gōmeʾ* derives not from *qmȝ* but from *gmy*, which he contends is a biform of *qmȝ*. Muchiki is probably correct in arguing that the two lexemes are biforms, for they are used synonymously in parallel contexts (Muchiki 1999, 242; see also Keimer 1927, 146).[47] Muchiki's argument that *gōmeʾ* derives from *gmy*, however, is not without problems. First, excluding the term *gmy* (or *qmȝ*), we know of only two other Egyptian words containing *g* that entered Hebrew, so the evidence is scant. Second, in both cases, Egyptian *g* was rendered in Hebrew as *q*, not *g*; the available examples are *qôp* 'ape, monkey' < *g(ỉ)f* and *qeset* 'scribal palette' < *gst(ỉ)* (Muchiki 1999, 254–55). Muchiki mentions another two Egyptian words containing *g* which entered Aramaic: *pqrqptḥ* < *p(ȝ)-grg-ptḥ*, GN (163) and *pq* < *pg(ȝ)* 'piece of wood' (171). In both cases, Egyptian *g* entered Aramaic as *q*. Additionally, Egyptian *y* was realized as [y], not [ʾ] (Allen 2013, 37–38, 53); accordingly, it is difficult to see how ʾ of *gōmeʾ* could have derived from *y* of *gmy*. In sum, Muchiki's claim that *gōmeʾ* must have derived from *gmy* and not *qmȝ* is not compelling.

This issue is complicated even more by Hoch's study of Semitic loanwords in Egyptian. Hoch (1994, 431) shows that when Semitic words containing *q* were borrowed into Egyptian, they were usually rendered in Egyptian with *q*, but also less frequently with *g* and *k*. Specifically, there are seventeen cases in which Semitic *q* entered Egyptian as *q*:

ya=ʿ=q=b < **yaʿqub-* 'to succeed' (50)
ʿa=m=qu$_2$ < **ʿamq-* 'valley' (69)
ʿa=ša=q < **ʿašaqa* 'to extort' (80)
ʿa=ša=qu < **ʿašaq-* or **ʿašūq-* 'act of oppression' (80–81)
ba=–r=qa < **baraqa* 'to sparkle' (101)
bi=qa=ʿa < **biqaʿ-* or **biqʿ-* 'ravine' (112)
ma=–n=q=ta < **manṣiqt-* 'large vessel' (131)
ma=ga < **maqʿar-* 'bottom of the oven' (165)
ma$_2$*=qi*$_2$*=ra* < **maqqīl-* 'staff, stick' (166)
ma=ḏ=q=ta < **māṣiqt-* or *manṣiqt-* 'large vessel' (180)

47. Two different papyri with the same content use the words *qmʾ* and *gmy* interchangeably. Papyrus Lansing contains *qmȝ*, while Papyrus Anastasi 4 has *gmy* (Keimer 1927, 146; Caminos 1954, 167–68).

_ḫi=ra=qa=ta_ < *_ḫilqat-_ or _ḫalaqōt-_ ‘slippery ground’ (251)
_ša=ḥa=qa_ < *_šaḥaq-_ ‘dust cloud; pulverized grain’ (287–88)
_qa=–r=ta_ < *_qart-_ ‘town’ (302)
_qu$_4$=da=ru$_2$=ta_ < *_qutōrt-_ or *_quṭārōt-_ ‘incense’ (305)
qid=šu$_4$ < *_qidš-_ ‘sanctuary’ (306)
_ḏa=ʿu=q_ < *_ṣaʿaqa_ and *_zaʿaqa-_ ‘cry out’ (380)
_ḏa=ʿa=qa=ta_ < *_ṣaʿaqāt-/zaʿaqāt-_ and *_ṣaʿaqōt-/zaʿaqōt-_ ‘cries’ (381)

There are five cases in which Semitic _q_ entered Egyptian as _g_:

_ʿ=š=g_ < *_ʿašaqa_ ‘to extort; to oppress’ (79–80)
_ma=gi$_2$=w=t_ < *_maqqīl-_ ‘staff, rod’ (166)
_ra=ga=ta_ < *_riqāt-_ ‘compartments; hollow spaces’ (211–12)
_ma=ga_ < *_maqʿar-_ ‘bottom of the oven’ (165)
_ga=wa=ša_ < *_qawaša_ ‘to be crooked’ (347–48)

And in another two cases Semitic _q_ entered Egyptian as _k_: _ka=ra=ta_ < *_qart-_ ‘town, city’ (303) and _ka=ma=ḥa_ < *_qamḥ-_ ‘a type of bread’ (321–22). These data indicate that Egyptian _q_ was most similar to Semitic _q,_ not Semitic _g_. Nevertheless, Hoch’s study suggests that Egyptian _q_ also resembled Semitic _g_.

Hoch (1994, 431) points out that when Semitic words containing _g_ entered Egyptian, the _g_ of Semitic usually entered Egyptian as _q_, but also less frequently as _g_ and _k_. Hoch lists seven examples of Semitic _g_ entering Egyptian as _q_:

_ʾa$_2$=–r=qa=bi=sa_ < *_ʾalgabīt-_ ‘precious stone; crystal’ (30)
_sa=ra=qu$_2$_ < *_θalg-_ ‘snow’ (264)
_q=b=ʿu$_2$_ < *_gibʿ-_ ‘hill’ (292)
_q=–n=ta_ < *_gint-_ ‘winepress’ (293)
_qa=ra=ḏi=na_ < *_garzin-_ ‘axe’ (304)
_qa=ḏa; qi$_2$=ḏa_ < *_gaṣṣ-_ or *_giṣṣ-_ ‘gypsum, plaster’ (307)
_qa=ḏa=ya_ < *_gaṣṣay-_ ‘plasterer’ (309)[48]

In four cases it entered as _g_:

_ʿa=ga=ra=ta_ < *_ʿagalt-_ ‘knob, handle’ (83)
_ma$_4$=ga=di=r_ <*_magdal-_ ‘tower’ (170)
_n=g=bu; n=g=bi_ < *_nagb-_ ‘the Negeb’ (196)
_g=ru$_2$=n=ʾa; g=ru$_2$=n_ < *_gurn-_ ‘threshing floor’ (352)

48. Hoch (1994, 431) states that there are eight examples in which Semitic _g_ entered Egyptian as _q_, but I have not been able to locate the eighth in his work.

Finally, there are five examples in which Semitic *g* entered Egyptian as *k*:

ma₃=k=ta=ra < **magdal-* 'tower' (170)
k=b=ʿ < **gibʿ-* 'hill' (292)
k=n=tu₂ < **gint-* 'winepress' (293)
ka=ma=–r < **garm-* or *gilam-* 'tusks, ivory' (321)
ka=–r=ka=–r < **galgal-* 'stone heap' (333)

While these correspondences between Semitic and Egyptian consonants demonstrate how Semitic *g* was perceived in Egyptian, they also reveal in part the realization of the Egyptian consonants that were used to transcribe Semitic *g*. Because Semitic *g* entered Egyptian as *q* in the majority of cases, it seems likely that the realization of Egyptian *q* resembled that of Semitic *g*.[49]

Allen attempts to synthesize the available evidence for the realization of Egyptian consonants. In view of Hoch's work, Allen argues that Egyptian *q* and *g* had a number of different realizations. Allen claims that Egyptian *q* was realized as [q] in the Old Kingdom (2663–2160 BCE), but as [k], and in certain dialects as [g], in Late Egyptian.[50] On the other hand, Egyptian *g* was realized as [k] and perhaps as [g] in some dialects (Allen 2013, 46–48; 53).[51] In other words, *q* and *g* were realized in a number of different ways, among which [g] was a viable option. It is possible, then, that *gōmeʾ* does derive from *qmꜣ*. In such a case, the lending Egyptian dialect must have pronounced *q* as [g]. It is puzzling, however, why this term and *gābiaʿ* (< *qbḥw*) are the only two words that came into any Northwest Semitic language with *g* rather than *q*. Nevertheless, because there is at least one case of Egyptian *q* entering Hebrew as *g* (*gābiaʿ*), and because there are phonological difficulties in deriving Hebrew *g* and *ʾ* from Egyptian *g* and *y*, respectively, it is preferable to view *gōmeʾ* as deriving from *qmꜣ*, not *gmy*.

2.7.3. *Penetration of* qmꜣ *into Hebrew*

The term *gōmeʾ* was presumably borrowed from Egyptian by the eleventh century BCE, since in the eleventh century BCE the technology of writing on

49. On the other hand, the existence of examples in which Semitic *g* entered Egyptian as *g* as well as *k* suggests that certain realizations of Egyptian *g* also resembled the realizations of Semitic *g* and *k*.

50. The transcription of Egyptian *q* as *k* in Phoenician supports the claim that Egyptian *q* was realized as [k]. Additionally, Allen (2013, 53) states that Egyptian *q* was even palatalized in certain words, becoming [k̠] and [ḡ]; according to Allen's peculiar transliteration system, *k̠* and *ḡ* are equivalent to IPA *kʲ* and *gʲ* respectively.

51. Egyptian *g* was also probably realized as [k̠] (= IPA kʲ) or [ḡ] (= IPA gʲ) in certain dialects (Allen 2013, 53).

papyrus was already known in the Levant, as is confirmed by the Report of Wenamun, which recounts the arrival of five hundred rolls of papyrus in Byblos from Thebes (Redford 2000, 2228; Breasted 1905, 102, 107). If we accept that *gōme*ʾ derives from Egyptian *qm3*, then the borrowing must have taken place after the fourteenth century, when *q* began to be realized as [g] in certain dialects of Late Egyptian. The phonology of *qm3* and *gōme*ʾ suggests that *qm3* would have entered Canaanite/Hebrew in the mid- to late second millennium BCE. As will be discussed in chapter 6, this was the period when Egypt ruled Canaan, and it was probably at this time that Egypt introduced the use of papyrus, as well as the lexeme designating papyrus, into Canaan.

2.7.4. Biblical Usage of gōmeʾ

The term *gōme*ʾ appears only four times in the biblical text. Of the four passages, two refer to certain items that are made of *gōme*ʾ. In Exod 2:3, one reads of the well-known basket made of *gōme*ʾ into which the infant Moses was placed: וְלֹא־יָכְלָה עוֹד הַצְּפִינוֹ וַתִּקַּח־לוֹ תֵּבַת **גֹּמֶא** וַתַּחְמְרָה בַחֵמָר וּבַזָּפֶת וַתָּשֶׂם בָּהּ אֶת־הַיֶּלֶד וַתָּשֶׂם בַּסּוּף עַל־שְׂפַת הַיְאֹר ‘She could no longer hide him, so she took for him a basket of ***gōme***ʾ and daubed it with bitumen and pitch, and she put the child into it, and put (it) in the marsh of reeds (*sûp*) on the bank of the Nile river’. Similarly, Isa 18:1–2 speaks of envoys traveling upon water in vessels made of *gōme*ʾ: הוֹי אֶרֶץ צִלְצַל כְּנָפָיִם אֲשֶׁר מֵעֵבֶר לְנַהֲרֵי־כוּשׁ׃ הַשֹּׁלֵחַ בַּיָּם צִירִים וּבִכְלֵי־**גֹמֶא** עַל־פְּנֵי־מַיִם ‘Oh, land of the buzzing of wings, which is across the rivers of Kush, the one that sends envoys in vessels of ***gōme***ʾ on the water’.

On the other hand, Isa 35:7 speaks of *gōme*ʾ, along with *qāne* ‘wild reed plant’, springing up from desolate places: וְהָיָה הַשָּׁרָב לַאֲגַם וְצִמָּאוֹן לְמַבּוּעֵי מָיִם בִּנְוֵה תַנִּים רִבְצָהּ חָצִיר לְקָנֶה **וָגֹמֶא** ‘The parched ground shall turn into a pool of water and the thirsty ground into streams of water; in the pasture of jackals, which is their dwelling place, the grass (will turn) into reeds [*qāne*] and ***gōme***ʾ’. Additionally, Job 8:11 discloses the habitat of *gōme*ʾ by asking rhetorically whether *gōme*ʾ can grow up without a *biṣṣā* ‘swamp, marsh’: הֲיִגְאֶה־**גֹּמֶא** בְּלֹא בִצָּה יִשְׂגֶּה־אָחוּ בְלִי־מָיִם ‘Will the ***gōme***ʾ grow without a swamp [*biṣṣā*]? Will sedges [*ʾāḥû*] increase without water?’. In these passages, *gōme*ʾ is clearly referring to the wild reed plant.

The above verses show that the term *gōme*ʾ refers to a reed plant (Isa 35:7; Job 8:11) and that this reed plant can be used to manufacture boats (Isa 18:2) and baskets (Exod 2:3). Exodus 2:3 is particularly instructive because it differentiates between two types of reeds. The verse uses the term *sûp* to refer to the marsh of wild reeds growing in the Nile, and the lexeme *gōme*ʾ is used in the same verse to designate the material of which a basket is made. Furthermore, in discussing the use of *gōme*ʾ in Exod 2:3 and Isa 18:2, I would point out that the two items mentioned in these verses—a basket and aquatic vessels—are very different items, yet the term *gōme'* is used to refer to the material utilized to produce both of these items. As mentioned earlier, the papyrus plant was indeed used in Egypt to manufacture items such as baskets, boats, mattings, sandals, and other items (Leach and Tait 2000, 228; Wendrich 2000, 255). It therefore seems plausible that the term *gōme'*, consistent with its use in Exod 2:3 and Isa 18:2, was the specific ancient Hebrew lexeme that referred to the papyrus material used for the production of various goods, including boats and baskets, and probably items such as matting, sandals, and other items listed above. Moreover, it is not difficult to imagine how this same word could also have been the ancient Hebrew term that designated manufacturable papyrus utilized to make writing material.

2.7.5. Translation of gōme' *in the Septuagint*

That *gōme'* may have referred to manufacturable papyrus paper is supported by the translation of the word in the Septuagint. When translating the passages containing *gōme'*, the Septuagint and its hexplaric revisions render *gōme'* with various terms. First, we will consider the two passages (Exod 2:3; Isa 18:2) in which *gōme'* refers to manufacturable papyrus material. In the Septuagint's translation of Isa 18:2—which seems to reflect a Hebrew *Vorlage* that differed slightly from the Masoretic Text—*gōme'* is rendered as an adjectival form of βύβλος 'Egyptian papyrus' (LSJ 333; Muraoka 2009, 117, 124). In the Masoretic Text, Isa 18:2 refers to aquatic vessels made of *gōme'*, but in the Septuagint the passage speaks of letters written on papyrus; both, however, refer to manufacturable papyrus. In Greek literature, βύβλος is used to refer to the reed material of which various items are made (Lewis 1974, 14–15). The term βίβλος 'scroll, book' is, of course, connected to βύβλος, which demonstrates that βύβλος refers not only to the reed plant generally, but particularly to the manufacturable papyrus material that was used in the production of papyrus scrolls (LSJ 333; Muraoka 2009, 117, 124).

It is noteworthy that the Greek term πάπυρος 'papyrus' usually refers to the wild plant itself, not the manufacturable material (LSJ 1302; Muraoka 2009, 522; Lewis 1974, 15).[52] Nevertheless, Symmachus and Theodotion both render *gōme'* of Isa 18:2 as πάπυρος (LSJ 1302; Muraoka 2009, 522; Ziegler 1939, 187).

52. According to Lewis (1974, 14–15), the distinction between πάπυρος and βύβλος can be seen in the manner in which Theophrastus uses these words in his work on plants. Lewis states that "πάπυρος designates the plant in its capacity as a foodstuff, while βύβλος generally denotes the plant as a source of fibres for manufacturing woven articles and writing-paper." While it is true that Theophrastus uses πάπυρος as referring to the plant as a foodstuff, it seems reasonable to suggest that one does not need to restrict the meaning of πάπυρος as referring only to the plant as a foodstuff. Rather, the term probably refers to the wild plant in general, whether it was used for food or not. After all, when used as a foodstuff, the plant was not manufactured but eaten in its natural form.

Similarly, while the Septuagint's rendition of Exod 2:3—which speaks of a basket of *gōme*ʾ—does not have a Greek term that corresponds to *gōme*ʾ, the word is rendered in this passage according to the Syro-Hexapla as πάπυρος (LSJ 1302; Muraoka 2009, 522; Wevers and Quast 1991, 72). Additionally, Aquila and Symmachus render *gōme*ʾ in this passage as πάπυρος (Wevers and Quast 1991, 72); however, there is also a variant in which βύβλος is used to render *gōme*ʾ (Wevers and Quast 1991, 72). The evidence from the Greek revisions suggests, then, that the Greek lexeme πάπυρος could also refer to manufacturable material, because it is used in contexts that clearly refer to manufacturable papyrus material.

Whereas *gōme*ʾ in Exod 2:3 and Isa 18:2 refers to manufacturable papyrus material, in Isa 35:7 and Job 8:11 the term designates the wild reed plant. In the Greek translation of Isa 35:7, the lexeme is rendered as ἕλος 'marshy meadow, marshy ground' (LSJ 537; Muraoka 2009, 224), and in Aquila's version of the passage *gōme*ʾ is rendered as λίμνη 'pool of standing water, marshy lake' (LSJ 1050; Muraoka 2009, 432; Ziegler 1939, 248). In the Septuagint's translation of Job 8:11, the term πάπυρος is used to render *gōme*ʾ (LSJ 1302; Muraoka 2009, 522; Ziegler 1982, 246).

While the Septuagint and the hexplaric revisions use a number of terms to translate *gōme*ʾ, the various translations suggest that the word was understood as referring to the wild papyrus plant as well as to manufacturable papyrus material. Accordingly, based on the evidence of the Greek translations of *gōme*ʾ and the use of the term in the Bible, it is reasonable to suggest that it was this term that designated the manufacturable papyrus material utilized in ancient Israel for various purposes, including writing.

2.8. Definitions of Terms Designating Reeds, Marshes, and Papyrus

Having analyzed the ancient Hebrew words that designate reeds, marshes, and papyrus, I suggest the following definitions for these terms.

***ʾēbe*:** A term that probably refers to reeds, perhaps papyrus, that were used for producing boats. The term may be Common Semitic.

***ʾăgam* and *ʾagmôn*/*ʾagmōn*:** The term *ʾăgam* entered Hebrew from Aramaic, which borrowed the lexeme from Akkadian, and Akkadian borrowed the word from Sumerian. It refers to swamps and reed marshes, while the augmented form *ʾagmôn*/*ʾagmōn* designates the reeds that grew near pools of water.

***ʾāḥû*:** An Egyptian loanword that refers to pastureland as well as sedges and reeds.

biṣṣā: A term deriving from Proto-Semitic that signifies a swamp or marshy area.

gebeʾ: A term that derives from the West Semitic root *g-b-ʾ* 'to gather, to collect'. The word carries the meaning 'pool of water, pond'.

gōmeʾ: Probably an Egyptian loanword that refers to workable reed material used to manufacture boats, baskets, and perhaps writing material. Besides referring to manufacturable papyrus material, this term also signifies wild reeds; the lexeme probably designates the specific plant *Cyperus papyrus* L.

ḥāṣîr: A term inherited from Proto-Semitic that refers primarily to grass and vegetation.

sûp: Probably an Egyptian loanword that denotes marshes of reeds as well as the reeds themselves, and it is possible that the term designates the wild papyrus plant.

ʿārôt: Probably an Egyptian loanword that refers to wild reeds, perhaps papyrus plants, growing in and near the Nile.

qāne: A term inherited from Proto-Semitic that refers to reeds. Due to semantic shift, the term also came to signify tubular items such as a measuring reed.

CHAPTER 3

Stone and Plaster

IN THIS CHAPTER I WILL EVALUATE Hebrew terms that designate various types of stone surfaces used for writing purposes as well as other terms that designated mud, clay, plaster, and whitewash, which were also used as surfaces for writing.

3.1. Stone

3.1.1. Writing on Stone in the Ancient World

Inscriptions on stone were common in the ancient Near East. In Egypt, one does not need to look far to see a stone inscription. The stone walls of Egyptian temples and tombs are covered with inscribed writing. Egyptian hieroglyphics on stone began to appear during the reign of Pharaoh Djoser (ca. 2700 BCE) and soon spread throughout Egyptian society, appearing on temples, monuments, and tombs (Vernus 2002, 46). Hieroglyphic writing was either inscribed with a chisel or painted with a brush (Black and Tait 2000, 2200–204; Wente 2000, 2211–12). An example of a stone inscription with engraved writing is the Merneptah stela, which was found in Thebes. The stela is of black granite and dates to the thirteenth century BCE (Petrie 1896, 26).

Due to the lack of stone within Mesopotamia, there are fewer stone inscriptions in Mesopotamia than in Egypt. Demsky (2007, 236) points out that the stone used for inscriptions needed to be imported to Mesopotamia. During Sargon's reign, in the late third millennium BCE, stone began to be imported into Mesopotamia proper from the mountains (Ashton 2008, 21). Stone inscriptions were engraved by masons using chisels (Pearce 2000, 2266; Ashton 2008, 44–45). Among the Mesopotamian lapidary inscriptions, the code of Hammurabi is perhaps the most famous. Initially erected in Sippar but later moved to Susa, the code of Hammurabi dates to the eighteenth century BCE and is inscribed on polished black diorite (Prince 1904, 601; Huehnergard 2011, 160; see figure 3.1 below).

FIGURE 3.1. Code of Hammurabi, eighteenth century BCE. Louvre Museum. Photo: Creative Commons.

FIGURE 3.2. Tel Dan stele, ninth century BCE. Israel Museum. Photo: © A. D. Riddle/BiblePlaces.com.

Many stone inscriptions have survived from ancient Greece. Some of the earliest lapidary inscriptions date to the seventh century BCE. Dating to 650–600 BCE is an inscription on gray schist from Dreros (Meiggs and Lewis 1988, 2–3). Originally situated in a wall of the temple of Apollo Delphinios, the inscription contains a law concerning the length of time one could serve as *kosmos*, a civil service office in Crete. Another inscription dating to 625–600 BCE appears on a marble block, which is perhaps an altar (Meiggs and Lewis 1988, 3–4); the inscription consists of a poem addressed to Glaukos, son of Leptines, who was a prominent figure in Thasos. Finally, we may mention the inscribed cylindrical limestone cenotaph that was found in a suburb of Corcyra; the inscription dates to around 650–600 BCE (Meiggs and Lewis 1988, 4–5).

Writing on stone is also attested from the Levant and specifically from ancient Israel. The Tel Dan stela, which dates to the ninth century BCE, consists of several fragments of a slab of basalt stone. Once pieced together, the fragments, which are engraved with writing, are about 12.5 inches in height and 8.6 inches in width, but the original stela is estimated to have been about 1 yard in height and 1.6 feet in width (Biran and Naveh 1993, 84; see figure 3.2). The Mesha stone from Dhiban, which also dates to the ninth century BCE, is of basalt stone (Aḥituv 2008, 387; Graham 1989, 72). The inscription was about 1 yard high and 2 feet wide (Graham 1989, 72) (see figure 3.3). Fragments of

FIGURE 3.3. Mesha stele, ninth century BCE. Louvre Museum. Photo: © Todd Bolen/BiblePlaces.com.

FIGURE 3.4. Siloam tunnel inscription, circa 700 BCE. Istanbul Archaeology Museums. Photo: © A.D. Riddle /BiblePlaces.com.

similar stelae were also found in Jerusalem, Samaria, Philistia, and Ammon (Aḥituv 2008, 25, 30–32, 257, 335–40, 367–70).

In addition to engraved stelae, there are also inscriptions etched directly on rock surfaces. The Siloam inscription, for instance, was incised on a smoothed surface of the western end of Hezekiah's tunnel just before the Siloam pool. The smoothed surface is about 2.2 feet high and 2.1 feet wide, but the inscription itself, which occupies the lower half of this area, is about 7.5 inches in height and 1.9 feet in width (Sayce 1881, 142; Conder 1881, 286; see figure 3.4). Also, two tomb inscriptions were discovered on the rocky cliff on the eastern side of the Kidron Valley (Aḥituv 2008, 44–49). The Siloam tunnel inscription and the Kidron Valley tomb inscriptions date to around 700 BCE (Dobbs-Allsopp et al. 2005, 500, 507, 510).

With the exception of a few royal inscriptions on basalt stelae, the majority of stone inscriptions found in Israel and its vicinity were incised on limestone.[1]

1. The following monumental inscriptions from ancient Israel and Transjordan were incised on basalt: the Tel Dan stela (Biran and Naveh 1993, 81), the Mesha inscription (Graham 1989, 72), the Kir Moab inscription (Reed and Winnett 1963, 1), the royal Moabite inscription (Aḥituv 2008, 419), and the Amman theater inscription (Aufrecht 1989, 151). Most inscriptions appearing on stone, however, were incised on limestone. Monumental inscriptions appearing on limestone include the Siloam inscription (Gill 1996, 23), the Ophel stela fragment (Aḥituv 2008, 30), the stela fragment

This, of course, is not surprising, because limestone was readily available in ancient Israel; in fact, "[m]ost of the rock exposed in Israel is limestone" (Reich 1992, 1). The mountainous areas of Israel consist of various types of limestone, especially in the karst systems and the exposed limestone bedrock (Gill 1996, 2, 11–12); limestone is also common in ancient Ammon (Najjar 1999, 106). Ancient limestone quarries have been identified in Ramat Raḥel, Samaria, Jerusalem, and Megiddo (Shiloh and Horowitz 1975, 39–44; Keimer 2014, 339–40). Admittedly, these quarries were used primarily to extract ashlar stones used in building projects. Nevertheless, it is not difficult to imagine that slabs of limestone used for inscribing purposes were also taken from such quarries. While limestone is commonly found in the highlands of Israel, basalt is also found in Israel, particularly in upper Galilee, the Golan, and Bashan (Reich 1992, 2); it was also common in ancient Ammon (Najjar 1999, 106).

3.1.2. Geological Properties of Limestone and Basalt

Limestone is a sedimentary rock made primarily of calcite, which is a rather soft mineral. According to the ten-point Mohs hardness scale (10 being the hardest and 1 being the softest), calcite is ranked 3.[2] This, of course, means that limestone is a soft rock that can be quarried and used for various purposes without much difficulty. Basalt is harder than limestone. It consists primarily of the mineral plagioclase, which is ranked 6–6.5 on the Mohs scale, but also includes pyroxene and olivine, which are ranked 5.5–6 and 6.5–7, respectively, according to the Mohs scale.

As mentioned above, both types of rock were used in ancient Israel as surfaces for writing. The material used to inscribe limestone and basalt must have ranked higher than these two stones on the Mohs scale. Perhaps an iron tool along with a hammer were used to chisel the larger inscriptions. Smaller inscriptions may have been engraved with a metal pen, and the graffiti on cave walls may have been incised with a knife or a sharp stone such as flint. We will return to the question of writing instruments in chapter 5.

---

from the City of David (Dobbs-Allsopp et al. 2005, 227), the royal stela from Samaria (Dobbs-Allsopp et al. 2005, 496), the Amman citadel inscription (Aufrecht 1989, 154), the royal dedicatory inscription from Ekron (Gitin, Dothan, and Naveh 1997, 7), and the Kidron cliff inscriptions (Ussishkin 1993, 283). Other inscriptions appearing on limestone surfaces include the inscriptions in the caves of Makkedah (Aḥituv 2008, 220), graffiti in a cave near Amaziah (Dobbs-Allsopp et al. 2005, 125), the Gezer calendar (Aḥituv 2008, 252), and the Tel Zayit abecedary (Aḥituv 2008, 17). Another noteworthy inscription was discovered in a cave at En Gedi. The inscription is unique inasmuch as it is written with black ink upon a rock surface—for that matter, upon a stalactite (Bar-Adon 1975, 227; Renz and Röllig 1995–2003, 1:173–75).

2. All rankings according to the Mohs scale are taken from the website Geology.com: Geoscience News and Information (http://www.geology.com).

3.1.3. The Terms **ʾeben, maṣṣēbā/maṣṣebet,** ***and*** **gāzît**

3.1.3.1. The Term ʾeben

3.1.3.1.1. ETYMOLOGY AND BIBLICAL USAGE

With cognates in various Semitic languages, the term *ʾeben* ‘rock, stone’ (GMD 9; *DCH* 2018, 1:117–21; *HALOT* 1:7–8) derives from Proto-Semitic **ʾabn-* (e.g., Akkadian *abnum*, *CAD* 1/1:54; Geʿez *ʾəbn*, *CDG* 4; Ugaritic *abn*, *DULAT* 1:9–10). In the Bible, the word occurs a total of 276 times. There are also around 44 instances of the term in the Dead Sea Scrolls, excluding cases that involve reconstructed letters (*DSSC* 1:6); and there are probably 8 cases of the term in Ben Sira, including once case with a restored *bet* (6, 21; 42, 4 [2x]; 43, 15; 45, 11 [2x]; 46, 5; 50, 9). In the Bible, the word refers to smaller-sized stones (e.g., Exod 20:25; 1 Sam 17:40) as well as larger stones used for construction or other purposes (e.g., Lev 14:40; Josh 10:18; 1 Kgs 5:31–32; Hag 2:15; Neh 3:35). It also refers to the rock from which building stones are quarried (e.g., 2 Kgs 12:13; 22:6; 1 Chr 22:15). According to the biblical text, the Mosaic law was inscribed on tablets of stone (i.e., *lūḥōt ʾeben*; Exod 24:12; 31:18; 34:1, 4; Deut 4:13; 5:22; 9:9–11; 10:1, 3; 1 Kgs 8:9). These passages will be discussed in 4.2.4.1–4.2.4.2 along with the term *lûaḥ* ‘tablet’. For the use of *ʾeben* in reference to engraved precious stones, see 5.3.

3.1.3.1.2. WRITING ON STELES IN THE BIBLE

While the term *ʾeben* refers to engraved precious stones (see 5.3), it also refers to erected stelae that served various purposes. The term designates stone carved statues that the Israelites were prohibited from possessing (Lev 26:1); it is also used to speak of boundary stones (Josh 15:6; 18:17) and stones erected by Israelites as commemorative markers of certain events (Gen 35:14; Josh 4:3–9, 20–21; 24:26–27). In a few passages, the term refers to stones that are used as surfaces for writing (Deut 27:1–12; Josh 8:30–35; Zech 3:9).

In Deut 27:1–12, which will be discussed in depth in 3.2.6.2, the Israelites are instructed to erect large stones, cover them with plaster, and write on the plaster the words of the law. The fulfillment of this instruction on the part of the Israelites is depicted in Josh 8:30–35, but this passage does not mention the process of covering the stones with plaster. Deuteronomy 27:1–3a reads:

> וַיְצַו מֹשֶׁה וְזִקְנֵי יִשְׂרָאֵל אֶת־הָעָם לֵאמֹר שָׁמֹר אֶת־כָּל־הַמִּצְוָה אֲשֶׁר אָנֹכִי מְצַוֶּה אֶתְכֶם הַיּוֹם׃
> וְהָיָה בַּיּוֹם אֲשֶׁר תַּעַבְרוּ אֶת־הַיַּרְדֵּן אֶל־הָאָרֶץ אֲשֶׁר־יְהוָה אֱלֹהֶיךָ נֹתֵן לָךְ וַהֲקֵמֹתָ לְךָ **אֲבָנִים**
> גְּדֹלוֹת וְשַׂדְתָּ אֹתָם בַּשִּׂיד׃ וְכָתַבְתָּ עֲלֵיהֶן אֶת־כָּל־דִּבְרֵי הַתּוֹרָה הַזֹּאת בְּעָבְרֶךָ

> Moses and the elders of Israel commanded the people, saying, “Keep all the law that I command you today. On the day that you cross the Jordan

> to the land that YHWH your God is giving you, you shall erect for yourself large *ʾăbānîm* and you shall cover them with quicklime plaster.[3] You shall write on them all the words of this instruction in your crossing"

While Deut 27:1–12 describes a process of writing on erected stones covered with plaster, as (presumably) does Josh 8:30–35, Zech 3:9 may refer to the process of engraving writing upon the surface of an actual stone. The passage reads: כִּי ׀ הִנֵּה **הָאֶבֶן** אֲשֶׁר נָתַתִּי לִפְנֵי יְהוֹשֻׁעַ עַל־**אֶבֶן** אַחַת שִׁבְעָה עֵינָיִם הִנְנִי מְפַתֵּחַ פִּתֻּחָהּ נְאֻם יְהוָה צְבָאוֹת וּמַשְׁתִּי אֶת־עֲוֺן הָאָרֶץ־הַהִיא בְּיוֹם אֶחָד '"For on the *ʾeben* that I have set before Joshua, on one *ʾeben* there are seven eyes [sides (?)]; I will engrave its engraving [*məpattēaḥ pittūḥāh*]," says YHWH of hosts, "and I will remove the iniquity of that land in one day"'. It is not clear whether this verse is speaking of the engraving of words or the engraving of images. The verb used in this verse (*piel* of *p-t-ḥ*) is employed elsewhere to refer to the engraving of images (e.g., 2 Chr 2:6, 13; 3:7), but the same verb is also used to speak of the engraving of words (Exod 28:36).[4] It is therefore possible that Zech 3:9 depicts the engraving of words upon a stela erected before Joshua.

As mentioned earlier, inscribed stelae were erected throughout the ancient Near East, including ancient Israel and its vicinity. It is possible that such stelae from ancient Israel are designated by the term *ʾeben*. Because the term signifies erected stones and refers to plaster-covered stones used for writing purposes, it may be that it also designates stelae with writing engraved directly upon them. If Zech 3:9 indeed refers to the engraving of writing upon a stela, the verse would also support such a suggestion.

3.1.3.2. The Term maṣṣēbā/maṣṣebet

3.1.3.2.1. ETYMOLOGY AND BIBLICAL USAGE

The lexeme *maṣṣēbā* 'erected stone' appears thirty-four times in the Bible, while its biform *maṣṣebet* appears four times, two times each in two passages (2 Sam 18:18; Isa 6:13; GMD 722; *DCH* 5:442–43; *HALOT* 1:620–21).[5] In the Dead Sea Scrolls, the term *maṣṣēbā* occurs five times with reference to erected stones (4Q368 2, 5; 11Q19 II, 6; LI, 20; LII, 2; PAM 43.675 1, 2; *DSSR* 1:618, 632, 688; 2:1108; *DSSC* 1:481); one of the five instances is perhaps *maṣṣebet* (PAM 43.675 1, 2). Both forms were derived from the root *n-ṣ-b* 'to erect' (GMD 837).

3. See 3.2.6 for discussion of *śîd* 'quicklime plaster'.

4. Edelman (2013, 197–224) connects the stone of Zech 3:9 to Mesopotamian eye stones that signified the seeing capacity of deities and served as good-luck charms.

5. The word *maṣṣēbā* (34x) occurs in the following passages: Gen 28:18, 22; 31:13, 45, 51–52 (3x); 35:14 (2x), 20 (2x); Exod 23:24; 24:4; 34:13; Lev 26:1; Deut 7:5; 12:3; 16:22; 1 Kgs 14:23; 2 Kgs 3:2; 10:26–27; 17:10; 18:4; 23:14; Isa 19:19; Jer 43:13; Ezek 26:11; Hos 3:4; 10:1–2; Mic 5:12; 2 Chr 14:2; 31:1.

Noun forms that were derived from *n-ṣ-b* are well attested in West Semitic languages: for instance, Arabic *nuṣba* 'post, pillar' (Lane 1968, 8:2799), Old South Arabian *mnṣbt* 'pillar' (GMD 722; *DNWSI* 2:750), and Old Aramaic *nṣbʾ* 'stela' (GMD 722; *DNWSI* 2:750). In the Bible, *maṣṣēbā/maṣṣebet* designates stones erected for various purposes (LaRocca-Pitts 2001, 205–228). Such stones were erected for cultic worship of various gods (e.g., Deut 12:3; 2 Kgs 10:26–27; Jer 43:13); stelae were also set up to commemorate encounters with YHWH (e.g., Gen 28:18, 22; 31:13; 35:14) and to mark burial sites (Gen 35:20).

Nowhere in the Bible is *maṣṣēbā/maṣṣebet* used in a context that involves the engraving of standing stones with writing. Nevertheless, in Phoenician and Palmyrene Aramaic, *mṣbh* often refers to inscribed funerary stelae (*DNWSI* 2:676). Other nouns derived from *n-ṣ-b* carry similar meanings in Phoenician and Old Aramaic (*DNWSI* 2:750). It is therefore possible that the Hebrew term *maṣṣēbā/maṣṣebet* designates inscribed stelae. The obvious parallel between the erecting of a *maṣṣēbā/maṣṣebet* and the erecting of an inscribed stela suggests the idea that the latter may have been designated in ancient Hebrew by the term *maṣṣēbā/maṣṣebet*. Richter (2007, 343–49, 358–61) notes the pairing of altars and stelae in Levantine religion and makes a case that the term *maṣṣēbā* refers to stelae inscribed with the names of deities; indeed, it is possible to understand *maṣṣēbā* in certain passages as referring to such cultic stelae (Deut 12:1–3; Isa 19:19–20).[6]

3.1.3.3. Translation of ʾeben *and* maṣṣēbā/maṣṣebet *in the Septuagint*

Of the 276 occurrences of *ʾeben* in the Bible, the Septuagint translates 220 of them as λίθος 'stone' (e.g., Gen 2:12; 1 Kgs 1:9; Zech 5:4; LSJ 1049; Muraoka 2009, 431). Another 24 times *ʾeben* is translated as an adjective or verb derived from λίθος (e.g., Gen 35:14; Exod 15:16; 28:11, 17). In eight cases where *ʾeben* refers to weights, the Septuagint translated it as στάθμιον 'weight' (e.g., Lev 19:36; Deut 25:13; Prov 11:1; LSJ 1632; Muraoka 2009, 632). In translating *ʾeben* when it is connected to writing (i.e., Exod 28:9–12, 17, 21; 39:6, 14 [36:13, 21 LXX]; Deut 27:1–12; Zech 3:9), the Septuagint renders the lexeme as λίθος or a form related to λίθος.[7] Of the 38 times that *maṣṣēbā/maṣṣebet* appears in the

6. The biblical text, however, does not offer concrete evidence in this regard. It may be that *maṣṣēbā/maṣṣebet* refers only to uninscribed erected stones (Graesser 1972, 34–35).

7. In several passages, *ʾeben* is rendered with a number of other Greek terms (Muraoka 2010, 140). It is rendered once as χάλιξ 'pebble' (Job 8:17; see LSJ 1972; Muraoka 2009, 727), once as πετροβόλος 'throwing rocks, catapult' (Job 41:20; LSJ 1397–98; Muraoka 2009, 555), once as σίκλος 'shekel' (2 Sam 14:26; LSJ 1596; Muraoka 2009, 621), and once as κατισχύω 'to strengthen' (Gen 49:24; LSJ 928; Muraoka 2009, 390). In certain passages, the Septuagint does not have a corresponding word for *ʾeben*.

biblical text, the Septuagint renders 30 such cases with the word στήλη 'perpendicular block, boundary stone' (e.g., Gen 28:18; 2 Sam 18:18; Isa 19:19; LSJ 1643; Muraoka 2009, 636). In the remaining examples, *maṣṣēbā/maṣṣebet* is rendered with a number of Greek words that are usually connected to the meaning 'stone'.[8] In sum, the Septuagint renders the words *ʾeben* and *maṣṣēbā/maṣṣebet* with terms that correspond in meaning with the Hebrew terms.

3.1.3.4. The Term gāzît

3.1.3.4.1. Etymology and Biblical Usage

The term *gāzît* 'hewn stone' (GMD 210; *DCH* 2:339; *HALOT* 1:186) occurs eleven times in the biblical text (Exod 20:25; 1 Kgs 5:31; 6:36; 7:9, 11–12; Isa 9:9; Ezek 40:42; Amos 5:11; Lam 3:9; 1 Chr 22:2). The word also occurs twice in the Dead Sea Scrolls with the same meaning (4Q158 7–8, 8; 11Q19 III, 7; *DSSR* 1:634, 736; *DSSC* 1:177). The Old South Arabian feminine noun *gḏwt* 'stone' is related (Biella 1982, 66). In the Bible, the lexeme refers to stones utilized in the construction of various structures such as an altar (Exod 20:25), the temple (1 Chr 22:2), and a house (Amos 5:11). Indeed, hewn stones (i.e., ashlars) are attested from various regions of ancient Israel (Shiloh and Horowitz 1975; Reich 1992, 3–5).

3.1.3.4.2. Translation of *Gāzît* in the Septuagint

In the Septuagint, *gāzît* is usually translated with terms referring to hewn or polished stones. The term is rendered once (Exod 20:25) as τμητός 'shaped by cutting' (LSJ 1801; Muraoka 2009, 682) and twice (Amos 5:11; 1 Chr 22:2) as ξυστός 'shaved, trimmed' (LSJ 1193; Muraoka 2009, 482). Another time (Exod 40:42) it is translated with the verb λαξεύω 'to hew in stone' (LSJ 1029; Muraoka 2009, 425); once more, in Isa 9:9, it is rendered as λίθος 'stone', which functions as the object of the verb λαξεύω in this passage. The Septuagint's translation of Lam 3:9 does not include a corresponding word for *gāzît*, but this word is rendered as μάρμαρον 'marble' (LSJ 1081) in the Hexapla's fifth column and in the Lucianic recension; according to the Syro-Hexapla, the term is rendered as λίθον λατομήτον 'hewn stone' (LSJ 1031, 1049) by Symmachus and as *lapidibus caesis* 'hewn stone' (Andrews 1958, 265, 1035) by Aquila (Ziegler 1957, 481). Another four times (1 Kgs 5:31 [6:1 LXX]; 6:36; 7:11–12 [7:48–49 LXX]), *gāzît*

8. In the four examples where *maṣṣēbā/maṣṣebet* is not translated as στήλη 'perpendicular block, boundary stone' in the Septuagint, the term is rendered with four words (Muraoka 2010, 261): once as λίθος 'stone' (Exod 24:4; LSJ 1048; Muraoka 2009, 431), once as στῦλος 'pillar' (Jer 43:13 [50:13 LXX]; LSJ 1657; Muraoka 2009, 640), once as ὑπόστασις 'foundation; support' (Ezek 26:11; LSJ 1895; Muraoka 2009, 705), and once as θυσιαστήριον 'altar' (Hos 3:4; LSJ 812; Muraoka 2009, 335). In a few cases, the Septuagint does not include a corresponding word for *maṣṣēbā/maṣṣebet*.

is rendered as ἀπελέκητος 'unhewn' (LSJ 185; Muraoka 2009, 67); similarly, ἀπελέκητος is used to render *gāzît* in a variant reading of 1 Kgs 7:9 (7:46 LXX; Brooke, McLean, and Thackeray 1906–40, 2:233), although the Septuagint does not have a corresponding word for *gāzît*. It is not clear why in these five cases *gāzît* is translated as ἀπελέκητος, which clearly carries the opposite meaning of *gāzît*.

Because the term *ʾeben* refers to stones of various sizes that served diverse purposes (e.g., boundary stones, commemorative stones), and because the lexeme refers to plaster-covered standing stones used for writing, it is possible that *ʾeben* also designates stelae with writing incised directly upon them. The term *maṣṣēbā*/*maṣṣebet* may have also carried this meaning, but biblical evidence for this is lacking. This is not to say that these terms carried the specific meaning 'inscribed stone'; rather, they refer to various types of stones, probably also including stones with writing inscribed directly upon them. While both *ʾeben* and *maṣṣēbā*/*maṣṣebet* may refer to inscribed stelae, the lexeme *gāzît* designates hewn stones that were used in construction.

3.1.4. The Terms **selaʿ** *and* **ṣûr**

3.1.4.1. Etymology and Biblical Usage

The lexeme *selaʿ* has cognates in West Semitic languages including Arabic (*silʿ*, *salʿ* 'crack, cleft'; Lane 1968, 4:1406) and Ugaritic (*slʿ* 'cliff' [?]; Huehnergard 2008, 157). The word occurs sixty-three times in the biblical text. It also occurs fourteen times in the Dead Sea Scrolls (e.g., CD X, 12; 1QH^a^ XV, 1; 4Q381 24a+b, 7; *DSSR* 1:98; 2:308, 426; *DSSC* 2:531) and twice in Ben Sira (40, 15; 41, 3) with meanings similar to those in the Bible. Like *selaʿ*, the term *ṣûr* also has cognates in West Semitic languages: for instance, Aramaic (*ṭwr* 'mountain'; *CAL*) and Ugaritic (*ġr* 'mountain'; *DULAT* 1:324). A cognate of Hebrew *ṣûr* may also exist in Akkadian (*ṣūrum* 'mountain path; cliff, rock'; GMD 1111; *AHw* 3:1115; Black, George, and Postgate 2007, 342).[9] Accordingly, we can reconstruct **θ̣ūr-* 'cliff, rock' in Proto-Semitic. In the Bible, *ṣûr* occurs a total of seventy-three times. In the Dead Sea Scrolls, the lexeme occurs at least seven times, including one case with an uncertain *vav* (e.g., 1QpHab V, 1; 4Q377 2ii8; 1QH[a] XVI, 23; *DSSR* 1:448, 1048; 2:314; *DSSC* 2:636).

Within the biblical text, *selaʿ* and *ṣûr* appear in similar contexts and carry similar meanings (GMD 890, 1111; *DCH* 6:164–65; 7:108; *HALOT* 1:758; 2:1016–17). Both terms refer to cliffs and rocks that have caves and clefts where people may hide (Exod 33:22; Judg 15:8; 2 Sam 13:6; Isa 2:10, 19, 21; Jer 49:16; Obad

9. Alternatively, the Akkadian example may be a loan from West Semitic (*CAD* 16:261).

3; Song 2:14). Both lexemes stand in parallel with the term *har* 'mountain' (Job 14:18; 1 Kgs 19:11). The two words refer to large stones (Judg 6:20–21; Isa 8:14; Isa 32:2), appear in contexts of hewing and quarrying in connection with the root *ḥ-ṣ-b* in the *qal* and *pual* stems (Isa 22:16; 51:1), and designate the rock that Moses strikes to provide water for the Israelites (Exod 17:6; Num 20:8, 10–11; Deut 8:15; Isa 48:21; Pss 78:16, 20; 105:41; Neh 9:15). Finally, both words are epithets of YHWH (Deut 32:31; 1 Sam 2:2; 2 Sam 22:2–3, 32, 47; Pss 18:3–4; 31:3; 42:10; 71:3). In short, it is difficult to establish a semantic difference between these two lexemes.

3.1.4.2. Writing on Stone in the Bible

Writing on stone is mentioned in Job 19:23–24. The passage reads: מִֽי־יִתֵּ֣ן אֵ֭פוֹ וְיִכָּתְב֣וּן מִלָּ֑י מִֽי־יִתֵּ֖ן בַּסֵּ֣פֶר וְיֻחָֽקוּ׃ בְּעֵט־בַּרְזֶ֥ל וְעֹ֑פָרֶת לָ֝עַ֗ד **בַּצּ֥וּר** יֵחָצְבֽוּן 'Oh that my words were written down, oh that they were inscribed in a document. With a pen of iron and lead, may they be engraved forever in the ***ṣûr***'. This passage is probably not speaking of an inscription on a large stela. Rather, the presence of the term *ʿēṭ barzel* 'pen of iron' suggests that the passage may be referring to the incising of words with a pen upon the side of a mountainous cliff, similar to the inscriptions on cave walls in Makkedah and near Amaziah (Aḥituv 2008, 220–36). We should also mention that the term *ṣûr* appears in the Siloam inscription in reference to the rock upon which the inscription was engraved (Aḥituv 2008, 19–25), which also suggests that the intended writing surface of Job 19:24 is that of a stone wall. On the other hand, the passage may be referring to the incising of writing on a smaller stone tablet, similar to the Gezer Calendar (Aḥituv 2008, 252–57). Ultimately, the point of Job's exclamation is that his words be recorded on stone rather than on a perishable material such as papyrus; whether Job's words are recorded on a stone tablet or a stone wall appears to be of secondary importance.

Also relevant for this discussion on writing executed upon stone is Jer 17:1. The passage speaks of writing that is incised on the horns of Judean altars. The verse reads: חַטַּ֣את יְהוּדָ֗ה כְּתוּבָ֛ה בְּעֵ֥ט בַּרְזֶ֖ל בְּצִפֹּ֣רֶן שָׁמִ֑יר חֲרוּשָׁה֙ עַל־ל֣וּחַ לִבָּ֔ם וּלְקַ֖רְנ֥וֹת **מִזְבְּחוֹתֵיכֶֽם** 'The sin of Judah is written with a pen of iron [*ʿēṭ barzel*], with a point of the hardest stone [*ṣippōren šāmîr*]; it is incised on the tablet of their heart [*lûaḥ libbām*] and on the ***qarnôt mizbəḥôtêkem***'. The reference to the engraving of Judah's sin upon the horns of an altar is, of course, figurative. The idea is that Judah's sins were directly related to altars, presumably because they were used by the Israelites to offer sacrifices to gods other than YHWH. Altars, including horned altars, have survived from ancient Israel (King and Stager 2001, 328–40, 339–46). A four-horned incense altar made of limestone was found at Tel Dan (King and Stager 2001, 328–40). It would have been quite simple to incise words with an

FIGURE 3.5. Beer-Sheba horned altar, eighth century BCE. Israel Museum. Photo: © Mark Bolen/BiblePlaces.com.

iron pen upon such an altar, as depicted in Jer 17:1. While no inscribed altars have been found in Israel, an inscribed limestone incense altar was discovered in Moab (Aḥituv 2008, 423–26; Dion and Daviau 2000). Also, the sandstone horned altar of Beer-sheba has an engraving of a snake on one of its stones (Aharoni 1974, 4) (see figure 3.5). Thus, while this passage is clearly symbolic, its description of writing and engraving upon altars seems to reflect an ancient practice.

3.1.4.3. Translation of selaʿ and ṣûr in the Septuagint

In the Septuagint, *selaʿ* is predominantly translated as πέτρα 'rock, cliffs' (e.g., Num 20:8; Deut 32:13; Isa 2:21; LSJ 1397; Muraoka 2009, 555; Muraoka 2010, 290).[10] In the passages that use *selaʿ* as an epithet for YHWH, the term is rendered with a number of Greek words that depict YHWH as strong (Muraoka 2010, 290).[11] Of the seventy-three occurrences of *ṣûr*, thirty are rendered

---

10. Of the sixty-three times that *selaʿ* occurs in the biblical text, fifty examples are translated in the Septuagint as πέτρα 'rock, cliffs'. In other cases (Muraoka 2010, 290), *selaʿ* is translated four times as λεωπετρία 'bare rock' (Ezek 24:7–8, 26:4, 14; LSJ 1034–35, 1043, 1397–98; Muraoka 2009, 428), twice as κρημνός 'beetling cliff' (2 Chr 25:12; LSJ 994; Muraoka 2009, 412), and once as σπήλαιον 'cavern' (Judg 15:8; LSJ 1627; Muraoka 2009, 631).

11. In translating *selaʿ* when it is used as an epithet of YHWH (Muraoka 2010, 290), the Septuagint renders the word twice as στερέωμα 'solid body' (Pss 18:3; 71:3 [17:3; 70:3 LXX]; LSJ 1640;

in the Septuagint as πέτρα (e.g., Exod 17:6; Judg 13:19; Isa 48:21), including Job 19:24.[12] In nineteen cases, all of which use *ṣûr* as an epithet of YHWH, it is translated as θεός 'god' (e.g., Deut 32:4; Isa 30:29; Ps 18:32; LSJ 791; Muraoka 2009, 327); in other passages that use *ṣûr* as an epithet of YHWH, it is translated by a number of Greek words (Muraoka 2010, 290).[13] In short, the Septuagint translates the terms *selaʿ* and *ṣûr* with Greek words that for the most part correspond to the meaning of *selaʿ* and *ṣûr* in the Hebrew text.

It is difficult to differentiate the meanings of the terms *selaʿ* and *ṣûr*. Both are used primarily to refer to rocky cliffs or unworked stone. The latter, however, is also used in relation to writing (Job 19:24), but the word does not refer to a specific type of stone surface (e.g., a stone tablet, a stone wall, or a stela). Rather, in this passage, *ṣûr* simply refers to the surface of writing in general—that is, a stone surface.

3.1.5. Definitions of Terms Designating Stone Surfaces

Having analyzed the ancient Hebrew words that designate stone surfaces, I suggest the following definitions for these terms.

***ʾeben*:** A term that carries the general meaning 'rock, stone' but also designates plaster-covered stones and probably also stelae with writing inscribed directly upon them. The term also denotes precious stones and weights that were used in ancient Israel (see 5.3.2 and 5.3.6).

gāzît: A term that denotes hewn stone used for construction purposes.

maṣṣēbā/māṣṣebet: A term that means 'erected stone', but that may refer to inscribed stelae as well.

***selaʿ* and *ṣûr*:** Both terms carry the meaning 'rock, stone, cliff'. The latter, however, is used once in a context involving the process of writing upon a stone surface (Job 19:24).

Muraoka 2009, 635), once as κραταίωμα 'strength' (Ps 31:4 [30:4 LXX]; LSJ 990; Muraoka 2009, 410), and once as ἀντιλήμπτωρ 'helper' (Ps 42:10 [41:10 LXX]; LSJ 158; Muraoka 2009, 59).

12. Another three times, *ṣûr* is translated as ὄρος 'mountain' (Num 23:9; Job 18:4; 29:6; LSJ 1255; Muraoka 2009, 507).

13. In translating *ṣûr* when it is used as an epithet of YHWH (Muraoka 2010, 290), the Septuagint renders the word four times as βοηθός 'assistant' (Pss 18:3; 19:15; 78:35; 94:22; LSJ 320; Muraoka 2009, 119), four times as φύλαξ 'guard' (2 Sam 22:3, 47 (2x); 23:23; LSJ 1960; Muraoka 2009, 722), once as κτίστης 'founder, creator' (2 Sam 22:32; LSJ 1003; Muraoka 2009, 417), once as δίκαιος 'righteous' (1 Sam 2:2; LSJ 429; Muraoka 2009, 169), once as κύριος 'lord' (Isa 17:10; LSJ 1013; Muraoka 2009, 419), once as μέγας 'great' (Isa 26:4; LSJ 1088; Muraoka 2009, 445), and once as ἀντιλήμπτωρ 'supporter' (Ps 89:27; LSJ 158; Muraoka 2009, 59).

3.2. Mud, Clay, Plaster, and Whitewash

Clay and plaster were used for various purposes in the ancient world. They were used most commonly in construction projects, but they were also painted and written upon from the earliest periods. I will review the types of plaster used as well as the purposes for which they were utilized in the ancient world in order to establish a context in which to consider Hebrew terms that carry meanings such as 'mud', 'clay', 'plaster', and 'whitewash'. Within this discussion of Hebrew terms, I will focus on two passages which mention plaster utilized for construction purposes (Lev 14:33–54; Ezek 13:9–15), and I will also evaluate Deut 27:1–12, which refers to the process of writing upon plaster-covered stones.

3.2.1. Mud, Clay, Plaster, and Whitewash in the Ancient World

In discussing the plaster of ancient Egypt, Lucas (1962, 74–79, 353–56) identifies three types of plaster or whitewash: clay plaster, gypsum plaster, and plaster and whitewash made of crushed limestone or actual quicklime (calcium hydroxide). Clay plaster is attested already in the Predynastic Period (5000–3050 BCE). It consisted of Nile alluvium mixed with straw and either sand or limestone. The walls of homes were made of such clay. While certain paintings are executed directly on clay plaster walls, clay plaster was rather coarse (Kemp 2000, 92). For this reason, walls made of clay plaster were often covered with a final layer of gypsum plaster in order to cover the unevenness and produce a smooth surface upon which painting could be executed.

Although clay plaster was used in the construction of walls from early times in Egyptian history, the most common wall plaster of Egypt was not clay plaster but gypsum plaster. Like clay plaster, gypsum plaster was used from the Predynastic Period (Aston, Harrell, and Shaw 2000, 22). Gypsum is a soft mineral consisting of hydrated calcium sulfate, which appears white, grey, or light brown in color. It is found in the Mariout region west of Alexandria and near the Red Sea coast (Lucas 1962, 78). Gypsum plaster is produced when gypsum is heated to a temperature of 100–200 degrees Celsius and mixed with water to create a paste. This plaster was used on walls and ceilings of houses, palaces, tombs, and temples (Aston, Harrell, and Shaw 2000, 22). It was applied to walls in a layer about 0.1 inch thick (van der Kooij 1976a, 27). A layer of gypsum plaster was sometimes used to cover stone statues; it was also used to cover the bodies of the deceased and to make masks for Egyptian mummies.

Besides clay and gypsum plaster, Lucas considers plaster with a base of crushed limestone or quicklime, and he also discusses whitewash with a base of crushed limestone. Crushed limestone was mixed with a small quantity of gypsum to produce a whitewash. This whitewash was utilized as a finishing coat on walls as well as the plasters mentioned above (Lucas 1962, 77). Concerning plaster, Lucas (1962, 353–56) states that, in addition to the use of clay and gypsum to produce plaster, crushed limestone was also combined with glue to produce plaster. This type of plaster was utilized already in the Third Dynasty (2663–2597 BCE) and was frequently employed in the Eighteenth Dynasty (1549–1297 BCE). It was later used as a coating on wooden objects to make a surface smooth enough to be painted upon (Aston, Harrell, and Shaw 2000, 22). While crushed limestone mixed with glue was employed quite early in ancient Egypt, it seems that there is no evidence for the use of quicklime until the Ptolemaic Period (332–30 BCE) (Lucas 1962, 74–79, 353–56; Aston, Harrell, and Shaw 2000, 22). The process of making quicklime requires limestone to be heated to a temperature of 900 degrees Celsius in order to calcine the limestone, thereby producing quicklime. Thereafter, the quicklime is slaked with water, which results in the production of a plaster.

Plaster is well attested in Mesopotamia. Mud plaster, which was used for construction purposes, consists of mud mixed with reinforcing ingredients such as straw. Today, two coats of mud plaster are applied to walls; the initial layer is mixed with straw, while the outer layer has a finer consistency and is applied as a very thin coating (Moorey 1999, 329). Plaster in Mesopotamia was also made of gypsum or quicklime. While it is difficult to distinguish between gypsum plaster and quicklime plaster, the differentiation between the two kinds can be achieved by a scientific examination. These examinations have shown that both types were used in ancient Mesopotamia, although gypsum plaster was more common than quicklime plaster, at least in southern Mesopotamia, because gypsum was locally available and because gypsum plaster required a simpler process of preparation than quicklime plaster. Specifically the preparation of gypsum plaster required less fuel than the production of quicklime plaster, which needed to be heated to high temperatures; gypsum plaster was therefore preferred in Mesopotamia (Moorey 1999, 328–32).

Moorey writes that the use of plaster was so common in Mesopotamia that a detailed survey of its use is superfluous (Moorey 1999, 331). Remains from Mari, Khorsabad, Til Barsib, and Arslan Tash, for example, attest to the use of thick white plaster (van der Kooij 1976a, 28). From the earliest periods, mud plaster was used in walls and floors of houses (Moorey 1999, 329); the archive at Garshana details the preparation of plaster and its use for various construction purposes.[14] Likewise, gypsum and quicklime plaster were used from early

14. Heimpel (2009, 125–29, 133, 142, 156–58, 162–63, 169, 172–74, 189–90, 197–98, 239–48, 261–62, 266–74, 277–81) discusses the plaster in the Garshana archive. I thank David Owen for bringing this work to my attention at the 226th American Oriental Society meeting.

times to cover walls and produce smooth surfaces on which painting and writing could be executed. Indeed, plastered walls with paintings have been discovered in various Mesopotamian palaces (Moorey 1999, 330–31).

The use of plaster is also attested in the ancient Mediterranean world. Brysbaert (2008, 77–110) extensively catalogs finds of painted plaster in ancient Greece, Anatolia, the northern Levant, and the Egyptian Delta. Cities attesting to the use of painted plaster include Knossos, Melos, Mycenae, Thebes, Alalakh, Miletus, Hattusha, Qatna, Tell Sakka, and Tell el-Dabʾa. Also, Stager (1980) writes that plaster seems to have been used as a writing surface for funerary purposes in Carthage. In the Aegean and eastern Mediterranean regions, it was quicklime plaster that was primarily used.

Plaster was also utilized in ancient Israel. Like Mesopotamia and Egypt, the ancient Israelites used plaster to coat the outside of homes as a form of weatherproofing (King and Stager 2001, 28). Mud plaster was applied to mud brick walls or to walls made of stones and rubble. In certain sections of such walls the mud plaster layer is nearly an inch thick (Wright 1985, 1:421). Mud was also used as mortar for mudbricks; for such purposes, mud was mixed with grit, straw, and sand and utilized to keep bricks in place (Wright 1985, 1:359–60, 420). Quicklime plaster was also used for various plastering purposes in ancient Israel. Indeed, the land of Israel has an abundance of friable limestone, which was employed to produce plaster (King and Stager 2001, 21). Quicklime plaster was utilized to coat walls and cisterns (Wright 1985, 1:371). Floors of quicklime plaster have been found at Megiddo (Wright 1985, 1:372, 437), and quicklime was commonly utilized to produce a whitewash that was applied to the outer layer of a plastered wall (Wright 1985, 1:420).[15] Painting and writing were usually done upon such whitewash (Wright 1985, 1:420–21). The Deir ʿAlla inscription and the Kuntillet ʿAjrud inscriptions, which will be discussed in 3.2.6 in connection with the word *śîd*, are examples of writing executed on plaster surfaces that have survived

15. Additionally, in Megiddo, from the Early Bronze Age through the Iron Age, a crushed limestone paste was used to cover floors and walls, as well as for other purposes (Keinan 2013, 34; Adams 2013, 55, 64, 66, 71, 76, 95, 111, 113; Adams and Bos 2013, 122, 125–26, 132, 136–40; Friesem and Shahack-Gross 2013, 144–47; Arie and Nativ 2013, 170–74; Franklin 2013a, 183–84, 189, 192, 198, 205; Pechuro 2013, 223; Finkelstein 2013, 234–37; Cline and Samet 2013, 276, 281–84; Franklin 2013b, 290). Quicklime was also used to cover mudbrick wall surfaces at Megiddo during the Iron Age (Franklin 2013a, 197). Plastered floors and walls are also attested at Kuntillet ʿAjrud (Meshel and Goren 2012), Khirbet Qeiyafa (Hasel 2014, 300; Fichter and Chang 2014, 451–52; Kang 2014, 457; Thompson 2014, 459; Freikman 2014, 486), Lachish (primarily quicklime; Ussishkin 2004a, 1:195–99, 202–206, 212–214; Ussishkin 2004b, 1:149, 154–55, 157, 162–64, 169–72, 174–87; Shimron 2004, 2620–55; Barkay and Ussishkin 2004, 423–25, 436–37, 440–44, 467, 473, 480–82, 497–500), Gezer (Dever and Lance 1986, 1:15, 30, 36, 47–48), Ekron (Meehl, Dothan, and Gitin 2006, 45, 49), Ashkelon (Stager et al. 2008, 258, 279), and Shechem (Campbell 2002, 1:174, 177–80, 189, 192–93, 198, 224, 239–40, 254, 261, 295).

from ancient Israel and Transjordan.[16] The former inscription was written upon quicklime plaster while the latter inscriptions were executed on gypsum plaster.

I will now evaluate several terms that refer to unworked mud as well as workable mud (i.e., clay and plaster). I will also examine other terms and certain verbal roots used in reference to different types of plaster and whitewash.

3.2.2. *The Terms* **bōṣ** *(and* **biṣṣā***),* **repeš**, *and* **yāwēn**

3.2.2.1. *The Term* bōṣ *(and* biṣṣā*)*

3.2.2.1.1. ETYMOLOGY AND BIBLICAL USAGE

The term *bōṣ* 'mud, mire' (GMD 166; *DCH* 2:244; *HALOT* 1:147) occurs once in the Bible (Jer 38:22). It also occurs once in 1QHodayot[a] (1QH[a] XV, 5; *DSSR* 2:308; *DSSC* 1:156) where it clearly refers to mud. A related word, *biṣṣā* 'swamp, marsh', occurs three times in the Hebrew Bible (Ezek 47:11; Job 8:11; 40:21).[17] Because East and West Semitic contain lexemes that are etymologically related to *bōṣ* and *biṣṣā*—Akkadian *baṣṣum*/*bāṣum* 'sand' and *b-ṣ-ṣ* 'to trickle' (*CAD* 2:134–35) and Arabic *baḍḍat* 'soft, tender, plump' and *b-ḍ-ḍ* 'to trickle, to ooze' (Lane 1968, 1:213)—these two terms probably derive from Proto-Semitic.[18] Additionally, the forms *biṣṣā* and *bwṣ'* (*būṣā* [?], *bōṣā* [?], *buṣṣā* [?]) 'swamp, pond' are attested in Jewish and Christian Palestinian Aramaic (*HALOT* 1:147; Jastrow 1926, 1:183). These forms, however, must be loans from Hebrew, because one would expect the Aramaic forms to possess ʿ in place of *ṣ* if the Aramaic forms were cognates with the aforementioned forms of Akkadian, Arabic, and Hebrew.

If the Hebrew, Akkadian, and Arabic forms are cognates, perhaps they derive from Proto-Semitic *qvtl* biforms (*qatl*, *qitl*, *qutl*).[19] The Hebrew term *biṣṣā* thus

16. Ink-on-plaster inscriptions may have also existed in Shechem and Arad (Richter 2007, 358–61).

17. See 2.2.2 for a fuller discussion of the meaning of *biṣṣā*.

18. The Akkadian term *baṣṣum*/*bāṣum* 'sand' (*CAD* 2:134–35) is attested as early as Old Babylonian (2000–1500 BCE). Variant spellings such as *ba-aṣ-ṣa* (*baṣṣu*) and *ba-a-ṣi* (*bāṣu*) indicate that two biforms of this lexeme existed (*CAD* 2:134–35). I will argue that the form *baṣṣu* derived from Proto-Semitic; the form *bāṣu*, however, must have been a secondary development within Akkadian. The root *b-ṣ-ṣ* 'to trickle' is used verbally in Neo-Babylonian (*CAD* 2:134). The noun *biṣṣum* 'tear' (?) appears to be related to this meaning of the root (*CAD* 2:268). Arabic *baḍḍat* and Akkadian *baṣṣum*/*bāṣum* resemble each other inasmuch as both derive from the same Proto-Semitic root (**b-ṣ́-ṣ́*) and appear to be of the *qatl* pattern. However, Arabic *baḍḍat* is a feminine lexeme, whereas Akkadian *baṣṣum*/*bāṣum* is masculine. Moreover, Arabic *baḍḍat* seems to have undergone its own semantic development, which does not correspond entirely to that of Akkadian *baṣṣum*/*bāṣum*.

19. The alternation of the theme vowel within *qvtl* patterns is attested in various *qvtl* nouns in Semitic. For instance, such vowel variation is clearly seen in the reflexes of the words meaning 'arrow' (Geʿez *ḥaṣṣ* < **ḥaθθ-*; Heb *ḥēṣ*, *ḥiṣṣî* < **ḥiθθ-*; Akk *uṣṣum* < **ḥuθθ-*) and 'wild-ox' (Syr *raymā* < **raʾm-*; Akk *rīmum* < **riʾm-*; Ug *rum* < **ruʾm-*) (J. Fox 2003, 78, 80).

may have been derived from a feminine *qitl* form (**biṣ̌ṣ-at-*), while the term *bōṣ* was derived from a masculine *qutl* form (**buṣ̌ṣ-*). Moreover, **buṣ̌ṣ-* may have been a secondary development from **biṣ̌ṣ-*. That is, **buṣ̌ṣ-* arose because the *i* vowel of **biṣ̌ṣ-* became a *u* vowel as a result of the assimilation of the *i* vowel to the first radical *b* (**biṣ̌ṣ-* > **buṣ̌ṣ-* > **buṣṣ* > **boṣṣ* > **boṣ* > *bōṣ*).[20] The Aramaic word *biṣṣā* would have been borrowed from the feminine Hebrew term *biṣṣā*, and the Aramaic term *bwṣ'* would have been borrowed from the Hebrew term *bōṣ*.[21] On the other hand, the Akkadian form *baṣṣum*/*bāṣum* must have derived from a *qatl* form (**baṣ̌ṣ-* > *baṣṣum*/*bāṣum*); likewise, the Arabic form derived from a feminine *qatl* form (**baṣ̌ṣ-at-* > *baḍḍat*).

Jeremiah 38:22, which contains the term *bōṣ*, is part of an oracle of Jeremiah against King Zedekiah. The oracle compares Zedekiah to someone who has been abandoned by his friends while he is sinking in mire. The verse reads: וְהִנֵּה כָל־הַנָּשִׁים אֲשֶׁר נִשְׁאֲרוּ בְּבֵית מֶלֶךְ־יְהוּדָה מוּצָאוֹת אֶל־שָׂרֵי מֶלֶךְ בָּבֶל וְהֵנָּה אֹמְרוֹת הִסִּיתוּךְ וְיָכְלוּ לְךָ אַנְשֵׁי שְׁלֹמֶךָ הָטְבְּעוּ **בַבֹּץ** רַגְלֶךָ נָסֹגוּ אָחוֹר 'All the women that remained in the house of the king of Judah were being taken out to the officials of the king of Babylon, and they were saying, "Your friends of peace have misled you and have overcome you. Your feet have sunk in the ***bōṣ***, they have moved back away from you"'. Needless to say, this passage uses *bōṣ* to refer to wet mud. A passage in 1QHodayot[a] (1QH[a] XV, 5; *DSSR* 2:308; *DSSC* 1:156) uses *bōṣ* in a similar manner. The passage reads: ותטבע <ב>בץ רגלי 'my foot sank in *bōṣ*'; *bōṣ* here designates wet mud.

3.2.2.1.2. TRANSLATION OF *BŌṢ* IN ANCIENT VERSIONS

The Septuagint's translation of Jer 38:22 (45:22 LXX) seems to render the term *bōṣ* with the Greek verb ὀλίσθημα 'to slip, to fall' (LSJ 1216; Muraoka 2009, 493). Although the verb is not equivalent to the noun *bōṣ*, the idea of slipping and perhaps sinking is connoted in the Septuagint's rendition of this verse. In the Peshitta, *bōṣ* is rendered as *syn'* 'mud', but Targum Jonathan apparently renders the word metaphorically as *bahtā* 'shame' (Sokoloff 2009, 1005; *CAL*).

In sum, while *bōṣ* and *biṣṣā* are related terms, they carry slightly different meanings. The former refers to wet mire that was presumably located near

20. The alternation between *qatl* or *qitl* forms with *qutl* forms within the Semitic languages often happens when one of the radicals, usually the second, is a bilabial. Thus, the *a* of *qatl* or the *i* of *qitl* becomes *u* as a result of assimilation to the bilabial radical (J. Fox 2003, 108).

21. While the Hebrew form *biṣṣā* is a feminine *qitl* form, the gender seems to have been reanalyzed as a masculine when this lexeme was borrowed into Targumic Aramaic (feminine Heb *biṣṣā* > masculine emphatic Aram *biṣṣā*). According to Jastrow (1926, 1:147) *bwṣ'* should be vocalized as *būṣā* (e.g., Ps 69:3). If so, this means that the *ō* vowel of Hebrew *bōṣ* was perceived in Targumic Aramaic as a *ū* vowel. On the other hand, it may be that *bwṣ'* was vocalized as *bōṣā* (Levy 1867–68, 1:108) or even *buṣṣā*. Another possibility is that *bwṣ'* was realized as *buṣṣā* as a dialectal variant of *biṣṣā*/*biṣṣā*, not as a loan of *bōṣ*.

bodies of water such as rivers; the latter designates mire specifically characterized by the reeds that grew there (i.e., 'swamp, marsh').

3.2.2.2. The Term repeš

3.2.2.2.1. ETYMOLOGY AND BIBLICAL USAGE

The term *repeš* 'mud, mire, foam (?), froth (?)' (GMD 1263; *DCH* 7:540; *HALOT* 2:1280) occurs once in the Bible (Isa 57:20).[22] It also appears three times in 1QHodayot[a] (1QH[a] X, 14; XI, 33; XVI, 16; *DSSR* 2:288, 294, 312; *DSSC* 2:690). The etymology of *repeš* is a bit dubious, but the Akkadian terms *rupuštu* and *rupšu* 'spittle, saliva, froth' may be related (*CAD* 14:414).

Isaiah 57:20, wherein *repeš* occurs, compares wicked people with the raging sea that casts up *repeš* along with mud (*ṭîṭ*). The verse reads: וְהָרְשָׁעִים כַּיָּם נִגְרָשׁ כִּי הַשְׁקֵט לֹא יוּכָל וַיִּגְרְשׁוּ מֵימָיו **רֶפֶשׁ** וָטִיט 'The wicked shall be like the tossing sea, for it cannot rest. Its waters shall toss up ***repeš*** and mud [*ṭîṭ*]'. The three 1QHodayot[a] passages, which resemble the Isaiah passage, also refer to waves that cast up *repeš*; in one passage, the term stands in parallel with *ṭîṭ* (1QH[a] X, 14; *DSSR* 2:288). Because the term *repeš* stands in parallel with *ṭîṭ* 'mud, mire' in Isa 57:20 and in one of the Hodayot[a] passages, one may conclude that *repeš* probably designates 'mud, mire'. If the word is related to the Akkadian forms that carry the meaning 'spittle, saliva, froth', it is possible that *repeš* also meant 'foam, froth'.

3.2.2.2.2. TRANSLATION OF *REPEŠ* IN ANCIENT VERSIONS

Although the Septuagint's rendering of Isa 57:20 does not include a corresponding word for *repeš*, the word is translated in the revisions of Aquila, Symmachus, and Theodotion as καταπατήμα 'that which is trampled underfoot' (LSJ 904; Muraoka 2009, 379; Ziegler 1939, 336). Similarly, in Targum Jonathan *repeš* is translated as *səyān* 'mud, mire' (*CAL*). In the Peshitta, however, *repeš* is translated as *rḥš* 'creeping thing' (Sokoloff 2009, 1459), which suggests that the ancient translators of the passage may have inferred the meaning of the word in view of the context.

3.2.2.3. The Term yāwēn

3.2.2.3.1. ETYMOLOGY AND BIBLICAL USAGE

The term *yāwēn* 'mud, mire' (GMD 454; *DCH* 4:186; *HALOT* 1:402) occurs twice in the biblical text (Pss 40:3; 69:3) and once in 4QVision of Samuel

22. GMD also suggests 'seaweed' as a meaning for *repeš* (1263), but this is difficult to prove because the use of the word in the Hebrew Bible (as well as its translation in the Septuagint) and in the Dead Sea Scrolls suggests the meaning 'mud, mire, grime', rather than seaweed.

(4Q160 5, 1; *DSSR* 1:826; *DSSC* 1:306). The Mandaic word *yaunā* 'clay' appears to be related (Drower and Macuch 1963, 185). The biblical passages suggest the meaning 'mud, mire' for the term *yāwēn*. Psalm 40:3 reads: וַיַּעֲלֵנִי ׀ מִבּוֹר שָׁאוֹן מִטִּיט הַיָּוֵן וַיָּקֶם עַל־סֶלַע רַגְלָי כּוֹנֵן אֲשֻׁרָי 'He lifted me up from the pit of destruction, from the mud (*ṭîṭ*) of the ***yāwēn***, and he set my feet upon a rock and established my steps'. In this verse, *yāwēn* appears in a genitive relationship with *ṭîṭ*. The same is true of the occurrence of the word in 4QVision of Samuel (4Q160 5, 1; *DSSR* 1:826). It seems strange, however, to understand this phrase as meaning 'mud of mire'. More likely, *yāwēn* does not modify *ṭîṭ*. Rather, the construct chain *ṭîṭ hayyāwēn* is probably a tautological construction similar to *məgillat sēper*; such constructions are not uncommon in Late Biblical Hebrew (Hurvitz 1996, 43*–44*).[23] The phrase *ṭîṭ hayyāwēn* would then be a stylistic formulation that simply connotes mud and mire. Indeed, that *yāwēn* means mud and mire is also suggested in Ps 69:3, which speaks of sinking in *yāwēn*. The text reads: טָבַעְתִּי ׀ בִּיוֵן מְצוּלָה וְאֵין מָעֳמָד בָּאתִי בְמַעֲמַקֵּי־מַיִם וְשִׁבֹּלֶת שְׁטָפָתְנִי 'I sink in ***yāwēn*** of depths, and there is no foothold; I have come into the depths of water and the rushing stream washes over me'.

3.2.2.3.2. TRANSLATION OF *YĀWĒN* IN ANCIENT TRANSLATIONS

The interpretation of *yāwēn* as referring to mud and mire is perhaps supported by the Septuagint's translation of Pss 40:3 and 69:3 (39:3; 68:3 LXX); in both cases, *yāwēn* is rendered as ἰλύς 'mud, slime' (LSJ 829; Muraoka 2009, 340), although both renderings may be inferences. Targum Psalms renders *yāwēn* of Ps 40:3 as *ṭyšṭwš*ʾ 'filth', but in Ps 69:3, the targum translates it metaphorically as *glwt*ʾ 'exile' (*CAL*). The Peshitta's translation is not helpful inasmuch as in both passages *yāwēn* is untranslated.

While the terms *bōṣ*, *repeš*, and *yāwēn* occur very infrequently, their meaning seems to be 'mud, mire'. Based on the Bible's use of these terms, they do not refer to workable clay used in construction but designate wet mud found along bodies of water.

3.2.3. The Term ʿāpār

3.2.3.1. Etymology and Biblical Usage

A number of Hebrew terms carry the meaning 'dust, dirt, earth' (GMD 996; *DCH* 6:515–18; *HALOT* 1:861–62). For example, the terms *ʾădāmā*, *ʾēper*, *ʾābāq*, and *ʿāpār* have this meaning. Of these terms, *ʿāpār* is also used on three

23. See 4.2.1.2 for a brief discussion of tautological constructions including those in *ṭîṭ hayyāwēn* and *məgillat sēper*.

occasions to refer to wall plaster that is presumably made of dirt. The use of *ʿāpār* in the Bible will be briefly summarized here, but its usage to refer to mud plaster will be discussed in 3.2.5.3.1.

The term *ʿāpār* 'dust, soil', which occurs a total of 110 times in the Bible, derives from Proto-Semitic **ʿapar-*. The word also occurs at least sixty-three times in the Dead Sea Scrolls, including six cases with an uncertain letter (e.g., CD XII, 16; 1QH^{a} V, 21; *DSSR* 1:102; 2:294; *DSSC* 2:588–9). Cognates of this word exist in various Semitic languages such as Akkadian (*eperum*; *CAD* 4:184), Arabic (*ʿafar*; Lane 1968, 5:2090), Syriac (*ʿaprā*; Sokoloff 2009, 1124 *CAL*), and Ugaritic (*ʿpr*; *DULAT* 1:174).

In the majority of biblical passages that use *ʿāpār*, the term refers to dust or the ground (e.g., Gen 13:16; 18:27; Isa 2:19; Job 28:2). For instance, Gen 13:16 reads: וְשַׂמְתִּי אֶת־זַרְעֲךָ **כַּעֲפַר** הָאָרֶץ אֲשֶׁר ׀ אִם־יוּכַל אִישׁ לִמְנוֹת אֶת־**עֲפַר** הָאָרֶץ גַּם־זַרְעֲךָ יִמָּנֶה׃ 'I will make your seed as the ***ʿāpār*** of the earth, so that if anyone would be able to count the ***ʿāpār*** of the earth, so your seed shall be numbered'. In several other cases, the word refers to soil or dirt (e.g., Gen 26:15; Lev 17:13; Neh 3:34). This meaning is clear in Gen 26:15: וְכָל־הַבְּאֵרֹת אֲשֶׁר חָפְרוּ עַבְדֵי אָבִיו בִּימֵי אַבְרָהָם אָבִיו סִתְּמוּם פְּלִשְׁתִּים וַיְמַלְאוּם **עָפָר** 'All the wells that his father's servants had dug in the days of Abraham his father, the Philistines had stopped and filled them up with ***ʿāpār***'. In a few passages, the word refers to the netherworld (e.g., Ps 22:16, 30; Job 5:6; 17:16; Dan 12:2). For example, Ps 22:30 reads: אָכְלוּ וַיִּשְׁתַּחֲוּוּ ׀ כָּל־דִּשְׁנֵי־אֶרֶץ לְפָנָיו יִכְרְעוּ כָּל־יוֹרְדֵי **עָפָר** וְנַפְשׁוֹ לֹא חִיָּה 'All the prosperous of the earth ate and worshipped; before him bowed down all those who descend to ***ʿāpār*** and the one who did not revive his own soul'.

3.2.3.2. Translation of ʿāpār *in the Septuagint*

In the Septuagint, the term *ʿāpār* is translated with a number of Greek terms (Muraoka 2010, 305–6), although, for the most part, the Greek words χοῦς 'soil' (40x; e.g., Gen 2:7; Josh 7:6) and γῆ 'earth, land' (40x; e.g., Gen 3:14, 19) are used (LSJ 347, 2000; Muraoka 2009, 129, 735).[24] In the Septuagint's translation of Lev 14, which uses *ʿāpār* to refer to mud plaster, *ʿāpār* is rendered with the term χοῦς 'soil'.

24. Other Greek terms are also used to translate *ʿāpār* (Muraoka 2010, 305–6): χῶμα 'mass of soil' (9x, e.g., Exod 8:12–13; LSJ 2014; Muraoka 2009, 739), ἔδαφος 'ground, foundation' (4x: Isa 25:12; 26:5; 29:4; Ps 119:25 [118:25 LXX]; LSJ 477; Muraoka 2009, 189), ἄμμος 'sandy ground' (2x: Gen 13:16; 28:14; LSJ 84; Muraoka 2009, 32), κονιορτός 'dust cloud' (2x: Deut 9:21; LSJ 977; Muraoka 2009, 406), κονία 'plaster, dust' (Job 38:38; LSJ 977; Muraoka 2009, 406), οἰκέω 'to colonize, to dwell' (Prov 8:26; LSJ 1202; Muraoka 2009, 487), πέτρα 'rock' (Job 14:8; LSJ 1397; Muraoka 2009, 555), πηλός 'mud, mire' (Job 4:19; LSJ 1401; Muraoka 2009, 556), σπέρμα 'seed' (Num 23:10; LSJ 1626; Muraoka 2009, 630–31), and σποδιά 'ashes' (Num 19:17; LSJ 1629; Muraoka 2009, 631).

In sum, the term *ʿāpār* is a common term used to designate dust, soil, and earth, as well as the netherworld. Although the term can refer to mud plaster, this is not the usual meaning of the term.

3.2.4. The Terms **ṭîṭ** *and* **ḥōmer**

3.2.4.1. The Term ṭîṭ

3.2.4.1.1. ETYMOLOGY

The etymology of Hebrew noun *ṭîṭ* 'mud' (GMD 423; *DCH* 3:363–64; *HALOT* 1:374) is debated. The attested cognates of this term pose a number of phonological difficulties when one attempts to reconstruct a Proto-Semitic form from which all other forms derived. Some West Semitic cognates of this word display a final *-n* (Arab *ṭīn*, Lane 1968, 5:1906; Aram *ṭyn*ʾ, *CAL*; Mehri *ṭayn*, Johnstone 1987, 414), while a few West Semitic cognates display a final *-ṭ* (Heb *ṭîṭ* and Jewish Aram *ṭyṭ*ʾ; Mankowski 2000, 57; *CAL*). Akkadian forms display a final *-ṭ* or *-d* (*ṭīṭu*/*ṭīdu* and *ṭiṭṭu*/*ṭiddu*) (*CAD* 19:106); in Akkadian, this word, which is designated by the logogram IM, occurs already in Old Babylonian (2000–1500 BCE; Huehnergard 2011, xxv). According to *HALOT* (1:374), the final *-ṭ* of the Akkadian forms derives from a feminine *-t* affix. Mankowski (2000, 57) therefore offers the following phonological development: **ṭin-t-u* > **ṭittu* (*ṭiddu* [?]) > *ṭiṭṭu* > *ṭīṭu*. Similarly, J. Fox (2003, 81) suggests that the Akkadian forms derived from **ṭiyntum*, while the Proto-Semitic form was **ṭiyn-*. According to Mankowski (2000, 57), the problem with both of these explanations, which depend on a feminine *-t* affix, is that none of the forms with final *-ṭ* or *-d* are feminine in any of the languages; rather, all such forms are masculine.[25] Mankowski therefore argues that the origin of the final *-ṭ* is not connected to a feminine affix *-t*.

Mankowski's approach seems to offer a coherent method of resolving the aforementioned difficulties. He suggests that *ṭīn* represents an original West Semitic form, while the form *ṭiṭ(ṭ)* represents an Akkadian innovation; whenever *ṭīṭ* occurs in Northwest Semitic, it is an Akkadian loanword (Mankowski 2000, 57). J. Fox (2003, 81) rightly states, then, that the Proto-Semitic form was **ṭiyn-*. This form developed into the West Semitic forms that have a final *-n* (**ṭiyn-* > *ṭīn*, *ṭyn*ʾ, and *ṭayn*). On the other hand, within Akkadian, the form developed independently of the West Semitic forms, thus producing the existing

25. *CAD* 19:108 gives one example in which the Akkadian form is modified by a masculine singular adjective. The given example reads: *ša* IM *ilta u qēma ballu teppuš* 'you made (it) of mud that is mixed with chaff and flour'. The adjective modifying IM (i.e., *ballu*) is a masculine singular form, which demonstrates that IM is also masculine. The Hebrew form *ṭîṭ* is presumably also masculine because it does not display a feminine marker, but the biblical passages in which the term occurs do not contain any modifiers of *ṭîṭ* that would unequivocally disclose the gender of the lexeme.

forms (*ṭiyn- > *ṭiyṭ- > *ṭīṭu/ṭīdu* > *ṭiṭṭu/ṭiddu*).[26] Hebrew *ṭîṭ* thus seems to be an Akkadian loanword.

3.2.4.1.2. USAGE OF *ṬĪṬU/ṬĪDU* IN AKKADIAN

In Akkadian texts, *ṭīṭu/ṭīdu* (written IM) usually refers to workable mud that was utilized for various purposes. For instance, one text uses the term in connection with temple construction: *mušlāla ša bīt Aššur . . . ša ina pānâ itti pīli u ṭīdi epšu ēnaḫma* 'the gatehouse of the Aššur temple, . . . which had originally been made of limestone and mud, had fallen into disrepair' (*CAD* 19:106). In another text the logogram IM refers to clay used in the production of figurines: *ina* IM-*ki ṣalam Ninšubur abanni* 'I will make an image of Ninšubur from your clay' (*CAD* 19:107). Nevertheless, the word also refers to mud or dust that one treads upon, as in this example: *umma* PN *ardūka epru ša šēpēka u ṭīdu ša kapāšīka* 'thus says PN, your servant, the dust at your feet, and the mud on which you tread' (*CAD* 19:110). While *ṭīṭu/ṭīdu* in Akkadian texts usually refers to clay, *ṭîṭ* in Biblical Hebrew primarily refers to actual mud and, in a few passages, to workable clay.

3.2.4.1.3. BIBLICAL USAGE OF *ṬÎṬ*

Within the Bible, *ṭîṭ* occurs a total of thirteen times. It also probably occurs five times, including two times with a restored *tet* and an uncertain *yod*, in the Dead Sea Scrolls in contexts similar to those in the Bible (4Q169 5, 3; 4Q160 5, 1; 1QH[a] X, 15; 4Q509 1–2, 3; 1Q28b V, 27; *DSSR* 1:442, 826; 2:288, 518, 634; *DSSC* 1:284). In the Bible, the term refers eleven times to unworked mud (2 Sam 22:43; Isa 57:20; Jer 38:6 [2x]; Mic 7:10; Zech 9:3; 10:5; Pss 18:43; 40:3; 69:15; Job 41:22) and twice to workable clay (Isa 41:25; Nah 3:14). When referring to the former, the Bible speaks of *ṭîṭ ḥûṣôt* 'mud of the streets' (2 Sam 22:43; Mic 7:10; Zech 9:3; 10:5; Ps 18:43). The word also refers in a number of passages to wet mud found in pits and near bodies of water (Isa 57:20; Jer 38:6; Pss 40:3; 69:15; Job 4:22). On the other hand, when the term *ṭîṭ* designates workable clay, the term stands in parallel with *ḥōmer* 'clay', and a clear reference is made within the text to processes of working *ṭîṭ* for a particular purpose (Isa 41:25; Nah 3:14).

26. In an effort to explain the presence of final *-ṭ/d* in Akkadian forms, Mankowski (2000, 58) offers a solution that is not tied to normal phonological processes: it is possible that the Akkadian forms with final *-ṭ/d* as well as the Ge'ez term *ṣoṭ* 'mud' and the Arabic term *ḍawīṭa* 'slime' are all related semantically and are similar acoustically but are not derived from one form according to regularly operating sound rules. Rather, the existence of these similar forms in different languages may be a case of onomatopoeia in which these various forms, which sound alike, carry a similar meaning but cannot be explained as developing according to regular phonological sound rules. On the other hand, the development within Akkadian of *ṭīṭu/ṭīdu* > *ṭiṭṭu/ṭiddu* is a phonological change that, although infrequent, occurs in other lexemes. The change is comparable to the development of *būnu* > *bunnu* 'goodness', *ḫīṭu* > *ḫiṭṭu* 'error', *kūṣu* > *kuṣṣu* 'coldness, winter', *pīdu* > *piddu* 'imprisonment', *ṭīru* > *ṭirru* 'impression, stamp', and *ṭūdu* > *ṭuddu* 'way, path'.

Speaking of the mud of the streets, Zech 10:5 reads: וְהָיוּ כְגִבֹּרִים בּוֹסִים **בְּטִיט** חוּצוֹת בַּמִּלְחָמָה וְנִלְחֲמוּ כִּי יְהוָה עִמָּם וְהֹבִישׁוּ רֹכְבֵי סוּסִים 'They shall be like warriors trampling on the ***ṭîṭ*** of the streets in war. They shall fight because YHWH is with them, and they will put to shame the riders on horses'. Also describing wet mud, Jer 38:6 reads: וַיִּקְחוּ אֶת־יִרְמְיָהוּ וַיַּשְׁלִכוּ אֹתוֹ אֶל־הַבּוֹר ׀ מַלְכִּיָּהוּ בֶן־הַמֶּלֶךְ אֲשֶׁר בַּחֲצַר הַמַּטָּרָה וַיְשַׁלְּחוּ אֶת־יִרְמְיָהוּ בַּחֲבָלִים וּבַבּוֹר אֵין־מַיִם כִּי אִם־**טִיט** וַיִּטְבַּע יִרְמְיָהוּ **בַּטִּיט** 'They took Jeremiah and cast him into the pit of Malciah, the king's son, which was in the court of the guard, and they sent Jeremiah (down) by ropes, but there was no water in the pit, but only ***ṭîṭ***, and Jeremiah sank in the ***ṭîṭ***'. On the other hand, Isa 41:25 refers to workable clay: הַעִירוֹתִי מִצָּפוֹן וַיַּאת מִמִּזְרַח־שֶׁמֶשׁ יִקְרָא בִשְׁמִי וְיָבֹא סְגָנִים כְּמוֹ־חֹמֶר וּכְמוֹ יוֹצֵר יִרְמָס־**טִיט** 'I stirred up from the north, and he came; from the rising of the sun he called upon my name. He marched [literally, 'came'] upon rulers as upon clay [*ḥōmer*], and as a potter treads ***ṭîṭ***'. While the use of *ṭîṭ* within the Bible is limited, it generally refers to mud, although it can also refer to workable clay.

3.2.4.2. The Term ḥōmer

3.2.4.2.1. ETYMOLOGY AND BIBLICAL USAGE

It is difficult to establish with certainty the etymology of *ḥōmer* 'clay, mud plaster, mortar' (GMD 368; *DCH* 3:259; *HALOT* 1:330). In Hebrew, there are several terms consisting of a supposed *ḥ-m-r* root; examples include *ḥămôr* 'donkey', *ḥămôr* 'heap', *ḥōmer* 'a dry measure', *ḥōmer* 'foaming', *ḥemer* 'wine', *ḥēmār* 'bitumen', *ḥ-m-r* 'to smear bitumen' (denominative of *ḥēmār*), *ḥ-m-r* 'to foam', and *ḥ-m-r* 'to be red'. Comparative Semitics helps in untangling this group of words and roots that, on the surface, appear to derive from one triradical base, *ḥ-m-r*.

We can separate out a number of the aforementioned terms. The word *ḥămôr* 'donkey' (with etymological *ḥ*) can be viewed as the first lexical item with cognates in various Semitic languages, including Akkadian *imērum* (*CAD* 7:110), Arabic *ḥimār* (Lane 1968, 2:641), and Ugaritic *ḥmr* (*DULAT* 1:363). The terms *ḥōmer* 'a dry measure' and *ḥămôr* 'heap' (both with etymological *ḥ*) form a second lexical group with a number of cognates: for example, Akkadian *amaru* 'pile of bricks' (*CAD* 1/2:4) and Ugaritic *ḥmr* 'heap, load' (*DULAT* 1:364). The verbal root *ḥ-m-r* 'to be red' (with etymological *ḥ*) pertains to yet another distinct group with cognates: for example, Ugaritic *ḥmr* 'reddish' (*DULAT* 1:364) and Ethiopic *ḥamar* 'red berry' (*CDG* 234). All of the aforementioned lexemes may derive from the same *ḥ-m-r* root, which carries the general meaning 'reddish'. This meaning is clear in the verbal root *ḥ-m-r* 'to be red'. The term *ḥămôr* 'donkey' may have derived from this root because donkeys were of a brownish-reddish color, and the word *ḥōmer* 'a dry measure' may have been the measure that a donkey carried (King and Stager 2001, 200). It is possible that the lexeme *ḥămôr* 'heap' is etymologically connected to the term *ḥōmer* 'a dry measure', as well as *ḥămôr* 'donkey', because *ḥămôr* 'heap', like *ḥōmer* 'a dry measure', refers to a quantity or amount.

The verbal root *ḥ-m-r* 'to foam', from which *ḥōmer* 'foaming' is derived, is distinct from the aforementioned lexemes. It is not clear whether *ḥ-m-r* 'to foam' is derived from an etymological *ḥ* or *ḫ* in first position; it is therefore difficult to determine the root's possible cognates. The root may be related to the Akkadian verb *emērum* 'to swell' (Black, George, and Postgate 2007, 72). If this is indeed the case, it would mean that the discussed Hebrew root has an etymological *ḥ* in first position, not *ḫ*.

In discussing the Hebrew root *ḥ-m-r* 'to be red', J. Fox (2003, 216) has suggested that the terms *ḥemer* 'wine', *ḥēmār* 'bitumen', and *ḥōmer* 'clay, mud plaster, mortar' may all be related to this verbal root. This is, however, unlikely. Comparative Semitic evidence reveals that *ḥemer* has an etymological *ḫ* as its first radical, as in Ugaritic *ḫmr* (*DULAT* 1:395) and Arabic *ḫamr* (Lane 1968, 2:808). If *ḥemer* is related to *ḥēmār*, *ḥōmer*, and *ḥ-m-r* 'to foam', then all these lexemes would also derive from an etymological *ḫ* in first position. On the other hand, if the Hebrew root *ḥ-m-r* 'to foam' is related to the Akkadian verb *emērum* 'to swell' (with etymological *ḥ*), Hebrew *ḥ-m-r* 'to foam' would also have an etymological *ḥ* in first position, and this would preclude any connection of Hebrew *ḥ-m-r* 'to foam' with *ḥemer* 'wine', because the latter clearly has *ḫ* in first position. In view of these difficulties, perhaps it is necessary to consider a different approach to resolve the etymological questions for these lexemes.

First, we will assume that the Akkadian verb *emērum* 'to swell' and the Hebrew root *ḥ-m-r* 'to foam' are connected. The similarity in meaning suggests that the roots are etymologically related. The term *ḥemer* 'wine' must therefore be unrelated to the aforementioned Hebrew or Akkadian roots. Rather, *ḥemer* 'wine' stands as an individual lexical item. Furthermore, the word *ḥēmār* 'bitumen' seems to be connected to Arabic *ḥumar* 'tamarind', because both meanings refer to dark, sticky, resin-like material (Lane 1968, 2:640); if this connection is correct, both the Hebrew and Arabic lexemes would have an etymological *ḥ* in first position. Finally, I would argue that the word *ḥōmer* 'clay, mud plaster, mortar' is also related to Hebrew *ḥēmār* and Arabic *ḥumar* because *ḥōmer*, like *ḥēmār* and Arabic *ḥumar*, consisted of a dark, viscous material. A possible outline of the meanings of the Hebrew root *ḥ-m-r* is given in table 3.1.

While the etymology of *ḥōmer* is debated, the meaning of this term in the biblical text is quite clear. The lexeme *ḥōmer* occurs a total of seventeen times in the Bible. In all but two cases, the term refers to workable mud that is used for a variety of purposes; it refers twice to unworked mud. When referring to workable mud, *ḥōmer* is used six times with a clear reference to a potter (Isa 29:16; 41:25; 45:9; 64:7; Jer 18:4, 6). In another seven passages, the word is used in connection to potter's clay or to clay that is used for construction purposes

TABLE 3.1. The Root *ḥ-m-r* in Biblical Hebrew

Root	Lexeme	Meaning	Cognates
I. *ḥ-m-r* 'reddish' (with etymological *ḥ*)	1. *ḥ-m-r*	1. 'to be red'	1. Ugaritic *ḥmr* 'reddish' Ethiopic *ḥamar* 'red berry'
	2. *ḥămôr*	2. 'donkey'	2. Akkadian *imērum* Arabic *ḥimār* Ugaritic *ḥmr*
	3. *ḥămôr*	3. 'heap'	3. Ugaritic *ḥmr* 'heap, load' Akkadian *amaru* 'pile of bricks'
	4. *ḥōmer*	4. 'a dry measure'	
II. *ḥ-m-r* 'viscous material' (with etymological *ḥ*)	1. *ḥōmer*	1. 'clay, mud plaster, mortar'	
	2. *ḥēmār* > *ḥ-m-r* (denominative of *ḥēmār*)	2. 'bitumen' 'to smear bitumen'	2. Arabic *ḥumar* 'tamarind'
III. *ḥ-m-r* 'to foam' (with etymological *ḥ*)	1. *ḥ-m-r*	1. 'to foam'	1. Akkadian *emērum* 'to swell'
	2. *ḥōmer*	2. 'foaming'	
IV. *ḥ-m-r* (with etymological *ḫ*)	*ḥemer*	'wine'	Ugaritic *ḫmr* Arabic *ḫamr*

(Nah 3:14; Job 4:19; 10:9; 13:12; 30:19; 33:6; 38:14). Twice, *ḥōmer* refers to the mortar utilized to bind bricks (Gen 11:3; Exod 1:14). Finally, in two cases, the term refers to unworked mud (Isa 10:6; Job 27:16).

In Isaiah 64:7, *ḥōmer* refers to potter's clay: וְעַתָּה יְהוָה אָבִינוּ אָתָּה אֲנַחְנוּ **הַחֹמֶר** וְאַתָּה יֹצְרֵנוּ וּמַעֲשֵׂה יָדְךָ כֻּלָּנוּ 'Now, YHWH, you are our father; we are the ***ḥōmer*** and you are our potter, and we are all the work of your hand'. In Job 4:19, however, *ḥōmer* refers to mud plaster used in the construction of houses: אַף ׀ שֹׁכְנֵי בָתֵּי־**חֹמֶר** אֲשֶׁר־בֶּעָפָר יְסוֹדָם יְדַכְּאוּם לִפְנֵי־עָשׁ 'Even those who dwell in houses of ***ḥōmer*** whose foundation is in the dust, they shall be crushed like the moth'. In Gen 11:3, one reads of the use of *ḥōmer* as mortar: וַיֹּאמְרוּ אִישׁ אֶל־רֵעֵהוּ הָבָה נִלְבְּנָה לְבֵנִים וְנִשְׂרְפָה

לְשְׂרֵפָ֑ה וַתְּהִ֨י לָהֶ֤ם הַלְּבֵנָה֙ לְאָ֔בֶן וְהַ֣חֵמָ֔ר הָיָ֥ה לָהֶ֖ם **לַחֹֽמֶר** 'They said to each other, "Let us make bricks and burn them with fire." The bricks served them as stone, and the bitumen served them as ***ḥōmer***'. Finally, Isa 10:6 uses *ḥōmer* to speak of the mud of the streets (*ḥōmer ḥûṣôt*); this usage of *ḥōmer* resembles the use of *ṭîṭ* to refer to the mud of the streets (*ṭîṭ ḥûṣôt*). Isaiah 10:6 reads: בְּג֤וֹי חָנֵף֙ אֲשַׁלְּחֶ֔נּוּ וְעַל־עַ֥ם עֶבְרָתִ֖י אֲצַוֶּ֑נּוּ לִשְׁלֹ֤ל שָׁלָל֙ וְלָבֹ֣ז בַּ֔ז ולשימו וּלְשׂוּמ֥וֹ מִרְמָ֖ס **כְּחֹ֥מֶר** חוּצֽוֹת 'Against a godless nation I shall send him, and against the people of my wrath I shall command him, to take spoil and to take plunder, and to set them for treading like the ***ḥōmer*** of the streets'. These examples show that *ḥōmer* was used to speak of workable clay as well as mud, although the former meaning was more common than the latter.

3.2.4.3. Translation of ṭîṭ *and* ḥōmer *in the Septuagint*

The Septuagint's translation of *ṭîṭ* is quite homogeneous. In all passages except for Jer 38:6 (45:6 LXX), the word is rendered as πηλός 'clay, earth' (LSJ 1401; Muraoka 2009, 556). The Greek term refers to workable clay as well as unworked mud. In translating the two occurrences of *ṭîṭ* in Jer 38:6 (45:6 LXX), the Septuagint renders the term as βόρβορος 'mire, filth' (LSJ 322; Muraoka 2009, 120), although Aquila and Symmachus both render the word as πηλός (Ziegler 1957, 405), and, in a variant reading of Ps 40:3 (39:3 LXX), *ṭîṭ* is also rendered as βόρβορος (Holmes and Parsons 1798–1827, 3:249). In another passage (Isa 57:20), there is not a corresponding Greek word for *ṭîṭ*, but it is rendered as πηλός in the Lucianic recension and the revisions of Aquila, Symmachus, and Theodotion (Isa 57:20; Ziegler 1939, 336).

The translation of *ḥōmer* in the Septuagint is comparable to the Septuagint's translation of *ṭîṭ*. In all but two cases, the Septuagint renders *ḥōmer* as πηλός (LSJ 1401; Muraoka 2009, 556) or as πήλινος 'made of clay' (LSJ 1400; Muraoka 2009, 556). In Isa 10:6, on the other hand, *ḥōmer* is rendered as κονιορτός 'dust, cloud of dust' (LSJ 977; Muraoka 2009, 406), while it is translated as ἄχυρον 'chaff, straw' in Nah 3:14 (LSJ 298; Muraoka 2009, 110). In one more passage (Jer 18:4), *ḥōmer* does not have a corresponding Greek word, but πηλός is provided in the Lucianic recension and in the revisions of the passage by Aquila and Theodotion (Ziegler 1957, 239).

Unfortunately, the Septuagint's rendering of *ṭiṭ* and *ḥōmer* is not particularly helpful in disclosing the unique meanings of these two terms. For the most part, both terms are translated by the same Greek term (i.e., πηλός). While this sheds light on the meaning of the Greek word πηλός—specifically, that it designated both clay and mud—this does not refine our knowledge of the individual Hebrew lexemes.

In sum, the Hebrew term *ṭîṭ* carries the general meaning 'mud' and means 'clay' less frequently. While clay was commonly used for various construction projects in the ancient Near East, the Hebrew term *ṭîṭ* does not usually refer to workable mud material. Rather, *ḥōmer* is the term that designates the clay material used for pottery and other construction purposes.

3.2.5. The Terms ṭîaḥ *(and* ṭ-w-ḥ*) and* tāpēl *(and* ṭ-p-l*)*

3.2.5.1. The Term ṭîaḥ *(and* ṭ-w-ḥ*)*

3.2.5.1.1. ETYMOLOGY

The noun *ṭîaḥ* 'coating, overlay' (GMD 423; *DCH* 3:363; *HALOT* 1:374) occurs only once in the Hebrew Bible (Ezek 13:12). The term reflects a *qīl*/*qitl* noun pattern built upon the verbal root *ṭ-w-ḥ* 'to overlay, to daub' (GMD 421; *DCH* 3:360; *HALOT* 1:372). Thus, *ṭîaḥ* probably meant 'that which is daubed or overlayed' (i.e., 'coating, overlay').[27] The verbal root is attested elsewhere in Semitic, in Arabic *muṭayyaḫ* 'smeared with tar' (Lane 1968, 5:1906) and Ugaritic *ṭḫ* 'to plaster' (*DULAT* 2:889). Within the Bible, the Hebrew verbal root is used eleven times (Lev 14:42–43, 48; Ezek 13:10–12, 14–15 [3x]; 22:28; 1 Chr 22:28).[28] While primarily used in contexts that speak of daubing mud and plaster, the verbal root also refers to the overlaying of walls with gold and silver. The root also occurs six times in the Dead Sea Scrolls in reference to plastered vessels and to the act of plastering (CD VIII, 12; XI, 9; XIX, 25; 4Q271 5i5; 4Q424 1, 3; 1QH^{a} XII, 24; *DSSR* 1:94, 98, 110, 198; 2:238, 298; *DSSC* 1:284).

3.2.5.2. The Term tāpēl *(and* ṭ-p-l*)*

3.2.5.2.1. ETYMOLOGY

The nominalized adjective *tāpēl* occurs seven times in the biblical text. Five times, the word seems to refer to a form of plaster (Ezek 13:10, 11, 14–15; 22:28). It is used once to speak of food as being 'tasteless, unsalted' (Job 6:6); another time the word refers to the deceptive promises of false prophets (Lam 2:14; GMD 1452; *DCH* 8:665; *HALOT* 2:1775–76). The feminine *qitl* noun *tiplā*

27. The *qitl* pattern is frequently used to derive nouns from transitive verbs. These nouns tend to denote the result of the verbal action. Examples of such nouns include *zebaḥ* 'sacrifice' (i.e., 'that which is sacrificed'), *ṭebaḥ* 'slaughter' (i.e., 'that which is slaughtered'), and *neder* 'vow' (i.e., 'that which is vowed') (Lambdin and Huehnergard 2000, 33).

28. Isaiah 44:18 contains perhaps another case of a verbal form of the root *ṭ-w-ḥ*. The verse reads: לֹא יָדְעוּ וְלֹא יָבִינוּ כִּי טַח מֵרְאוֹת עֵינֵיהֶם מֵהַשְׂכִּיל לִבֹּתָם 'They did not discern, and they did not understand, for he daubed [*ṭaḥ*] their eyes from seeing, their hearts from understanding'. BDB (376) takes *ṭaḥ* as related to the supposed root *ṭ-ḥ-ḥ*. Alternatively, it may be that the text is incorrectly pointed and should read *ṭāḥ*, which would mean that the word is related to the root *ṭ-w-ḥ*. Another option is to view *ṭaḥ* as indeed being connected to the root *ṭ-ḥ-ḥ* while understanding this root as secondarily derived from the root *ṭ-w-ḥ* (*HALOT* 1:372–74; GMD 422).

'unseemliness', which occurs three times in the Bible (Jer 23:13; Job 1:22; 24:12; GMD 1452; *DCH* 8:665; *HALOT* 2:1775–76), seems to be related to the term *tāpēl*. Perhaps the root *t-p-l* carried the basic meaning 'without substance'. Under this general meaning seem to fall the meanings 'tasteless', 'deceptive', and 'unseemliness', all of which can be understood as connoting a lack of substance.[29] The use of *tāpēl* to designate plaster can perhaps also be related to this meaning in that the plaster designated by *tāpēl* was unmixed with straw and other hardening elements and was thus lacking in substance (Greenberg 1983, 237–38).

Prior to further discussing the etymology of this word, let us first look at the root *ṭ-p-l*. The verbal root *ṭ-p-l* occurs three times in the biblical text (Ps 119:69; Job 13:4; 14:17). The root carries the meaning 'to slander' in two instances (Ps 119:69; Job 13:4) and once means 'to cover up, to smear over' (Job 14:17) (GMD 428; *DCH* 3:373; *HALOT* 1:379). The root also occurs once with the meaning 'to slander' in Ben Sira (41, 5). The two meanings may reflect two distinct homophonous roots, but this is uncertain. Connected with the first meaning ('to slander') is the Akkadian verb *ṭapālum*, which means 'to scorn, to treat scornfully, with disrespect' (*CAD* 19:47–48; Tawil 2009, 134).[30] Related to the second meaning ('to cover up, to smear over') are a number of terms in Aramaic and Arabic which mean 'paste, mud, dirt'; see the Aramaic lexemes *ṭəpāl* 'dirt, paste', *ṭəpēl* 'paste, plaster', and *ṭ-p-l* 'to plaster' (Jastrow 1926, 1:547–48; *CAL*) and the Arabic terms *ṭufāl* and *ṭafāl* 'clay, dirt' (Lane 1968, 5:1860). Whether or not Hebrew *ṭ-p-l* reflects two homophonous roots, its meanings connected to plaster and dirt are probably Common Semitic, because such meanings are attested in a number of Semitic languages.

The etymology of Hebrew *tāpēl*, *tiplā* is a bit murky. While there are lexemes of the root *t-p-l* in other languages, it is not entirely clear if the words are cognates with Hebrew or loanwords from Hebrew. The Omani Arabic term *tfil* 'unsalted' is probably cognate with Hebrew *tāpēl* (GMD 1452). The Arabic term *tufl* 'saliva' as well as the verb *tafala* 'to spit' (Lane 1968, 1:308), which is presumably a denominative verb of *tufl*, are probably related to Hebrew *tāpēl* in that the saliva refers to a tasteless substance.[31] Likewise, the Aramaic terms *tāpēl*

29. Some, however, suggest that *tāpēl* and *tiplā* reflect two different roots (*HALOT* 2:1775–76; Salters 2010, 155; Albrektson 1963, 109–10). This is certainly possible, but it may simply be that the two words derive from one root that carried the general meaning 'lacking substance'.

30. The Aramaic verbal root *t-p-l* 'to slander', which has an initial *t*, is problematic. It may be, as Propp (1990, 407 n. 22; see also Jastrow 1926, 2:1686) suggests, that *t-p-l* acquired the meaning 'to slander' as a secondary development.

31. On the other hand, it is possible that the Arabic term *tufl* 'saliva' as well as the verb *tafala* 'to spit' (Lane 1968, 1:308) are onomatopoeic in nature and unrelated to Hebrew *tāpēl*. Indeed, Propp (1990, 405 n. 7) writes that in various languages the terms carrying the meaning 'to spit; spittle' possess the consonants *p* and *t*. In support of his claim, Propp mentions the English verb 'to spit' as well as the following examples: Greek πτύω; Latin *spūto*; Aramaic *t-p-p*/*t-p-y*; Ethiopic *taf'a*; and Hebrew *tōpet* (Job 17:6). The three Semitic examples are so similar that it is tempting to view them

TABLE 3.2. The Roots *t-p-l* and *ṭ-p-l* in Biblical Hebrew

Root	**Lexeme**	**Meaning**	**Cognates (or Loanwords)**
t-p-l 'without substance'	1. *tāpēl*	1. 'tasteless, unsalted; deception'	1. Omani Arabic *tfil* 'unsalted' Arabic *tufl* 'saliva', *tafala* 'to spit' Aramaic *tāpēl* 'tasteless matter'
	> *tāpēl*	> 'mud-based plaster without reinforcing elements'	Aramaic *t-p-l* 'to paste' Mandaic *tapala* 'mud, slime, adhesive'
	2. *tiplā*	2. 'unseemliness'	2. Aramaic *tiplā* 'indecency'
ṭ-p-l	1. *ṭ-p-l*	1. 'to slander'	1. Akkadian *ṭapālum* 'to scorn'
	2. *ṭ-p-l*	2. 'to cover up, to smear over'	2. Aramaic *ṭəpāl* 'dirt, paste' Aramaic *ṭəpēl* 'paste, plaster' Aramaic *ṭ-p-l* 'to plaster' Arabic *ṭufāl* and *ṭaffāl* 'clay, dirt'

'tasteless matter' and *tiplā* 'indecency' seem to be connected to the Hebrew terms (Jastrow 1926, 2:1686). The Mandaic term *tapala* 'mud, slime, adhesive' also appears to be related (Drower and Macuch 1963, 480). According to Jastrow (1926, 2:1686), Aramaic also uses the verbal root *t-p-l* to mean 'to paste'. In sum, the root *t-p-l* carries meanings such as 'mud, plaster' and 'tasteless, without substance' in a number of West Semitic languages.

We can outline the meanings of Hebrew *t-p-l* and *ṭ-p-l* in the following manner. The nominal root *t-p-l* did not initially denote mud-based plaster without reinforcing elements; this meaning was a secondary development from the primary meaning 'without substance'. The verbal root *ṭ-p-l* carries two distinct meanings: one meaning was 'to slander' and the other was 'to cover up; to smear over'. A possible outline of the meanings of the Hebrew roots *t-p-l* and *ṭ-p-l* is given in table 3.2.

3.2.5.3. Biblical Usage of ṭîaḥ *(and* ṭ-w-ḥ*),* tāpēl*, and* ʿāpār

3.2.5.3.1. LEVITICUS 14:33–54

An examination of the verbal forms of the root *ṭ-w-ḥ* demonstrates that this root means 'to overlay, to daub'. In Lev 14, the root is used a number of times in reference to wall construction. The passage focuses on the priestly responsibility to identify and remove a plague, presumably mold, that appears on the walls of houses. The passage (14:36b–48) reads:

---

as related. To the aforementioned examples we can also add lexemes in Slavic languages that begin with a *pl* sequence (e.g., Russian плюнуть [plyunut'], Ukrainian плювати [pl'uváty]).

וְאַחַר כֵּן יָבֹא הַכֹּהֵן לִרְאוֹת אֶת־הַבָּיִת׃ וְרָאָה אֶת־הַנֶּגַע וְהִנֵּה הַנֶּגַע בְּקִירֹת הַבַּיִת שְׁקַעֲרוּרֹת
יְרַקְרַקֹּת אוֹ אֲדַמְדַּמֹּת וּמַרְאֵיהֶן שָׁפָל מִן־הַקִּיר׃ וְיָצָא הַכֹּהֵן מִן־הַבַּיִת אֶל־פֶּתַח הַבָּיִת וְהִסְגִּיר
אֶת־הַבַּיִת שִׁבְעַת יָמִים׃
וְשָׁב הַכֹּהֵן בַּיּוֹם הַשְּׁבִיעִי וְרָאָה וְהִנֵּה פָּשָׂה הַנֶּגַע בְּקִירֹת הַבָּיִת׃ וְצִוָּה הַכֹּהֵן וְחִלְּצוּ אֶת־הָאֲבָנִים
אֲשֶׁר בָּהֵן הַנָּגַע וְהִשְׁלִיכוּ אֶתְהֶן אֶל־מִחוּץ לָעִיר אֶל־מָקוֹם טָמֵא׃ וְאֶת־הַבַּיִת יַקְצִעַ מִבַּיִת סָבִיב
וְשָׁפְכוּ אֶת־**הֶעָפָר** אֲשֶׁר הִקְצוּ אֶל־מִחוּץ לָעִיר אֶל־מָקוֹם טָמֵא׃ וְלָקְחוּ אֲבָנִים אֲחֵרוֹת וְהֵבִיאוּ
אֶל־תַּחַת הָאֲבָנִים **וְעָפָר** אַחֵר יִקַּח **וְטָח** אֶת־הַבָּיִת׃
וְאִם־יָשׁוּב הַנֶּגַע וּפָרַח בַּבַּיִת אַחַר חִלֵּץ אֶת־הָאֲבָנִים וְאַחֲרֵי הִקְצוֹת אֶת־הַבַּיִת וְאַחֲרֵי **הִטּוֹחַ**׃
וּבָא הַכֹּהֵן וְרָאָה וְהִנֵּה פָּשָׂה הַנֶּגַע בַּבָּיִת צָרַעַת מַמְאֶרֶת הִוא בַּבַּיִת טָמֵא הוּא׃ וְנָתַץ אֶת־הַבַּיִת
אֶת־אֲבָנָיו וְאֶת־עֵצָיו וְאֵת כָּל־**עֲפַר** הַבָּיִת וְהוֹצִיא אֶל־מִחוּץ לָעִיר אֶל־מָקוֹם טָמֵא׃ וְהַבָּא אֶל־
הַבַּיִת כָּל־יְמֵי הִסְגִּיר אֹתוֹ יִטְמָא עַד־הָעָרֶב׃ וְהַשֹּׁכֵב בַּבַּיִת יְכַבֵּס אֶת־בְּגָדָיו וְהָאֹכֵל בַּבַּיִת יְכַבֵּס
אֶת־בְּגָדָיו׃ וְאִם־בֹּא יָבֹא הַכֹּהֵן וְרָאָה וְהִנֵּה לֹא־פָשָׂה הַנֶּגַע בַּבַּיִת אַחֲרֵי **הִטֹּחַ** אֶת־הַבָּיִת וְטִהַר
הַכֹּהֵן אֶת־הַבַּיִת כִּי נִרְפָּא הַנָּגַע׃

Afterwards, the priest shall come to inspect the house. He shall inspect the plague and if the plague is on the walls of the house with reddish and greenish spots, and they appear deeper than the wall, then the priest shall exit from the house toward the door of the house, and he shall close the house for seven days.

The priest shall return on the seventh day and he shall inspect; if the plague has spread on the walls of the house, then the priest shall command and they shall remove the rocks upon which appears the plague, and they shall cast them outside of the city to an impure place. He shall have the house scraped all around, and the *ʿ**āpār*** ['dust, soil' > 'mud plaster'] which they had scraped they shall pour outside of the city to an unclean place. They shall take other stones and they shall bring (them) in place of the (former) stones, and he shall take other *ʿ**āpār*** ['dust, soil' > 'mud plaster'] and he shall daub [***weṭāḥ***] the house.

If the plague returns and breaks out in the house after he has removed the stones and after the scraping of the house and after the daubing [***hiṭṭôaḥ***], then the priest shall come and inspect. If the plague has spread in the house, then it is a malignant leprosy in the house; it is unclean. He shall tear down the house, its stones, and its wood, and all the *ʿ**āpār*** ['dust, soil' > 'mud plaster'] of the house, and he shall remove (it) outside of the city to an unclean place. The one who comes into the house all the days that it is shut, he shall be unclean until the evening. The one who lies in the house shall wash his clothes and the one who eats in the house shall wash his clothes. If the priest comes and sees that the plague has not spread in the house after the daubing [***hiṭṭôaḥ***] of the house, then the priest shall purify the house, for the plague has been healed.

According to this passage, several steps are involved in removing mold from a house. The stones wherein the mold first appeared are to be removed from the wall and discarded. Next, the outer layer of mud plaster is to be scraped off the walls of the house. Then, new stones are to replace the former stones, and the entire house is be daubed with a new coating of mud plaster. In short, the passage does not appear to be describing a quick job of applying a finishing whitewash on the walls of a house. Rather, what is involved is a partial dismantling of a wall and a rebuilding of it with new materials.

In view of the process described in Lev 14, we may suggest a more specialized meaning for the verbal forms of *ṭ-w-ḥ* in this passage: the verbal forms of *ṭ-w-ḥ* refer to the (re-)plastering of a thick mud-based plaster that protected the wall from weather damage and increased the rigidity of the wall structure itself (Wright 1985, 1:420). That the verbal root *ṭ-w-ḥ* is employed to refer to a mud-based plaster is made clear by use of the word *ʿāpār* ('dust, soil' > 'mud plaster') in this passage to speak of the plaster. Nevertheless, the root *ṭ-w-ḥ* was not only used to speak of the daubing of mud plaster. In 1 Chr 29:4, the root refers to the application of gold and silver coatings to the walls of the temple: שְׁלֹשֶׁת אֲלָפִים כִּכְּרֵי זָהָב מִזְּהַב אוֹפִיר וְשִׁבְעַת אֲלָפִים כִּכַּר־כֶּסֶף מְזֻקָּק **לָטוּחַ** קִירוֹת הַבָּתִּים '3,000 talents of gold, of the gold of Ophir, and 7,000 talents of refined silver for the overlaying [***laṭṭûaḥ***] of the walls of the houses'. While *ṭ-w-ḥ* seems to mean 'to daub with mud-based plaster' in the Leviticus passage, the verbal root also carries the more general meaning 'to overlay, to daub', as is made clear by the passage in 1 Chronicles.

3.2.5.3.2. EZEKIEL 13:9–15

The process of plastering a wall is also described in the book of Ezekiel. Ezekiel 13:9–15 records a critique of false prophets, comparing them to irresponsible builders of a wall that, like the unreliable promises of false prophets, is unstable and will inevitably collapse. This passage uses verbal forms of *ṭ-w-ḥ* as well as the noun *ṭîaḥ* to speak of the plastering process. Additionally, the lexeme *tāpēl* is used in this passage to refer to the quality of the plaster used—that is, one that is probably unmixed with reinforcing ingredients such as straw and sand. The passage reads:

> וְהָיְתָה יָדִי אֶל־הַנְּבִיאִים הַחֹזִים שָׁוְא וְהַקֹּסְמִים כָּזָב בְּסוֹד עַמִּי לֹא־יִהְיוּ וּבִכְתָב בֵּית־יִשְׂרָאֵל
> לֹא יִכָּתֵבוּ וְאֶל־אַדְמַת יִשְׂרָאֵל לֹא יָבֹאוּ וִידַעְתֶּם כִּי אֲנִי אֲדֹנָי יְהוִה׃ יַעַן וּבְיַעַן הִטְעוּ אֶת־עַמִּי
> לֵאמֹר שָׁלוֹם וְאֵין שָׁלוֹם וְהוּא בֹּנֶה חַיִץ וְהִנָּם **טָחִים** אֹתוֹ **תָּפֵל**׃ אֱמֹר אֶל־**טָחֵי תָפֵל** וְיִפֹּל הָיָה
> ׀ גֶּשֶׁם שׁוֹטֵף וְאַתֵּנָה אַבְנֵי אֶלְגָּבִישׁ תִּפֹּלְנָה וְרוּחַ סְעָרוֹת תְּבַקֵּעַ׃ וְהִנֵּה נָפַל הַקִּיר הֲלוֹא יֵאָמֵר
> אֲלֵיכֶם אַיֵּה **הַטִּיחַ** אֲשֶׁר **טַחְתֶּם**׃
> לָכֵן כֹּה אָמַר אֲדֹנָי יְהוִה וּבִקַּעְתִּי רוּחַ־סְעָרוֹת בַּחֲמָתִי וְגֶשֶׁם שֹׁטֵף בְּאַפִּי יִהְיֶה וְאַבְנֵי אֶלְגָּבִישׁ
> בְּחֵמָה לְכָלָה׃ וְהָרַסְתִּי אֶת־הַקִּיר אֲשֶׁר־**טַחְתֶּם תָּפֵל** וְהִגַּעְתִּיהוּ אֶל־הָאָרֶץ וְנִגְלָה יְסֹדוֹ וְנָפְלָה

וּכְלִיתֶם בְּתוֹכָהּ וִידַעְתֶּם כִּי־אֲנִי יְהוָה׃ וְכִלֵּיתִי אֶת־חֲמָתִי בַּקִּיר וּבַטָּחִים אֹתוֹ **תָּפֵל** וְאֹמַר לָכֶם אֵין הַקִּיר וְאֵין **הַטָּחִים** אֹתוֹ׃

My hand shall be against the prophets who see false visions and who divine deception. They shall not be in the counsel of my people, and they will not be written down in the record of the house of Israel, and they shall not enter the land of Israel. You shall know that I am the lord, YHWH. Since they have misled my people saying, "Peace," but there is no peace, when one builds a wall and when they daub it [*ṭāḥîm*] with ***tāpēl***, tell those who daub it with ***tāpēl*** [***ṭāḥê tāpēl***] that it will fall; there will be flooding rain, and you, O hailstones, shall fall and a stormy wind will break out. When the wall has fallen, will it not be said to you, "Where is the ***ṭîaḥ*** which you daubed [***ṭaḥtem***]?"

Therefore, thus says the lord, YHWH, "I will cause a stormy wind to break out in my wrath, and there will be a flooding rain in my anger, and hailstones in my wrath for complete destruction. I shall destroy the wall which you daubed [***ṭaḥtem***] with ***tāpēl***. I shall strike it [the wall] to the ground and its foundation will be exposed, and when it falls, you shall be destroyed within it, and you shall know that I am YHWH. I will achieve my wrath on the wall and on those who daubed it [***ûbaṭṭāḥîm***] with ***tāpēl***. I will say to you, 'There is no wall, and those who daubed [***haṭṭāḥîm***] it are no more.'"

This passage comprises a critique of prophets who promise false hope for Judah. The prophecies given are of peace, but the reality is an absence of peace. Thus, the prophets' words are a mere covering of the truth—namely, that disaster is near. The author of this passage is comparing the false prophets with builders who plaster up a wall that is in actuality damaged and doomed to fall under pressure. In essence, the false words of the prophets are comparable to the unmixed plaster (*tāpēl*) that merely covers up the deficiencies of the wall in order to make the wall more attractive but does not in fact strengthen the durability of the wall.

3.2.5.3.3. USAGE OF *TĀPĒL* IN OTHER BIBLICAL PASSAGES

While *tāpēl* refers to a form of plaster in the Ezekiel passage, in two other passages the term is used with a meaning that generally means 'without substance'. In Job 6:6, *tāpēl* is utilized to speak of food that seems to be tasteless: הֲיֵאָכֵל **תָּפֵל** מִבְּלִי־מֶלַח אִם־יֶשׁ־טַעַם בְּרִיר חַלָּמוּת 'Will ***tāpēl*** be eaten without salt? Or is there any taste in the liquid of the mallow?'. In Lam 2:14, on the other hand, *tāpēl* refers to the empty promises of false prophets. The passage reads: נְבִיאַיִךְ חָזוּ לָךְ שָׁוְא **וְתָפֵל** וְלֹא־גִלּוּ עַל־עֲוֹנֵךְ לְהָשִׁיב שביתך שְׁבוּתֵךְ וַיֶּחֱזוּ לָךְ מַשְׂאוֹת שָׁוְא וּמַדּוּחִים 'Your prophets have envisioned for you emptiness and ***tāpēl*** and did not disclose your iniquity in order to restore your fortune; rather, they envisioned for you oracles that are vain and misleading'. While the more original meaning of *tāpēl* was probably 'without substance, bland', the term also came to denote plaster unmixed with reinforcing elements.

3.2.5.4. Translation of ṭîaḥ *(and* ṭ-w-ḥ*) and* tāpēl *(and* ṭ-p-l*) in the Septuagint*

In the Septuagint, the noun *ṭîaḥ* and the verbal forms of *ṭ-w-ḥ* are rendered with Greek words that derive from one root—that is, the word *ṭîaḥ* (Ezek 13:12) is translated as ἀλοιφή 'ointment, paint' (LSJ 72; Muraoka 2009, 29). Similarly, the verbal forms of *ṭ-w-ḥ* are translated with the verb ἀλειφω 'to anoint, to polish, to daub, to plaster' in the Ezekiel passage (LSJ 62; Muraoka 2009, 25), while the verbal forms are rendered in the Greek with the verb ἐξαλείφω 'to plaster; to wash over' in Lev 14:36b–48 and 1 Chr 29:4 (LSJ 583; Muraoka 2009, 245). According to the Syro-Hexapla, *ṭîaḥ* in Ezek 13:12 is rendered by Symmachus as χρῖσμα 'anointing, plaster, coating' (LSJ 2007; Muraoka 2009, 737), while the verbal form of *ṭ-w-ḥ* is rendered by the Greek verb ἐπιχρίω 'to anoint, to plaster' (LSJ 673; Ziegler 1952, 138). The verb ἐπιχρίω is also used to render *ṭ-w-ḥ* in a variant reading of Lev 14:43 (Wevers and Quast 1986, 170). For two other passages, there are variant readings that render the Hebrew verb *ṭ-w-ḥ* with the Greek verbs χρῖω 'anoint' (Lev 14:42–43; LSJ 2007; Muraoka 2009, 737; Wevers and Quast 1986, 170–71) and καταχρίω 'smear over' (1 Chr 29:4; LSJ 921; Muraoka 388; Brooke, McLean, and Thackeray 1906–40, 2:472).[32]

In translating *tāpēl* when it seems to refer to plaster (Ezek 13:10–11, 14–15; 22:28), the Septuagint apparently understood the word to be connected with the Hebrew root *n-p-l* 'to fall' because the term is rendered with forms of the verb πίπτω 'to fall' (LSJ 1406; Muraoka 2009, 558; Barthélemy 1992, 82).[33] The Greek translation therefore does not allow us to conclude anything specific about the meaning of the Hebrew word itself. However, in the hexaplaric translation known as ὁ ἑβραῖος, *tāpēl* in Ezek 22:28 is translated as πηλός ανευ ἄχυρον 'mud without straw' (LSJ 298, 1401; Muraoka 2009, 110, 556; Ziegler 1952,

32. In Targum Jonathan, *ṭîaḥ* is translated as *šəyāʿā* 'sealing clay' (*CAL*), and in the Peshitta, the word is rendered as *tryʾ* 'plaster, stucco' (Sokoloff 2009, 552).

33. In the hexaplaric revisions or the Syro-Hexapla of some of the passages (Ezek 13:10, 15; 22:28), the term is also rendered with three other terms: ἄναλος 'without salt' (LSJ 112), ἀφροσύνη 'folly, thoughtlessness' (LSJ 294; Muraoka 2009, 109), and ἀνάρτυτος 'unseasoned food' (LSJ 120; Ziegler 1952, 137–38, 190–91; Ziegler 1982, 236; Ziegler 1957, 477). In Job 6:6, the Septuagint renders *tāpēl* as ἄρτος 'loaf of wheat bread' (LSJ 250; Muraoka 2009, 93), although Symmachus's revision has ἀνάρτυτος (LSJ 120; Ziegler 1982, 236); in Lam 2:14, the Septuagint renders *tāpēl* as ἀφροσύνη (LSJ 294; Muraoka 2009, 109), while, according to the Syro-Hexapla, Aquila's version has ἄναλος (LSJ 112; Ziegler 1957, 477).

190–91). Similarly, Targum Jonathan renders *tāpēl* with the phrase *ṭîn paṭṭîr dəlāʾ təban* 'unmixed mud without straw', which perhaps supports the claim that *tāpēl* refers to mud-based plaster that lacks hardening material (e.g., Ezek 13:10–11; 22:28; *CAL*).[34]

The translation of *ṭ-p-l* in the Septuagint is not particularly helpful. Once (Ps 119:69 [118:69 LXX]) the root is translated as πληθύνω 'to multiply' (LSJ 1418; Muraoka 2009, 563), while, according to the Syro-Hexapla (Field 1875, 2:274), Symmachus renders the same case as ἀφάπτω 'to fasten' (LSJ 287; Muraoka 2009, 106). Another two times, the root is translated in a free manner according to the context of the passage. In one case (Job 13:4), *ṭ-p-l* is rendered as ἰατρός 'healer, physician' (LSJ 816; Muraoka 2009, 336), although Aquila and Symmachus render it as the adjective ἐπίπλαστος 'plastered over' (LSJ 651). Another time (Job 14:17), the root *ṭ-p-l* is rendered as ἐπισημαίνω 'to mark, to recognize' (LSJ 655; Muraoka 2009, 279).

In sum, I suggest that the Hebrew term *ṭîaḥ* carries the general meaning 'coating, overlay'. The verbal root *ṭ-w-ḥ* 'to overlay, to daub' was used to speak of daubing or plastering with mud-based plaster (e.g., Lev 14:33–54; Ezek 13:9–15), as well as overlaying a wall with a finishing coat (e.g., 1 Chr 29:4). The term *tāpēl*, as used in the Ezekiel passages, probably refers to a type of mud plaster that lacks reinforcing materials such as sand, straw, or grit.

3.2.6. The Term **śîd** *(and* **ś-y-d***)*

3.2.6.1. Etymology and Biblical Usage

The noun *śîd* 'quicklime plaster and whitewash' (GMD 1282; *DCH* 8:124; *HALOT* 2:1319) appears four times in the Bible (Deut 27:2, 4; Isa 33:12; Amos 2:1). It also occurs once in a fragment of 4QMysteries[a] (4Q299 65, 2; *DSSR* 2:200; *DSSC* 2:696). The verbal form *ś-y-d* 'to daub with quicklime plaster' (GMD 1282; *DCH* 8:124; *HALOT* 2:1319), probably a derived denominative form, occurs twice (Deut 27:2, 4). The term *śîd* has cognates in other West Semitic languages, which also possess verbal forms of this lexeme: Arabic *šīd*, *šāda* (Lane 1968, 4:1629–30), Jewish Aramaic *sîdā*, *s-w-d* (*CAL*; Jastrow 1926,

34. In translating *tiplā*, the Septuagint renders it once as ἀφροσύνη 'thoughtlessness' (Job 1:22; LSJ 294; Muraoka 2009, 109) and once as ἀνόμημα 'lawlessness' (Jer 23:13; LSJ 146; Muraoka 2009, 55), although, according to the Syro-Hexapla, the latter case is rendered by Aquila as ἄναλος 'without salt' (LSJ 112) and by Symmachus as ἀφροσύνη (LSJ 294; Muraoka 2009, 109; Ziegler 1957, 264). Another time, the Septuagint translates *tiplā* as ἐπισκοπή 'investigation; visitation' (Job 24:12; LSJ 657; Muraoka 2009, 280), although, according to the Syro-Hexapla, Theodotion renders this case as ἀφροσύνη (LSJ 294; Muraoka 2009, 109; Ziegler 1982, 319).

2:961, 976), and Syriac *saydā, sayyed* (Sokoloff 2009, 999). With the exception of the Arabic lexemes that refer to gypsum, these Semitic nouns and verbs all refer to quicklime and the process of plastering with quicklime. The different Semitic verbal forms may have developed coevally, deriving from a denominative verb in Central Semitic.

3.2.6.2. Biblical Usage

Deuteronomy 27:1–12 preserves an account of the utilization of plaster for writing purposes. The Deuteronomy passage describes the erection of large stones, which are to be plastered over and subsequently written upon. The relevant verses (27:1–4, 8) read:

וַיְצַ֤ו מֹשֶׁה֙ וְזִקְנֵ֣י יִשְׂרָאֵ֔ל אֶת־הָעָ֖ם לֵאמֹ֑ר שָׁמֹר֙ אֶת־כָּל־הַמִּצְוָ֔ה אֲשֶׁ֧ר אָנֹכִ֛י מְצַוֶּ֥ה אֶתְכֶ֖ם הַיּֽוֹם׃
וְהָיָ֣ה בַיּוֹם֮ אֲשֶׁ֣ר תַּעַבְר֣וּ אֶת־הַיַּרְדֵּן֒ אֶל־הָאָ֕רֶץ אֲשֶׁר־יְהוָ֥ה אֱלֹהֶ֖יךָ נֹתֵ֣ן לָ֑ךְ וַהֲקֵמֹתָ֤ לְךָ֙ אֲבָנִ֣ים
גְּדֹל֔וֹת וְ**שַׂדְתָּ֥** אֹתָ֖ם **בַּשִּֽׂיד**׃ וְכָתַבְתָּ֣ עֲלֵיהֶ֗ן אֶת־כָּל־דִּבְרֵ֛י הַתּוֹרָ֥ה הַזֹּ֖את לְמַ֣עַן אֲשֶׁ֣ר תָּבֹ֗א
אֶל־הָאָ֜רֶץ אֲשֶׁר־יְהוָ֣ה אֱלֹהֶ֣יךָ ׀ נֹתֵ֣ן לְךָ֗ אֶ֤רֶץ זָבַ֤ת חָלָב֙ וּדְבַ֔שׁ כַּאֲשֶׁ֥ר דִּבֶּ֛ר יְהוָ֥ה אֱלֹהֵי־אֲבֹתֶ֖יךָ
לָֽךְ׃ וְהָיָה֙ בְּעָבְרְכֶ֣ם אֶת־הַיַּרְדֵּ֔ן תָּקִ֣ימוּ אֶת־הָאֲבָנִ֣ים הָאֵ֗לֶּה אֲשֶׁ֨ר אָנֹכִ֜י מְצַוֶּ֥ה אֶתְכֶ֛ם הַיּ֖וֹם בְּהַ֣ר
עֵיבָ֑ל וְ**שַׂדְתָּ֥** אוֹתָ֖ם **בַּשִּֽׂיד**׃ . . . וְכָתַבְתָּ֣ עַל־הָאֲבָנִ֗ים אֶת־כָּל־דִּבְרֵ֛י הַתּוֹרָ֥ה הַזֹּ֖את בַּאֵ֥ר הֵיטֵֽב׃

Moses and the elders of Israel commanded the people, saying, "Keep all the law that I command you today. It shall be on the day that you cross the Jordan to the land that YHWH, your God, is giving you, that you shall erect for yourself large stones and you shall plaster [*wəśadtā*] them with *śîd*. You shall write on them all the words of this instruction in your crossing so that you would come into the land which YHWH, your God, is giving to you, a land flowing with milk and honey, just as YHWH, the God of your father, spoke to you. It shall be that in your crossing the Jordan, you shall erect these stones which I command you today in Mount Ebal, and you shall plaster [*wəśadtā*] them with *śîd* . . . You shall write on the stones all the words of this instruction very clearly."

This passage describes the process of covering large stones with plaster in order to write upon them the words of YHWH's instruction to Moses. The need to coat the stones with plaster or whitewash is clear—it is to cover up the uneven surface of the stones and produce a smooth surface which could be written upon.[35]

---

35. The fulfillment of Deut 27:1–12 is described in Josh 8:30–35, which depicts Joshua writing a copy of the law of Moses upon stones erected at Mount Ebal. Unlike Deut 27:1–12, however, Josh 8:30–35 does not explicitly mention the plastering of the erected stones.

The term *śîd* is used in two additional passages, Isa 33:12 and Amos 2:1. Isaiah 33:12 reads: וְהָיוּ עַמִּים מִשְׂרְפוֹת **שִׂיד** קוֹצִים כְּסוּחִים בָּאֵשׁ יִצַּתּוּ ‘The nations will be like the burning of ***śîd***, like cut-down thorns that burn in fire’. Amos 2:1 reads: כֹּה אָמַר יְהוָה עַל־שְׁלֹשָׁה פִּשְׁעֵי מוֹאָב וְעַל־אַרְבָּעָה לֹא אֲשִׁיבֶנּוּ עַל־שָׂרְפוֹ עַצְמוֹת מֶלֶךְ־אֱדוֹם **לַשִּׂיד** ‘Thus says YHWH, “For three evils of Moab and for four, I will not forgive him, for burning the bones of the king of Edom into ***śîd***” ’. Both passages refer to the process of burning. Whereas Isaiah intimates that nations will be burned like *śîd*, Amos refers to the burning of the bones of the king of Edom into *śîd*. Although *sîd* seems to mean ‘ash’ in Amos, the mention of burning in these two passages seems to be a reference to the process of making quicklime, which involved the burning of limestone at very high temperatures that resulted in the production of quicklime.[36]

3.2.6.3. Gypsum Plaster, Quicklime Plaster, or Whitewash?

It is impossible to know with certainty whether Deut 27:1–12 is referring to gypsum plaster, quicklime plaster, or a quicklime whitewash. There are, however, good reasons for understanding the term *śîd* as referring to a thick quicklime plaster. To begin with, the surface that is covered in the passage is a stone, which presumably has a rough texture. A mere whitewash solution would not produce a surface smooth enough to write upon. A thicker plaster would indeed produce the necessary smooth surface. Furthermore, because the Deir ʿAlla inscription attests to the use of quicklime plaster in Transjordan, and because much of the ancient Mediterranean world attests to the use of quicklime plaster for writing or painting purposes, it is reasonable to hold that such plaster was also used in ancient Israel for such purposes. Indeed, limestone was very plentiful in ancient Israel, so it seems likely that the *śîd* was made of quicklime. Also, as stated above, the use of *śîd* in Isaiah and Amos seems to recall the processes of producing quicklime; this further supports the supposition that *śîd* refers to a plaster made of quicklime.

In essence, Deut 27:1–12 seems to describe a writing technology that very much resembles the one employed in the production of the Deir ʿAlla inscription. It involves the use of plaster, probably a quicklime plaster similar to that of

36. In Amos, the lexeme *śîd* is probably used figuratively to refer to quicklime. However, both quicklime plaster and gypsum plaster were produced by the process of burning, so one may argue that Amos’s use of *śîd* in connection with burning can refer to either gypsum plaster or quicklime plaster. Nevertheless, it is likely that *śîd* designates quicklime here, because it is mentioned in relation to the burning of bones, which required high temperatures just like the process of burning limestone into quicklime. For bones to disintegrate, they must be burned at about 700 degrees Celsius, while limestone must be burned at 900 degrees Celsius to become quicklime; gypsum, on the other hand, can be heated to 100–200 degrees Celsius to make it suitable for use in gypsum plaster.

the Deir ʿAlla inscription. Moreover, we read in the Deuteronomy passage that this plaster is to be applied to large stones, which are then to be set up where passers-by could view it. As will be discussed in 3.2.6.5, the Deir ʿAlla inscription consisted of a plaster surface that was probably also attached to a stela that hung on a wall for public viewing (Franken and Ibrahim 1977–78, 65–68; van der Kooij 1976a, 25–28).

3.2.6.4. Translation of śîd *(and* ś-y-d*) in the Septuagint*

The Septuagint's rendering of *śîd* and its denominative verb (*śadtā*) seems to support the view that these lexical items were used in connection with a type of plaster. In translating the noun *śîd* (Deut 27:2, 4; Amos 2:1), the Septuagint employs the term κονία 'dust, sand, plaster, stucco' (LSJ 977; Muraoka 2009, 406). Likewise, the Septuagint renders the denominative verb form of *śîd* (Deut 27:2, 4) with the verb κονιάω 'to plaster (with lime or stucco)' (LSJ 977; Muraoka 2009, 406). In a variant reading of Deut 27:4, *śîd* and its denominative verb (*śadtā*) are rendered with the words χρῖσις 'anointing, smearing' and χριστηρίον 'bottle of ointments', respectively (LSJ 2007; Wevers and Quast 1977, 287).[37] In the Septuagint's translation of Isa 33:12, however, the Greek word corresponding to *śîd* is ἀγρός 'field' (LSJ 15–16), which suggests that the translator read *śāde* 'field' in place of *śîd.*

3.2.6.5. Writing on Plaster in Ancient Israel and Transjordan

Perhaps the most famous ink-on-plaster inscription is the Deir ʿAlla inscription. Dating to the eighth century BCE, this inscription was discovered in the temple of Deir ʿAlla, which is biblical Succoth (Hoftijzer 1976, 271) (see figure 3.6). It is possible that the inscription collapsed from a wall due to an earthquake (Hackett 1984, 3), although it was probably attached to a stela that was suspended on a wall rather than directly to the wall itself (Franken and Ibrahim 1977–78, 65–68; van der Kooij 1976a, 25–28). The inscription consists of two layers. The top layer is primarily a quicklime plaster about 0.3 inches thick. It was applied to a lower layer of clay plaster, as is confirmed by the remainder of pieces of clay in the back side of the outer quicklime layer. The writing on the inscription is executed in red and black ink (Mehra and Voskuil 1976, 20–21; Mosk 1976; van der Kooij 1976a, 23–24). The fact that quicklime plaster was used in Deir ʿAlla, which is situated just south-east of Beth Shean across the Jordan river, further

37. Wevers and Quast (1977, 287) also cite that *ś-y-d* in Deut 27:4 is rendered as *gypsabitis* 'to cover with gypsum; to plaster' (see also Andrews 1958, 52) in the Ethiopian and Armenian translations.

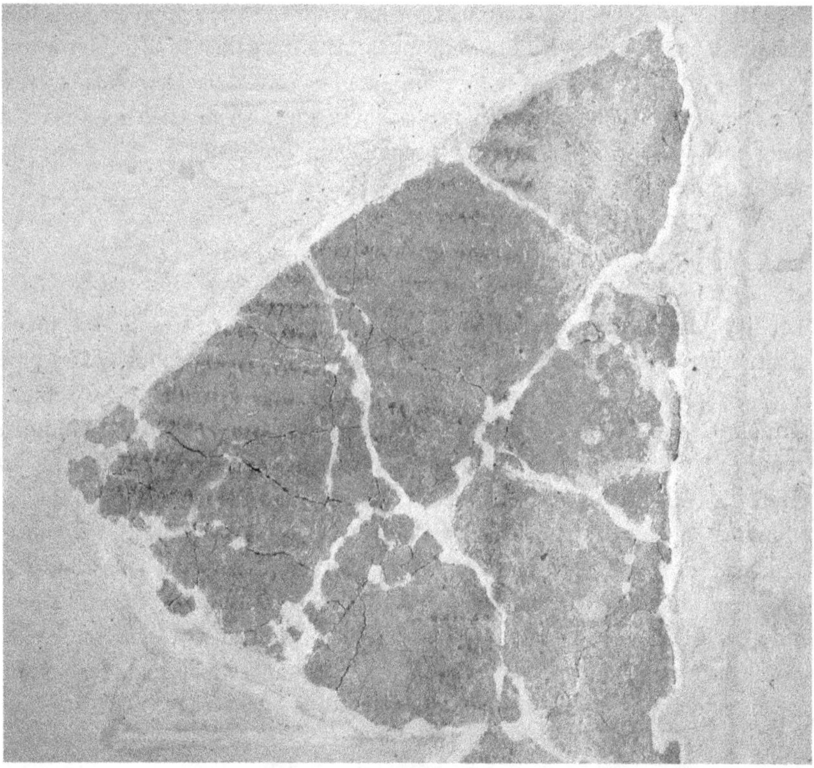

FIGURE 3.6. Balaam son of Beor inscription from Deir ʿAlla, eighth century BCE. Amman Citadel Museum. Photo: © Todd Bolen/BiblePlaces.com.

attests to the use of quicklime plaster for various purposes throughout ancient Israel and the Levant.

While the Deir ʿAlla inscription was found in Transjordan, a number of inscriptions on plaster have been found within Israel proper. Of particular interest are those found at Kuntillet ʿAjrud, an ancient fortress located between Elath and Kadesh Barnea. Among the inscriptions discovered, there were a few fragments of plaster that contain inscriptions dating to about 800 BCE (Aḥituv 2008, 313). These ink-on-plaster inscriptions were attached to the walls and doorways of the main building at Kuntillet ʿAjrud (King and Stager 2001, 305). The ink on these inscriptions was red and black (Meshel 1978, 53). The plaster on which these inscriptions were written consisted of 90 percent unslaked gypsum, while the outer layer consisted of 90 percent slaked gypsum (Wright 1985, 1:421).[38]

38. The initial reports of the discovery of the Kuntillet ʿAjrud inscriptions (Meshel 1978) do not contain information on the makeup of the plaster, nor does the more recent collection of articles on

It is not surprising that gypsum plaster rather than quicklime plaster was used at Kuntillet ʿAjrud. The site is, after all, in the vicinity of Egypt, which, as mentioned in 3.2.1, predominantly used gypsum plaster prior to the Ptolemaic Period (332–30 BCE).

The lexeme *śîd* probably denotes quicklime plaster and a thin quicklime whitewash. The plaster that *śîd* designates is probably of a thick composition and was used for purposes such as weatherproofing a wall. Additionally, this is the type of plaster that was utilized to create smooth surfaces upon which writing or painting could be executed. Archeological evidence from the ancient world confirms that surfaces with painting or writing on them were usually comprised of a quicklime plaster or quicklime whitewash. Gypsum plaster was also written and painted upon in ancient Israel, as attested by the Kuntillet ʿAjrud inscriptions. It is possible, then, that while the primary meaning of *śîd* was 'quicklime plaster', the term also carried a more general meaning ('plaster') and could therefore be used to refer to quicklime as well as gypsum plaster.

3.2.7. Definitions of Terms Designating Mud, Clay, Plaster, and Whitewash

Having analyzed the ancient Hebrew words that designate mud, clay, plaster, and whitewash, I suggest the following definitions for these terms.

***bōṣ*:** A term that occurs only once in a poetical text (Jer 38:22), it was used to refer to wet mire located near bodies of water such as rivers. The term derives from Proto-Semitic.

***ḥōmer*:** A term that refers to workable mud and designates clay used for pottery as well as mud plaster and mortar utilized for construction purposes.

***ṭîaḥ* (and *ṭ-w-ḥ*):** A term that carries the general meaning 'coating, overlay'. The verbal root *ṭ-w-ḥ*, from which *ṭîaḥ* was derived, means 'to overlay, to daub'. In the Bible, *ṭîaḥ* refers specifically to a coating of a mud consistency, but it seems reasonable to hold that *ṭîaḥ* could also refer to coatings of a makeup other than mud.

***ṭîṭ*:** A term that carries the general meaning 'mud' and, less frequently, 'clay'. It seems to be a loan of the Akkadian term *ṭīṭu*/*ṭīdu*.

***ṭ-p-l*:** A verbal root that probably means 'to insult, to slander' as well as 'to cover up, to smear over'. The root is not related to the Hebrew term *tāpēl*, which denotes mud-based plaster that lacks reinforcing ingredients.

***yāwēn*:** This term occurs twice in poetical texts (Pss 40:3; 69:3) and probably means 'mud, mire'.

---

these inscriptions (Aḥituv, Eshel, and Meshel 2012). Wright (1985, 1:421), however, states that these inscriptions were executed upon gypsum plaster.

***ʿāpār*:** A common term derived from Proto-Semitic that carries the meaning 'dust, soil, earth' as well as some specific meanings such as 'netherworld' and 'mud plaster'. Although on three occasions the term refers to 'mud plaster', this is not the usual meaning of the term.

***repeš*:** A term that appears once in a prophetic text (Isa 57:20), where it probably means 'mud, mire', or 'foam'.

***śîd* (and *ś-y-d*):** A term derived from Central Semitic that denotes quicklime plaster. This type of plaster, probably of a thick composition, was used for purposes such as weatherproofing a wall. This type of plaster was also utilized to create smooth surfaces upon which writing or painting could be executed. The term *śîd* probably also refers to the thin quicklime whitewash that was applied to walls of ancient houses and structures. The verbal root *ś-y-d*, which is derived from *śîd*, means 'to daub with quicklime plaster'. Both the noun *śîd* and the verbal root *ś-y-d* may also have been used to refer to gypsum plaster.

***tāpēl*:** A term that probably refers to a type of mud-based plaster that lacks reinforcing materials such as sand, straw, or grit. The term is etymologically unrelated to the verbal root *ṭ-p-l*.

CHAPTER 4

Skins, Scrolls, Tablets, Ostraca, and Uncommon Writing Surfaces

4.1. Animal Skins (*ʿôr*)

Although the Bible does not record the use of animal skins for writing purposes, the biblical text contains references to various items made of leather (e.g., clothing, vessels). The term *ʿôr* carries the meaning 'skin, leather'; if vellum was indeed used as a writing surface in ancient Israel, which is quite possible, it seems reasonable to suggest that the term *ʿôr* designates vellum as well, although it designates only the material, while the term *məgillā* carries the meaning 'scroll, roll'.

4.1.1. Use of Leather in the Ancient World

Lucas (1962, 36) writes that leather was used in Egypt for a variety of purposes. It was utilized in the production of "bags, bracelets . . . cushion covers, chariot parts . . . dog collars and leashes, harness, quivers, ropes and cords, sandals, seats of chairs and stools, and sheaths for daggers, as well as for writing upon, which was quite common, and for various other purposes." Skins were also employed for covering shields and to manufacture water containers and clothing (Lucas 1962, 37). Gazelle skin was used for producing loincloths, leopard skin for robes, and crocodile skin for ritual garments (van Driel-Murray 2000, 302). Scenes in tombs from the Old Kingdom (2663–2160 BCE) even depict the slaughter of animals and the processing of animal hide (van Driel-Murray 2000, 300–302).

Akkadian texts reveal that leather served many purposes in Mesopotamia (Stol 1980–83). Leather was used to make pouches for holding water, wine, dry goods, and money (Stol 1980–83, 536–38), as well as sandals, boots, clothing, whips, belts, ropes, buckets, armor, shields, quivers, and chairs (Stol 1980–83, 539, 541). Animal skins were also utilized in the production of boats and tents (Stol 1980–83, 538, 540). Several workshops for leather have been identified at a number of Mesopotamian sites, although actual evidence of leather is absent (Moorey 1999, 111).

4.1.2. The Term ʿôr

4.1.2.1. Etymology and Biblical Usage

The Hebrew term *ʿôr* 'skin' (GMD 940; *DCH* 6:317–18; *HALOT* 1:803) derives from Proto-Semitic **ʿawr-*. Ugaritic also has a reflex of this term, namely, [*ú*?]-*ru* in singular vocalized as /*ʿōru*/ and ^{túg}*ú-ra-tu* in plural vocalized as /*ʿōrātu*/ 'skins, hides' (Huehnergard 2008, 47–48, 159). The Punic term *ʿrh* 'hide' is also cognate with the Hebrew and Ugaritic lexemes (*DNWSI* 2:887).[1]

In the Bible, the term *ʿôr* carries the general meaning 'skin, leather'. The term occurs a total of ninety-nine times in the biblical text. The lexeme can refer to the actual skin of a person (e.g., Lev 13:4; Jer 13:23; Ezek 37:6) or the hide of an animal (e.g., Lev 8:17; Num 19:5; Job 40:31). In the Dead Sea Scrolls, the word occurs over twenty times with meanings similar to those of Biblical Hebrew (e.g., 4Q271 2, 10; 11Q19 XXVI, 8; XLVII, 17; *DSSR* 1:195, 658, 680; *DSSC* 2:556).

The term *ʿôr* refers to the skin of a human in Jer 13:23: הֲיַהֲפֹךְ כּוּשִׁי **עוֹרוֹ** וְנָמֵר חֲבַרְבֻּרֹתָיו גַּם־אַתֶּם תּוּכְלוּ לְהֵיטִיב לִמֻּדֵי הָרֵעַ 'Would the Cushite change his ***ʿôr*** and the leopard its spots? If so, then you also would be able to do good, you who are accustomed to do evil!'. It refers to the hide of an animal in Lev 8:17: וְאֶת־הַפָּר וְאֶת־**עֹרוֹ** וְאֶת־בְּשָׂרוֹ וְאֶת־פִּרְשׁוֹ שָׂרַף בָּאֵשׁ מִחוּץ לַמַּחֲנֶה כַּאֲשֶׁר צִוָּה יְהוָה אֶת־מֹשֶׁה 'The bull, and its ***ʿôr***, and its flesh, and its dung, you shall burn with fire outside of the camp, as YHWH had commanded Moses'. The Bible also refers to tanned skins used as coverings in the tabernacle (Exod 26:14; 36:19; 39:34). For instance, Exodus 26:14 reads: וְעָשִׂיתָ מִכְסֶה לָאֹהֶל **עֹרֹת** אֵילִם מְאָדָּמִים וּמִכְסֵה **עֹרֹת** תְּחָשִׁים מִלְמָעְלָה 'You shall make a covering for the tabernacle of dyed-red ***ʿôrôt*** of rams, and a covering of the ***ʿôrôt təḥāšîm*** above that'.[2] The term ***ʿôr*** can also refer to items made of leather such as clothing (Gen 3:21), utensils or vessels (Lev 13:53), and a belt (2 Kgs 1:8).[3]

1. If Hebrew *ʿôr* and Ugaritic [*ú*?]-*ru* and ^{túg}*ú-ra-tu* derive from Proto-Semitic **ʿawr-*, then Old Assyrian *āru* 'hide' (?) cannot be cognate with the Hebrew and Ugaritic lexemes (*CAD* 1/2:318). An Akkadian lexeme deriving from Proto-Semitic **ʿawr-* would be realized not as *āru* but as ***ūru*, because the Proto-Semitic diphthong *aw* becomes *ū* in Akkadian (Huehnergard 2011, 591).

2. There is debate regarding the meaning of the term *təḥāšîm*. Suggestions for its meaning include 'dolphin', 'giraffe', and 'crocodile', as well as 'bluish', 'blackish', and 'beaded' (Propp 2006, 374–75). More recently, Noonan (2012, 589) has argued that *təḥāšîm* derives from Egyptian *ṯḥs*, a term that referred to a type of leather; Mastnjak (2016, 9), however, connects the Hebrew term with the Akkadian term *duḫšum*/*dušû*, arguing that the Hebrew term refers to a greenish-bluish color.

3. When referring to skins used as water pouches, the Bible uses the specific term *ḥēmet* (Gen 21:14–15, 19). The Hebrew term *ḥēmet* is related to Akkadian *ḫimtu* (*CAD* 6:192–93), Ugaritic *ḥmt* (*DULAT* 1:365), and Arabic *ḥamīt* (GMD 369), all of which denote skins used to store goods.

4.1.2.2. Translation of ʿôr *in the Septuagint*

In the Septuagint, the term *ʿôr* is predominantly translated as δέρμα 'skin, hide' or δερμάτινος 'of skin' (LSJ 379–80; Muraoka 2009, 143–44; Muraoka 2010, 298). In fact, of the ninety-nine occurrences of *ʿôr* in the Hebrew Bible, it is rendered as δέρμα seventy-three times (e.g., Exod 22:26) and δερματίνος thirteen times (e.g., Gen 3:21). Another three times, *ʿôr* is rendered as βύρσα 'skin, hide' (e.g., Lev 8:17; LSJ 333; Muraoka 2009, 124), and once as χρῶμα 'complexion, skin' (Exod 34:29; LSJ 2012; Muraoka 2009, 738). In a few instances, the Septuagint seems to paraphrase the Hebrew text; in these cases, *ʿôr* is translated with a Greek word unrelated to the meaning 'skin, hide'.[4]

4.1.3. Archeological Evidence for Writing on Animal Skins

Diringer (1953, 172) writes that leather was used as a writing material in Egypt, Mesopotamia, and the Levant.[5] The earliest Egyptian leather scroll is a fragmentary roll from the Fourth Dynasty (2597–2471 BCE). Another scroll dates to the Twelfth Dynasty (1994–1781 BCE), while a scroll with a mathematical text on it dates to the Eighteenth Dynasty (1549–1298 BCE); a different leather document from the reign of Rameses II dates to the Nineteenth Dynasty (1298–1187 BCE). Egyptian reliefs also depict skins being stretched on frames. These scenes may represent the process in which skins were prepared to be used for writing (van Driel-Murray 2000, 303–4). While the aforementioned Egyptian leather records have been preserved to the modern day, no leather scrolls have survived from Mesopotamia; nevertheless, a few reliefs from Mesopotamia appear to depict scribes writing on leather sheets (Pearce 2000, 2267).[6]

The skins used in the ancient world as writing material were prepared through the process of tanning—that is, animal skins were treated with solutions made of plant extracts, lime, and tree bark. These solutions, called tannins, helped clean dirt, blood, hair, fat, and flesh from the skins. The hides were also soaked in water with salt or in urine to help in the process of depilation (King and Stager 2001, 162). Ash and pastes of flour mixed with salt were also used to depilate the skins (van Driel-Murray 2000, 302). The skins could also be dyed during the process of depilation or afterwards. Once the skins were cleared of hair,

4. In Exod 22:26, *ʿôr* is rendered as ἀσχημοσύνη 'shameful act' (LSJ 267; Muraoka 2009, 100); *ʿôr* in this passage was presumably understood by the Septuagint translators as connected to the term *ʿerwā* 'nakedness'. In Job 7:5, *ʿôr* is translated as ἰχώρ 'blood, pus' (LSJ 846; Muraoka 2009, 346) and as πούς 'foot' in Job 18:13 (LSJ 1456; Muraoka 2009, 580).

5. Leather scrolls were also used for writing in ancient Greece, Persia, and pre-Islamic Arabia (Maraqten 1998, 287–92).

6. Alternatively, the Mesopotamian reliefs may be depicting papyrus sheets.

FIGURE 4.1. Great Isaiah Scroll (1QIsaa), first century BCE. Israel Museum. Photo: public domain.

they were stretched on frames to produce smooth writing materials (van Driel-Murray 2000, 302–8).

The largest collection of ancient leather texts is that of the Dead Sea Scrolls from Qumran. Of about 930 Qumran texts, nearly 800 were written on leather (Tov 2004, 31). The leather of the scrolls came from sheep, goats, gazelles, and ibexes (Tov 2004, 33). Various scholars discuss the physical makeup of the scrolls at Qumran (Tov 2004, 31–43; Bar-Ilan 2000; Hicks 1983, 57–66). Scrolls consisted of individual sheets that were stitched together to form a complete roll. Sheets could be between 4.7 and 12.5 inches in height and 10.2 inches to 2.9 feet in length (Bar-Ilan 2000, 996). Sheets were lined before they were written upon (Tov 2004, 36). The edges of the sheets were butted against each other and sewn together with thread; most of the stitching at Qumran consists of sinews (Tov 2004, 38). Scrolls were fastened together with thongs and could also be placed in linen wrappings (Tov 2004, 40–41).

In his examination of various biblical scrolls from Qumran, Hicks (1983, 61–62) focuses on the layout of the written text upon the scrolls. He points out that individual sheets contained three or four columns of text.[7] Hicks (1983, 62) further points out that the majority of the Qumran texts involve columns that consist of some thirty or so lines. This would be equivalent to approximately one and one-third chapters of the Masoretic Text per column (Hicks 1983, 63). The length of each scroll was determined, of course, by the length of the content.

7. See 4.2.2 for a discussion on the term *delet* and the number of columns that Jeremiah's scroll contained (Jer 36:23).

The Great Isaiah Scroll (1QIsa[a]) is the longest biblical scroll from Qumran. It contains all sixty-six chapters of what would become the Masoretic Text and is about twenty-four feet long, consisting of seventeen sheets with fifty-four columns (Hicks 1983, 61; *DSSSMM* 1:xiv; see figure 4.1.). The Temple Scroll, on the other hand, was originally almost twenty-nine feet long, consisting of nineteen sheets (Bar-Ilan 2000, 997).

In sum, animal skins were used for a variety of purposes in the ancient world, including as writing surfaces. It is quite possible that animal skins were employed for writing purposes in ancient Israel during Iron Age II, but actual evidence to confirm this usage is still lacking. If, however, vellum was indeed used in ancient Israel, it is plausible that it was designated by the lexeme *ʿôr*.

4.2. Scrolls, Tablets, and Ostraca

Having discussed the term designating leather (*ʿôr*), we can now consider more specific Hebrew lexemes that designate scrolls, tablets, and ostraca.

4.2.1. The Term **məgillā** *(and* **məgillat sēper***)*

4.2.1.1. Etymology and Biblical Usage

The lexeme *məgillā* 'scroll, roll' is connected to the root *g-l-l* 'to roll' (GMD 628; *DCH* 5:134; *HALOT* 1:545). The term falls into the noun pattern *maqtil-(a)t* (geminate pattern *maqlil-(a)t* > *maqill-at*), which is the common pattern used for nouns of instrument (Lambdin and Huehnergard 2000, 47). The word *məgillā* also occurs in Aramaic and in Akkadian as *magallatu* (*CAL*; *CAD* 10/1:31). In fact, both the Hebrew and Akkadian terms are loans from Aramaic (Hurvitz 1996, 42*, 45*–46*; Abraham and Sokoloff 2011, 40).

In Akkadian, *magallatu* is first attested in Neo-Babylonian (1000–600 BCE). Hurvitz (1996, 41*) points out that *məgillā* is not attested in Ugaritic or in any other Canaanite language. In his view, these various data suggest that the term is a late loanword that entered the Hebrew lexicon near the end of the First Temple Period.

While the majority of Aramaic influence upon Hebrew occurred during and after the Babylonian exile, scholars also argue for Aramaic influence upon Hebrew during and after the time of Sennacherib's siege of Jerusalem (ca. 700 BCE). At this time period, the upper class of Judah knew Aramaic, while the common people did not know how to speak or write in Aramaic (Hurvitz 2014, 6; 2003, 27; Wagner 1966, 6). The book of Jeremiah is usually dated to the seventh–sixth centuries BCE (Lundbom 1999, 92–101; Hornkohl 2014,

371), when Aramaic was beginning to influence the Hebrew language. Aramaic influence was at its peak in the postexilic period (Hurvitz 2014, 2–3, 6; Hornkohl 2013, 321–22), but it is felt already in the book of Jeremiah.[8]

The term *məgillā* occurs a total of twenty-two times in the biblical text.[9] In one case, *məgillā* occurs in the Aramaic portion of Ezra (6:2). It probably also occurs in at least one text in the Dead Sea Scrolls, in which two letters need to be restored (4Q421 8, 2; *DSSR* 1:216; *DSSC* 1:425).[10] In the Bible, the lexeme appears most often in Jer 36 (14x). For instance, Jer 36:28 reads: שׁוּב קַח־לְךָ **מְגִלָּה** אַחֶרֶת וּכְתֹב עָלֶיהָ אֵת כָּל־הַדְּבָרִים הָרִאשֹׁנִים אֲשֶׁר הָיוּ עַל־**הַמְּגִלָּה** הָרִאשֹׁנָה אֲשֶׁר שָׂרַף יְהוֹיָקִים מֶלֶךְ־יְהוּדָה 'Again, take for yourself another ***məgillā*** and write upon it all the former words that were on the first ***məgillā*** which Jehoiakim the king of Judah burned'.

It is not necessary to expound on the meaning of *məgillā*; the term simply means 'scroll' or 'roll', as the root *g-l-l* suggests. The Aramaic term *mglh*, as well as the Akkadian word *magallatu*, designates scrolls made of leather (*CAL*; *CAD* 10/1:31), so it stands to reason that Hebrew *məgillā*, which derives from Aramaic *mglh*, probably also refers to leather scrolls. It may also denote rolls of papyrus, because papyrus rolls were commonly used in ancient Israel, and because the meaning of *məgillā* ('scroll, roll') does not imply the material of which a scroll consists.[11] Indeed, as will be shown shortly, the Septuagint rendered *məgillā* and *məgillat sēper* with Greek words that specifically denote papyrus rolls, which shows that both of these lexemes—at least according to the translators of the Septuagint—could refer to rolls of papyrus. In sum, although the Bible does not specify the material comprising a *məgillā*, it seems reasonable to conclude that the term could refer to scrolls of leather as well as papyrus.[12]

8. The language of Jeremiah is best coined as Transitional Biblical Hebrew (Hornkohl 2013, 322) because it falls between Classical Biblical Hebrew and Late Biblical Hebrew. Transitional Biblical Hebrew, while consisting predominantly of Classical Biblical Hebrew, is interspersed with features that become common in Late Biblical Hebrew. Aramaic influence is a key feature of Late Biblical Hebrew (Hurvitz 2013, 329), but it also occurs in Jeremiah (Hornkohl 2014, 53, 56–58). Jeremiah 10:11, written entirely in Aramaic, comprises the clearest example of Aramaic influence in the book of Jeremiah. Additionally, the high frequency of second person feminine singular *qāṭaltī* forms as *ketiv* writings (e.g., 2:33; 3:4–5; 4:19; 22:23; 31:21; 46:11) as well as the high frequency of third person feminine plural *qāṭəlā* forms as *ketiv* writings (e.g., 2:15; 22:6; 51:56) seems to be a result of Aramaic influence upon Hebrew (Hornkohl 2014, 118–19, 144–45, 371; Morag 1971, 140–41; 1972, 300).

9. The passages using *məgillā* are Jer 36:2, 4, 6, 14 (2x), 20–21, 23, 25, 27–29 (4x), 32; Ezek 2:9, 3:1–3; Zech 5:1–2; Ps 40:8; Ezra 6:2.

10. Assuming the restoration is correct, the text reads: [. . . מג]לת ספר לקרוא '[. . . scr]oll of a book to read'. The lexeme may also appear in 4Q264a 1, 4 (*DSSR* 1:210; *DSSC* 1:425).

11. Arabic *majallah* 'scroll', which is also a loan of Aramaic *mglh*, can refer to leather or papyrus material (Maraqten 1998, 310). Needless to say, this suggests that Aramaic *mglh*, and probably Hebrew *məgillā*, may have designated scrolls of leather as well as papyrus.

12. See 2.1.2–2.1.3 and 4.1.1–4.1.3 for discussion on the use of papyrus and leather as a writing material in ancient Israel and the ancient world.

4.2.1.2. *The Phrase* məgillat sēper

Of the twenty-two occurrences of *məgillā* within the biblical text, there are four examples in which *məgillā* stands in construct with *sēper* (*məgillat sēper*; Jer 36:2, 4; Ezek 2:9; Ps 40:8). For instance, Jer 36:2 reads: קַח־לְךָ֙ מְגִלַּת־סֵ֔פֶר וְכָתַבְתָּ֣ אֵלֶ֗יהָ אֵ֣ת כָּל־הַדְּבָרִ֞ים אֲשֶׁר־דִּבַּ֧רְתִּי אֵלֶ֛יךָ עַל־יִשְׂרָאֵ֥ל וְעַל־יְהוּדָ֖ה וְעַל־כָּל־הַגּוֹיִ֑ם מִיּ֞וֹם דִּבַּ֤רְתִּי אֵלֶ֙יךָ֙ מִימֵ֣י יֹאשִׁיָּ֔הוּ וְעַ֖ד הַיּ֥וֹם הַזֶּֽה 'Take for yourself a ***məgillat sēper*** and write on it all the words that I spoke to you about Israel and about Judah and about all the nations from the day that I spoke to you, from the days of Josiah and until this day'. The noun phrase *məgillat sēper* is difficult to translate. Usually, the second element of a construct chain modifies the first element, as in the phrase *sēper mōše* 'the book of Moses' (Neh 13:1) or *dibrê hattōrā* 'the words of the Torah' (Josh 8:34). Therefore, the phrase *məgillat sēper* should be translated as 'scroll of a book' or 'scroll of a document'. But it is not clear what, in fact, 'scroll of a book' or 'scroll of a document' would mean.

Hurvitz (1996, 43*–44*) analyzes the phrase *məgillat sēper* and concludes that it is tautological—that is, the second element *sēper* does not add anything to the meaning of the first element, *məgillat*. Hurvitz (1996, 44*) explains that tautological constructions are not uncommon in late books of the Bible. Examples include *ṣûp dəbāš* 'honey-comb of honey' (Prov 16:24), *kōaḥ ḥāyil* 'strength of might' (2 Chr 26:13), and *məṭar gešem* 'shower of rain' (Zech 10:1).[13] This phenomenon also occurs in the documents of the Dead Sea Scrolls; for instance, *'bl ygwn* 'mourning of sorrow', *ḥsdy rḥmym* 'lovingkindness of compassion', and *k's ḥmtw* 'the anger of his wrath' (Hurvitz 1996, 44*). Such phrases, Hurvitz argues, are stylistic formulations that became prevalent in Late Biblical Hebrew.

According to Hurvitz, the difference between *məgillā* and *məgillat sēper* is one of chronology, not semantics. Although the noun phrase *məgillat sēper* probably emerged later within Hebrew than did *məgillā*, Hurvitz would presumably contend that both simply meant 'scroll'. Indeed, when looking at the passages that use these two expressions, it is difficult to see any difference between them. In Jer 36:2, Jeremiah is told by yhwh to take a *məgillat sēper* and write upon it. In Jer 36:4, Baruch is depicted as writing down on a *məgillat sēper* all the words that Jeremiah dictates to him. Subsequently, this document is called a *məgillā* all throughout the chapter (Jer 36:6, 14, 20–21, 23, 25, 27). One may suggest, then, that the phrase *məgillat sēper* refers to the blank scroll, while *məgillā* refers to the inscribed scroll. Yet this view is complicated by the fact that, when Jeremiah is commanded to take a second document (Jer 36:28), the word used to speak of this second, presumably blank, scroll is *məgillā*, not

---

13. See 3.2.2.3 for discussion of the term *yāwēn* and the tautological phrase *ṭîṭ hay-yāwēn* (Ps 40:3).

məgillat sēper, and this second document is subsequently referred to by the term *məgillā* (Jer 36:28–29, 32). A difference between *məgillat sēper* and *məgillā* is equally difficult to detect when these expressions are used in Ezek 2:9–3:3.

4.2.1.3. Translation of məgillā *(and* məgillat sēper*) in the Septuagint*

The Septuagint uses a number of different words to translate *məgillā*. Within Jer 36 (Jer 43 LXX), the Septuagint translates *məgillā* with the term χαρτίον in all but one case (36:23 [43:23 LXX]), where the related term χάρτης is used instead. The term χάρτης designates a roll of papyrus (LSJ 1980; Muraoka 2009, 729), while χαρτίον, a diminutive of χάρτης, designates "a piece of paper of any size, up to and including a roll" (Lewis 1974, 77). In translating the two occurrences of the phrase *məgillat sēper* in Jeremiah (36:2, 4 [43:2, 4 LXX]), the Septuagint renders it as χαρτίον βιβλίον 'roll of a scroll' (LSJ 333, 1980; Muraoka 2009, 117, 124, 729). In the Septuagint, the term *məgillā* is also rendered with the word κεφαλίς, which is the diminutive of κεφαλή 'head, top' (LSJ 945; Muraoka 2009, 396). The term κεφαλίς carries the meaning 'little head', but, in the Greek passages where *məgillā* is rendered as κεφαλίς (Ezek 2:9; 3:1–3; Ps 40:8 [39:8 LXX]; Ezra 6:2), the context may refer to a small papyrus roll (LSJ 945; Muraoka 2009, 396). The Septuagint renders *məgillat sēper* in Ezek 2:9 and Ps 40:8 (39:8 LXX) as κεφαλίς βιβλίον 'roll/volume of a scroll' (LSJ 333, 945; Muraoka 2009, 117, 124, 396).[14]

In two cases (Zech 5:1–2), the Septuagint renders *məgillā* with the term δρέπανον 'pruning knife' (LSJ 449; Muraoka 2009, 178); the translators apparently read the text as *maggāl* 'sickle', not as *məgillā*.[15] Nevertheless, according to the Syro-Hexapla, Aquila and Theodotion render *məgillā* in Zech 5:1 as διφθέρα 'prepared leather, hide' (LSJ 438). Symmachus, according to the Syro-Hexapla, renders *məgillā* in Zech 5:1–2 as εἴλημα 'roll' (LSJ 486), although he renders the same case as κεφαλίς 'little head; small papyrus roll' according to Jerome (Ziegler 1943, 299). Furthermore, almost all passages containing *məgillā* involve variant readings among manuscripts as well as diverse translations of the word in hexaplaric revisions (Ziegler 1957, 391–99; Ziegler 1952, 98; Ziegler 1943, 299; Field 1875, 151); the terms χάρτης 'roll of papyrus', βιβλίον 'roll of a scroll', and κεφαλίς 'little head; small papyrus roll' (usually a Lucianic recension) all occur as translations of *məgillā* in the Septuagint, in variant readings, and in hexaplaric revisions.[16] The lexemes τόμος 'roll of papyrus' (LSJ 1804;

14. Targum Onkelos, Targum Jonathan, and Targum Psalms render *məgillat sēper* as *mglt spr'* (Jer 36:2, 4 [43:2, 4 LXX]; Ezek 2:9; Ps 40:8 [39:8 LXX]).

15. The Hebrew term *maggāl* occurs once in Jer 50:16 (27:16 LXX), which the Septuagint also renders as δρέπανον.

16. The term χάρτης 'roll of papyrus' occurs as a variant reading or in hexaplaric revisions in Jer 36:4, 6, 25, 28 (43:4, 6, 25, 28 LXX); βιβλίον 'roll of a scroll' occurs in Jer 36:14, 20–21, 25, 27–29

Muraoka 2009, 683), εἴλημα 'roll' (LSJ 486), and τεῦχος 'rolled writing material' (LSJ 1784) also appear as renderings of *məgillā* in variant readings of the passages and in hexaplaric revisions.[17] In general, then, the term *məgillā* and the phrase *məgillat sēper* were understood in the Septuagint and in the hexaplaric revisions to designate scrolls made of papyrus.

4.2.1.4. Leather or Papyrus?

It is not surprising that the Septuagint renders *məgillā* with Greek terms that designate papyrus rolls. After all, the Septuagint was written during the third century BCE–first century CE, a time when papyrus was in common use throughout the Mediterranean world. While several biblical books were translated into Greek in Palestine, the Torah and some additional books were produced in Alexandria of Egypt, which was the heart of the papyrus industry (Tov 2012, 128, 131; Fernández Marcos 2000, 50; Lewis 1974, 116), and evidence from the Dead Sea Scrolls library (ca. 250 BCE–68 CE; Tov 2012, 99) confirms that papyrus was also used as a writing material in Israel during the production of the Septuagint; as mentioned earlier, of 930 Qumran texts, 131 are written upon papyrus (Tov 2004, 31). Among the Dead Sea Scrolls, there are even biblical texts written on papyrus.[18] This is noteworthy because it suggests that biblical texts may have been written on papyrus even during Iron Age II in Israel, as is also suggested by the Septuagint's use of χαρτίον, χάρτης, and κεφαλίς to translate *məgillā*. However, it is also conceivable that the composers of the Septuagint were merely influenced by the milieu in which they lived and therefore translated *məgillā* with Greek terms designating papyrus rolls. Whether Jeremiah's scroll, or any biblical scroll, was indeed made of papyrus during Iron Age II is an issue that has inspired scholarly debate.

Some scholars suggest that biblical texts were initially written on papyrus and then on leather during and after the Persian Period (Haran 1983; Lemaire 1992, 1003; Whitt 2000, 2393). Indeed, we have firm evidence attesting to the use of papyrus as a writing material in ancient Israel as early as the seventh

---

[43:14, 20–21, 25, 27–29 LXX]); and κεφαλίς 'small papyrus' occurs in Jer 36:2, 4, 6, 14, 32 (43:2, 4, 6, 14, 32 LXX) and in Zech 5:1 (Ziegler 1957, 391–99; Ziegler 1943, 299).

17. The lexeme τόμος 'roll of papyrus' occurs in Jer 36:2, 4 (43:2, 4 LXX) and Ps 40:8 (39:8 LXX), εἴλημα 'roll' occurs in Jer 36:14 (43:14 LXX) and Ps 40:8 (39:8 LXX), and τεῦχος 'rolled writing material' occurs in Ezek 2:9 and 3:1 (Ziegler 1957, 391–99; Ziegler 1952, 98; Field 1875, 151).

18. In the Dead Sea Scrolls library were found Greek papyrus fragments of biblical texts that date to the second–first centuries BCE (Tov 2004, 32–33, 289–94; Bar-Ilan 2000, 996); examples of such texts are 4QSeptuagint Leviticus^{b} (4Q120), 4QSeptuagint Numbers (4Q121), and 4QSeptuagint Exodus (7Q1). Biblical texts on papyrus written in Hebrew also appear among the Dead Sea Scrolls; e.g., 4QIsaiah^{p} (4Q69), 6QKings (6Q4), and 6QDaniel (6Q7) (Bar-Ilan 2000, 996; Tov 2004, 289–94).

century BCE.[19] Rollston (2010, 75) states that papyrus was widely used not only in ancient Israel but all over the Levant, especially for legal documents (e.g., contracts, marriage licenses, divorce certificates). Archeological finds confirming the use of papyrus in ancient Israel and the ancient Near East are used as evidence by scholars to bolster the claim that biblical texts were written on papyrus scrolls even during Iron Age II.

Not all scholars hold this view, however. Others contend that biblical texts were written on leather even from the First Temple Period (Demsky 2007, 238; Hicks 1983, 60–61). In Israel, the use of leather as a writing material, especially for biblical texts, is first attested at Qumran. As mentioned above, the Dead Sea Scrolls library consists primarily of leather scrolls—about 85 percent (Tov 2004, 31; 2012, 99).[20] It is difficult, however, to make absolute claims about the physical makeup of biblical scrolls in Iron Age II by solely relying on evidence from Qumran, although the absence of earlier leather documents does not preclude the possibility that leather was used as a writing material in earlier periods. The question of whether biblical texts were written on leather scrolls in ancient Israel will remain open until other physical evidence is discovered.

In sum, the term *məgillā* is a Late Biblical Hebrew word that designates a scroll made of papyrus or leather.[21] The term is a loanword from Aramaic, and it supplanted the older Standard Biblical Hebrew term *sēper*, which was used to designate various types of writing, including scrolls. The phrase *məgillat sēper* seems to be a stylistic variant of the term *məgillā*.

4.2.2. The Term **delet**

4.2.2.1. Etymology and Biblical Usage

The term *delet* 'door' (GMD 252; *DCH* 2:441–42; *HALOT* 1:223–24), which derives from Proto-Semitic **dal-t-*, has cognates in Akkadian (*daltum*; *CAD* 3:52–56), Ugaritic (*dlt*; *DULAT* 1:271), Phoenician (*dl*, *dlt*; *DNWSI* 1:250), and Galilean Aramaic (*daltā*; J. Fox 2003, 72). The noun pattern of *delet* can be classified as a *qal-t* pattern (Lambdin and Huehnergard 2000, 30).

In the Bible, *delet* occurs a total of eighty-eight times. The word also occurs in reference to doors at least sixteen times in the Dead Sea Scrolls (e.g., CD

19. For evidence confirming the use of papyrus in ancient Israel see 2.1.3.

20. It is also worth mentioning that according to rabbinic prescriptions the biblical text was to be written only upon leather (Tov 2004, 31–33). These rabbinic instructions, however, date to a time much later than the Iron Age.

21. In discussing scrolls and the term *məgillā*, I would be remiss not to mention the Copper Scrolls discovered in Qumran as well as the Ketef Hinnom amulets, which were miniature metal scrolls. Presumably, these types of scrolls were also designated by the term *məgillā*. Both of these finds are discussed in more detail in 4.3.3.3, which relates to writing on metal surfaces.

VI, 13; 11Q19 XXXVI, 11; 1QH[a] XI, 19; *DSSR* 1:90, 668; 2:292; *DSSC* 1:192), excluding cases with restored or uncertain letters; and *delet* also occurs once in Ben Sira (49, 13). In seventy-nine cases, the term refers to a type of door or gate (e.g., Gen 19:6; Judg 19:22; 1 Sam 3:15). In the remaining nine examples, *delet* is used figuratively or with a specialized meaning. In seven of these nine examples, the term refers to an opening, closure, or passageway.[22] In one verse (Song 8:9), *delet* is used figuratively to speak of a woman who is open to sexual activity. Finally, *delet* appears in Jer 36:23 with the meaning 'column'. How *delet* came to connote a column of a scroll will be discussed below. Prior to considering this issue, I will first evaluate the context of Jer 36:23.

Jeremiah 36 is well known for its description of the production of a written oracle. The chapter tells how Baruch composed a scroll, Jehoiakim burned that scroll, and Baruch subsequently rewrote that scroll. This chapter is of interest in that it raises questions about the process of producing a scroll as well as questions about the composition of that initial scroll of Jeremiah. What concerns us, however, is the use of *delet* in Jer 36:23 to refer to the columns of the scroll. In this verse, we read of Jehudi, a servant of Jehoiakim, reading Jeremiah's scroll, which is subsequently cut and burned. The verse reads: וַיְהִי ׀ כִּקְרוֹא יְהוּדִי שָׁלֹשׁ **דְּלָתוֹת** וְאַרְבָּעָה יִקְרָעֶהָ בְּתַעַר הַסֹּפֵר וְהַשְׁלֵךְ אֶל־הָאֵשׁ אֲשֶׁר אֶל־הָאָח עַד־תֹּם כָּל־הַמְּגִלָּה עַל־הָאֵשׁ אֲשֶׁר עַל־הָאָח 'As Jehudi read three or four ***dəlātôt***, he would cut it up with a scribal knife, throwing (it) into the fire in the brazier, until all the scroll was consumed on the fire on the brazier'. It is not clear whether it was Jehudi or Jehoiakim who was cutting the scroll and tossing it into the brazier. The text simply states, "he would cut it with a scribe's knife, throwing it into the fire in the brazier." Verses 27, 28, 29, and 32 attribute the burning of the scroll to Jehoiakim. Traditionally, therefore, the actions of cutting and burning the scroll have been attributed to King Jehoiakim, but even if it was Jehudi who cut and burned the scroll, one can be sure that Jehoiakim sanctioned these actions (Koller 2012, 223 n. 15).

4.2.2.2. Writing Boards, Ancient Scrolls, and the Translation of delet *in Ancient Versions*

One may argue that the natural interpretation of *delet*/*dəlātôt* within this text is to view the term as referring to the sheets that were stitched together to form the scroll. A scroll consisted of a number of sheets that resembled doors, reminiscent of the polyptych writing boards that were common in ancient Mesopotamia.

22. The term *delet* refers to Jerusalem as a gateway to the nations (Ezek 26:2). It can also refer to the opening or the doors of heaven (Ps 78:23) and to the closure or the doors of the sea (Job 38:8, 10). It may also speak of a man's lips (Eccl 12:4) and the mouth, or perhaps teeth, of Leviathan (Job 41:6). Finally, it is used once in reference to a woman's vulva (Job 3:10).

Examples of such writing boards, made of wood and ivory, were discovered at Nimrud (Wiseman 1955, plates 1 and 2; see figure 4.4 in 4.2.4.7). Another diptych writing board connected with ivory hinges was found off the Turkish coast of Uluburun near Kaç (Payton 1991; Warnock and Pendleton 1991).[23] One may argue, then, that an ancient scroll—which was comprised of many sheets stitched together as if with hinges—resembled a polyptych writing board, which, of course, consisted of connected hinged doors.

While it is possible to compare Jeremiah's scroll with a polyptych board, thereby equating the term *delet*/*dəlātôt* with the sheets of a scroll, this view is not supported by the Septuagint's translation of Jer 36:23 (43:23 LXX). Here *delet*/*dəlātôt* is rendered as σελίς 'scroll column' (LSJ 1590; Muraoka 2009, 619).[24] Similarly, Targum Jonathan and the Peshitta have *pṣ* 'column or page of a scroll' (*CAL*; Sokoloff 2009, 1220). Arguing in favor of interpreting *delet*/*dəlātôt* as 'columns', Hicks (1983) offers evidence from the Dead Sea Scrolls library as support for this view. While discussing the meaning of *delet*/*dəlātôt* in Jer 36:23, he suggests that the number of *dəlātôt* ('three or four *dəlātôt*') mentioned in this passage is not random, because an ancient scroll consisted of sheets that usually contained three or four columns of text per sheet. When Jehudi or Jehoiakim cut Jeremiah's scroll, then, this was done at the sutures between the sheets. In essence, according to Hicks, Jeremiah's scroll was cut up sheet by sheet and cast into the fire until it was entirely consumed. This explanation fits nicely with the evidence from the actual Qumran scrolls, several of which had three or four columns per sheet (Hicks 1983, 61–63).

4.2.2.3. The Term delet *in Epigraphic Finds*

While Jer 36:23 is the only biblical attestation of the use of *delet* to mean 'column', Hicks (1983, 51–57) persuasively argues that a few extrabiblical sources use *delet* with the meaning 'writing board, tablet'.[25] This is probably the meaning of *delet* in Lachish letter 4, which reads: *ktbty ʿl hdlt kkl ʾšr šlḥ[t ʾ]ly* 'I wrote on the *dlt* according to all that you have sent me' (Aḥituv 2008, 70). While it is possible that *delet* in this letter refers to an actual door, it seems more natural to read

23. A more thorough discussion of ancient writing boards appears in 4.2.4.7, which analyzes the term *lûaḥ*/*lûḥôt*.

24. Of the seventy-seven occurrences of *delet*/*dəlātôt* in the Bible, the Septuagint renders only the occurrence in Jer 36:23 (43:23 LXX) with the term σελίς. In most cases, *delet*/*dəlātôt* is rendered with the term θύρα 'door' (e.g., Gen 19:6, 9; LSJ 811; Muraoka 2009, 334). In other cases, the term is rendered with the following words (Muraoka 2010, 181): θύρωμα 'doorway, panel' (e.g., Ezek 41:23, 24; LSJ 812; Muraoka 2009, 334), πύλη 'swinging door, gate' (e.g., Deut 3:5; Josh 6:26; LSJ 1553; Muraoka 2009, 607), and σανίς 'plank' (2 Kgs 12:10; LSJ 1583; Muraoka 2009, 617).

25. Eshel (2000, 185–87) suggests that *delet* in Prov 8:34 also refers to a column of a scroll, but this is difficult to prove.

the passage as referring to a writing board or tablet.[26] Hicks also mentions that the Greek term δέλτος/δάλτος, which is a loanword from Semitic (Galling 1971, 210; Masson 2007, 737), carries the meaning 'writing board, tablet' (LSJ 377; Muraoka 2009, 142); δέλτος/δάλτος is attested already in the fifth century BCE (Hicks 1983, 55). It occurs, for instance, in 1 Maccabees in reference to metal writing boards (8:22; 14:18, 26, 48). The term *dlt* also appears to be associated with writing in Phoenician (Dobbs-Allsopp et al. 2005, 315). Finally, in Akkadian, *daltu* seems to refer to the leaves of a polyptych writing board (Hicks 1983, 55–57).

The extrabiblical use of Hebrew *dlt* to signify a writing board or tablet—as well as similar use of the cognates of *delet* in other Semitic languages and the use of δέλτος/δάλτος in Greek—suggests that Hebrew *delet* does carry a secondary meaning of 'writing board, tablet'. Indeed, both Eusebius (*Praep. ev.* 10.5.4) and Jerome (*Epist.* XXX.5) note that the fourth letter of the Hebrew alphabet, *dalet*, refers to writing tablets. It is this meaning that may have given rise to the meaning of *delet* as 'column' (Lundbom 2004a, 605). The semantic development of *delet* probably underwent the following progression: 'door of diptych writing board, tablet' > 'one side of diptych writing board' > 'column'. Thus, Lachish letter 4 probably preserves an earlier meaning of *delet* ('door of diptych writing board, tablet') whereas Jer 36:23 reflects a further semantic development of *delet* that resulted in the meaning 'column'.

There seem to be only two ways to understand the meaning of the term *delet*/*dəlātôt* in Jer 36:23. The lexeme can refer to the sheets of a scroll or the columns of a scroll. The earliest translation of the Bible supports the latter view. Furthermore, based on Hicks's analysis of specific scrolls from Qumran, it seems most reasonable to understand *dəlātôt* in Jer 36:23 as referring to columns of a scroll sheet. The semantic narrowing from 'door' to 'column' is rooted in the use of hinged diptych writing boards in the ancient Near East and probably in ancient Israel.

4.2.3. The Term gillāyôn

4.2.3.1. Etymology

The term *gillāyôn*/*gilyônîm* occurs only twice in the biblical text (Isa 3:23; 8:1).[27] For this reason, the exact meaning of this lexeme is difficult to establish

26. Another example, although not entirely convincing, is the use of *delet* in the Amman citadel inscription. The passage reads: []*n'l tdlt bdlt bṭn krh* []. Hicks (1983, 55) understands *tdlt* as a denominative *piel* verb of *delet* and therefore understands the phrase *tdlt bdlt* as meaning "to write (upon a door or tablet)." Aḥituv, however, views the passage as speaking of an actual door (2008, 357–58). More recently, Burlingame (2016, 63) has defended the view that *tdlt bdlt* should be interpreted as meaning "equip with a door."

27. *Gillāyôn* and *gilyônîm* are biforms that differ only in the presence of gemination in the middle radical of the former and the absence of it in the latter (*gilyônîm* < **gilləyônîm*). Examples of

with certainty (GMD 218; *HALOT* 1:191–93). Nevertheless, I will cautiously argue that, in Isa 8:1, *gillāyôn* means 'blank scroll', whereas it is not clear what *gilyônîm* means in Isa 3:23.

The lexeme *gillāyôn* is related to the verbal root *g-l-y* 'to uncover' (*DCH* 2:348–52; GMD 191–93; *HALOT* 1:191–92). The noun pattern of *gillāyôn* is *qittal-ān* (> *qittālōn* in Hebrew).[28] This pattern, which carries an abstract meaning of the root from which it derives, appears in nouns of strong roots such as *zikkārōn* 'remembrance' (< *z-k-r* 'to remember'; e.g., Exod 12:14) and *šibbārōn* 'breaking' (< *š-b-r* 'to break'; e.g., Jer 17:18); and in III-*y* roots such as *ḥizzāyôn* 'vision' (< *ḥ-z-y* 'to see'; e.g., 2 Sam 7:17), *bizzāyôn* 'contempt' (< *b-z-y* 'to despise'; e.g., Esth 1:18), and *niqqāyôn* 'innocence' (< *n-q-y* 'to clean'; Hos 8:5).[29] Just as these nouns carry an abstract meaning of their corresponding verbal root, so *gillāyôn* must have initially carried an abstract meaning of *g-l-y* 'to uncover'. It is possible, then that *gillāyôn* first meant 'uncovering, disclosure, revelation', but this abstract meaning does not appear in the Bible. Nevertheless, the Syriac term *gelyānā*/*gelyōnā*, which is clearly related to Hebrew *gillāyôn*, does mean 'revelation', and this suggests that Hebrew *gillāyôn* may also have also had this meaning (Sokoloff 2009, 236; *CAL*; GMD 218).[30] In Isa

similar biforms: *ḥizzāyôn* 'vision' (2 Sam 7:17) and *ḥezyōnôt* (Joel 3:1, plural), *niqqāyôn* 'innocence' (Hos 8:5) and *niqyôn* (Amos 4:6, construct state), and *timmāhôn* 'confusion' (Zech 12:4) and *timhôn* (Deut 28:28, construct state).

28. J. Fox (2003, 280) lists *qittal* as a very rare pattern in Hebrew and provides *ʾissār* 'bond' as an example; *ʾikkār* 'farmer' also belongs to this pattern (e.g., Isa 61:5; Jer 14:4). The pattern also has reflexes in Arabic: *ʾimmar* 'weak-minded', *dinnab* 'dwarf' (Lane 1968, 1:97; J. Fox 2003, 280). *Qittal-ān* (> *qittālōn* in Hebrew) is, of course, the same pattern as *qittal*, although augmented with the sufformative *-ān* (> *-ōn* in Hebrew). Joüon (J-M §88) incorrectly ascribes nouns such as *gillāyôn* and *zikkārōn* to the *qatal-ān* (> *qatalōn* in Hebrew) pattern, which appears to be the pattern of *rəʿābōn*. He suggests that in words such as *gillāyôn* and *zikkārōn* the pattern underwent gemination of the second radical and then a weakening of the initial *a* vowel to an *i* vowel. He explains the gemination of the second radical as an ad hoc change and the weakening of the *a* vowel as a result of its rather far position from the long *-ōn* syllable. More likely, the discussed forms simply derive from the *qittal-ān* (> *qittālōn*) pattern.

29. It is noteworthy that the sequence *-yôn*, which appears in *gillāyôn*, occurs in nouns that primarily derive from III-*y* roots. Besides *gillāyôn*, there are twenty-three other Hebrew words with this ending. Of this number, two words are perhaps loanwords: *siryôn* 'coat of mail' and *širyôn* 'army'. Another two words are proper names which may not derive from a III-*y* root: *ʿeṣyôn* 'Ezion' and *ṣipyôn* 'Ziphion'. The remaining nineteen examples, however, all derive from III-*y* roots: *ʾebyôn* 'needy' (< *ʾ-b-y*), *bizzāyôn* 'contempt' (< *b-z-y*), *gaʾăyôn* 'proud' (< *g-ʾ-y*), *dimyôn* 'likeness' (< *d-m-y*), *higgāyôn* 'talking, meditation' (< *h-g-y*), *hērāyôn* 'pregnancy' (< *h-r-y*), *ḥebyôn* 'hiding' (< *ḥ-b-y*), *ḥezyôn* 'Ḥezion' (< *ḥ-z-y*), *ḥizzāyôn* 'vision' (< *ḥ-z-y*), *kilyôn* 'Chilion' (< *k-l-y*), *killāyôn* 'annihilation' (< *k-l-y*), *niqqāyôn* 'innocence' (< *n-q-y*), *ʿelyôn* 'upper' (< *ʿ-l-y*), *pidyôn* 'redemption' (< *p-d-y*), *qišyôn* 'Kishion' (< *q-š-y*), *raʿyôn* 'striving' (< *r-ʿ-y*), *ripyôn* 'feeble' (< *r-p-y*), *rišyôn* 'authorization' (< *r-š-y*), and *šiggāyôn* 'Shiggaion' (< *š-g-y*). These data strongly suggest that *gillāyôn* also derives from a III-*y* root.

30. The lexeme *gelyōnā*/*gellāyōnā* also appears in the Peshitta's translation of Isa 8:1, where the word appears to mean 'scroll' (Sokoloff 2009, 236; *CAL*); this meaning, assuming it is credible,

8:1, however, *gillāyôn* certainly has a more tangible meaning; the context of the verse suggests that it designates a surface used for writing.

Indeed, in Mishnaic Hebrew, *gillāyôn* carries the meaning 'blank parchment, margin of scrolls' (Jastrow 1926, 1:248–49). The word is even used as a satirical adaptation of the Greek term εὐαγγέλιον 'gospel' (LSJ 705; Muraoka 2009, 297; Jastrow 1926, 1:249); that is, because εὐαγγέλιον acoustically resembles the term *gillāyôn*, the latter was used as a pejorative designation for the former as a type of wordplay, implying that the Christian scriptures were 'blank'. Also, it is noteworthy that Geʿez *gəlyat*, which derives from *galaya* 'to cut off, to separate, to reveal', carries the meaning 'lateral margin of a page' (*CDG* 192–93). Needless to say, Geʿez *gəlyat* and Mishnaic Hebrew *gillāyôn* confirm that nouns derived from *g-l-y* could designate scrolls or sections of scrolls. It is possible, then, that Mishnaic Hebrew has correctly preserved the intended meaning of *gillāyôn* in Isa 8:1. I would argue, then, that Biblical Hebrew *gillāyôn* designates a blank scroll, and the semantics of the word are extended in Mishnaic Hebrew to include 'margin of scrolls'.[31] To understand how the meaning of *gillāyôn* as 'blank scroll' developed, it is necessary to look at the meaning of the verbal root *g-l-y* in Hebrew and other Semitic languages.

The general meaning of the Hebrew verbal root *g-l-y* is 'to uncover'. This meaning is very clear in the *piel* stem (e.g., Lev 18:6; Jer 49:10; Prov 11:13). The *hiphil* stem of this root, however, carries the primary meaning 'to deport' (e.g., 2 Kgs 17:6; Jer 29:4; Ezra 2:1). As in the *piel* stem, in the *qal* stem *g-l-y* carries the meaning 'to uncover' (e.g., Amos 3:7; Prov 20:19); this meaning is especially common in the idiom 'to uncover one's ear' (i.e., 'to disclose information'; e.g., Job 33:16; 1 Sam 22:8). The more common meaning of *g-l-y* in the *qal* stem, however, is 'to depart, to go into exile'. Often, the verb refers to the people of Israel and Judah going into exile (e.g., 2 Kgs 7:23; Jer 52:27; Ezek 39:23). The verb can also refer to the disappearance or removal of joy (Isa 24:11), grass (Prov 27:25), possessions (Job 20:28), or glory (Hos 10:5).[32]

In other Semitic languages, the root *g-l-w/y* appears with meanings such as 'to cut off, to separate, to reveal' (Geʿez *galaya*; *CDG* 192–93), 'to uncover, to emigrate' (Aramaic *g-l-y*; *CAL*), 'to become clear, uncovered' (Arabic *g-l-w*;

---

is probably borrowed from Hebrew.

31. Haran (1980–81, 82 n. 34) argues that *gillāyôn* specifically designated a leather scroll; although difficult to prove, this view is plausible because *gillāyôn* does refer to blank parchment in Mishnaic Hebrew. Galling (1971, 222), on the other hand, holds that *gillāyôn* can also refer to a papyrus scroll. It is possible that *gillāyôn* simply refers to a blank scroll that could be of leather or papyrus.

32. In the *niphal*, the root *g-l-y* carries the meaning 'to reveal oneself, to appear' (e.g., Gen 35:7; 1 Sam 2:27; *HALOT* 1:191–92), and the *hithpael* carries a similar meaning (Gen 9:21; Prov 18:2). The *pual* and *hophal* stems carry the passive meanings of *piel* and *hiphil*, respectively (*pual*, Nah 2:8; Prov 27:5; *hophal*, e.g., Jer 13:19; Esth 2:6).

Lane 1968, 2:446) and 'to clean, polish, clear' (Modern Standard Arabic *g-l-w/y*; Wehr 1976, 132), and 'to present oneself' (Ugaritic *g-l-y*; *DULAT* 1:299). Leslau (*CDG* 192) concludes that "the various meanings of the Semitic root *g-l-w/y* can be explained by one root with the meaning 'cut, uncover, separate, emigrate'." I would suggest that Leslau's suggested definition of *g-l-w/y* can be further reduced to one meaning: 'to remove'.

In view of this comparative evidence, I would argue that *gillāyôn* may carry two distinct meanings. The meaning of *gillāyôn* as 'uncovering, disclosure, revelation', assuming such a meaning existed, reflects an abstract meaning of the root *g-l-y*. On the other hand, the more tangible meaning of *gillāyôn* as 'blank scroll' may be connected to the more general meaning of *g-l-y* 'to remove' in that a *gillāyôn* is a scroll from which all writing has been 'removed' or 'cleared'—hence, the meaning 'blank parchment' in Mishnaic Hebrew. Alternatively, if *gillāyôn* specifically refers to a blank scroll of leather, the lexeme may be connected with the meaning 'to remove' in that a *gillāyôn* was a piece of leather from which all hair, blood, flesh, and dirt were removed in preparation for the writing of the text. These suggested semantic shifts are, admittedly, not entirely satisfying. Nevertheless, *gillāyôn* clearly refers to a writing surface in Isa 8:1 and, with the scant evidence available, it may be reasonable to allow Mishnaic Hebrew to inform our understanding of the meaning of *gillāyôn* in this passage.

4.2.3.2. Biblical Usage of gillāyôn *(Isaiah 8:1) and Its Translation in Ancient Versions*

Isaiah 8:1 reads: וַיֹּאמֶר יְהוָה אֵלַי קַח־לְךָ **גִּלָּיוֹן** גָּדוֹל וּכְתֹב עָלָיו בְּחֶרֶט אֱנוֹשׁ לְמַהֵר שָׁלָל חָשׁ בַּז 'YHWH said to me, "Take for yourself a large ***gillāyôn*** and write upon it with a *ḥereṭ ʾĕnôš* [stylus?], 'belonging to *māhēr šālāl ḥāš baz*'"'. Regarding the translation of Isa 8:1 into Greek, van Wieringen (2011a, 3–4) argues that the Greek translations incorrectly derive *gillāyôn* from the root *g-l-l* 'to roll'. He contends that this is clear because the Septuagint renders *gillāyôn gādôl* as τόμον καινοῦ μεγάλου 'roll of a new large (scroll)' (LSJ 858, 1088, 1804; Muraoka 2009, 355, 445, 683), while Symmachus renders it as τεῦχος 'roll of writing material' (LSJ 945, 1784; Ziegler 1939, 149) and Theodotion as κεφαλίς 'little head; small papyrus roll' (LSJ 945; Muraoka 2009, 396); Aquila also translates *gillāyôn* as διφθέρωμα 'hide', which, of course, is related to the meaning of scroll (LSJ 438; van Wieringen 2011a, 3; Ziegler 1939, 149). It is possible that the translators of the Greek versions incorrectly derived *gillāyôn* from the root *g-l-l* as a type of folk etymology that emerged due to the superficial similarity between *gillāyôn* and the root *g-l-l*. This, however, does not preclude the possibility that the term designates a blank scroll. The word may indeed carry this meaning although it is etymologically unconnected to the root *g-l-l*. This would mean, of course, that the meaning ‘blank scroll’ must have emerged from the root *g-l-y*, perhaps as described above.[33]

4.2.3.3. Biblical Usage of gilyônîm *(Isaiah 3:23) and Its Translation in Ancient Versions*

Isaiah 3:18–23 reads: בַּיּוֹם הַהוּא יָסִיר אֲדֹנָי אֵת תִּפְאֶרֶת הָעֲכָסִים וְהַשְּׁבִיסִים וְהַשַּׂהֲרֹנִים׃ הַנְּטִיפוֹת
וְהַשֵּׁירוֹת וְהָרְעָלוֹת׃ הַפְּאֵרִים וְהַצְּעָדוֹת וְהַקִּשֻּׁרִים וּבָתֵּי הַנֶּפֶשׁ וְהַלְּחָשִׁים׃ הַטַּבָּעוֹת וְנִזְמֵי הָאָף׃ הַמַּחֲלָ־
צוֹת וְהַמַּעֲטָפוֹת וְהַמִּטְפָּחוֹת וְהָחֲרִיטִים׃ **וְהַגִּלְיֹנִים** וְהַסְּדִינִים וְהַצְּנִיפוֹת וְהָרְדִידִים ‘In that day the Lord will take away the glory of the anklets, the headbands, the crescent ornaments, the pendants, the bracelets, the veils, the headdresses, the leg ornaments, the sashes, the perfume boxes, the amulets, the rings, the nose rings, the festal robes, the outer mantels, the cloaks, the purses, the ***gilyônîm***, the linen garments, the turbans, and the veils’. In order to ascertain the meaning of *gilyônîm* in Isa 3:23, Van Wieringen (2011a, 3–4) exams how the passage was rendered in the earliest translations of the Bible. The Septuagint’s translation of *gilyônîm* reveals that *gilyônîm* was understood to derive from the root *g-l-y* ‘to uncover’. The term is rendered in Greek as τα διαφανῆ Λακωνικὰ ‘the translucent Laconian dresses’ (LSJ 417, 1025; Muraoka 2009, 162, 422). Following the Greek translations, the Syriac Peshitta has *nḥtyhyn* ‘their long mantels’ (Sokoloff 2009, 910; *CAL*). Rabbinic Hebrew also understands *gilyônîm* in Isa 3:23 as referring to garments for women (Jastrow 1926, 1:249). On the other hand, Aquila’s revision of the verse renders *gilyônîm* as the plural of κάτοπτρον ‘mirror’ (LSJ 929; Ziegler 1939, 135). Similarly, Targum Onkelos has *mḥzyt’*, *mḥzy’t’* ‘mirrors’ (*CAL*) and the Latin Vulgate has *specula* ‘mirror’ (Weber and Gryson 2007). Thus, according to ancient translations of Isa 3:23, *gilyônîm* designates either dresses or mirrors.

Isaiah 3:23 falls within the greater passage of Isa 3:16–26, which contains a denouncement of Judean women. This larger context derides Judean women for their supposed pride. In response, YHWH promises to humble these women by taking away their decorations, including anklets, earrings, and bracelets. It is not surprising, then, that verse 23 should include ‘dresses’ or ‘mirrors’ as one of the items to be confiscated.[34] Indeed, while the meaning of *gilyônîm* is not clear,

33. Following the Septuagint, the Vulgate renders *gillāyôn gādôl* as *librum grandem* ‘large book’ (Weber and Gryson 2007). The Syriac Peshitta renders the Hebrew as *glywn’ rb’* ‘large scroll’, while Targum Jonathan has *lwḥ rb* ‘large tablet’ (van Wieringen 2011b, 3–4; *CAL*; Sokoloff 2009, 236, 1425). It is noteworthy that, with the exception of Targum Jonathan, *gillāyôn* is usually translated in ancient Bibles with a word that is connected to scrolls.

34. Evidence exists for the use of mirrors in the ancient world. Mirrors have been discovered in ancient Israel, Mesopotamia, Egypt, and Anatolia. They are first known in Anatolia and Canaan

translating the term as 'dresses' or 'mirrors' fits well within the context of Isa 3:16–26.

It is difficult to know with certainty the meaning of *gillāyôn* and *gilyônîm*. Based on a comparison of *gillāyôn* with nouns of the same nominal pattern, the word may originally have meant 'uncovering, disclosure, revelation'; this seems to be supported by Syriac *gelyānā*/*gelyōnā* 'revelation' (Sokoloff 2009, 236, *CAL*). In Isa 8:1, however, *gillāyôn* clearly refers to some type of a writing surface, perhaps a blank scroll, and the meaning of *gilyônîm* is uncertain.

4.2.4. The Term **lûaḥ**

4.2.4.1. Etymology and Biblical Usage

The term *lûaḥ* 'tablet, board, plank' is a primary noun with cognates in various Semitic languages (J. Fox 2003, 76; GMD 600–601; *DCH* 4:524–25; *HALOT* 1:522–23). Cognates exist in Akkadian (*lēʾu*, *lēḫu* 'board, writing board'; *CAD* 9:156–61), Ugaritic (*lḥ* 'missive, message'; *DULAT* 2:494–95), Aramaic (*lwḥʾ* 'tablet, board'; *CAL*), Arabic (*lawḥ* 'board, tablet, plate'; Lane 1968, 7:2679), and Ethiopic (*lawḥ* 'board, tablet, parchment'; *CDG* 320). The term seems to have referred to a type of board or plank originally and later developed the meaning 'writing board, tablet'. The Hebrew form *lûaḥ* is in the *qūl* pattern, ultimately deriving from Proto-Semitic **lawḥ-* (Lambdin and Huehnergard 2000, 31; J. Fox 2003, 76).[35]

In the Bible, the term *lûaḥ*/*lûḥôt* occurs forty-three times. Of this number, thirty-three examples refer to the stone tablets of the ark of the covenant.[36] In ten more passages, *lûaḥ*/*lûḥôt* refers to tablets or planks made of wood or metal. The term also occurs at least seven times in the Dead Sea Scrolls (*DSSC* 1:414), including one case with a restored *khet.* Three of the seven occurrences, which appear in a pesher or in 4QReworked Pentateuch[b], refer to writing boards or tablets (4Q177 1–4, 12; 1QpHab VI, 15; 4Q364 26bii+e, 5, 8; *DSSR* 1:378, 450, 762). I will first evaluate the biblical cases in which *lûaḥ*/*lûḥôt* refers to the stone tablets of the covenant and then the cases in which the term refers to other wooden and metal boards.

---

around 6,000 BCE and in Mesopotamia and Egypt in the late third millennium BCE. Mirrors were first made of obsidian and later of polished metals such as bronze, copper, silver, gold, or electrum (King and Stager 2001, 283–84; Nemet-Nejat 1993).

35. Steiner (1987) points out that *ū* is the normal reflex of **aw* following *l* in Hebrew and Aramaic (e.g., *lûz* < **lawz-* 'almond tree').

36. Thirty-three times the term *lûaḥ* refers to the tablets of stone: Exod 24:12; 31:18; 32:15–16, 19; 34:1, 4, 28–29; Deut 4:13; 5:22; 9:9–11, 15, 17; 10:1–5; 1 Kgs 8:9; 2 Chr 5:10.

4.2.4.2. Biblical Usage of lûaḥ/lûḥôt *as the Tablets of Stone*

Among the thirty-three passages that use *lûaḥ/lûḥôt* to refer to the tablets of the covenant, thirteen explicitly state that the tablets are made of stone.[37] In these instances, the term *lûaḥ/lûḥôt* is modified by the term *ʾeben/ʾăbānîm* 'stone(s)'. Other passages portray the tablets as being hewn out of stone (Exod 34:1, 4; Deut 10:1, 3). It seems reasonable to hold that the author of the accounts involving the two tablets wrote these stories in light of actual ancient Near Eastern writing practices. It is thus worthwhile to consider the details of these passages in order to understand the writing technology indicated in the passages.

The text not only depicts the tablets of the covenant as comprised of stone but also seems to imply their size. In five passages, Moses holds the two tablets in one hand (Exod 32:15, 19; 34:4, 29; Deut 10:3), and in two passages he is said to be holding the two tablets with two hands (Deut 9:15, 17). The author of the text thus seems to depict tablets that could not have been larger than what can be carried in one or two hands. Finally, the text also pictures these tablets as being inscribed on both sides (Exod 32:15). The description of these tablets fits well within what we know about ancient Near Eastern writing technologies. In order to establish a better historical context for the use of stone tablets as a writing surface, we will consider the use of tablets and writing boards in the ancient Near East.

4.2.4.3. Hittite Law Tablets of Clay

One may compare the tablets of the covenant with the Hittite law tablets of clay.[38] The collection of two hundred Hittite laws, dating to 1650–1400 BCE, is written in cuneiform on fragments of two clay tablets (Neufeld 1951, 70–75). Writing appears on both sides of the clay tablets (Neufeld 1951, 73). In comparing the clay tablets of the Hittite laws with the tablets of the covenant described in the Bible, some have suggested that the author of the biblical text imagined the tablets of the covenant to have been made of clay (van Wieringen 2011b, 1, 5). Nevertheless, the tablets of the covenant are clearly depicted as hewn from stone. While clay tablets are similar to stone tablets in that they become as hard as stone after drying, the process of writing on wet clay is, of course, different

37. Thirteen times the tablets are stated to be of stone: Exod 24:12; 31:18; 34:1, 4 (2x); Deut 4:13; 5:22; 9:9–11; 10:1, 3; 1 Kgs 8:9.

38. Just as Hammurabi's law collection was etched on stone in the Code of Hammurabi, so the Bible depicts Moses's law collection as being inscribed on the stone covenant tablets. Nevertheless, the biblical tablets as portrayed in the text and the Code of Hammurabi are quite different in size, so the Code of Hammurabi was mentioned earlier in connection with royal and nonroyal lapidary inscriptions.

FIGURE 4.2. Gezer calendar, tenth century BCE. Istanbul Archaeology Museums. Photo: © Todd Bolen/BiblePlaces.com.

from the process of inscribing letters upon stone. For this reason, we turn to consider some finds of stone tablets and stelae that will hopefully shed some light on the stone tablets of the covenant.

4.2.4.4. Gezer Calendar and Amman Citadel Inscription

The Gezer calendar and the Amman citadel inscription were etched upon stone. Discovered by Macalister in 1908, the Gezer calendar from the tenth century BCE consists of a small limestone tablet, measuring 4.2 inches high, 2.7 inches wide, and 0.6 inches thick (Dobbs-Allsopp et al. 2005, 156; see figure 4.2). The tablet is a record of agricultural activities, including ingathering and sowing, and the corresponding months for each activity. The obverse side of the tablet contains the text, but the tablet is a palimpsest and has signs of writing on the reverse side as well (Dobbs-Allsopp et al. 2005, 156). It has been suggested that the tablet was an exercise tablet written by a student (Albright 1934, 21).

Almost three times larger than the Gezer calendar is the Amman citadel inscription. It measures 10.2 inches in height and 7.6 inches in width and it is also executed upon limestone (Aḥituv 2008, 357). Dating to the ninth century BCE, this inscription is probably from a stela erected by an Ammonite king for the god Milkom (Aḥituv 2008, 359). The original inscription was larger than the portion that has been preserved (see figure 4.3). Perhaps the tablets of the covenant as portrayed in the text can be compared in their composition and format to that of the Gezer calendar or the Amman citadel inscription.

FIGURE 4.3. Amman citadel inscription, ninth century BCE. Amman Citadel Museum. Photo: © Todd Bolen /BiblePlaces.com.

4.2.4.5. Biblical Usage of lûaḥ/lûḥôt *to Refer to Wooden Planks and Writing Tablets*

Besides referring to the tablets of the covenant, *lûaḥ/lûḥôt* is used ten times to designate boards of wood or metal. Four times the term refers to planks of wood (Exod 27:8; 38:7; Ezek 27:5; Song 8:9) and once to a plank of metal (1 Kgs 7:36).[39] In the remaining five passages, *lûaḥ/lûḥôt* refers to tablets that are written upon (Isa 30:8; Jer 17:1; Hab 2:2; Prov 3:3; 7:3), although the occurrences of *lûaḥ/lûḥôt* in Jeremiah and in Proverbs are used in a figurative sense to refer to the "tablet of the heart." Still, in at least the Jeremiah passage, useful information can be gleaned regarding the use of boards for writing in ancient Israel. The passages in Proverbs, however, do not contain any information that would inform us about the processes of writing on stone tablets or writing boards.

4.2.4.6. Stone Tablets or Wooden Writing Boards?

It is difficult to know whether the tablets mentioned in the Isaiah, Jeremiah, and Habakkuk passages refer to tablets of stone or wood. The Jeremiah and Isaiah

39. Twice, the term *lûaḥ/lûḥôt* refers to wooden planks of the tabernacle (Exod 27:8; 38:7). Once, *lûaḥ/lûḥôt* refers to wooden planks of a ship (Ezek 27:5) and once *lûaḥ/lûḥôt* is used in a poetical passage to refer to a wooden plank utilized to cover up a door (Song 8:9). In one passage, *lûaḥ/lûḥôt* refers to metal planks of a cart situated in the temple (1 Kgs 7:36).

passages seem to imply that the tablets were made of stone, but the Habakkuk passage does not provide any clue as to the composition of the tablets mentioned there.

Jeremiah 17:1 reads: חַטַּאת יְהוּדָה כְּתוּבָה בְּעֵט בַּרְזֶל בְּצִפֹּרֶן שָׁמִיר חֲרוּשָׁה עַל־לוּחַ לִבָּם וּלְקַרְנוֹת מִזְבְּחוֹתֵיכֶם 'The sin of Judah is written with a pen of iron, with a point of the hardest stone, it is incised on the ***lûaḥ*** of their heart, and on the horns of their altars'. Clearly, this verse is stressing the hardness of the Judeans' heart. According to this verse, a tool that was commonly used to inscribe on stone—namely, an iron pen, a point of the hardest stone—is the instrument used to engrave the sin of Judah upon the tablet of the Judeans' heart. Furthermore, one of the terms used to describe the writing on the tablet is *ḥărûšā* 'inscribed', which bespeaks a process of engraving upon stone. The verse is, of course, using the term *lûaḥ*/*lûḥôt* in an allegorical sense. Nevertheless, even in this poetical usage of *lûaḥ*, we may conclude that a tablet of stone, not wood, is intended by the author of this passage.

I suggest that the use of *lûaḥ*/*lûḥôt* in the Isaiah passage also refers to a stone tablet rather than a wooden tablet. Isaiah 30:8 reads: עַתָּה בּוֹא כָתְבָהּ עַל־לוּחַ אִתָּם וְעַל־סֵפֶר חֻקָּהּ וּתְהִי לְיוֹם אַחֲרוֹן לָעַד עַד־עוֹלָם 'Now, go write it on a ***lûaḥ*** with them, and on a document inscribe it, so that it will be for the last day, forever and ever'. Based on this verse, the writing on the tablet was to remain for eternity. This seems to imply that the writing surface was a stone tablet rather than a wax-covered wooden board.

While the Jeremiah and Isaiah passages may imply a stone tablet, the Habakkuk passage does not have this implication. Habakkuk 2:2 reads: וַיַּעֲנֵנִי יְהוָה וַיֹּאמֶר כְּתוֹב חָזוֹן וּבָאֵר עַל־הַלֻּחוֹת לְמַעַן יָרוּץ קוֹרֵא בוֹ 'YHWH answered me and said, "Write a vision and expound on the ***lûḥôt***, so that the one who reads in it will run"'. Because the passage refers to the boards in the plural form *lûḥôt*, perhaps a diptych or polyptych writing board is meant. While this understanding of this passage is possible, it is difficult to prove. Nevertheless, because the possibility exists, it would be beneficial to mention here the extant evidence for the use of such boards in the ancient world.

4.2.4.7. Writing Boards

The boards mentioned in the aforementioned three passages, or at least in the Habakkuk passage, may have been wax-covered boards used for writing.[40] After all, *lûaḥ*/*lûḥôt* does refer to wooden planks, so it is not difficult to imagine that

40. Driver (1976, 79–80) holds that *lûaḥ*/*lûḥôt* refers to wooden writing boards in Isa 30:8 and Hab 2:2. Likewise, Moore (2011, 55–57) presents a strong argument that these passages use *lûaḥ*/*lûḥôt* to speak of wooden wax boards. Moore (2011, 43–59) also has a nice survey of evidence for the use of wax-covered wooden boards in the ancient Near East.

lûaḥ/lûḥôt may also have designated a wooden writing board. In Akkadian texts, wax-covered writing boards were called by the term *lēʾum* (*CAD* 9:158). This is significant, of course, because the use of *lēʾum* in Akkadian to denote wax-covered writing boards further supports the supposition that *lûaḥ/lûḥôt* may refer to similar boards in the Levant.

In ancient Mesopotamia, cuneiform texts were inscribed on flat pieces of ivory, single wooden writing boards, and wooden diptych boards connected with hinges (Black and Tait 2000, 2199). Writing boards of gold and silver, although rare, were also used (Driver 1976, 15; Wiseman 1955, 3). Such boards were covered with wax which contained orpiment. The wax could be written upon and erased for reuse. Often, a text was initially impressed into the wax of a writing board and then copied onto a clay tablet, whereupon the wax tablet was erased and reused for a new text (Pearce 2000, 2269).

Some writing boards have survived to the present day. For instance, a writing board dating to about 1300 BCE was found in the wreck of a merchant ship off the Turkish coast of Uluburun near Kaç (Payton 1991; Warnock and Pendleton 1991). The diptych is made of boxwood (*Buxus*) and consists of two boards connected by ivory hinges. Wooden and ivory boards have also been found in a well at Nimrud (Wiseman 1955, plates 1 and 2). A total of sixteen ivory boards and at least an equal number of wooden boards were found. The ivory boards, as well as the boards made of walnut wood, comprised polyptychs. Dating to about 707–705 BCE, these polyptychs were types of a "deluxe edition of a book specially copied for the royal palace of Sargon II at Khorsabad" (Wiseman 1955, 3; see figure 4.4).

Writing boards were also utilized in Egypt already in the Old Kingdom (2663–2160 BCE) and continued to be used throughout Egyptian history (Hagen 2013, 83; for an example, see figure 4.5). Hagen examines a writing board from Thebes which dates to the Eighteenth Dynasty (1549–1298 BCE); the board, like others from the New Kingdom (1549–1069 BCE), served a didactic purpose for scribal training. Gunter (2000, 1541–42, figure 1) mentions another writing board, also from the Eighteenth Dynasty. The board, which is probably from Thebes, is covered with gesso and has a grid drawn with red paint. The grid assisted the Egyptian scribes in drawing human figures according to the prescribed system of proportions. The surviving board has a depiction of King Thutmose III and a hieroglyph of a quail chick.[41]

An Etruscan wooden writing board was found in Marsiliana (Wiseman 1955, 9–10, plate 1). The find consists of one unhinged board with an Etruscan inscription on it. Remains of wax were seen on the board upon its discovery.

41. Diringer (1953, 22, 27) refers to another two wooden boards recovered from Egypt. The boards have demotic writing on them. Additionally, Pritchard (1974, 83) mentions two wooden boards with inscribed hieroglyphs. Egyptian writing boards or fragments of boards can be viewed at the Metropolitan Museum of Art (http://metmuseum.org, search for "writing boards").

FIGURE 4.4. Assyrian ivory writing boards, circa 721–705 BCE. Metropolitan Museum of Art, New York. Photo: public domain.

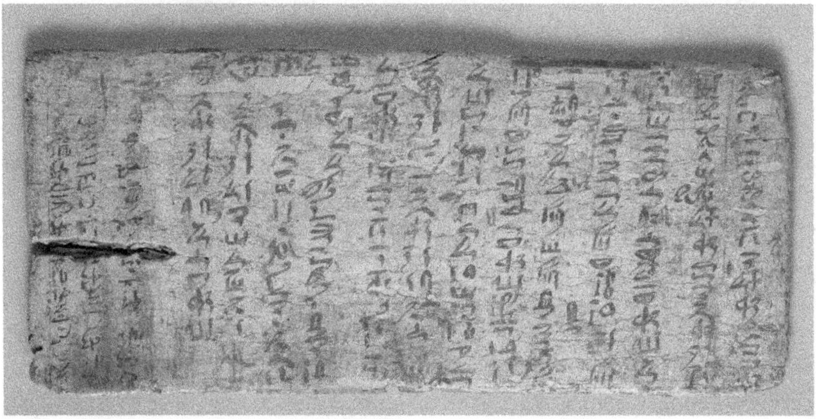

FIGURE 4.5. Egyptian wooden writing board, circa 1981–1802 BCE. Metropolitan Museum of Art, New York. Photo: public domain.

This Etruscan find dates to 700 BCE, and Wiseman (1955, 10) considers it to be "directly inspired from the Orient if not an actual import."

Ancient Near Eastern reliefs also depict scribes writing on wooden boards. A notable example comes from the Southwest Palace at Nineveh, which depicts two scribes recording booty. One is writing on a papyrus or leather scroll, while the other is recording booty on a wooden tablet (King and Stager 2001, 310). Diptych boards are also represented on Neo-Hittite reliefs from the eighth century BCE, for instance, in a depiction of the young scribe Tarhunpias (Lemaire 1992, 1002). A relief from Zincirli represents the king Barrakib with a minister possessing a diptych (Lemaire 1992, 1002). Finally, there is textual evidence for the use of writing boards in Ugarit (Symington 1991, 121–23). In sum, the use of wax-covered writing boards was a common practice in the ancient Near East, so it is possible that biblical passages contain references to such writing boards.

4.2.4.8. Translation of lûaḥ/lûḥôt *in the Septuagint*

The Septuagint uses a number of words to render *lûaḥ/lûḥôt* in Greek. In the cases where *lûaḥ/lûḥôt* refers to the stone tablets of the ark of the covenant, the Hebrew is almost always rendered with the term πλάξ 'flat stone, tablet' (e.g., Exod 31:18; 32:15; LSJ 1411; Muraoka 2009, 561). Yet in Exod 24:12, when *lûaḥ/lûḥôt* refers to the tablets of stone, the term is rendered as πυξίον 'tablet of boxwood' (LSJ 1554; Muraoka 2009, 608). It is not clear why the Septuagint uses this rendering here, because this passage clearly depicts the tablets given to Moses by YHWH as tablets of stone.

When the term *lûaḥ/lûḥôt* refers to wooden or metal planks, the Septuagint renders it twice as σανίς 'board, plank, timber' (Ezek 27:5; Song 8:9; LSJ 1583) and once as σανιδωτός 'planked, boarded over' (Exod 27:8; LSJ 1583; Muraoka 2009, 617). Another time, when the Hebrew text refers to a metal board, the Septuagint appears to have ἀρχή 'beginning, origin' (1 Kgs 7:36 [7:21–22 LXX]; LSJ 252; Muraoka 2009, 94) which, of course, does not correspond to the meaning of *lûaḥ/lûḥôt*. Finally, there is not a corresponding Greek translation for *lûaḥ/lûḥôt* in the Septuagint's translation of Exod 38:7.

Of the five passages that use *lûaḥ/lûḥôt* to denote writing boards or tablets, the lexeme is rendered twice as πυξίον 'tablet of boxwood' (Isa 30:8; Hab 2:2; LSJ 1554; Muraoka 2009, 608), although, according to Jerome, Symmachus translates *lûaḥ/lûḥôt* as πτύχιον 'folding tablet' in Isa 30:8 (LSJ 1549; Ziegler 1939, 227) and as σελίδιον 'column of a papryus' in Hab 2:2 (LSJ 1590; Ziegler 1943, 264). In translating the phrase *lûaḥ libbekā/libbām* 'the tablet of your/their heart' (Prov 3:3, 7:3; Jer 17:1), the Septuagint and its revisions use three words—πλάτος, στῆθος, and πλάξ—to render *lûaḥ*. In the Septuagint's translation of Prov 7:3, *lûaḥ* is rendered as πλάτος 'breadth' (i.e., 'breath of heart'; LSJ 1413; Muraoka 2009, 561) and, according to the Syro-Hexapla, the quinta renders the term as στῆθος 'breast' (i.e., 'breast of the heart'; LSJ 1643; Muraoka 2009, 636; Field 1875, 2:323). However, a variant reading of the verse has πλάξ 'flat stone, tablet' (LSJ 1411; Muraoka 2009, 561), and the same is true for the versions of this verse by Aquila, Symmachus, and Theodotion, as reflected in the Syro-Hexapla (Field 1875, 2:323; Holmes and Parsons 1798–1827, 3:412).

While the Septuagint text does not include Jer 17:1, the passage is included in the hexaplaric revisions. Thus, according to Origen, *lûaḥ* in this passage is rendered as στῆθος 'breast' by Aquila, Symmachus, and Theodotion (Ziegler 1957, 233); alternatively, according to the Syro-Hexapla, Aquila and Symmachus translate the same case as πλάξ 'flat stone, tablet' (Ziegler 1957, 233). Also, although the Septuagint does not include the latter half of Prov 3:3, various manuscripts add a translation of the second part of the verse. In such manuscripts, *lûaḥ* is rendered as πλάτος 'breadth' and πλάξ 'flat stone, tablet' (Holmes and Parsons 1798–1827, 3:406). Finally, Symmachus renders *lûaḥ* in this verse as στῆθος 'breast', while Theodotion renders it as πλάξ 'flat stone, tablet' (Field 1875, 2:315).

The Septuagint does display slight distinctions in the way it translates *lûaḥ/lûḥôt*. When the biblical passage refers to the stone tablets, the Septuagint predominantly uses πλάξ because this word connotes stone material. On the other hand, when *lûaḥ/lûḥôt* is used to speak of wooden planks, the Septuagint renders the term with a form of the word σανίς, which implies a wooden material. Similarly, in Isa 30:8 and Hab 2:2, *lûaḥ/lûḥôt* is rendered as πυξίον 'tablet of boxwood'. The translators of the Septuagint seem to have understood these instances of *lûaḥ/lûḥôt* as referring to wooden writing boards.

To sum up, the term *lûaḥ/lûḥôt* means 'board' or 'tablet'. This is clear because the Hebrew term refers to boards used for various building purposes and because it refers to tablets or boards upon which writing was executed. While stone tablets are clearly designated as such in the biblical text and perhaps also implied in a couple of passages (Isa 30:8; Jer 17:1), writing boards made of wood or another material are not mentioned explicitly. Nevertheless, because the term *lûaḥ/lûḥôt* does refer to boards of wood (Exod 27:8; 38:7; Ezek 27:5; Song 8:9) and metal (1 Kgs 7:36)—although these boards were not used for writing purposes—it is not unreasonable to suggest that the term could also refer to wax-covered writing boards. The Septuagint seems to support this view, because it translates *lûaḥ/lûḥôt* in Isa 30:8 and Hab 2:2 with the term πυξίον, which usually refers to a wooden writing board. Moreover, because writing boards were used in Egypt, Mesopotamia, and the ancient Mediterranean world, it is reasonable to conclude that such boards were also used in ancient Israel. In sum, when referring to writing surfaces, the term *lûaḥ/lûḥôt* designates tablets of stone, and it is quite possible that the same lexeme also designates wax-covered writing boards made of wood or another material.

4.2.5. The Term ḥereś

4.2.5.1. Writing on Ostraca in the Ancient World

The use of ostraca, or potsherds, for writing purposes was commonplace in the ancient world. Deir el-Medina is the most significant Egyptian site in this regard because hundreds of ostraca were discovered there (McDowell 1999, 18, 25), and thousands more were acquired from local dealers (McDowell 1999, 27). In total, there are between 17,000 and 20,000 finds belonging to the corpus of Deir el-Medina (Hagen 2011, 1 n. 1), consisting of limestone pieces as well as potsherds. The size of the ostraca varies (e.g., 4.3 × 2.3 inches; 5.9 × 3.1 inches; 7.8 × 3.9 inches) and the writing on them appears in black or red ink (Hagen 2011, 1–42). These hieratic inscriptions, which date to the New Kingdom (1549–1069 BCE), consist of private letters, economic records, legal records, testaments, magical spells, and other types of texts (McDowell 1999, 4, 28).[42] While Egypt has yielded a surplus of inscribed ostraca, such finds have been uncovered elsewhere in the ancient world.

The use of ostraca as a writing material is also attested in ancient Greece, where they were used in the practice of ostracism (ὀστρακισμός). As is well known, the ancient Greek practice of ostracism—the procedure of exiling a Greek politician from Athens—is named after the material (ὄστρακον 'potsherd'; LSJ 1264) that was inscribed with the name of a Greek politician to be exiled. In Athens, this method of exile primarily dates to the fifth century BCE (Forsdyke 2005, 146–49, 165–205). More than 11,000 inscribed ostraca have been found in Athens (Lang 1990, 7; Brenne 2001, 28; 2002, 40).

Ostraca were also used for writing purposes in ancient Canaan. In 1988, Sass (1988, 51–52) could write that, of the various Old Canaanite and early Phoenician inscriptions discovered in Canaan, eleven were written on potsherds. These ostraca were found primarily in southern Canaan, but some were discovered in the north; these finds come from various sites, including Lachish (Sass 1988, 60–64, 96, 100), Gezer (Sass 1988, 55–56), Reḥov (Sass 1988, 69–70), and Hazor (Sass 1988, 71–72, 97–98). While these Old Canaanite inscriptions date to the sixteenth–twelfth centuries BCE (Cross 2003a), the practice of writing on potsherds continued into the period of the Israelite monarchy.

Although writing in ancient Israel appeared on many different materials, King and Stager (2001, 307) state that, due to the vast availability and affordability of ostraca, they comprised the most widespread writing material used for communication in Israel. Indeed, Israel has yielded a large number of inscribed potsherds from Samaria, Lachish, and Arad. The ostraca from Samaria date to the eighth century BCE, prior to the fall of Samaria to Assyria in 722 BCE. Over one hundred inscribed potsherds were discovered at Samaria (Dobbs-Allsopp et al. 2005, 423–26). At Lachish, thirty-four ostraca inscriptions were unearthed. The finds date to the sixth century BCE, just prior to the fall of Jerusalem to Babylon in 586 BCE (Dobbs-Allsopp et al. 2005, 299). The Arad ostraca date to the same time period and consist of nearly one hundred finds (Dobbs-Allsopp et al. 2005, 5–6; see figure 4.6). The writing on most of the ostraca discovered

42. In Egyptian, ostraca were designated by the term *nḏr*, and in Demotic by the term *blḏ(ʿ)* (Gestermann 1984, 701–2).

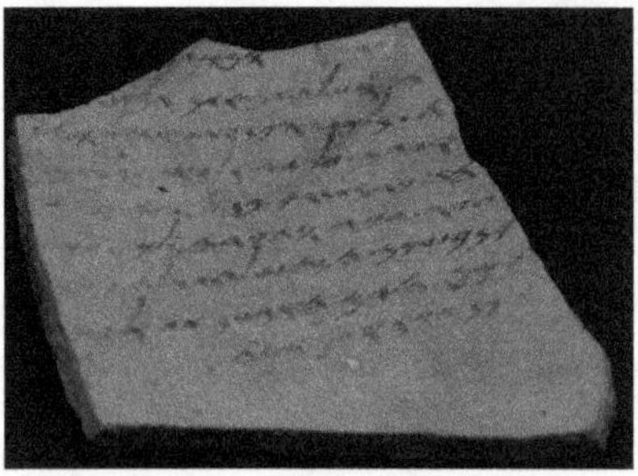

FIGURE 4.6. Arad letter 24, sixth century BCE. Israel Museum. Photo: © Todd Bolen/BiblePlaces.com.

in Israel appears in ink; however, there are also potsherds with writing incised upon them (Aḥituv 2008, 154–55, 310). Other sites in the vicinity of ancient Israel have also yielded inscribed potsherds (e.g., Philistia, Edom, and Ammon; Aḥituv 2008, 346–56, 370–86).

4.2.5.2. Etymology and Biblical Usage

The term *ḥereś* carries the meaning 'earthenware, potsherd' (GMD 402; *DCH* 3:323; *HALOT* 1:357). While the meaning of this word is clear, the etymology is not. Perhaps the Arabic term *ḫars* 'wine jar' and the obscure Punic term *chirs*, *ers* 'potsherd' are related to the Hebrew word (Noonan 2019, 105; Lane 1968, 2:722; Friedrich and Röllig 1999, 35c, 193a, 220b).[43]

Evaluating the etymology of Hebrew *ḥereś*, Rabin (1963, 118–20; see also Noonan 2019, 105 and Friedrich, Kammenhuber, and Hoffmann 2001, 3/2:367–69) suggests that the term is a loanword deriving from Hittite *ḫarši* 'bowl, jar'. In arguing that Hebrew *ḥereś* derives from Hittite *ḫarši*, however, one must address two issues. First, according to Mazar (1992, 49–55), pottery is attested in Canaan as early as the Neolithic Period (8500–4300 BCE). One would assume, then, that the Canaanites possessed a word of their own and would not need to borrow a Hittite word designating pottery. Second, because we do not know how Hittite *š* was pronounced, it is not certain that Hebrew *ś* would have corresponded phonologically to Hittite *š* (*GHL* 1:38). The realization may have been as a dental-alveolar [s], alveo-palatal [ʃ], or palatal [ç] (*GHL* 1:38). Presumably,

43. Arabic *ḫars* cannot be cognate with Hebrew *ḥereś* because the sibilants do not line up; Arabic *s* derives from Proto-Semitic **s* or **ṯ*, whereas Hebrew *ś* derives from **ɬ*. Consequently, if the forms are indeed related, the Arabic form can only be a loanword, but it is difficult to imagine that Arabic borrowed the word directly from Hebrew. Additionally, because the Punic forms appear in Latin transcription, we cannot know which sibilant is present in these terms. If the Punic terms are cognate with Hebrew *ḥereś*, the final sibilant can only derive from **ɬ* (Huehnergard 2002, 32; Hackett 2008, 87).

if the realization of Hittite *š* was [s], it would have entered Hebrew as *s* and, if Hittite *š* was pronounced as [ʃ], it would have entered Hebrew as *š*. If, however, Hittite *š* was realized as [ç] or something similar, it is possible that a Hittite loanword with this phoneme would have entered Hebrew as *ś*. However, neither the realization of Hittite *š* nor the possibility of it entering Hebrew as *ś* can be established with certainty. The evidence at hand does not allow us to decide conclusively whether there is a connection between Hittite *ḫarši* and Hebrew *ḥereś*.

Although ostraca were a very common form of communication in ancient Israel, no biblical passage mentions them in connection with writing. Nevertheless, it is plausible that the pieces of pottery that were used for epistolary purposes were referred to by the same Hebrew term that carries the meaning 'earthenware, potsherd'—namely, *ḥereś*.

The term *ḥereś* occurs twenty times in the Hebrew Bible. It also occurs at least four times in the Dead Sea Scrolls in reference to vessels of clay or to a brick of clay (4Q274 3ii10; 4Q276 3; 11Q19 XLIX, 8; L, 18; *DSSR* 1:318, 362, 682, 686; *DSSC* 1:278).[44] The word refers to a geographical location three times in the Bible (Isa 16:11; Jer 48:31, 36). Another twelve times, it is used to speak of vessels of clay (Lev 6:21; 11:33; 14:5, 50; 15:12; Num 5:17; Isa 45:9 [2x]; Jer 19:1; 32:14; Prov 26:23; Lam 4:2). For example, Lam 4:2 reads: בְּנֵי צִיּוֹן הַיְקָרִים הַמְסֻלָּאִים בַּפָּז אֵיכָה נֶחְשְׁבוּ לְנִבְלֵי־**חֶרֶשׂ** מַעֲשֵׂה יְדֵי יוֹצֵר 'The precious sons of Zion, whose weight is measured in gold, how they are regarded as pots of ***ḥereś***, a work of the hands of a potter'. In another five passages, the term refers to potsherds (Ps 22:16; Job 2:8; 41:22; Isa 30:14; Ezek 23:34). The plural form of the term is used in Ezek 23:34, where Judah is depicted as a woman scraping her breasts with potsherds. Similarly, the term *ḥereś* is used to speak of the potsherd that Job uses to scrape boils from his skin (Job 2:8). Job 2:8 reads: וַיִּקַּח־לוֹ **חֶרֶשׂ** לְהִתְגָּרֵד בּוֹ וְהוּא יֹשֵׁב בְּתוֹךְ־הָאֵפֶר 'He took for himself a ***ḥereś*** with which to scrape himself while he sat in the ashes'. In Isa 30:14, the term refers to a potsherd that is utilized to remove coals from a fire, and in Job 41:22, the term is compared to the scales of Leviathan, presumably because the scales are sharp like a potsherd.

This survey shows that the term *ḥereś* can designate both pottery vessels and potsherds. Moreover, the use of this term is not restricted to a specific book or genre within the biblical corpus. Rather, although the term occurs only seventeen times with the meaning 'earthenware, potsherd', it appears in the Torah, the Writings, and the Prophets. It is not unreasonable to conclude that *ḥereś* was a fairly common term in the ancient Hebrew lexicon. After all, *ḥereś* designates an item that was commonplace in ancient Israelite society—namely, a pottery vessel or a broken piece of earthenware. I tentatively suggest that, in ancient Israel,

44. Perhaps also in 5Q20 1, 1 (*DSSR* 2:1096; *DSSC* 1:278).

this term not only designated intact pottery vessels or broken potsherds, but also potsherds that were inscribed with writing and used as epistolary documents.

4.2.5.3. Translation of ḥereś *in the Septuagint*

The term *ḥereś* is translated with a number of Greek words in the Septuagint. When *ḥereś* refers to earthenware, it is usually translated with the term ὀστράκινος 'made of clay' (e.g., Lev 6:21; Jer 19:1; LSJ 1263; Muraoka 2009, 510). In one case, the word ὄστρακον 'earthen vessel, potsherd' is used to render *ḥereś* (Prov 26:23; LSJ 1264; Muraoka 2009, 510). In another verse (Isa 45:9), the Septuagint does not have semantically corresponding renderings of the two occurrences of *ḥereś*; according to Eusebius, however, Symmachus translates the words as ὄστρακον (Ziegler 1939, 292).[45] Similarly, in three of five cases in which *ḥereś* refers to a potsherd, the Septuagint renders the term as ὄστρακον (Isa 30:14; Ps 22:16 [21:16 LXX]; Job 2:8). In another two cases (Ezek 23:34; Job 41:22), the Septuagint seems to translate *ḥereś* with Greek terms unrelated to the meaning of *ḥereś*, although the hexaplaric revisions of the two passages render *ḥereś* as ὄστρακον.[46] When *ḥereś* appears as part of the geographical designation *qîr ḥāreś*, the Septuagint transliterates two such cases with Κιραδας 'Kir Hareseth' (Jer 48:31; 36 [31:31; 43 LXX]); another time the Septuagint seems to equate *qîr ḥāreś* with a form of the verb ἐγκαινίζω 'to restore, to inaugurate' (Isa 16:11; LSJ 469; Muraoka 2009, 186). For the passages in which *ḥereś* designates a geographical location, the hexaplaric revisions equate the word with ὄστρακον.[47] In general, the translations of *ḥereś* in the Septuagint are unsurprising; when *ḥereś* refers to earthenware or to potsherds, ὀστράκινος or ὄστρακον is usually used to render *ḥereś*.

45. In translating Isa 45:9, which uses *ḥereś* twice to denote earthenware, the Septuagint translators seem to equate *ḥereś* once with πηλός 'clay' (LSJ 1401; Muraoka 2009, 556); another time, they seem to have read *ḥereś* as deriving from the root *ḥ-r-š*, rendering it in Greek as the participial form of ἀροτριάω 'plower' (LSJ 245; Muraoka 2009, 92).

46. In the Septuagint's translation of Ezek 23:34, *ḥereś* seems to be equated with the plural form of ἑορτή 'festival' (LSJ 601; Muraoka 2009, 256). In Aquila's revision of the verse, *ḥereś* is translated as ὄστρακον 'earthen vessel, potsherd' (Ziegler 1952, 197–98). In the Septuagint's rendering of Job 41:22, *ḥaddûdê ḥāreś* 'sharp potsherds' is translated as the plural form of ὀβελίσκος 'small spit, nail' (LSJ 1196; Muraoka 2009, 484), which seems to reflect the sharp edges of a potsherd. However, in Aquila's version of the passage, ὄστρακον 'earthen vessel, potsherd' is used to render *ḥereś* (Ziegler 1982, 406).

47. The term *ḥereś* is equated with ὄστρακον 'earthen vessel, potsherd' in the revisions of Jer 48:31 (31:31 LXX) by Aquila and Symmachus (Ziegler 1957, 321) and in Theodotion's version of Jer 48:36 (31:36 LXX) (Ziegler 1957, 323); according to the Syro-Hexapla, this is also the case in the versions of Jer 48:36 (31:36 LXX) by Aquila and Symmachus (Ziegler 1957, 323). Similarly, according to Eusebius, Symmachus renders *ḥereś* as ὄστρακον in Isa 16:11 (Ziegler 1939, 183).

While the Bible refers to earthen vessels and potsherds by the term *ḥereś*, it does not preserve any record of writing on such potsherds. Nevertheless, the many finds of potsherds inscribed with ancient Hebrew writing confirm that ostraca were widely used in ancient Israel as a means of epistolary communication. The term *ḥereś* designates both intact vessels and pottery sherds. It probably also refers to an inscribed potsherd, although not to the epistolary document itself; terms such as *sēper* and *ʾiggeret* refer to the letters themselves.

4.2.6. Definitions of Terms Designating Scrolls, Tablets, and Ostraca

Having analyzed the ancient Hebrew words that designate scrolls, tablets, and ostraca, I suggest the following definitions for these terms.

***delet*:** A term that generally means 'door'. In Jer 36:23, however, it means 'column'. The semantic narrowing from 'door' to 'column' is rooted in the use of hinged diptych writing boards in the ancient Near East and in ancient Israel. The term probably also designates writing boards.

***gillāyôn*:** A term that perhaps means 'uncovering, disclosure, revelation' as well as 'blank scroll' (Isa 8:1). In Isa 3:23, the plural form *gilyônîm* may mean 'dresses' or 'mirrors'.

***ḥereś*:** A term that refers to intact pottery vessels as well as sherds. Regarding inscribed ostraca in ancient Israel, the term *ḥereś* probably refers only to the material that was inscribed with writing, and not to the potsherd as an epistolary document (i.e., it does not mean 'ostracon').

***lûaḥ*:** A term that carries the meaning 'tablet, board, plank'. In the context of writing technology, it designates tablets, whether of stone, wood, or another material.

***məgillā*:** A Late Biblical Hebrew word that designates a scroll made of papyrus or leather. The term is a loanword from Aramaic, and it supplanted the older Standard Biblical Hebrew term *sēper*, which was used to designate all types of writing, including scrolls. The phrase *məgillat sēper* is a stylistic variant of *məgillā* but carries the same meaning: 'scroll'.

***ʿôr*:** A term that refers to animal skins used for various purposes; it may also designate vellum employed as writing material.

4.3. Uncommon Writing Surfaces

In the above discussion, we considered a number of different surfaces used for writing purposes in ancient Israel. Here, we will evaluate a few biblical passages that describe writing on uncommon surfaces such as a staff (Num 17:16–26), staff-like wooden sticks (Ezek 37:15–20), and golden rosettes (Exod 28:36–38).

4.3.1. Writing on a Staff, maṭṭe (Numbers 17:16–26)

4.3.1.1. Etymology and Biblical Usage

The term *maṭṭe* 'tribe, staff' derives from the root *n-ṭ-y* 'stretch out, extend' (GMD 663; *DCH* 5:235–37; *HALOT* 1:573).[48] The word belongs to the *maqtil* pattern, which is the common pattern for nouns of instrument (Lambdin and Huehnergard 2000, 47). Ugaritic *mṭ* and *mṭh* of Deir ʿAlla are perhaps cognate with the Hebrew form (*DULAT* 2:602; *DNWSI* 2:617). Within the Hebrew Bible, *maṭṭe* occurs a total of 252 times. Of this number, there are 68 cases in which the term refers specifically to a staff (e.g., Gen 38:18; Ex 4:2; 1 Sam 14:27) or rod-like object (e.g., Ezek 4:16; 19:12; Hab 3:9).[49] The term also occurs over 25 times in the Dead Sea Scrolls with the meaning 'tribe' (e.g., CD X, 5; 11Q19 XIX, 14–15; *DSSR* 1:96, 659; *DSSC* 1:442), and four times in Ben Sira (32, 23; 45, 6, 25; 48, 2). The term can also refer figuratively to the power of a ruler or kingdom (e.g., Isa 14:5; Ezek 7:11; Ps 110:2).

In Num 17:16–26, *maṭṭe* refers to a staff. This passage contains a colorful account that portrays the choice of Aaron over Korah as YHWH's legitimate priest. A *maṭṭe* was requested from the head of each Israelite tribe, and each staff was inscribed with one of the names of the tribal heads. An additional staff was added for the Levites, and Aaron's name was written upon this one (Levine 2000, 421–22). The staves were then placed into the tent of testimony. The following day, Moses discovered that Aaron's staff had budded, blossomed, and produced ripe almonds, signifying the choice of Aaron as YHWH's priest. The passage reads:

וַיְדַבֵּ֣ר יְהוָ֔ה אֶל־מֹשֶׁ֖ה לֵּאמֹֽר׃ דַּבֵּ֣ר ׀ אֶל־בְּנֵ֣י יִשְׂרָאֵ֗ל וְקַ֣ח מֵֽאִתָּ֡ם **מַטֶּ֣ה מַטֶּה֩** לְבֵ֨ית אָ֜ב מֵאֵ֣ת כָּל־נְשִׂיאֵהֶ֗ם לְבֵ֤ית אֲבֹתָם֙ שְׁנֵ֣ים עָשָׂ֣ר **מַטֹּ֑ות** אִ֗ישׁ אֶת־שְׁמ֙וֹ תִּכְתֹּ֖ב עַל־**מַטֵּֽהוּ**׃ וְאֵת֙ שֵׁ֣ם אַהֲרֹ֔ן תִּכְתֹּ֖ב עַל־**מַטֵּ֣ה** לֵוִ֑י כִּ֚י מַטֶּ֣ה אֶחָ֔ד לְרֹ֖אשׁ בֵּ֣ית אֲבוֹתָ֑ם׃ וְהִנַּחְתָּ֣ם בְּאֹ֣הֶל מוֹעֵ֔ד לִפְנֵי֙ הָ֣עֵד֔וּת אֲשֶׁ֧ר

---

48. Because *maṭṭe* can be explained as deriving from a Semitic root, it seems best to view the term as native to Hebrew rather than a loanword deriving from Egyptian *mdw* (Muchiki 1999, 249).

49. Sixty-eight times *maṭṭe* refers to a staff or rod-like object: Gen 38:18, 25; Exod 4:2, 4, 17, 20; 7:9–10, 12 (3x), 15, 17, 19–20; 8:1, 12–13; 9:23; 10:13; 14:16; 17:5, 9; Lev 26:26; Num 17:17–18 (6x), 20–25 (11x); 20:8–9, 11; 1 Sam 14:27, 43; Isa 9:3; 10:5, 15, 24, 26; 14:5; 28:27; 30:32; Jer 48:17; Ezek 4:16; 5:16; 7:10–11; 14:13; 19:11–12, 14 (2x); Mic 6:9; Hab 3:14; Pss 105:16; 110:2. In this list are included the five occurrences of the phrase *maṭṭe leḥem* 'staff of bread', which perhaps designated the rod upon which bread was hung (Lev 26:26; Ezek 4:16; 5:16; 14:13; Ps 105:16; *HALOT* 1:573). In the remaining 184 cases, *maṭṭe* means 'tribe' (e.g., Lev 24:11).

אִוָּעֵד לָכֶם שָׁמָּה׃ וְהָיָה הָאִישׁ אֲשֶׁר אֶבְחַר־בּוֹ **מַטֵּהוּ** יִפְרָח וַהֲשִׁכֹּתִי מֵעָלַי אֶת־תְּלֻנּוֹת בְּנֵי
יִשְׂרָאֵל אֲשֶׁר הֵם מַלִּינִם עֲלֵיכֶם׃ וַיְדַבֵּר מֹשֶׁה אֶל־בְּנֵי יִשְׂרָאֵל וַיִּתְּנוּ אֵלָיו ׀ כָּל־נְשִׂיאֵיהֶם **מַטֶּה**
לְנָשִׂיא אֶחָד **מַטֶּה** לְנָשִׂיא אֶחָד לְבֵית אֲבֹתָם שְׁנֵים עָשָׂר **מַטּוֹת וּמַטֵּה** אַהֲרֹן בְּתוֹךְ **מַטּוֹתָם**׃ וַיַּנַּח
מֹשֶׁה **אֶת־הַמַּטֹּת** לִפְנֵי יְהוָה בְּאֹהֶל הָעֵדֻת׃ וַיְהִי מִמָּחֳרָת וַיָּבֹא מֹשֶׁה אֶל־אֹהֶל הָעֵדוּת וְהִנֵּה פָּרַח
מַטֵּה־אַהֲרֹן לְבֵית לֵוִי וַיֹּצֵא פֶרַח וַיָּצֵץ צִיץ וַיִּגְמֹל שְׁקֵדִים׃ וַיֹּצֵא מֹשֶׁה אֶת־כָּל־**הַמַּטֹּת** מִלִּפְנֵי
יְהוָה אֶל־כָּל־בְּנֵי יִשְׂרָאֵל וַיִּרְאוּ וַיִּקְחוּ אִישׁ **מַטֵּהוּ**׃
וַיֹּאמֶר יְהוָה אֶל־מֹשֶׁה הָשֵׁב אֶת־**מַטֵּה** אַהֲרֹן לִפְנֵי הָעֵדוּת לְמִשְׁמֶרֶת לְאוֹת לִבְנֵי־מֶרִי וּתְכַל
תְּלוּנֹּתָם מֵעָלַי וְלֹא יָמֻתוּ׃ וַיַּעַשׂ מֹשֶׁה כַּאֲשֶׁר צִוָּה יְהוָה אֹתוֹ כֵּן עָשָׂה׃

YHWH spoke to Moses, saying, "Speak to the Israelites and take from them ***maṭṭe maṭṭe***, one for each father's house from all their leaders according to their fathers' houses, twelve ***maṭṭôt***. Write the name of each man on ***maṭṭēhû***. Write the name of Aaron on the ***maṭṭe*** of Levi, for there is one ***maṭṭe*** for the head of their fathers' house. You shall place them in the tent of meeting before the testimony where I meet you. The person whom I choose, ***maṭṭēhû*** will sprout. I will cause to cease from before me the grievances of the Israelites that they make against you."

Moses spoke to the Israelites, and all of their leaders gave him a ***maṭṭe*** for each leader, a ***maṭṭe*** for each leader according to their fathers' house, twelve ***maṭṭôt***; and the ***maṭṭe*** of Aaron was among ***maṭṭôtām***. Moses placed the ***maṭṭôt*** before YHWH in the tent of meeting.

On the next day, Moses entered into the tent of the testimony, and the ***maṭṭe*** of Aaron according to the house of Levi had budded, put forth flowers, produced blossoms, and bore almonds. So, Moses brought out all of the ***maṭṭôt*** from before YHWH to all of the Israelites, and they saw, and each man took ***maṭṭēhû***.

God said to Moses, "Put back the ***maṭṭe*** of Aaron before the testimony to be kept as a sign for the rebels, that you may make an end of their grievances before me so they do not die." Moses did (this); just as YHWH commanded him, so he did.

While this passage certainly contains colorful elements, the references to the inscribing of staves appear to denote an actual ancient Near Eastern writing practice.

4.3.1.2. The Septuagint's Translation of maṭṭe *in Numbers 17:16–26*

In the majority of cases (about 170; e.g., Exod 31:6), the Septuagint renders *maṭṭe* as φυλή 'tribe' (LSJ 1562, 1961; Muraoka 2009, 723). All occurrences of *maṭṭe* in Num 17:16–26, however, are rendered as ῥάβδος 'stick, rod' (LSJ 1562,

1961; Muraoka 2009, 611). Indeed, there are over fifty cases in which the Septuagint renders *maṭṭe* as ῥάβδος.[50] Needless to say, it seems that the translators of the Septuagint understood *maṭṭe* of Num 17 to designate a staff.

4.3.1.3. Inscribed Staves from Egypt

Eleven wooden staves, each about 5 feet long, dating to the period of Thutmose III (1479–1425 BCE) were found in burial chambers in Thebes. Two of these staves are inscribed with the owners' names (Hayes 1990, 118, 215). Staves and scepters were common in the ancient Near East. Initially, they were used by shepherds and later adopted as divine and royal symbols of authority (Hayes 1968, 286; Wiggerman 1985–86, 15; Fischer 1978, 21–25).[51] Indeed, it is very clear in Num 17:16–26 that the staff represents authority.

The staff used by a shepherd in ancient Israel was presumably made of wood, but this is not stated in any of the biblical passages listed above.[52] If Num 17:16–26 indeed refers to wooden staves, the writing described in this passage would have been accomplished by incising the wood with a metal tool. As we shall see shortly, incising writing in wooden sticks was commonplace in ancient South Arabia.[53] The etching of names on wood as depicted in this passage can thus be understood in light of evidence for this practice in the ancient world.

4.3.2. Writing on a Wooden Stick, ʿēṣ *(Ezekiel 37:15–20)*

4.3.2.1. Etymology and Biblical Usage

The term *ʿēṣ* 'wood, tree' (GMD 998; *DCH* 6:519–25; *HALOT* 1:863–64), which derives from Proto-Semitic **ʿiṣ́-* (Huehnergard 2008, 211), has cognates in languages including Akkadian (*iṣum*; *CAD* 7:214–19), Aramaic (ʾʿ; *CAL*), and

50. The Septuagint also renders *maṭṭe* as στήριγμα 'support' (5x; Ps 105:16 [104:16 LXX]; Ezek 4:16; 5:16; 7:11; 14:13; LSJ 1644; Muraoka 2009, 636), σκῆπτρον 'staff, scepter' (3x; 1 Sam 14:27, 43; Hab 3:9; LSJ 1609; Muraoka 2009, 264), βακτηρία 'staff, cane' (1x; Jer 31:17 [38:17 LXX]; LSJ 303; Muraoka 2009, 111), and ζυγός 'crossbar, yoke' (1x; Isa 14:5; LSJ 757; Muraoka 2009, 315). In a few cases, *maṭṭe* does not have a corresponding word in the Septuagint (Muraoka 2010, 252).

51. Scepters and shepherd staves were associated with rulership because the king was viewed as the ruler who shepherded his people (Wiggerman 1985–86, 15; Fischer 1978, 21–25). Many depictions of gods and kings holding scepters, maces, and hooked staves have survived from the ancient Near East (Wiggerman 1985–86; Ambos and Krauskopf 2010). At least six full ceremonial staves have been found in ancient Egyptian tombs in el-Lisht from the early Twelfth Dynasty (1994–1781 BCE). These rods are made of wood and measure between 4.5 and 5 feet in length. Some of the staves have a hooked top and forked ending to prevent the staves from sinking into the ground (Hayes 1968, 285).

52. In Hos 4:12, *ʿēṣ* 'wood, tree' stands in parallel with *maqqēl* 'rod, staff', which suggests that in ancient Israel staves were indeed made of wood.

53. See 4.3.2.3 and Figure 4.7.

Ethiopic (*ʿəḍ*; *CDG* 57). In the Bible, *ʿēṣ*/*ʿēṣîm* appears a total of 330 times. The word also occurs around 60 times in the Dead Sea Scrolls (e.g., CD XI, 19; 11Q19 LXIV, 8; 1QH[a] XVI, 6; *DSSR* 1:100, 706; 2:312; *DSSC* 2:589) and 6 times in Ben Sira (6, 3; 8, 3; 14, 18; 27, 6; 38, 5; 50, 10). The word can refer to a tree (e.g., Gen 1:11; 1:29), a specific type of tree or wood (e.g., Gen 6:14; Exod 25:5; Lev 14:4), wood of which a cart is made (e.g., 1 Sam 6:14), timber in a house (e.g., Zech 5:4; Hab 2:11), a wooden handle (e.g., Deut 19:5; 2 Sam 21:19), and firewood (e.g., Gen 22:3). In several instances, *ʿēṣ*/*ʿēṣîm* refers to wooden sticks or branches (e.g., 1 Kgs 17:10; 2 Kgs 6:6).

In 1 Sam 6:14, *ʿēṣ*/*ʿēṣîm* refers to the wood of which a cart is made: וְהָעֲגָלָה בָּאָה אֶל־שְׂדֵה יְהוֹשֻׁעַ בֵּית־הַשִּׁמְשִׁי וַתַּעֲמֹד שָׁם וְשָׁם אֶבֶן גְּדוֹלָה וַיְבַקְּעוּ אֶת־**עֲצֵי הָעֲגָלָה** וְאֶת־הַפָּרוֹת הֶעֱלוּ עֹלָה לַיהוָה ‘The cart came into the field of Joshua of Beth-Shemesh and it stood there. There was a large stone there, so they split up the ***ʿăṣê hāʿăgālā*** [‘wood of the cart’] and offered up the cows as an offering to YHWH’. In 1 Kgs 17:10, *ʿēṣ*/*ʿēṣîm* refers to wooden sticks: וַיָּקָם ׀ וַיֵּלֶךְ צָרְפַתָה וַיָּבֹא אֶל־פֶּתַח הָעִיר וְהִנֵּה־שָׁם אִשָּׁה אַלְמָנָה מְקֹשֶׁשֶׁת **עֵצִים** וַיִּקְרָא אֵלֶיהָ וַיֹּאמַר קְחִי־נָא לִי מְעַט־מַיִם בַּכְּלִי וְאֶשְׁתֶּה ‘He arose and went to Zarephath, and he came to the gate of the city and there was a widow gathering ***ʿēṣîm***. He called to her and said, “Get me a little water in a vessel that I may drink”’.

In Ezek 37:15–20, as in 1 Kgs 17:10, *ʿēṣ*/*ʿēṣîm* seems to designate wooden sticks or branches. The passage reads:

> וַיְהִי דְבַר־יְהוָה אֵלַי לֵאמֹר׃ וְאַתָּה בֶן־אָדָם קַח־לְךָ **עֵץ** אֶחָד וּכְתֹב עָלָיו לִיהוּדָה וְלִבְנֵי יִשְׂרָאֵל חברו חֲבֵרָיו וּלְקַח **עֵץ** אֶחָד וּכְתוֹב עָלָיו לְיוֹסֵף **עֵץ** אֶפְרַיִם וְכָל־בֵּית יִשְׂרָאֵל חברו חֲבֵרָיו׃ וְקָרַב אֹתָם אֶחָד אֶל־אֶחָד לְךָ לְ**עֵץ** אֶחָד וְהָיוּ לַאֲחָדִים בְּיָדֶךָ׃ וְכַאֲשֶׁר יֹאמְרוּ אֵלֶיךָ בְּנֵי עַמְּךָ לֵאמֹר הֲלוֹא־תַגִּיד לָנוּ מָה־אֵלֶּה לָּךְ׃ דַּבֵּר אֲלֵהֶם כֹּה־אָמַר אֲדֹנָי יְהוִה הִנֵּה אֲנִי לֹקֵחַ אֶת־**עֵץ** יוֹסֵף אֲשֶׁר בְּיַד־אֶפְרַיִם וְשִׁבְטֵי יִשְׂרָאֵל חברו חֲבֵרָיו וְנָתַתִּי אוֹתָם עָלָיו אֶת־**עֵץ** יְהוּדָה וַעֲשִׂיתִם לְ**עֵץ** אֶחָד וְהָיוּ אֶחָד בְּיָדִי׃ וְהָיוּ **הָעֵצִים** אֲשֶׁר־תִּכְתֹּב עֲלֵיהֶם בְּיָדְךָ לְעֵינֵיהֶם׃

> The word of YHWH came to me, “You, son of man, take for yourself one ***ʿēṣ*** and write on it, ‘For Judah and for the sons of Israel, his companions’; and take one ***ʿēṣ*** and write on it, ‘For Joseph, the ***ʿēṣ*** of Ephraim and (for) all the house of Israel, his companions’. Bring them near each other for yourself into one ***ʿēṣ*** and they shall become one in your hand. When your people speak to you, saying, ‘Will you not tell us what are these (things) that you have?’ say to them, ‘Thus says the Lord, YHWH, I am taking the ***ʿēṣ*** of Joseph—which is in the hand of Ephraim—and (of) the tribes of Israel, his companions; I will set them on it, (on) the ***ʿēṣ*** of Judah, and I will make them into one ***ʿēṣ***, and they will become one in my hand’. The ***ʿēṣîm*** upon which you shall write will be in your hand before their eyes.”

This passage depicts Ezekiel handling staff-like sticks that probably represent royal scepters.[54] The merging of the two sticks symbolizes the reunification of the two kingdoms of Israel, Judah and Samaria.

4.3.2.2. Translation of ʿēṣ/ʿēṣîm *in the Septuagint*

In the Septuagint, *ʿēṣ*/*ʿēṣîm* is predominantly translated with ξύλον 'wood, tree' or a form of this word (LSJ 1191–92; Muraoka 2009, 481).[55] In fifteen cases, *ʿēṣ*/*ʿēṣîm* is translated as δένδρον 'tree' (e.g., Gen 18:4; Prov 11:30; LSJ 378; Muraoka 2009, 142). Another four times (1 Kgs 18:33–34 [3x], 38), *ʿēṣ*/*ʿēṣîm* is translated as σχίδαξ 'cut wood' (LSJ 1746; Muraoka 2009, 666). The Septuagint renders *ʿēṣ*/*ʿēṣîm* in Ezek 37:15–20 six times as ῥάβδος 'stick, rod' (37:16–17, 19–20; LSJ 1562; Muraoka 2009, 611), which suggests that *ʿēṣ*/*ʿēṣîm* could refer to a staff or stick that could be used as a staff.[56] Similarly, in Hos 4:12, *ʿēṣ* stands in parallel with *maqqēl* 'rod, staff', which also suggests that *ʿēṣ* may carry the meaning 'rod, staff' in addition to the more common meaning 'stick, branch'.[57]

4.3.2.3. Stick, Staff, or Writing Board?

Some have suggested that *ʿēṣ*/*ʿēṣîm* in Ezek 37:15–20 refers to a wooden tablet (Hyatt 1943, 75; Driver 1976, 80 n. 3; King and Stager 2001, 308). Although this interpretation is possible, it seems unlikely. There are a few reasons to believe that *ʿēṣ*/*ʿēṣîm* in this passage simply refers to sticks. First, the events of the passage are set in a valley, so it is likely that the text is depicting Ezekiel as lifting sticks or branches from the ground. Second, one does not have to manipulate

54. See 4.3.1.3 for a discussion of the royal symbolism of scepters and staves.

55. Of the 330 occurrences of *ʿēṣ*/*ʿēṣîm*, the Septuagint translates 270 of them with the word ξύλον 'wood, tree' (e.g., Gen 1:11; 1 Kgs 17:10).

56. While six cases of *ʿēṣ* in Ezek 37:15–20 are rendered as ῥάβδος 'stick, rod', two cases (37:19) appear to be rendered as φυλή 'tribe' (LSJ 1562, 1961; Muraoka 2009, 723). It is possible that in these two cases the Septuagint is superimposing the meaning of the Hebrew terms *šebeṭ* and *maṭṭe*—both of which mean 'staff' and 'tribe'—upon the term *ʿēṣ*/*ʿēṣîm*. Indeed, the terms *šebeṭ* and *maṭṭe* are rendered in the Septuagint as ῥάβδος (e.g., Ps 23:4 [22:4 LXX]; Num 17:17), while in other cases they are translated as φυλή (e.g., Exod 24:4; Num 18:2), so the Septuagint may have understood *ʿēṣ*/*ʿēṣîm* in Ezek 37:15–20 as carrying this dual meaning, too. Alternatively, the Septuagint's use of φυλή in these two cases may reflect a Hebrew *Vorlage* that actually had *šebeṭ* in this passage instead of *ʿēṣ*. In translating Ezek 37:15–20, Targum Onkelos renders *ʿēṣ*/*ʿēṣîm* as *lwḥ*ʾ 'tablet' (*CAL*). Greenberg (1997, 753; see also *CAL*) suggests that the Targum's translation of *ʿēṣ*/*ʿēṣîm* as *lwḥ*ʾ may have arisen by influence from Isa 8:1. In this passage, Isaiah is commanded to take a *gillāyôn*—which is rendered in Targum Onkelos as *lwḥ*ʾ—and write upon it.

57. In translating Hos 4:12, however, the Septuagint uses σύμβολον 'sign, seal', not ῥάβδος 'stick, rod', to render *ʿēṣ*/*ʿēṣîm* (LSJ 1676; Muraoka 2009, 646), apparently connecting the Hebrew lexeme with *ʿēṣā* 'counsel'. On the other hand, according to the Syro-Hexapla, the revisions of this passage by Aquila and Symmachus has ξύλον 'wood, tree' (Ziegler 1943, 155).

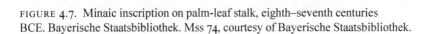

FIGURE 4.7. Minaic inscription on palm-leaf stalk, eighth–seventh centuries BCE. Bayerische Staatsbibliothek. Mss 74, courtesy of Bayerische Staatsbibliothek.

the passage for *ʿēṣ*/*ʿēṣîm* to mean 'stick, branch'. Rather, as mentioned above, *ʿēṣ*/*ʿēṣîm* carries the meaning 'stick, branch' in various passages in the Bible, so it is most natural to understand the word in this passage as also carrying this meaning. Third, if a writing board were meant, we would expect the term *lûaḥ* 'tablet' to be used. Finally, the translators of the Septuagint understood *ʿēṣ*/*ʿēṣîm* in this passage as referring to some type of stick or rod. If a wooden tablet were intended, the Septuagint would have rendered *ʿēṣ*/*ʿēṣîm* with the word πυξίον 'tablet of box-wood', because this is the term used to translate *lûaḥ*/*lûḥôt* in Isa 30:8 and Hab 2:2, which may indeed refer to writing boards. Consequently, it is best to understand *ʿēṣ*/*ʿēṣîm* in Ezek 37:15–20 as speaking of wooden sticks.

Writing on wooden sticks is attested from the ancient world, especially from ancient South Arabia (modern day northern Yemen).[58] There are about seven thousand inscriptions, known as minuscule inscriptions, that appear on wooden sticks and are written in Old South Arabian. Dating from the end of the tenth century BCE through the fifth century CE, the minuscule inscriptions consist of writing carved on sticks and palm leaf stocks that are about 4–8 inches in length; these inscriptions consist of letters, legal documents, name lists, writing exercises, and records from religious practices (Drewes and Ryckmans 2016; Drewes et al. 2013, 201; Stein 2005, 183–84). Stein (2005, 184) contends that such wooden pieces would have been the most common form of communication in ancient South Arabia due to the affordability and availability of such material. The process of writing on a stick as depicted in Ezek 37:15–20 may be comparable to the practice of engraving sticks with writing as was done in ancient South Arabia. This process involved etching words on a wooden stick with a metal tool or a stone point that was suitable for incising wood (see figure 4.7).[59] We should note, however, that the writing depicted in Ezek 37 is comparable to the minuscule inscriptions only in regard to the process of carving words on a wooden stick. In content and length, the writing in Ezek 37 is quite different from the minuscules. The former consists of a couple names, whereas the latter involve lengthier texts.

58. Such inscriptions appear in Sabaic, Minaic, Amirite dialect, and Ḥaḍramitic (Stein 2005, 184).

59. It is noteworthy that there was commercial contact between ancient Israel and ancient South Arabia. This is confirmed by a South Arabian inscription that mentions a trade expedition headed for Gaza, "towns of Judah," and Kition; the inscription dates to about 600 BCE (Bron and Lemaire 2009). It is possible that scribal practices were exchanged during these expeditions as well as goods.

In sum, *ʿēṣ*/*ʿēṣîm* is a common term designating trees, wood, and sticks. Contrary to some suggestions, *ʿēṣ*/*ʿēṣîm* probably does not mean 'writing board' in Ezek 37:15–20, but to rods or sticks that resemble royal scepters.

4.3.3. Writing on a Rosette of Pure Gold, **ṣîṣ zāhāb ṭāhôr** *(Exodus 28:36–38; 39:30–31)*

4.3.3.1. Etymology and Biblical Usage

Three passages speak of a *ṣîṣ zāhāb* 'golden rosette' on the headdress of the high priest. In Lev 8:9, *ṣîṣ zāhāb* is mentioned without an explicit reference to engraved words, but two passages in Exodus contain commands to engrave a *ṣîṣ zāhāb ṭāhôr* 'rosette of pure gold' with the words *qōdeš ləYHWH* 'holy to YHWH' (Exod 28:36–38; 39:30–31). For instance, Exodus 28:36–38 reads: וְעָשִׂ֥יתָ **צִּ֖יץ זָהָ֣ב טָה֑וֹר** וּפִתַּחְתָּ֤ עָלָיו֙ פִּתּוּחֵ֣י חֹתָ֔ם קֹ֖דֶשׁ לַיהוָֽה׃ וְשַׂמְתָּ֤ אֹתוֹ֙ עַל־פְּתִ֣יל תְּכֵ֔לֶת וְהָיָ֖ה עַל־הַמִּצְנָ֑פֶת אֶל־מ֥וּל פְּנֵֽי־הַמִּצְנֶ֖פֶת יִהְיֶֽה׃ וְהָיָה֮ עַל־מֵ֣צַח אַהֲרֹן֒ 'You shall make a ***ṣîṣ zāhāb ṭāhôr***. You shall engrave upon it (like) an engraving of a signet seal, "Holy to YHWH." You shall attach it to a blue cord on the turban. It shall be on the front of the turban. It shall be on Aaron's forehead'. It is not entirely apparent whether the text is prescribing the engraving to appear on the rosette itself or, as Propp (2006, 447) suggests, on a plaque above or below the rosette.

Another fourteen times the term *ṣîṣ* refers to a flower, either to an actual flower of the field (Num 17:23; Isa 28:1; 40:6–8; Ps 103:15; Job 14:2) or to a rosette carved in wood or metal (Exod 28:36; 39:30; Lev 8:9; 1 Kgs 6:18, 29, 32, 35). The word also occurs probably four times with these meanings in the Dead Sea Scrolls, including one case with an uncertain *tsade* (4Q372 12, 2; 4Q185 1–2i10–11 [2x]; 1QH^{a} XIV, 18; *DSSR* 1:1076; 2:242, 306; *DSSC* 2:637); in Ben Sira, *ṣîṣ* occurs three times in addition to one occurrence of the verbal root *ṣ-w-ṣ* (40, 4; 43, 19; 45, 12). While the lexeme *ṣîṣ* is connected to the verbal root *ṣ-w-ṣ* 'to blossom', the etymology of the root is not clear (GMD 1109–10, 1116; *DCH* 7:105, 118; *HALOT* 2:1013, 1023).

4.3.3.2. Translation of ṣîṣ *in the Septuagint*

When *ṣîṣ* refers to an actual flower (Num 17:23; Isa 28:1; 40:6–7; Ps 103:15 [102:15 LXX]; Job 14:2), it is rendered in the Septuagint as ἄνθος 'flower' (LSJ 140; Muraoka 2009, 51–52). When it refers to a metal rosette (Exod 28:36; 39:30 [36:37 LXX]; Lev 8:9; 1 Kgs 6:32, 35), it is rendered as πέταλον 'leaf of metal' (LSJ 1396; Muraoka 2009, 555).[60] In some cases, the Septuagint does not have a

60. In a variant reading of Lev 8:9, *ṣîṣ* is rendered as στέφανος 'crown' (LSJ 1642; Muraoka 2009, 636).

corresponding word for *ṣîṣ*. In Exod 28:36 and 39:30 (36:37 LXX), which specify that the *ṣîṣ* is made of pure gold, the Septuagint translates the words *zāhāb* and *ṭāhôr* as χρυσοῦς 'golden' (LSJ 2009; Muraoka 2009, 738) and καθαρός 'pure' (LSJ 850; Muraoka 2009, 348); χρυσοῦς is also used in the Septuagint's translation of *zāhāb* in Lev 8:9, but καθαρός does not appear in the translation because *ṭāhôr* is absent in the Hebrew text of this verse. In short, the Septuagint's rendering of *ṣîṣ* as πέταλον 'leaf of metal' in Exod 28:36; 39:30 (36:37 LXX); and Lev 8:9 suggests that the Greek translators understood the word as referring to a golden leaf or plaque.

4.3.3.3. Writing on Metal

The Ketef Hinnom inscriptions are relevant for our discussion of the engraving of a *ṣîṣ zāhāb ṭāhôr*. Discovered in the burial caves of Ketef Hinnom in Jerusalem, these inscriptions consist of two small rolled silver plaques with text very similar to the priestly benediction (Num 6:24–26) etched upon them. One plaque is about 1 inch wide and 4 inches long and the other is about 0.25 inches wide and 1.5 inches long (Barkay 1992, 149–50). The plaques date to the seventh through fifth centuries BCE (Barkay et al. 2004, 46; Na'aman 2011, 188). Three inscribed golden plates were also found at Pyrgi. The plates, which date to about 500 BCE, are around 3.5 inches in width and 7.5 inches in length. Two of the plates are Etruscan inscriptions, and one is a Phoenician inscription (Fitzmyer 1966, 285–86; Heurgon 1966, 6).[61] The process of engraving the Ketef Hinnom inscriptions and the Pyrgi plates involved a tool with a hard point that would have been used to etch words upon the metal surfaces. The author of the Exodus passages discussed here probably had in mind a similar process when depicting the engraving of the *ṣîṣ zāhāb ṭāhôr*.

Given that the engraving of words upon metal is attested in the ancient world, it is no surprise that the Bible makes reference to such texts. While the Bible only refers to the incising of words on a golden rosette, the process of engraving writing on other metal surfaces was certainly practiced in ancient Israel, as is attested by the Ketef Hinnom finds and the Copper Scrolls.

61. In discussing writing on metal in ancient Israel, I should also mention the Copper Scrolls from the Dead Sea Scrolls archive. Discovered in Qumran cave 3, these two copper scrolls are about 8 feet long and 11 inches wide, and they are engraved with writing in Hebrew (Baker 1962, 203). They date between the third century BCE and 73 CE (King and Stager 2001, 305).

CHAPTER 5

Scribal Instruments and Glyptics

IN PREVIOUS CHAPTERS, I CONSIDERED LEXEMES that designate writing surfaces such as papyrus and stone. In this chapter, I will evaluate terms referring to scribal writing utensils such as pens and palettes as well as terms referring to engraved seals and weights.

5.1. Writing Instruments

5.1.1. The Term ʿēṭ *(*ʿēṭ barzel, ʿēṭ sōpēr/sōpərîm*)*

5.1.1.1. Etymology and Biblical Usage

The etymology of *ʿēṭ* 'writing instrument' is unclear.[1] The noun pattern of *ʿēṭ* is either *qil* (*ʿēṭ* < **ʿiṭ-*) or *qitl* (*ʿēṭ* < **ʿiṭṭ-*) (Lambdin and Huehnergard 2000, 12, 30–31, 33–34). The Arabic verb *ġāṭa* 'to dig' (< *ġ-w-ṭ*) and the lexemes *ġāṭ*, *ġiyāṭ*, *ġauṭ* 'hollow, cavity' may be related (Lane 1968, 6:2309; Wehr 1976, 688; Jenner 2011a, 2).

In the Bible, *ʿēṭ* occurs four times (Jer 8:8; 17:1; Ps 45:2; Job 19:24) and probably carries the general meaning 'pen, writing instrument' (Driver 1976, 84–86). When modified by *barzel* 'iron', *ʿēṭ* refers to an engraving pen (Jer 17:1; Job 19:24); and when modified by *sōpēr/sōpərîm* 'scribe(s)', *ʿēṭ* probably refers to a rush pen as well as a reed pen (Jer 8:8; Ps 45:2) (Lundbom 1999, 514; Haran 1980–81, 83–84). The lexeme *ʿēṭ* occurs once as a quotation of Ps 45:2 in 4QPsalms Pesher[a] (4Q171 1–10iv26; *DSSR* 1:466; *DSSC* 2:559).

1. The lexeme *ʿēṭ* is usually glossed as 'stylus' (GMD 950; *DCH* 6:349; *HALOT* 1:813), but perhaps a more accurate gloss is 'writing instrument', because *ʿēṭ* can refer to a reed or rush pen as well as an engraving tool.

5.1.1.2. Iron Pen, ʿēṭ barzel *(Jeremiah 17:1; Job 19:24)*

The phrase *ʿēṭ barzel* occurs in two passages. Jeremiah 17:1 reads: חַטַּאת יְהוּדָה כְּתוּבָה **בְּעֵט בַּרְזֶל בְּצִפֹּרֶן שָׁמִיר** חֲרוּשָׁה עַל־לוּחַ לִבָּם וּלְקַרְנוֹת מִזְבְּחוֹתֵיכֶם ‘The sin of Judah is written with an ***ʿēṭ barzel***, with a ***ṣippōren šāmîr***; it is incised on the tablet of their heart and on the horns of their altars’. Also, Job 19:24 reads: מִי־יִתֵּן אֵפוֹ וְיִכָּתְבוּן מִלָּי מִי־יֻתַּן בַּסֵּפֶר וְיֻחָקוּ׃ **בְּעֵט־בַּרְזֶל וְעֹפֶרֶת** לָעַד בַּצּוּר יֵחָצְבוּן ‘Oh that my words were written down, oh that they were inscribed in a document. With an ***ʿēṭ barzel wəʿōpāret*** (‘pen of iron and lead’), may they be engraved forever in stone’. There is no doubt that, in both passages, *ʿēṭ* refers to a writing instrument used to engrave hard surfaces. This is initially clear because the verbal roots that accompany it connote a process of engraving: *ʿēṭ* appears alongside the word *ḥărûšā* ‘incised’ in Jer 17:1 and stands in relation with the verb *yēḥāṣəbûn* ‘be engraved’ in Job 19:24. Furthermore, both passages use *ʿēṭ* in reference to the engraving of stone surfaces, a horned altar in the former passage and an unidentified stone surface in the latter. Finally, in both passages, *ʿēṭ* is modified by the term *barzel* ‘iron’, which again points to the use of this tool for engraving.[2] Additionally, in Jer 17:1, *ʿēṭ barzel* stands in parallel with *ṣippōren šāmîr* ‘point of the hardest stone’, which may refer to the tip of an *ʿēṭ barzel* (King and Stager 2001, 305, 340).[3] In sum, according to these two passages, an *ʿēṭ barzel* was made of iron, perhaps with a hard tip, and was used to engrave writing on rock surfaces.

We may surmise that an *ʿēṭ barzel* was used to engrave nonmonumental inscriptions on stone surfaces as well as inscriptions on metal, ostraca, and other hard surfaces. The Gezer calendar (Aḥituv 2008, 252), a limestone tablet, would have been incised with an *ʿēṭ barzel*. This pen would also have been used to engrave bronze and stone weights and measures (Aḥituv 2008, 243–48, 333, 349–50), signet seals (Hestrin and Dayagi-Mendels 1979), and gemstones, as described in Exod 28:9–12, 17–21. Inscriptions on metal—such as those from Ketef Hinnom (Barkay 1992; Barkay et al. 2004), the Tell Sīrân bottle inscription (Aḥituv 2008, 363), or golden rosettes or plaques as portrayed in Exod 28:36–38—would also have been incised with an *ʿēṭ barzel*. Finally, an *ʿēṭ barzel* would have been the tool employed to incise ostraca (Aḥituv 2008, 154–55, 310),

2. In Job 19:24, *ʿēṭ* is modified by the phrase *barzel wəʿōpāret* ‘(pen) of iron and lead’, wherein the term *barzel* designates the material of which the *ʿēṭ* is made; however, it is not clear what *ʿōpāret* signifies in the passage. Some suggest that *ʿōpāret* ‘lead’ appears in Job 19:24 because lead may have been used to fill in the letters of an inscription engraved upon stone. Alternatively, *ʿōpāret* may stand in parallel with *ṣûr* ‘stone’, thereby designating the type of stone to be inscribed (Pope 1965, 134; Jenner 2011a, 1).

3. Because the identification of *šāmîr* is not certain, I follow the translation of this lexeme as ‘hardest stone’ as in Lundbom (1999, 774, 776).

pottery vessels (Aḥituv 2008, 330–31), and other surfaces such as ivory (Aḥituv 2008, 329). Graffiti appearing on rock surfaces may also have been engraved with an *ʿēṭ barzel* (Aḥituv 2008, 220, 233), but it is just as likely that they were incised with a knife, a piece of flint, or another sharp object.

5.1.1.3. Scribal Pen, ʿēṭ sōpēr/sōpərîm *(Jeremiah 8:8; Psalm 45:2)*

The term *ʿēṭ* clearly does not refer to an engraving tool in Jer 8:8 and Ps 45:2. In these two verses, *ʿēṭ* is not modified with *barzel*, verbs of engraving are absent, and no mention is made of a hard surface. There is no reason, therefore, to view this *ʿēṭ* as identical with the *ʿēṭ barzel* of Jer 17:1 and Job 19:24. What is noteworthy about the use of *ʿēṭ* in Jer 8:8 and Ps 45:2 is that, in both passages, it is modified by the term *sōpēr/sōpərîm* 'scribe(s)'—that is, the *ʿēṭ* mentioned in these verses refers to a writing instrument used particularly by scribes. Jeremiah 8:8 reads: אֵיכָה תֹאמְרוּ֙ חֲכָמִ֣ים אֲנַ֔חְנוּ וְתוֹרַ֥ת יְהוָ֖ה אִתָּ֑נוּ אָכֵן֙ הִנֵּ֣ה לַשֶּׁ֣קֶר עָשָׂ֔ה **עֵ֖ט שֶׁ֥קֶר סֹפְרִֽים** 'How will you say, "We are wise and the law of YHWH is with us"? For an ***ʿēṭ šeqer sōpərîm*** has made (it) into deception'. Also, Ps 45:2 reads: רָ֘חַ֤שׁ לִבִּ֨י ׀ דָּ֘בָ֤ר ט֗וֹב אֹמֵ֣ר אָ֭נִי מַעֲשַׂ֣י לְמֶ֑לֶךְ לְ֝שׁוֹנִ֗י **עֵ֤ט ׀ סוֹפֵ֬ר מָהִֽיר** 'My heart overflows with a good word, I will tell my deeds to the king; my tongue is an ***ʿēṭ sōpēr māhîr***'. Prior to evaluating these two passages as well as the meaning of *ʿēṭ sōpēr/sōpərîm*, it is important to briefly mention the difference between a rush pen and a reed pen.

The rush pen, which was common in ancient Egypt, was used to write on papyrus. One end of the rush pen was cut diagonally and chewed to produce a writing tip (Wente 2000, 2211). A rush pen was used like a brush to write in carbon ink (Black and Tait 2000, 2200–202). The rush pen was used in Egypt until the Ptolemaic Period (332–30 BCE), when the reed pen became much more common. A reed pen, which was used to write on ostraca (Lemaire 1992, 1002), was obliquely cut at its end; an incision was probably made at this end to be filled with ink (Tait 1988, 478–79). While Jer 8:8 and Ps 45:2 do not specify the material of which the *ʿēṭ sōpēr/sōpərîm* was made or how this pen was used, collation of a few passages in Jeremiah with epigraphic evidence that will be discussed shortly suggests that the *ʿēṭ sōpēr/sōpərîm* probably designates both a rush pen and a reed pen.

In Jer 36, Baruch is identified as a *sōpēr* (Jer 36:26, 32). The same chapter also identifies Elishama as a *sōpēr* (36:12, 20–21) and mentions that several other servants of the court were associated with scribal duties (e.g., Jehudi, Gemariah; 36:11–15, 20–21, 23, 25). In the next chapter, Jonathan is identified as a *sōpēr* (37:15, 20). It seems reasonable to infer that Baruch, Elishama, and Jonathan—each of whom is identified as a *sōpēr*—carried out similar scribal duties and used the same types of scribal tools: scrolls, ink, and pens. Moreover, there is no reason to doubt that the 'lying pen of scribes' (*ʿēṭ šeqer sōpərîm*) in Jer 8:8

was anything other than what Baruch, as well as Elishama and Jonathan, would have used as a writing instrument. According to Jer 36, Baruch wrote Jeremiah's oracles upon a scroll with ink. The fact that he used ink to write on a scroll suggests that his writing instrument was probably a rush or reed pen. Consequently, although Jer 8:8 does not state that the *ʿēṭ šeqer sōpərîm* was used with ink, it is not unreasonable to suggest that it was similar, if not identical, to Baruch's writing utensil.[4]

While an Israelite scribe (*sōpēr*) would presumably have been able to write on various types of surfaces—tablets of soft stone, wooden boards, ostraca, papyrus, vellum—the epigraphic record suggests that the majority of writing was done in ink with a rush or reed pen. The fifty-one bullae as well as fragments of 170 bullae from the City of David, all of which date to Iron Age II, point to the common use of rush pens and ink as writing instruments (Avigad 1997, 167; Reich, Shukron, and Lernau 2007, 156–57). After all, such bullae would have been attached to papyrus rolls, and writing on papyrus was done with ink and rush pens. The rush pen was probably also used to write on plaster inscriptions such as the Deir ʿAlla inscription (van der Kooij 1976b, 31–33) and the inscriptions from Kuntillet ʿAjrud. Additionally, the few hundred ostraca inscriptions from ancient Israel attest to the common use of ink, which, of course, implies the use of a rush or reed pen. Indeed, Lemaire (1992, 1002; see also van der Kooij 1976b, 31–36) writes that traces of both types of pens are visible in the ostraca from ancient Israel.[5] The ubiquity of ostraca finds with writing in ink suggests that the most common task of a *sōpēr* was to write with ink using a rush or reed pen. Therefore, the phrase *ʿēṭ sōpēr/sōpərîm* must designate the instrument that a scribe would have used to carry out his primary function of writing with ink on ostraca and papyrus—that instrument being a rush or reed pen.

5.1.1.4. Rush Pens in Ancient Egypt and Mesopotamia

Various rush pens and palettes have survived from ancient Egypt. The oldest discovered rush pens from Egypt date to the Fourth Dynasty (2597–2471 BCE) (Ashton 2008, 48; for an example of such pens, see figure 5.1 in 5.2.2.3). Other

4. If Jeremiah's scroll was made of papyrus, the pen that Baruch used to write Jeremiah's words would have been a rush pen, because this type of pen was utilized to write on papyrus; Haran (1980–81, 83–84) identifies the *ʿēṭ sōpēr/sōpərîm* specifically as the rush pen. If, however, Jeremiah's scroll was made of leather, it is possible that Baruch's writing implement was a reed pen.

5. That both rush and reed pens were used to write inscriptions on ancient Hebrew ostraca is confirmed by two pieces of evidence. First, van der Kooij (1976b, 31–36) argues that the strokes visible on inscribed ostraca point to the use of both types of pens. Second, the fact that two types of ink are attested from ancient Israel (carbon-based and metallic inks) suggests that both a reed and a rush pen were used, because each type of ink was associated with a particular type of pen: carbon-based ink was for rush pens, while metallic ink was for reed pens (Leach and Tait 2000, 238).

pens dating to the Eighteenth Dynasty (1549–1298 BCE) measure between 4.8 and 12 inches (Ashton 2008, 48; also, Hayes 1990, 274). Even a toy writing palette with a number of rush pens survives from the Eighteenth Dynasty (Hayes 1990, 296–97). An Aramaic palette with two pens dating to the fifth century BCE was found at Elephantine (Ashton 2008, 49). In addition to finds of actual pens, there is also art historical evidence attesting to the use of rush pens as well as palettes and other scribal accessories in ancient Egypt and Mesopotamia.

At Giza, there is a depiction of scribes holding rush pens in a tomb of Kani-nesut from the Fourth Dynasty (2597–2471 BCE) (Pritchard 1974, 73). Other depictions appear in the tomb of Ti at Saqqara from the Fifth Dynasty (2471–2355 BCE) (Pritchard 1974, 73; Black and Tait 2000, 2205). In both of these Egyptian examples, scribes are depicted as writing on sheets of papyrus with rush pens in hand and with rush pens placed behind both ears. The monuments and reliefs of the Neo-Assyrian empire also have representations of rush pens held by scribes recording booty (King and Stager 2001, 310; Pritchard 1974, 74).

5.1.1.5. Translation of ʿēṭ *in Ancient Versions*

The translation of *ʿēṭ* in the Greek Bible reflects the bifurcated meaning of *ʿēṭ* as suggested in 5.1.1.2 and 5.1.1.3. In the passages where *ʿēṭ* is modified by *sōpēr/sōpərîm* (Ps 45:2 [44:2 LXX]; Jer 8:8), it is rendered with terms that can refer to rush or reed material. In Ps 45:2 (44:2 LXX), *ʿēṭ* is translated as κάλαμος 'reed, reed pen' (LSJ 865–66; Muraoka 2009, 358) and, according to Eusebius and the Syro-Hexapla, Aquila's recension of the verse renders the term as σχοῖνος 'rush, reed used as pen' (LSJ 1747; Muraoka 2009, 667; Field 1875, 161). Similarly, in Jer 8:8, *ʿēṭ* is rendered as σχοῖνος. The lexeme *ʿēṭ* is also rendered with the term γραφεῖον, which carries the general meaning 'writing instrument' (LSJ 359; Muraoka 2009, 136), in Aquila's revision of Jer 8:8 and also in Symmachus's revision of Ps 45:2 (44:2 LXX) according to Eusebius and the Syro-Hexapla (Ziegler 1957, 191; Field 1875, 2:161).

The term γραφεῖον is also used to render *ʿēṭ* when it designates an engraving instrument. The phrase *ʿēṭ barzel*, which refers to an engraving instrument, is thus rendered as γραφεῖον σιδηροῦς 'iron graving tool' (LSJ 359, 359, 1597; Muraoka 2009, 136, 621) by Aquila, Symmachus, and Theodotion in Jer 17:1 according to Origen (Ziegler 1957, 233), although the passage is not included in the Septuagint. The Greek phrase γραφεῖον σιδηροῦς is also used in the Hexapla's fifth column to render *ʿēṭ barzel* in Job 19:24 (Ziegler 1982, 295; Jenner 2011a, 3) and in Theodotion's version of the verse according to the Syro-Hexapla, although Job 19:24, like Jer 17:1, is not included in the Septuagint. It seems, then, that γραφεῖον is an especially fitting translation of the Hebrew term *ʿēṭ*, for just as the Hebrew lexeme carries the general meaning 'writing instrument', inasmuch as it can refer to reed pens or to graving tools, so γραφεῖον can be used in contexts referring to reed pens or tools used for engraving.

In translating these four passages, three times the Targums render *ʿēṭ* with forms of the lexeme *qwlmws* 'reed pen', and once *ʿēṭ* is simply transliterated.[6] Targum Psalms renders *ʿēṭ sōpēr* of Ps 45:2 (44:2 LXX) as *qwlmws sprʾ* 'scribal reed pen' (*CAL*), and Targum Jonathan renders *ʿēṭ sōpərîm* in Jer 8:8 with the terms *qûlmas* 'reed pen' and *sāpar* 'scribe', although the words are rearranged so that *sāpar* stands before *qûlmas* (*CAL*). Targum Jonathan renders *ʿēṭ barzel* in Jer 17:1 as *ʿyṭ dbrzl* 'pen of iron' (*CAL*), while Targum Job renders *ʿēṭ* in Job 19:24 as *qlmn przlʾ* '(reed) pen of iron' (Stec 1994, 132*; *CAL*).[7] Although Job 19:24 renders *ʿēṭ* as *qlmn* (also *qwlmwz*), which usually connotes a pen of reed, *qlmn* is modified by *przlʾ*, signifying that *qlmn przlʾ* refers to an engraving tool.

In the Peshitta, *ʿēṭ* is rendered as *qnē*/*qanyā* in all four passages. In translating Ps 45:2 (44:2 LXX) and Jer 8:8, the Peshitta renders the phrase *ʿēṭ sōpēr* and *ʿēṭ šeqer sōpərîm* as *qnyʾ dsprʾ* 'reed pen of a scribe' and *qnyʾ dglʾ lsprʾ* 'false reed pen of a scribe' (Sokoloff 2009, 383–84, 274, 1035; *CAL*). In translating Jer 17:1 and Job 19:24, the Peshitta renders the phrase *ʿēṭ barzel* as *qnyʾ dprzlʾ* '(reed) pen of iron' (Sokoloff 2009, 383–84, 1235; *CAL*). The Septuagint and its revisions, the Targums, and the Peshitta thus preserve the bifurcated meaning of the Hebrew term *ʿēṭ*.[8]

In sum, the term *ʿēṭ* can refer to two very different writing tools: an iron tool used to engrave hard surfaces or a rush or reed pen used to write with ink.

5.1.2. *The Phrase* **ṣippōren šāmîr**

5.1.2.1. *Etymology and Biblical Usage*

The noun phrase *ṣippōren šāmîr* 'point of the hardest stone' appears in Jer 17:1. The passage reads: חַטַּאת יְהוּדָה כְּתוּבָה בְּעֵט בַּרְזֶל **בְּצִפֹּרֶן שָׁמִיר** חֲרוּשָׁה עַל־לוּחַ לִבָּם וּלְקַרְנוֹת מִזְבְּחוֹתֵיכֶם 'The sin of Judah is written with a pen of iron, with a ***ṣippōren šāmîr***; it is incised on the tablet of their heart and on the horns of their altars'. Scholars suggest that the noun phrases *ʿēṭ barzel* and *ṣippōren šāmîr* refer to one and the same writing implement, the former referring to the tool itself and the latter designating the tip of the same tool (Lundbom 1999, 776–77; King and Stager 2001, 305). As mentioned in 5.1.1.2, an *ʿēṭ barzel* with a *ṣippōren šāmîr* would have been used to engrave stone surfaces, metal, ostraca, and other hard

6. The Aramaic lexeme *qwlmws* is, of course, a loan of the Greek term κάλαμος 'reed, reed pen' (LSJ 865–66; Muraoka 2009, 358; *CAL*).

7. Both *brzl* and *przl* are attested in Aramaic (Jastrow 1926, 1:191; 2:1223).

8. See the final paragraph of 2.5.2 where I discuss the term *qāne* in relation to reed pens.

materials. In order to better understand the meaning of *ṣippōren šāmîr*, each element of this noun phrase will be examined.

5.1.2.1.1. THE TERM *ṢIPPŌREN*

Apart from Jer 17:1, *ṣippōren* 'nail, point' (GMD 1135; *DCH* 7:153; *HALOT* 2:1051; Jenner 2011d) also appears in Deut 21:12. The verse reads: וַהֲבֵאתָהּ אֶל־תּוֹךְ בֵּיתֶךָ וְגִלְּחָה אֶת־רֹאשָׁהּ וְעָשְׂתָה אֶת־**צִפָּרְנֶיהָ** 'You shall bring her into your house and she shall shave her head, and she shall make ***ṣipporne(y)hā***'. In this verse, *ṣippōren* appears in the plural form to refer to the fingernails of a woman. The lexeme *ṣippōren* also occurs twice in Temple Scroll[a], once in reference to claws and once in a paraphrase of Deut 21:12 (11Q19 LI, 4; LXIII, 12; *DSSR* 1:686, 706; *DSSC* 2:640). Cognates of the Hebrew term *ṣippōren* exist in other languages, including Akkadian (*ṣuprum*; *CAD* 16:250–53), Arabic (*ẓifr*, *ẓufr*; Lane 1968, 5:1912–13), Geʿez (*ṣəfr*; *CDG* 549), and Aramaic (*ṭpar*, *ṭeprā*, *ṭuprā*; Jastrow 1926, 1:525–26; *CAL*). The Arabic and Aramaic examples reveal that the initial sibilant of all these forms derives from a Proto-Semitic *$\underset{.}{\theta}$; accordingly, the aforementioned forms are reflexes of Proto-Semitic *$\underset{.}{\theta}$*ipr-* (J. Fox 2003, 81). The noun pattern of *ṣippōren* appears to be *quttul* (> *qittul* > *qittōl*), although with an anomalous *-en* (< *-n*) sufformative.

5.1.2.1.2. THE TERM *ŠĀMÎR*

The meaning and etymology of *šāmîr* 'flint (?), emery (?)' is not entirely clear (GMD 1379; *DCH* 8:443; *HALOT* 2:1562). Syriac *šmirā* 'flint, adamant' seems to be related (Sokoloff 2009, 1573; J. Fox 2003, 193). In the Bible, the term *šāmîr* occurs fifteen times, but only in three does it refers to a hard stone (Jer 17:1; Ezek 3:9; Zech 7:12). In another eight occurrences, *šāmîr* carries the meaning 'thorn' (Isa 5:6; 7:23, 24, 25; 9:17; 27:4; 32:13).[9] It is possible, though, that the meanings 'hardest stone' and 'thorn' derive from a single primary noun (Lambdin and Huehnergard 2000, 39). The Dead Sea Scrolls seem to contain three instances of the lexeme with the meaning 'thorn', including one case with a restored *yod* and *resh* (4Q162 I, 3; 4Q368 10ii5; 1QHa XVI, 26; DSSR 1:422, 620; 2:314; DSSC 2:736).

The biblical passages in which *šāmîr* refers to a stone point emphasize the hard nature of this stone. Ezekiel 3:9 states that God has made Ezekiel's forehead as strong as *šāmîr* so that he will not be afraid. The passage reads: **כְּשָׁמִיר** חָזָק מִצֹּר נָתַתִּי מִצְחֶךָ לֹא־תִירָא אוֹתָם וְלֹא־תֵחַת מִפְּנֵיהֶם כִּי בֵּית־מְרִי הֵמָּה 'Like ***šāmîr*** harder than flint [*ṣōr*] I have set your forehead. Do not fear them, and do not be dismayed by their faces, for they are a house of rebellion'. Similarly, Zech 7:12

9. The other four occurrences of *šāmîr* are cases in which *šāmîr* is either a geographical location (Josh 15:48; 10:1, 2) or a personal name (1 Chr 24:24).

states that the heart of the people of Israel is as hard as *šāmîr*. The passage reads: וְלִבָּם שָׂמוּ **שָׁמִיר** מִשְּׁמוֹעַ אֶת־הַתּוֹרָה וְאֶת־הַדְּבָרִים אֲשֶׁר שָׁלַח יְהוָה צְבָאוֹת בְּרוּחוֹ בְּיַד הַנְּבִיאִים הָרִאשֹׁנִים וַיְהִי קֶצֶף גָּדוֹל מֵאֵת יְהוָה צְבָאוֹת ‘They have set their hearts as ***šāmîr*** instead of hearing the law and the words which YHWH of hosts sent by his spirit into the hand of the former prophets; therefore, there was great wrath from YHWH of hosts’. Finally, according to Jer 17:1, Judah’s sin is engraved on the tablet of Israel’s heart and on the horns of Israel’s altars with a tip of *šāmîr*. Whether metaphorically or literally, these three passages imply that *šāmîr* was composed of a very hard material—one that could even be used to incise words on the horns of a stone altar.

5.1.2.2. Translation of ṣippōren *and* šamîr *in Ancient Versions*

The Septuagint renders *ṣipporne(y)hā* in Deut 21:12 with the verb περιονυχίζω ‘to trim nails’ (LSJ 1381; Muraoka 2009, 550). In the revisions of Jer 17:1 by Aquila, Symmachus, and Theodotion, however, *ṣippōren* is rendered as ὄνυξ ‘talon’ (LSJ 1234; Muraoka 2009, 499; Ziegler 1957, 233) and *šāmîr* as ἀδαμάντινος ‘adamantine’ (LSJ 20; Muraoka 2009, 9), which is, of course, related to ἀδάμας ‘hardest metal, diamond’ (LSJ 20; Muraoka 2009, 9). Similarly, Aquila’s revision of Isa 5:6 and 7:23 renders *šāmîr* as ἀδάμας (Ziegler 1939, 138, 149). In a few cases, there is no Greek word that corresponds to *šāmîr* (Isa 9:17; Ezek 3:9; Zech 7:12). The remaining occurrences of *šāmîr* are rendered in the Septuagint by a number of terms that do not elucidate the meaning of the *šāmîr*.[10] In translating the Jeremiah, Ezekiel, and Zechariah passages, Targum Jonathan transposes Hebrew *šāmîr* into Aramaic.

5.1.2.3. Engraved Seals and the Meaning of šāmîr

The exact meaning of *šāmîr* is not known. Some contend that it should be understood as referring to emery, a relatively hard stone (6–9 on the Mohs scale; Harrell, Hoffmeier, and Williams 2017, 45). The translation of *ṣippōren šāmîr* by Lundbom (1999, 774, 776) is perhaps most suitable; he renders the phrase as ‘point of the hardest stone’, leaving the identification of the stone unspecified.

10. When referring to a geographical location, the Septuagint transliterates *šāmîr* as Σαμιρ (Josh 15:48) and Σαμάρεια (Judg 10:1, 2). When referring to a thorn, *šāmîr* is rendered as χέρσος ‘dry land’ (Isa 5:6; 7:23, 24, 25; LSJ 1989; Muraoka 2009, 732); χέρσος ‘dry land’ is also used in Aquila’s revision of Isa 27:4 according to Eusebius, although Aquila has *spinam et vepram* ‘thorns and briers’ in the same verse according to Jerome (Andrews 1958, 1742, 1971; Ziegler 1939, 213). The term *šāmîr* is also rendered as ὕλη ‘wood, material’ (Isa 10:17; LSJ 1847–48; Muraoka 2009, 694), as φυλάσσω ‘to guard’ (Isa 27:4; LSJ 1961; Muraoka 2009, 722), and as χόρτος ‘grass’ (Isa 32:13; LSJ 2000; Muraoka 2009, 734).

TABLE 5.1. Seals from Iron Age II Israel

1. steatite: Mohs 1–2.5	5. carnelian: Mohs 6–7
2. limestone: Mohs 3	6. chalcedony: Mohs 6–7
3. serpentine: Mohs 3–6	7. agate: Mohs 7
4. dolerite: Mohs 5–7	8. jasper: Mohs 7

Still, an examination of the corpus of Iron Age II engraved seals may help us get closer to the meaning of *šāmîr*. Specifically, by considering the types of stones and materials out of which these seals were made, and by noting the Mohs scale ranking of these stones and materials, we can conclude how hard the stone tip of an engraving tool (i.e., *šāmîr*) needed to be in order to incise such seals. The types of stones of a number of the engraved seals found in excavations are listed above in table 5.1; an assortment of such seals appears in figure 5.3 in 5.3.1.[11]

The various seals that survive from ancient Israel range from 1 to 7 in their Mohs hardness ranking. Needless to say, the tool that produced these seals must have had a Mohs hardness ranking higher than that of the seals. It is also possible that tools of varying Mohs hardness rankings were used to produce these seals. Perhaps flint, which has a Mohs ranking of 7 and is found everywhere in Israel (Frachtenberg and Yellin 1992, 149), was the tip of engraving pens that were used to engrave the softer stones listed here. Flint tools were probably also used to make seals in ancient Egypt (Aston, Harrell, and Shaw 2000, 65) and perhaps in ancient Mesopotamia (Sax, McNabb, and Meeks 1998). For some of the harder stone seals listed here, however, a stone with a higher Mohs scale ranking, such as emery, would have been used.

To sum up, the noun phrase *ṣippōren šāmîr* refers to the hard stone tip of an *ʿēṭ barzel*. It is not entirely clear which stone is designated by the term *šāmîr*, but it is quite possibly flint. On the other hand, flint could not have been used to inscribe all the seals discovered in ancient Israel, because many of them are of stone that is just as hard as flint. Because diamonds were not known in the Near East until the Roman Period, diamond cannot be the correct identification of *šāmîr* (Harrell, Hoffmeier, and Williams 2017, 20). It is possible, however, that *šāmîr* designated emery (9 on the Mohs scale), which was a relatively hard stone (Harrell, Hoffmeier, and Williams 2017, 37–38). The term *šāmîr* may also be a general term that refers to a number of hard stones.

11. Table 5.1 lists a number of the seals discovered in excavations as listed in Avigad 1997, 49, 52, 68, 70, 77, 80, 85, 91, 99–100, 102, 116–17, 135–36, 144, 151, 154, 161–62. Many more seals were acquired from the antiquities market or purchased elsewhere (Hestrin and Dayagi-Mendels 1979; Avigad 1997); such seals have not been listed here. Also, see 5.3.2.1 for a discussion Exod 28:9–12, which depicts the engraving of precious stones.

5.1.3. *The Term* ḥereṭ

5.1.3.1. *Etymology and Biblical Usage*

The word *ḥereṭ* 'chisel (?)' appears twice in the biblical text (Exod 32:4; Isa 8:1).[12] It also occurs twice in the Dead Sea Scrolls (1Q33 XII, 3; 4Q382 25, 4; *DSSR* 1:260, 1056; *DSSC* 1:276). There may be a few related lexemes and verbal roots in other Semitic languages; for instance, Syriac contains the terms *ḥwrṭ'* 'incising' and *ḥwrṭt'* 'incision' as well as the verbal root *ḥ-r-ṭ* 'to cut in, to incise' (Sokoloff 2009, 433; *CAL*; *HALOT* 1:352). Also, the Tigre verbal root *ḥ-r-ṭ* 'scratch' may be related (Leslau 1958, 22). If these lexemes and roots are indeed connected with Hebrew *ḥereṭ*, the lexeme may mean 'chisel'.[13] The problem of determining the meaning of *ḥereṭ* results from the opaque nature of the passages that use this term.

In Exod 32:4, *ḥereṭ* refers to the tool that Aaron uses to shape the golden calf. The passage reads: וַיִּקַּח מִיָּדָם וַיָּצַר אֹתוֹ **בַּחֶרֶט** וַיַּעֲשֵׂהוּ עֵגֶל מַסֵּכָה וַיֹּאמְרוּ אֵלֶּה אֱלֹהֶיךָ יִשְׂרָאֵל אֲשֶׁר הֶעֱלוּךָ מֵאֶרֶץ מִצְרָיִם 'He took (the gold) from their hand and shaped it with the ***ḥereṭ*** and made it a calf of cast metal, and they said, "This is your god, O Israel, who brought you up from the land of Egypt"'. While the story of the golden calf is well known, the composition of the calf as depicted in the text is not entirely transparent. We do not know if Exod 32:4 is referring to a calf of pure gold or to a calf of wood covered with gold (Propp 2006, 549–50). Another possibility is that the reference is to a two-dimensional image of a calf on a gold plaque (Propp 2006, 549). Furthermore, it is difficult to know how the text imagines the *ḥereṭ* to have been used in the preparation of the calf. If the identification of the *ḥereṭ* as a chisel is correct, then perhaps the *ḥereṭ* is employed to draw up an image of a calf, either on wood or on a plaque of gold. Alternatively, the text may be suggesting that the *ḥereṭ* was used to carve out a mold that was later utilized to form a calf. According to Exod 32:4, all that can be known about the meaning of *ḥereṭ* is that it was some type of tool.

While *ḥereṭ* may refer to a chisel or a tool of some sort in Exod 32:4, in Isa 8:1 the term seems to refer to a writing instrument. The passage reads: וַיֹּאמֶר יְהוָה אֵלַי קַח־לְךָ **גִּלָּיוֹן** גָּדוֹל וּכְתֹב עָלָיו **בְּחֶרֶט אֱנוֹשׁ** לְמַהֵר שָׁלָל חָשׁ בַּז 'YHWH said to me, "Take for yourself a large ***gillāyôn*** ['blank scroll' (?)], and write upon it with a ***ḥereṭ ʾĕnôš***, 'belonging to *māhēr šālāl ḥāš baz*'"'. Admittedly, little can be ascertained about the meaning of *ḥereṭ ʾĕnôš* from the context of Isa 8:1. If 'chisel' is the correct

12. In addition to being glossed as 'chisel', the lexeme *ḥereṭ* is also often glossed as 'stylus' (GMD 396; *DCH* 3:316; *HALOT* 1:352). However, I argue here that the gloss 'stylus' is problematic.

13. Hebrew *ḥārîṭ* 'purse' (2 Kgs 5:23; Isa 3:22) is probably not related to *ḥereṭ*. Rather, *ḥārîṭ* seems to be connected to Arabic *ḫarīṭa* 'sack' (GMD 397; Lane 1968, 2:723).

meaning of *ḥereṭ*, then *ḥereṭ ʾĕnôš* perhaps carries the meaning 'common chisel, people's chisel' (?), but it is not self-evident how this tool would have been used to write on a blank scroll (*gillāyôn*).

Scholars generally understand *ḥereṭ* and *ḥereṭ ʾĕnôš* as a type of stylus (Jenner 2011b, 2; Haran 1980–81, 81–82; Blenkinsopp 2000, 237; GMD 396; *DCH* 3:316; *HALOT* 1:352). Yet the meaning of *ḥereṭ*/*ḥereṭ ʾĕnôš* as 'stylus' still poses difficulties in understanding how *ḥereṭ ʾĕnôš* was utilized to write on a *gillāyôn* as recorded in Isa 8:1. The problem lies in the fact that the suggested meanings of *ḥereṭ* and *gillāyôn*—the former perhaps designating some type of chisel or a stylus and the latter a blank scroll—do not fit together well in the context of this passage. If *ḥereṭ ʾĕnôš* refers to a chisel or a stylus, then we expect *gillāyôn* to designate a writing board or a tablet of some sort. In Mishnaic Hebrew, however, *gillāyôn* refers to blank parchment. If this is also the meaning of *gillāyôn* in Isa 8:1, then we expect *ḥereṭ* to refer to a rush pen, not a chisel or a stylus. Haran (1980–81, 81–82), who accepts the meaning of *gillāyôn* as 'leather scroll', insists that *ḥereṭ ʾĕnôš* refers to a stylus used to write on the *gillāyôn*. If Haran is correct, it is still not clear whether the *ḥereṭ ʾĕnôš* is used to somehow engrave the *gillāyôn*, or to write upon the *gillāyôn* with ink in similar fashion to a rush pen.

5.1.3.2. Usage of ḥereṭ *in the Dead Sea Scrolls*

The use of *ḥereṭ* in the War Scroll seems to suggest that the lexeme refers to a type of engraving tool. The relevant passage reads: וחסדי ברכו[תיכה] וברית שלומכה **חרתה** למו **בחרט** חיים למלוך [. . .] בכול מועדי עולמים '[Your] benevolent blessings and your covenant of peace you have engraved (**חרתה**) for them with a **חרט** of life to rule [. . .] in all times forever' (1Q33 XII, 3; *DSSR* 1:260). Although this passage contains symbolic language, the use of the verbal root *ḥ-r-t* 'to engrave' suggests that *ḥereṭ* designates a tool utilized for engraving. This, of course, lends itself to the interpretation that the word denotes a type of chisel. Another text contains the phrase חרט זהב 'golden *ḥereṭ*', which may point to the hard composition of the tool but does not say anything as to its use (4Q382 25, 4; *DSSR* 1:1056). If 'chisel' or even 'stylus' is the correct meaning of *ḥereṭ*, it is still not clear how to understand the use of the term in Isa 8:1.

5.1.3.3. Translation of ḥereṭ *in Ancient Versions*

In translating Exod 32:4 and Isa 8:1, the Septuagint renders both occurrences of *ḥereṭ* as γραφίς 'stylus, paintbrush, graving tool' (LSJ 360; Muraoka 2009, 136), although both cases may be inferences on the part of the Greek translators. Targum Onkelos, however, renders *ḥereṭ* of Exod 32:4 as *zêpā* 'mold, forgery, chisel' (?) (*CAL*; Jastrow 1926, 1:395); similarly, the Peshitta renders ḥereṭ in this passage as *ṭwps* 'mold' (Sokoloff 2009, 520; *CAL*). In translating Isa 8:1, Targum Jonathan renders *ḥereṭ 'ĕnôš* in a paraphrastic manner as *kətab məpāraš* 'clear writing' (*CAL*), and the Peshitta translates it as *ktbʾ dʾnwšʾ* 'a man's writing' (Sokoloff 2009, 65, 660–61), neither of which elucidates the meaning of the Hebrew term.

While it is difficult to know the meaning of *ḥereṭ* with certainty, it is possible that the lexeme designated a chisel that would have been utilized by a smith. The meaning of *ḥereṭ 'ĕnôš*, however, remains elusive.

5.1.4. The Term śered

5.1.4.1. Etymology and Biblical Usage

The exact meaning and etymology of *śered*, which occurs only once (Isa 44:13), is not known (GMD 1299; *DCH* 8:190; *HALOT* 2:1354).[14] The Hebrew verbal root *š-r-d* 'to leave behind' is probably unrelated (*HALOT* 2:1353). According to *HALOT*, Arabic *s-r-d* 'to pierce through' and *sirād, sarīd* 'awl, bradawl' are connected (*HALOT* 2:1353; see also Lane 1968, 4:1346–7), which suggests that Hebrew *śered* may refer to a sharp tool like an awl. The initial sibilants of Hebrew *śered* and the Arabic lexemes do not line up, though, so these forms cannot be cognates.

In Isa 44:13, the term *śered* is used alongside other specific terms that denote tools employed by a craftsman of wood to make an idol. The verse reads: חָרַשׁ עֵצִים֙ נָ֣טָה קָ֔ו יְתָאֲרֵ֙הוּ֙ **בַשֶּׂ֔רֶד** יַעֲשֵׂ֙הוּ֙ בַּמַּקְצֻע֔וֹת וּבַמְּחוּגָ֖ה יְתָאֳרֵ֑הוּ וַֽיַּעֲשֵׂ֙הוּ֙ כְּתַבְנִ֣ית אִ֔ישׁ כְּתִפְאֶ֥רֶת אָדָ֖ם לָשֶׁ֥בֶת בָּֽיִת 'A craftsman of wood stretches out a line, he marks it with the **śered**, he fashions it with carpenters' knives, and with a compass he fashions it; he fashions it like the form of a man, like the beauty of a man, to dwell in a house'. This text is situated within a passage (Isa 44:9–20) that ridicules idols and those who make them. Isaiah 44:12 describes how the blacksmith uses tools such as an adze (*maʿăṣād*) and hammers (*maqqābôt*) to make idols. On the other hand, Isa 44:13 states how the carpenter stretches out a line (*qāw*), then marks up the wood with a *śered*, fashioning the wood with carpenters' knives (*maqṣūʿôt*), marking it with a compass (*məḥûgā*), and making it into the form of a man. In short, the text depicts a workshop occupied by blacksmiths and carpenters, not scribes. We should therefore consider *śered* to be a tool that belonged to the tool set of a craftsman, in this case a carpenter.[15]

---

14. Clines glosses *śered* as 'stylus, scriber, marker' (*DCH* 8:190), which demonstrates that the exact meaning of the term remains elusive.

15. Blenkinsopp (2000, 238–39) holds that *śered* refers to chalk, which would have been used to mark up wood prior to it being cut into the outlined shape. Blau (1995, 689–95) points out, however, that the interpretation of *śered* as 'chalk' or a dye of some kind—which was a common interpretation

5.1.4.2. Translation of śered *in Ancient Versions*

The translation of Isa 44:13 in the Greek Bible does not line up entirely with the Hebrew text. In the Septuagint, *śered* appears to be rendered with the word κόλλα 'glue' (LSJ 972; Muraoka 2009, 405).[16] Aquila, however, renders it as παραγραφίς 'writing instrument' (LSJ 1306; Ziegler 1939, 287). In Targum Jonathan, *śered* is translated as *'ûzmêl* 'scalpel, knife' (*CAL*), and the Peshitta, like the Septuagint, renders *śered* as *tt* 'glue' (Sokoloff 2009, 1675; *CAL*). Needless to say, ancient Bible translations offer a number of interpretations of *śered*, but none is certain.

5.1.4.3. Awls from Ancient Egypt

Various carpentry tools were used in ancient Egypt. Awls and engraving tools dating to the First Dynasty (3050–2813 BCE) were discovered at Saqqara (Gale et al. 2000, 356). Other discovered tools include "hammers, chisels, knives, awls, rasps and levels" (Manuelian 2000, 1629). If *śered* indeed designates an awl, perhaps it is a type of scratch awl, which is used to mark up wood for cutting.

In sum, while the exact meaning of *śered* is uncertain, the lexeme probably refers to a tool used by a carpenter in the preparation of wood to be cut up.

5.2. Accessories of the Scribal Kit

5.2.1. The Term dəyô

5.2.1.1. Etymology and Biblical Usage

The lexeme *dəyô* 'ink' (GMD 248; *DCH* 2:433; *HALOT* 1:220), which occurs only once in the biblical text (Jer 36:18), probably derives from Egyptian *ry.t* 'color for writing and drawing, ink' (Lambdin 1953, 149; Muchiki 1999, 242; *WÄS* 2:399). In Egyptian, *ry.t* is attested since the Middle Kingdom (2066–1650) (*WÄS* 2:399). Aramaic *dəyûtā* 'ink' and Arabic *dawāt* 'ink horn' probably derive

in medieval Jewish texts—ultimately stems back to a misunderstanding of Saadya Gaon's Arabic translation of Isa 44:13. Blau (1995, 695) contends that *śered* refers to a carpenter's tool.

16. Jenner (2011c, 4) suggests, however, that the lines of verse 23 are misplaced so that the translation of *śered* actually appears in the previous verse. According to Jenner, *śered* is rendered as τέρετρον 'borer' (see also LSJ 1776; Muraoka 2009, 676). If Jenner is correct that τέρετρον is intended to translate *śered*, then *maqqābôt* 'mallets' of the previous verse is left without a translation, and, although τέρετρον does not correspond semantically to *maqqābôt*, the location of τέρετρον in the text does seem to correspond to that of *maqqābôt*, not *śered*.

from Hebrew *dəyô* (*CAL*; Jastrow 1926, 1:298; Lane 1968, 3:940). Because the correspondence of Egyptian *r* and Hebrew *d* is unexpected—one expects Egyptian *r* to correspond to Hebrew *r*, not *d*—Lambdin (1953, 149) has suggested that Hebrew *dəyô* derives from a graphic form ***rəyô*, due to the orthographic similarity of *d* and *r*.[17] I will argue, however, that Egyptian *r* may indeed have entered Canaanite as *d*, although this is not the expected correspondence.

The word *dəyô* appears in Jer 36, which describes Baruch writing Jeremiah's words upon a scroll. Jeremiah 36:18 reads: וַיֹּאמֶר לָהֶם בָּרוּךְ מִפִּיו יִקְרָא אֵלַי אֵת כָּל־הַדְּבָרִים הָאֵלֶּה וַאֲנִי כֹּתֵב עַל־הַסֵּפֶר בַּדְּיוֹ 'Baruch told them, "He would read to me with his (own) mouth all these words as I wrote on a document with the ***dəyô***"'. As mentioned earlier, Jer 36 contains a unique description of the composition of a biblical scroll. In this chapter, we read of the writing surface (*məgillā*; *məgillat sēper*), while the pen of the scribes is also mentioned earlier in the book (*ʿēṭ sōpərîm*; Jer 8:8). It is fitting, then, that ink is also mentioned in Jer 36:18.[18]

5.2.1.2. *Translation of* dəyô *in Ancient Versions*

Although Jer 36:18 does not indicate the meaning of *dəyô*, the meaning of the word is nevertheless suggested in ancient Bible translations. The Septuagint does not include a corresponding word for *dəyô* (Jer 43:18 LXX), but the term is rendered as μέλαν 'ink' in the Syro-Hexapla and the Lucianic recension (LSJ 1095; Ziegler 1957, 395; Fields 1875, 2:679). In Targum Jonathan and in the Peshitta, *dəyô* is rendered as *dəyûtā* 'ink' (Sokoloff 2009, 294; *CAL*). These renderings, however, may be based on an inference on the part of the translators.

5.2.1.3. *Phonology of Egyptian* ry.t *and Hebrew* dəyô*, and the Penetration of* ry.t *into Hebrew*

While there are no certain examples of Egyptian *r* entering Canaanite as *d*, some evidence suggests that the loan vector of Egyptian *r* > Canaanite *d* is not impossible. According to Muchiki (1999, 259, 261–62), there are sixteen sure cases of Egyptian *r* entering Canaanite as *r* and two examples in which Egyptian *r* entered Canaanite as *l* (Muchiki 1999, 260, 262). This demonstrates, of course,

17. The suggestion that *dəyô* is a graphic error for ***rəyô* is not convincing. To begin with, this argument assumes that every single manuscript that contains *dəyô* ultimately derives from a scribal error; we would expect at least one manuscript to preserve the correct reading, but *BHS* does not list any variants of *dəyô* written with *r* instead of *d*. Moreover, as I argue here, there may be a phonological explanation for *r* of Egyptian *ry.t* to have entered Canaanite as *d*; consequently, there is no need to rely on an explanation involving a graphic error.

18. For a different interpretation, see Cohen (2016), who presents a case that בַּדְּיוֹ is actually an inflected form of the preposition בְּדֵי. Cohen suggests the text should read, "for him," rather than "with the ink."

that Egyptian *r* generally entered Canaanite as *r*, not *d*. Nevertheless, Allen (2013, 40, 53; see also Hoch 1994, 406) holds that Egyptian *r* was realized as [ɾ], a single apical tap. It is possible, then, that the *r* of *ry.t* entered Canaanite as *d*, because Egyptian *r* (i.e., [ɾ]) is not that much different from [d].

Examining Semitic words that were borrowed into Egyptian, Hoch (1994, 431) shows that there are arguably twenty cases of Semitic *d* entering into Egyptian. Of this number, Semitic *d* was rendered fifteen times as *d*, four times as *t*, and once as *r* (*ʿa=–r=ši$_2$=na* < **ʿadašīn-* 'lentils'; Hoch 1994, 74).[19] Hoch also shows that there are thirty-six cases of Semitic *n* entering Egyptian as *r*. Admittedly, these data do not prove that Egyptian *r* could have entered Canaanite as *d*. Hoch's findings nevertheless demonstrate that Egyptian *r* may have resembled [d], because [n] and [d] are at least partially similar in that they are both produced in the alveolar ridge. Moreover, because there is one sure case of Semitic *d* that entered Egyptian as *r*, the reverse development may also be possible.

If *dəyô* is an Egyptian loanword in Hebrew, it seems likely that the lexeme entered Canaanite during the New Kingdom (1549–1069 BCE). Indeed, Allen (2013, 40, 53; see also Hoch 1994, 406) suggests that it is during the New Kingdom that Egyptian *r* came to be primarily realized as [ɾ]. For this reason, the New Kingdom seems like a fitting time period for the phonological correspondence of Egyptian *r* > Canaanite *d* to have occurred. Moreover, it was probably during the New Kingdom that papyrus paper was introduced into the Levant, so it seems plausible that *dəyô*—which denotes a material intrinsically linked with the technology of writing on papyrus—would have entered Canaanite around the same time.[20]

5.2.1.4. Ink in Ancient Egypt and the Levant

Ink utilized for writing in ancient Egypt was usually black or red. Black ink was carbon based (Leach and Tait 2000, 238; Lee and Quirke 2000, 108) and was used to write on papyrus with a rush pen (Black and Tait 2000, 2200–202; Leach and Tait 2000, 238); it was produced from the soot of cooking vessels and less often from charcoal (Diringer 1953, 547). Red ink was manufactured from red ocher (Leach and Tait 2000, 239).[21] Both forms of ink were mixed with gum

19. Another possible example of Semitic *d* entering Egyptian as *r* is *ʿpr*/*ʿpra* < **ʿabd-* 'servant' (Hoch 1994, 64), but this identification is uncertain.

20. See 2.6–2.7 for discussions concerning the terms *sûp* and *gōme'*, which probably also entered Canaanite during the New Kingdom. Also, see 2.1.2 as well as chapter 6 for discussion of when papyrus was introduced into the Levant.

21. While black and red ink was primarily used for writing, ancient Egyptian pigments utilized for painting included the colors white, yellow, brown, green, blue, grey, orange, pink, and purple (Diringer 1953, 549; Lee and Quirke 2000, 108–16).

and water and left to dry into ink cakes, which were used by dipping a rush pen into water and rubbing it in the ink cake (Wente 2000, 2211; Ashton 2008, 51). In addition to carbon-based ink, a metallic ink made of a mixture of oak galls and iron sulphate is attested in ancient Egypt; it was applied primarily with a reed pen (Leach and Tait 2000, 238).

Because ancient Israel borrowed its writing technology from Egypt, the composition of ink utilized in ancient Israel resembled that of Egypt. Carbon ink was probably used on papyrus (Lundbom 2004a, 602; Ashton 2008, 51). However, there are also traces of metallic ink from the ostraca discovered at Lachish (Lundbom 2004a, 602). Metallic ink would also have been used on leather scrolls, assuming they were used in ancient Israel, because common carbon ink would not have attached well to leather surfaces (Ashton 2008, 51). The Deir ʿAlla inscription attests to the use of black carbon-based ink and red ink made of iron oxide (van der Kooij 1976a, 25; Mosk 1976); black and red inks are also attested at Kuntillet ʿAjrud (Meshel 1978, 53). Although there is still insufficient research on the ink used in the Dead Sea Scrolls, Tov (2004, 53–55) writes that carbon-based, metallic, and red inks were all utilized on these documents.

To sum up, the lexeme *dəyô* designates ink in ancient Hebrew. It seems safe to assume that *dəyô* does not designate a specific type of ink but refers to the various forms of ink discussed above. After all, metallic ink is attested in the Lachish ostraca, and carbon ink is attested in the Dead Sea Scrolls; both types are also attested in the Deir ʿAlla inscription, which was discovered just across the Jordan river. Additionally, red ink is attested in Deir ʿAlla and at Kuntillet ʿAjrud. If we accept that Hebrew *dəyô* derives from Egyptian *ry.t*—which, in Egyptian, refers to ink of any color—it seems reasonable to conclude that *dəyô* also carries the general meaning ‘ink’ and designates ink of different colors and compositions.

5.2.2. *The Phrase* qeset hassōpēr

5.2.2.1. *Etymology and Biblical Usage*

The term *qeset* ‘scribal palette’ (GMD 1178; *DCH* 7:272; *HALOT* 2:1116), which occurs three times in the Bible (Ezek 9:2–3, 11), seems to derive from Egyptian *gstj* (Lambdin 1953, 154; Muchiki 1999, 255; *WÄS* 5:207).[22] In Egyptian, *gstj* is attested as early as the Old Kingdom (2663–2160 BCE) and refers to a scribe’s palette (*WÄS* 5:207). In the Bible, the term appears in Ezek 9:2–4, which reads:

22. Clines glosses *qeset* as ‘writing case, inkpot’ (*DCH* 7:272), which is possible, but *qeset* more likely designates a scribal palette.

וְהִנֵּה שִׁשָּׁה אֲנָשִׁים בָּאִים ׀ מִדֶּרֶךְ־שַׁעַר הָעֶלְיוֹן אֲשֶׁר ׀ מָפְנֶה צָפוֹנָה וְאִישׁ כְּלִי מַפָּצוֹ בְּיָדוֹ
וְאִישׁ־אֶחָד בְּתוֹכָם לָבֻשׁ בַּדִּים **וְקֶסֶת הַסֹּפֵר** בְּמָתְנָיו וַיָּבֹאוּ וַיַּעַמְדוּ אֵצֶל מִזְבַּח הַנְּחֹשֶׁת׃ וּכְבוֹד
׀ אֱלֹהֵי יִשְׂרָאֵל נַעֲלָה מֵעַל הַכְּרוּב אֲשֶׁר הָיָה עָלָיו אֶל מִפְתַּן הַבָּיִת וַיִּקְרָא אֶל־הָאִישׁ הַלָּבֻשׁ
הַבַּדִּים אֲשֶׁר **קֶסֶת הַסֹּפֵר** בְּמָתְנָיו׃
וַיֹּאמֶר יְהוָה אלו אֵלָיו עֲבֹר בְּתוֹךְ הָעִיר בְּתוֹךְ יְרוּשָׁלָםִ וְהִתְוִיתָ תָּו עַל־מִצְחוֹת הָאֲנָשִׁים הַנֶּאֱ־
נָחִים וְהַנֶּאֱנָקִים עַל כָּל־הַתּוֹעֵבוֹת הַנַּעֲשׂוֹת בְּתוֹכָהּ׃

Six people were coming from the way of the upper gate which faces north, and each had his weapon of slaughter in his hand; and with them was one man dressed in linen with ***qeset hassōpēr*** at his waist. They came and stood at the bronze altar. The glory of the God of Israel went up above the cherub upon which it had been to the threshold of the house. He called to the man dressed in linen with ***qeset hassōpēr*** at his waist.

YHWH said to him, "Pass through the city, through Jerusalem, and put a mark on the foreheads of the people sighing and groaning over all the abominations done in it."

According to this passage, a man with a *qeset hassōpēr* at his waist is commanded to place a mark, presumably with a pen and ink, on the foreheads of those who are to be spared destruction. While it seems reasonable to understand *qeset hassōpēr* as referring to a scribal palette, this passage does not preclude other possible interpretations of the phrase. Jenner (2011e, 4) argues that, because *qeset* is modified by *sōpēr*, it carries a general meaning such as 'equipment'; he suggests that *qeset* refers to a type of writing case. Indeed, a box dating to the Fourth Dynasty (2597–2471 BCE) that contains papyri, cakes of ink, and reeds has been discovered in Egypt (Piacentini 2001, 190), so it is possible that *qeset* designated such a container. Nevertheless, if *qeset* indeed derives from *gstj*, it would be reasonable to conclude that *qeset*, like *gstj*, designates a scribal palette, not a writing case.

5.2.2.2. Phonology of Egyptian gstj *and Hebrew* qeset

From a phonological perspective, there are no major difficulties in deriving Hebrew *qeset* from Egyptian *gstj*. As already mentioned in the discussion of the term *gōmeʾ*, Egyptian *g* does enter Semitic as *q*. Excluding *qeset*, the correspondence of Egyptian *g* > Hebrew *q* is confirmed in one other Hebrew term: *qôp* 'ape, monkey' < *g(ỉ)f* (Muchiki 1999, 254–55). There are also two cases of Egyptian *g* entering Aramaic as *q*.[23] This is not abundant evidence, but it does show that Egyptian *g* could be perceived in Semitic as *q*. There is also no

23. For a fuller discussion on the phonology of Egyptian *g*, see 2.7.2–2.7.3.

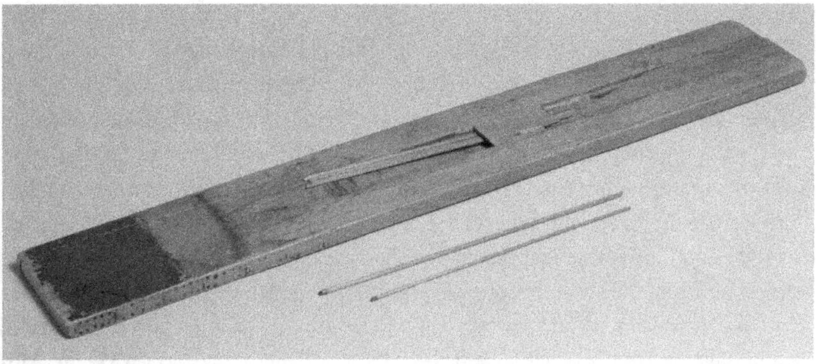

FIGURE 5.1. Egyptian palette and pens, circa 1045–992 BCE. Metropolitan Museum of Art, New York. Photo: public domain.

problem with deriving Hebrew *s* from Egyptian *s*.[24] Muchiki (1999, 261) offers twelve examples in which Egyptian *s* entered Hebrew as *s*.[25] Furthermore, in the majority of cases, Egyptian *s* entered other Semitic languages as *s*.[26]

It seems reasonable that the Egyptian word *gstj* was loaned into Canaanite during the New Kingdom (1549–1069 BCE), along with the technology of writing on papyrus.

5.2.2.3. Scribal Kits, Palettes, and Inkwells in Ancient Egypt and Israel

An Egyptian scribal kit consisted of a sack, a rectangular palette, and a reed tube. The sack contained pigments, the palette was used for mixing the ink and also held brushes, and the tube was an extra container for storing brushes (Wente 2000, 2212). Numerous scribal palettes have survived from ancient Egypt; see figure 5.1 for an example. The oldest such palette dates to the Fourth Dynasty (2597–2471 BCE) (Ashton 2008, 55). Palettes were usually made of wood and had rectangular depressions that held rush pens as well as round depressions to hold ink cakes. While a number of palettes have been discovered in Egypt,

24. In Egyptian, the phonemes *z* (initially pronounced as [θ]) and *s* (pronounced as [s] and alternatively transliterated as *ś*) merged into one phoneme /s/ (Allen 2013, 46). The *s* of Egyptian *gstj* is a reflex of an etymological *s* (i.e., *ś*) (*WÄS* 5:207).

25. There are, however, also three examples in which Egyptian *s* entered Hebrew as *š* (Muchiki 1999, 261) and one case in which Egyptian *s* entered Aramaic as *š* (Muchiki 1999, 182). Although Muchiki (1999, 261, 263) states that "Hebrew שׁ does not really correspond to Egyptian *ś*," he seems to imply that the three Hebrew examples of Egyptian *s* (alternatively transliterated as *ś*) > Hebrew *š* reflect a sound shift that supposedly occurred in Egyptian (i.e., *s* > *š*).

26. This is true for Phoenician (Muchiki 1999, 47, 49), Aramaic (Muchiki 1999, 182, 184), and Ugaritic (Muchiki 1999, 284).

Demsky (2007, 241) also speaks of an Egyptian ivory pen case dating to the time of Rameses III (1185–1153 BCE) that was found at Megiddo.[27]

In addition to actual finds of palettes, there are art historical depictions of scribal palettes, water jugs, and ink horns (Pritchard 1974, 73; Black and Tait 2000, 2205). To begin with, the hieroglyphic symbol for the word 'scribe' consists of a palette connected to a rush pen and a water jug (Avrin 1991, 89). Perhaps the most relevant find for Ezek 9:2–3 and 11 is a part of a wall painting from the tomb of Khaemhet. Dating to the fourteenth century BCE, the picture depicts an Egyptian scribe recording quantities of produce on a board or papyrus sheet with a rush pen. The scribe seems to be dressed in linen and has a scribal palette fastened to his waist, just as described in Ezek 9:2–3 and 11 (Mazar, Avi-Yonah, and Malamat 1958–61, 3:166). Syrian scribes also used scribal palettes, as attested by a monument from Zincirli that dates to about 730 BCE; the stela has a depiction of Barrakib and a scribe holding a palette in his hand (Driver 1976, 87; Ashton 2008, 55; Gilibert 2011, 85–86).

5.2.2.4. Translation of qeset hassōpēr *in Ancient Versions*

The Greek Bible and its revisions contain a number of different translations of *qeset hassōpēr*. The Septuagint renders *qeset* as ζώνη 'belt, girdle' in the three Ezekiel verses (9:2–3, 11; LSJ 759; Muraoka 2009, 316); *qeset hassōpēr* in Ezek 9:2 is rendered as ζώνη σαπφείρου 'sapphire belt' (LSJ 759, 1583; Muraoka 2009, 316, 617). According to Origen, *qeset hassōpēr* is rendered in the versions of Aquila and Theodotion as κάστυ γραμματέως: *qeset* is simply transliterated, while *sōpēr* is translated as γραμματέως 'of a scribe' (LSJ 358–59; Muraoka 2009, 136; Ziegler 1952, 122–24). According to Jerome, Aquila's revision of Ezek 9:2 and 9:11 renders *qeset* as μελανοδοχεῖον 'inkstand' (LSJ 1095; Ziegler 1952, 122–24) and, according to Origen, Jerome, and the Syro-Hexapla, Symmachus's revision of the same two verses renders *qeset* as πινακίδιον γραφέως 'scribal writing tablet' (LSJ 359, 1405; Ziegler 1952, 122–24). Finally, the Hebrew translation known as ὁ ἑβραῖος in the Hexapla renders *qeset hassōpēr* as μέλαν και κάλαμος γραφέως 'ink and a scribal reed pen' (LSJ 359, 865–66, 1095; Muraoka 2009, 358). Targum Jonathan renders *qeset* as *pênqas* 'tablet, account', which itself is a Greek loanword: *pênqas* < πίναξ 'writing tablet' (*CAL*; LSJ 1405). The Peshitta renders *sōpēr* as *spyl*' 'sapphire' (Sokoloff 2009, 1030; *CAL*), but it does not have a translation for *qeset*. Although these translations are quite different, it is clear that *qeset* was generally understood as a scribal accessory.

27. I should also mention that four inkwells, possibly five, were discovered at Qumran. Remains of dried ink are still present in two inkwells. Two inkwells are made of ceramic material, one from bronze, and the makeup of the other two is not stated (Tov 2004, 54–55).

While we cannot be certain what the noun phrase *qeset hassōpēr* means, if *qeset* derives from Egyptian *gstj* 'scribal palette', it is likely that *qeset* also carries this meaning.

5.2.3. *The Phrase* taʿar hassōpēr

5.2.3.1. Etymology and Biblical Usage

The phrase *taʿar hassōpēr* 'scribal knife' appears one time in the biblical text (Jer 36:23), although the term *taʿar* 'razor, knife, sheath' (GMD 1451; *DCH* 8:661; *HALOT* 2:1770–71) occurs thirteen times in the Bible. Six times it refers to a type of knife or blade (Num 6:5; 8:7; Isa 7:20; Jer 36:23; Ezek 5:1; Ps 52:4) and seven times to a sheath (1 Sam 17:51; 2 Sam 20:8; Jer 47:6; Ezek 21:8–10, 35). Some argue that *taʿar* is connected with the verbal root *ʿ-r-w/y* 'to uncover, to empty' (GMD 1450; *DCH* 8:661; Koller 2012, 224). But a formal and semantic connection between *taʿar* and *ʿ-r-w/y* is difficult to ascertain. Koller (2012, 224) suggests that *taʿar* and *ʿ-r-w/y* were related in that a *taʿar* was a tool that "uncovered" a head by shaving off the hair. *HALOT* (2:1770), on the other hand, considers *taʿar* to be unconnected with the verbal root. Ugaritic *yʿr* 'razor' and *tʿrt* 'sheath' are probably related to Hebrew *taʿar* (GMD 1451; *DULAT* 2:857, 947).

The meaning of *taʿar* is clear from the contexts of the passages that use the term. For instance, Num 6:5 uses *taʿar* in reference to a razor that is employed to shave one's head: כָּל־יְמֵי֙ נֶ֣דֶר נִזְר֗וֹ **תַּ֙עַר֙** לֹא־יַעֲבֹ֣ר עַל־רֹאשׁ֔וֹ עַד־מְלֹ֤את הַיָּמִם֙ אֲשֶׁר־יַזִּ֣יר לַיהוָ֔ה קָדֹ֣שׁ יִהְיֶ֔ה גַּדֵּ֥ל פֶּ֖רַע שְׂעַ֥ר רֹאשֽׁוֹ 'All the days of his vow of consecration a *taʿar* shall not pass over his head; until the completion of the days that he consecrated to YHWH, he shall be holy, letting the locks of the hair of his head to grow long'. In 1 Sam 17:51, *taʿar* refers to the sheath that holds Goliath's sword: וַיָּ֣רָץ דָּ֠וִד וַיַּעֲמֹ֨ד אֶל־הַפְּלִשְׁתִּ֜י וַיִּקַּ֣ח אֶת־חַ֠רְבּוֹ וַיִּֽשְׁלְפָ֤הּ **מִתַּעְרָהּ֙** וַיְמֹ֣תְתֵ֔הוּ וַיִּכְרָת־בָּ֖הּ אֶת־רֹאשׁ֑וֹ וַיִּרְא֧וּ הַפְּלִ֖שְׁתִּים כִּי־מֵ֥ת גִּבּוֹרָ֖ם וַיָּנֻֽסוּ 'David ran and stood over the Philistine, took his sword and removed it from its *taʿar*, and killed him and cut off his head with it. When the Philistines saw that their mighty man was dead, they fled'. Finally, in Jer 36:23, *taʿar* is modified by *hassōpēr*, signifying that this particular *taʿar* was used by scribes: וַיְהִ֣י ׀ כִּקְר֣וֹא יְהוּדִ֗י שָׁלֹ֣שׁ דְּלָתוֹת֮ וְאַרְבָּעָה֒ יִֽקְרָעֶ֙הָ֙ **בְּתַ֣עַר הַסֹּפֵ֔ר** וְהַשְׁלֵ֖ךְ אֶל־הָאֵ֛שׁ אֲשֶׁ֥ר אֶל־הָאָ֖ח עַד־תֹּם֙ כָּל־הַמְּגִלָּ֔ה עַל־הָאֵ֖שׁ אֲשֶׁ֥ר עַל־הָאָֽח 'As Jehudi read three or four columns, he would cut it up with *taʿar hassōpēr*, throwing (it) into the fire in the brazier, until all of the scroll was consumed on the fire on the brazier'.[28]

---

28. The use of the root *q-r-ʿ* in the *qal* stem to refer to the cutting of the scroll is a bit strange. The root occurs around sixty times and is predominantly used in connection with the tearing of clothing (e.g., Gen 37:29; 2 Sam 13:31). In the *niphal* stem, the root is used in connection with torn-down altars (1 Kgs 13:3; 13:5). One would expect the *qal* stem of *k-r-t* 'to cut' to be used in the context of Jer 36:23, because a *taʿar hassōpēr* is a cutting tool; *k-r-t* is used in 1 Sam 24:5–6, which depicts David

In this passage, the meaning of *taʿar hassōpēr* is clear; it refers to the knife that is utilized to cut up Jeremiah's scroll in order to have it burned.

5.2.3.2. Translation of taʿar *in Ancient Versions*

The Greek Bible generally translates *taʿar* in accordance with the Hebrew text. In the six cases where *taʿar* refers to a knife, it is rendered as ξυρόν 'razor' (e.g., Num 6:5; LSJ 1192–93; Muraoka 2009, 482). In the Septuagint's translation of Jer 36:23 (43:23 LXX), *taʿar hassōpēr* is rendered as ξυρόν τοῦ γραμματέως 'scribal razor' (LSJ 358–59, 1192–93; Muraoka 2009, 136, 482), although Symmachus's version and Lucian's recension render *taʿar* as σμίλη 'knife for cutting or carving' (LSJ 1619; Ziegler 1957, 396–97). When *taʿar* refers to a sheath, it is usually translated as κολεός 'sheath' (e.g., Jer 47:6 [29:6 LXX]; LSJ 972; Muraoka 2009, 404). In Ezek 21:35, *taʿar* is translated as καταλύω 'to destroy, to dissolve' (LSJ 899–900; Muraoka 2009, 376–77), although Lucian's recension renders the word as κολεός (Ziegler 1952, 185–86). There is not a Greek word corresponding to *taʿar* in 1 Sam 17:51, but a variant reading renders it as καλεός (Brooke and McLean 1906–40, 2:60). In translating Jer 36:23 (43:23 LXX), Targum Jonathan renders *taʿar hassōpēr* as *ʾūzmîl saprā* 'scribal knife' (*CAL*); similarly, the Peshitta translates the phrase as *zmlyʾ dsprʾ* 'scalpel of a scribe' (Sokoloff 2009, 385, 1035; *CAL*).

5.2.3.3. Scribal Knives in Ancient Egypt

In his study of Biblical Hebrew terms designating cutting tools, Koller connects the *taʿar hassōpēr* with Egyptian scribal knives (2012, 228). Two such knives have been discovered that date to the Eighteenth Dynasty (1549–1298 BCE) (Hayes 1990, 412); see figure 5.2 for an example. Both knives are made of bronze and have the names of their owners engraved upon them (Hayes 1990, 113, 219, 412). The knives have long, thin blades and were used to trim writing brushes and to cut sheets of papyrus (Hayes 1990, 113, 219; Koller 2012, 228). Hyatt (1943, 79) writes that such a knife was not part of the scribal kit carried by a scribe. Rather, this knife would have been used in the scribe's office and probably remained there.

cutting off a piece of Saul's garment unbeknownst to him. It is possible, however, that Jeremiah's scroll was both cut and torn. It may also be that the text is using *q-r-ʿ* as a wordplay of *q-r-ʾ*, which appears in the same verse, and of *q-r-ʿ*, which occurs in verse 24; thus, as Jehudi reads (*kiqərôʾ*) the scroll, he tears it (*yiqrāʿehā*), but those who listen to Jehudi read the scroll do not tear (*lōʾ⁽ʾ⁾ qārəʿû*) their clothes (Lundbom 2004a, 605).

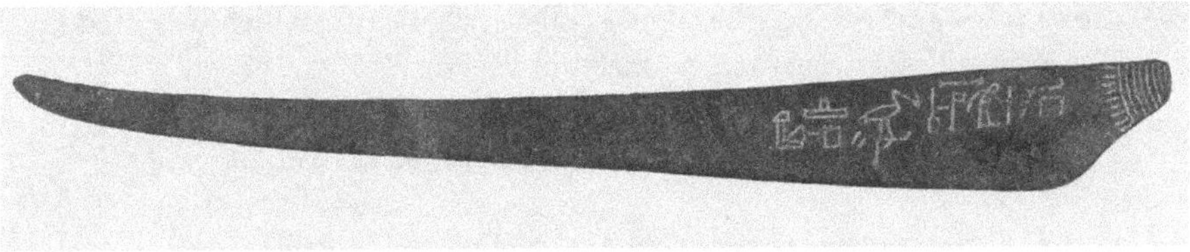

FIGURE 5.2. Egyptian scribal knife, circa 1479–1458 BCE. Metropolitan Museum of Art, New York. Photo: public domain.

In his discussion of the *taʿar hassōpēr*, Koller also mentions an Egyptian knife called the *dg3*, which resembles a razor (Hayes 1990, 64; Koller 2012, 231). Koller (2012, 235) argues that, because Hebrew *taʿar* and Egyptian *dg3* both refer to razors, and because *taʿar* can also refer to a scribal knife, the *taʿar hassōpēr* may have resembled the Egyptian *dg3* razor knife.

While the etymology of *taʿar* is uncertain, the meaning of *taʿar hassōpēr* is clear. It refers to the Israelite scribal knife, which was used for various scribal purposes.

5.2.4. Definitions of Terms Designating Writing Instruments and Accessories of the Scribal Kit

Having analyzed the ancient Hebrew words that designate writing instruments and accessories of the scribal kit, I suggest the following definitions for these terms.

***dəyô*:** Probably an Egyptian loanword that designates ink of different colors and compositions.

***ḥereṭ*:** A term perhaps denoting a chisel that would have been utilized by a smith. The meaning of *ḥereṭ ʾĕnôš*, however, remains elusive.

***ʿēṭ*:** A term that probably carries the general meaning ‘pen, writing instrument’. When modified by *barzel* ‘iron’, *ʿēṭ* refers to an engraving pen; when modified by *sōpēr/sōpərîm* ‘scribe(s)’, it refers to a rush pen as well as a reed pen.

***ṣippōren šāmîr*:** A phrase that refers to the hard stone tip of an engraving tool (i.e., point of an *ʿēṭ barzel*).

***qeset hassōpēr*:** A phrase that designates the scribal palette containing pens and ink. The lexeme *qeset* probably derives from Egyptian.

***śered*:** A term that probably refers to a tool, perhaps a scratch awl, used by a carpenter in the preparation of wood to be cut up.

taʿar hassōpēr: A phrase designating the scribal knife, which was used to trim writing brushes and cut sheets of papyrus.

5.2.5. *Note on Scribal Training in Ancient Israel and the Scribal Tool Set*

There is debate about whether schools existed in ancient Israel; some argue in favor (G. I. Davies 1995; Lemaire 1981), while others argue against (Golka 1993, 4–15; Jamieson-Drake 1991, 156).[29] I concur with Rollston that "there was a mechanism in ancient Israel (defined broadly) that facilitated formal, standardized scribal education" and that "the mechanism most responsible for the standardized education of professional scribes was the state" (2010, 95, 113; see also, 2015, 80–97, and 2006). Rollston (2010, 129) contends that the ability to read and write would have belonged to literate elites such as professional scribes and officials of the court and temple.[30] Rollston (2010, 91–113) presents several arguments for the existence of standardized education in ancient Israel. First, learning an altogether new writing system would have required a sufficient amount of time and practice, which suggests that Israelite scribes were formally trained in the Hebrew alphabet (Rollston 2010, 92–94). Second, the shape and stance of letters in Hebrew inscriptions, as well as the use of *matres lectiones*, is consistent both synchronically and diachronically from the eighth through sixth centuries BCE; this indicates that scribes were trained in a standardized system of writing (Rollston 2010, 95–110). Third, Egyptian hieratic numerals are used in Hebrew inscriptions, and learning this foreign numeric system would have required formal training on the part of Israelite scribes (Rollston 2010, 110). Finally, the existence of abecedaries from various sites in Israel and Judah further supports the claim that formal scribal education existed in ancient Israel (Rollston 2010, 111). Given the evidence for formal scribal training, we can only conclude that the scribal tools discussed above belonged to a kit that was used by professional scribes and in schools.

That the instruments evaluated here belonged to a professional scribal kit is reinforced by the fact that three of the relevant terms (*ʿēṭ sōpēr/sōpərîm*, *qeset hassōpēr*, and *taʿar hassōpēr*) are modified by the lexeme *sōpēr*. The term *dəyô* also appears in a context in which the term *sōpēr* occurs eight times (Jer 36:10, 12, 20–21, 23, 26), not to mention that the word *dəyô* is used by the scribe Baruch

29. A nice critique of Jamieson-Drake's arguments appears in the short study "Were There Schools in Ancient Israel?" by G. I. Davies (1995).

30. Rollston (2010, 127) believes, however, that "there were some in ancient Israel who should be classed as semi-literates . . . who were capable of reading the most remedial of texts with at least some modest level of comprehension and often the ability to pen some of the most common and simplest of words." He admits, though, that the data at hand do not allow one to determine the variation of literacy that existed in ancient Israel (Rollston 2010, 128).

(36:18). The phrase *ṣippōren šāmîr* (Jer 17:1) is used in the context of writing, which was the task of scribes; and the phrase *ḥereṭ ʾĕnôš* (Isa 8:1) also occurs in the context of writing, which suggests that it may have been a specific scribal tool, although this is not certain. In sum, the tools described here are either designated as scribal tools or used in the context of writing, which was the primary task of scribes. We must conclude, then, that these writing implements were specialized scribal tools employed for the specific purpose of writing by professional scribes in ancient Israel.

5.2.6. Production of Monumental Inscriptions and the Tools Involved

The biblical text does not describe the process of producing monumental lapidary inscriptions. Nevertheless, it is possible to reconstruct something of that process and perhaps to identify a number of Hebrew terms that designate the tools involved. We must rely on data from other, non-Semitic cultures such as the Greeks. Comparing the masonry of ancient Israel with that of Greece and the Mediterranean world is useful because these cultures had much in common when it came to their practice of masonry (Koller 2012, 129).

McLean (2002, 4–13) identifies the steps involved in the production of Greek lapidary inscriptions. First, the stone was quarried. In ancient Israel, most royal inscriptions were etched on limestone or basalt; both types of stone were quarried locally, in the land of Israel.[31] Next, the stone was manufactured by stone masons into a particular shape such as "statue bases, altars, tombs, sarcophagi, boundary markers, milestones, stelae, and so forth" (McLean 2002, 7–8). Once the stone was formed into the desired shape, it was polished in order to provide a smooth surface that would later be covered with the inscription. Before the stone was quarried, or while it was being quarried, the text that would appear on the stone was drafted by scribes in consultation with the king and royal dignitaries (McLean 2002, 9). Once the stone was quarried, formed into the desired shaped, and polished, the drafted text was transcribed onto the stone surface by a scribe. The transcription was done using "paint, charcoal, chalk, or a metal point" (McLean 2002, 11). Finally, the text was engraved, probably by a professional stonemason rather than a scribe.[32]

Koller's (2012, 129–61) study of masonry in the Levant is especially helpful for determining which tools weres used in the process of producing a lapidary inscription. He writes that ancient Israel's masonry tools consisted of "two

31. See 3.1 for discussion of specific inscriptions and their lapidary composition.

32. McLean (2002, 12–13) writes, however, that it was indeed the scribes that did the engraving, because this would have prevented mistakes. He admits, though, that others believe that, while scribes transcribed the text, the engraving was done by stonemasons (McLean 2002, 13).

picks, a number of different chisels, a mallet, and a saw" (Koller 2012, 129). The quarrying process was executed by the use of picks, some of which survive from as early as the twelfth century BCE (Koller 2012, 130–32). The Siloam tunnel inscription contains the lexeme that designates the pick used for quarrying rock: the *garzen* (Aḥituv 2008, 22). Koller (2012, 139–40) identifies the *garzen* as the 'heavy excavating pick' that was used for digging in rock. Indeed, the Bible uses *garzen* in connection with masonry in 1 Kgs 6:7. The verse states that the temple was built of dressed stones that had been brought to the construction site in a prepared state. Because it states that the stones were already dressed when they were brought to the site and highlights that the *garzen* was not used at the site, the verse implies that the *garzen* was the tool used to quarry the stones.

Once quarried, stones were dressed into ashlars (*ʾabnê gāzît*; 1 Chr 22:2). Koller (2012, 142–43) writes that *garzen* designates not only the heavy pick used to quarry stones but also the light pick used to dress them. The light pick was used along with mallets and chisels to shape the stone. The term *maqqebet*, which is mentioned in the Bible (Judg 4:21; 1 Kgs 6:7; Isa 44:12; 51:1; Jer 10:4), denotes the mallet (Koller 2012, 148). While the Bible does not identify the chisel that was used with the mallet, Koller holds that the *mapselet*, which is attested in Mishnaic Hebrew, was the chisel used in masonry (Koller 2012, 150; Jastrow 1926, 2:821). Koller (2012, 153–55) also identifies the saw employed in the preparation of ashlar stones: the *məgērā* was a heavy saw utilized to cut stone (2 Sam 2:31; 1 Kgs 7:9; 1 Chr 2:3). Smaller hammers were probably designated by the terms *paʿam* (Isa 41:7) and *paṭîš* (Isa 41:7; Jer 23:29; 50:23); these would have been used to smash stone.

Once the stone was fashioned into the desired shape, the scribe transcribed the text onto the smoothed surface. The initial transcription of the text was probably done with pen and ink. It is also possible that the text was transcribed with an *ʿēṭ barzel* that contained a *ṣippōren šāmîr* as its tip. The final engraving, however, would have been done with a chisel and hammer. It is possible that *ʿēṭ barzel* designates not only an engraving pen but also a particular chisel utilized for incising writing on stelae (Ashton 2008, 45); alternatively, perhaps the lexeme *ḥereṭ* designated such a chisel.

While the duties of an Israelite scribe did not include quarrying stone and shaping it into stelae fit for writing purposes, scribes were indeed involved in the transcription of the written text onto the stone.

5.3. Glyptics

Writing on stone can appear in various forms. Stone inscriptions may consist of engraved royal stelae or of smaller incised tablets such as the Gezer calendar, or even of graffiti on cave surfaces. Such inscriptions were considered in chapters 3–4. Below, we will consider inscribed stones of a much smaller size—namely, precious stones and weights, as well as seals and signets. We will also examine items such as bullae and jar impressions that have been impressed with seals and signets.

5.3.1. Seals in the Ancient World and Ancient Israel

While their origin can be traced back to Mesopotamia, stamp and cylinder seals were used throughout the ancient world: Mesopotamia and the Levant, Egypt, South Asia, and the Aegean (Ameri et al. 2018, 2). Cylinder seals first appear in Mesopotamia in the mid-fourth millennium BCE and were common in the ancient Near East for the next three thousand years (Pittman 2018, 13). Indeed, several thousand Mesopotamian cylinder seals fill museums and private collections (Collon 2005, 6, 99).[33] Most extant seals are cut from soft stone, but there are some seals made of wood and bone (Collon 2005, 6). Throughout the ancient world, seals served to authenticate documents, to certify quantities of commercial goods, or to assert ownership or authority; they were also used to decorate objects or functioned as gifts and good-luck amulets (Seevers and Korhonen 2016, 1–2).

In Egypt, cylinder seals emerged around 3400 BCE in the Predynastic Period (5000–3050 BCE) and were common until they were replaced by stamp seals near the end of the Old Kingdom (2663–2160 BCE). By the end of the Middle Kingdom (2066–1650 BCE), scaraboid seals became prevalent and continued to be the dominant form of Egyptian seal in subsequent millennia (Wegner 2018, 230, 237). Scarab seals functioned as amulets for funerary purposes but also in daily administrative sealing practices (Wegner 2018, 237–38; D. Ben-Tor 2018, 290). It was during the Middle Kingdom that scarabs began to be mass produced, as made clear by the thousands of seal impressions discovered from this period (D. Ben-Tor 2018, 289); the vast majority of these scarabs were carved from steatite (D. Ben-Tor 2018, 291).[34] As discussed below, many Egyptian scarabs dating to the Middle Kingdom have been discovered in Israel, confirming the close ties between ancient Canaan and ancient Egypt (D. Ben-Tor 2011; 2004; 2003). Whereas inscribed scarabs previously contained names of officials, scarabs with personal names became quite common during the Middle Kingdom, although scarabs inscribed with personal and official names receded from prevalence toward the end of that period (Wegner 2018, 240–41). In the

33. Ancient Near Eastern seals and their impressions are cataloged in many different volumes; see, e.g., Mitchell and Searight 2008, Collon 2001, Doumet 1992, Teissier 1984, Buchanan 1981.

34. Egyptian scarabs are cataloged and discussed in various volumes; see, e.g., D. Ben-Tor 2007, Bietak and Czerny 2004, Wiese 1996, Tufnell 1984, Ward 1978, Hornung and Staehelin 1976, G. T. Martin 1971.

FIGURE 5.3. Seals from Iron Age II Israel. Israel Museum. Photo: Creative Commons.

New Kingdom (1549–1069 BCE), signet rings mounted with a scarab as the ring bezel began to take precedence over scarabs previously worn on the wrist or neck (Wegner 2018, 243; Smith 2018, 306).

By about 2400 BCE, seals were used in mainland Greece for administrative purposes (Younger 2018, 335–36). They were usually made of softer materials such as clay, bone, or steatite, but harder stones such as agate and carnelian began to be used for the production of seals by 1800 BCE. While Mesopotamia preferred the cylinder seal and Egypt preferred the scaraboid type, a circular biconvex form was common for seals in the ancient Aegean (Younger 2018, 341). Younger (2018, 344–55) suggests that seals functioned primarily as funerary jewelry in Crete, while they were used for administrative sealing purposes in mainland Greece. Thousands of seals and impressions have been discovered in Greece and Crete, virtually all of which are cataloged in the *Corpus der minoischen und mykenischen Siegel* (*CMS*), which is available online.[35]

In view of the discovery of thousands of seals and impressions originating in the ancient Near East, Egypt, and the Aegean, it is not surprising that the utilization of seals was also a common practice in ancient Israel. Cylinder seals dating to the third–second millennia have been discovered in Israel (Ornan and Peri 2017; Peri 2010; Miroschedji 1997; Teissier 1997; A. Ben-Tor 1978). The

35. The Corpus der minoischen und mykenischen Siegel (The CMS) can be found on the website of Universität Heidelberg at https://www.uni-heidelberg.de/fakultaeten/philosophie/zaw/cms/.

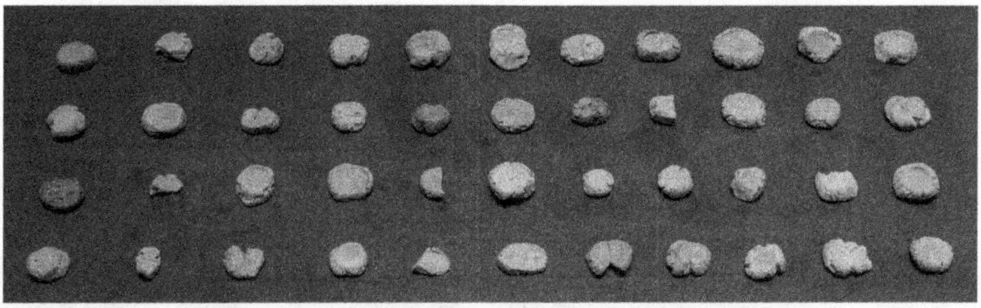

FIGURE 5.4. Seal impressions from Jerusalem, sixth century BCE. Israel Museum. Photo: © A.D. Riddle/BiblePlaces.com.

scaraboid seal, however, eventually became much more common in Canaan and Israel. Already in Middle Bronze Age II, a large number of Egyptian-influenced scarabs that were locally produced in Canaan began to appear in the southern Levant (D. Ben-Tor 2011, 27). The use of scarabs continued into the Late Bronze Age, although the bulk of them were imported from Egypt (D. Ben-Tor 2011, 32). As discussed below, Canaan was under Egyptian domination during the Late Bronze Age, so it is not surprising that aspects of Egyptian influence such as the use of scarabs were present in Canaanite culture.

The use of scaraboid seals in Canaan continued in the Iron Age. Avigad lists almost 400 Hebrew seals, including a few signet rings (1997, 69, 87, 120, 131, 160), as well as about 260 bullae, and almost 50 jar-handle impressions (1997, 49–263; see figures 5.3–5.5). Furthermore, fragments of over 170 clay bullae impressed with images have been discovered in the City of David (Reich, Shukron, and Lernau 2007, 156–57).[36] Additionally, Vaughn (1999, 166, 185–97) writes of 1,700 jars with the *lmlk* impression.[37] The majority of Iron Age II seals discovered in Israel are of scaraboid shape (Avigad 1997). Seals in the collection by Avigad and Sass that were discovered in digs are composed of the following stones: steatite, limestone, serpentine, dolerite, carnelian, chalcedony, agate, and jasper; the Mohs scale of these stones ranges from 1–2.5, which is quite soft, to 7, which is relatively hard.[38] Many ancient Near Eastern seals are anepigraphic and iconographic, while ancient Israelite seals usually bear private names with minor iconography (Avigad 1997, 33). Nevertheless, even Israelite

36. Among the finds were also several hundred unimpressed broken clay lumps that would have been attached to letters and package goods (Reich, Shukron, and Lernau 2007, 156–57).

37. In addition to the Hebrew seals, bullae, and jar-handle impressions, Avigad (1997, 264–461) lists about five hundred West Semitic seals (i.e., Phoenician, Aramaic, Ammonite, Moabite, and Edomite).

38. Seals can be found in Avigad 1997, 49, 52, 68, 70, 77, 80, 85, 91, 99–100, 102, 116–17, 135–36, 144, 151, 154, 161–62. See discussions in 5.1.1.2 and 5.1.2.3, which consider the engraving of such stones.

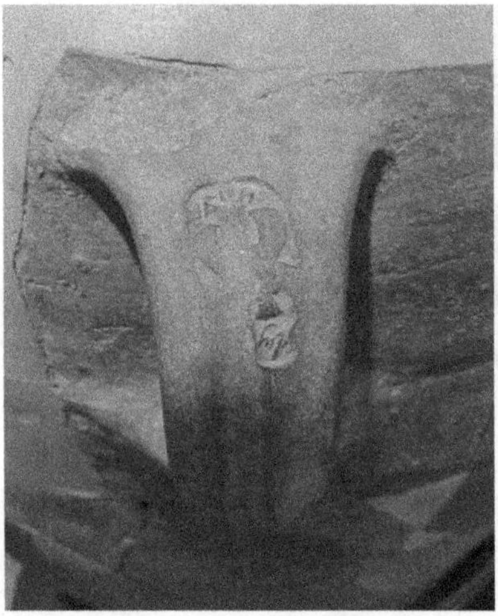

FIGURE 5.5. LMLK jar handle impression (writing is upside down). Eretz Israel Museum, Tel Aviv. Photo: Creative Commons.

seals bear imagery including that of creatures (mammals, reptiles, insects, fish, birds, fantastic animals), plants, celestial bodies, and even human and anthropomorphic figures (Sass 1993).

Having summarized the existence of seals in the ancient Near East in general and ancient Israel in particular, we now turn to examining Hebrew lexemes denoting seals, engraved precious stones, and inscribed weights and measures.

5.3.2. Engraved Precious Stones and Weights

5.3.2.1. The Term 'eben and Engraved Precious Stones

As mentioned above, the term 'eben can designate large stones as well as stones of a small size (e.g., Exod 20:25, 1 Sam 17:40). In a number of passages, 'eben also refers to precious stones (e.g., 1 Kgs 10:11; 1 Chr 29:2). In Exodus (28:9–12, 17–21; 39:6, 10–14), we read of the engraving of names upon precious stones, which were to be part of the priestly garments. Exodus 28:9–12 reads:

וְלָקַחְתָּ֗ אֶת־שְׁתֵּ֣י **אַבְנֵי־שֹׁ֔הַם** וּפִתַּחְתָּ֣ עֲלֵיהֶ֔ם שְׁמ֖וֹת בְּנֵ֣י יִשְׂרָאֵֽל: שִׁשָּׁה֙ מִשְּׁמֹתָ֔ם עַ֖ל הָאֶ֣בֶן הָֽאֶחָ֔ת וְאֶת־שְׁמ֞וֹת הַשִּׁשָּׁ֧ה הַנּוֹתָרִ֛ים עַל־הָאֶ֥בֶן הַשֵּׁנִ֖ית כְּתוֹלְדֹתָֽם: מַעֲשֵׂ֣ה חָרַשׁ֮ **אֶ֒בֶן֒** פִּתּוּחֵ֣י חֹתָ֗ם תְּפַתַּח֙ אֶת־שְׁתֵּ֣י הָֽאֲבָנִ֔ים עַל־שְׁמֹ֖ת בְּנֵ֣י יִשְׂרָאֵ֑ל מֻסַבֹּ֛ת מִשְׁבְּצ֥וֹת זָהָ֖ב תַּעֲשֶׂ֥ה אֹתָֽם: וְשַׂמְתָּ֞ אֶת־שְׁתֵּ֣י הָאֲבָנִ֗ים עַ֚ל כִּתְפֹ֣ת הָֽאֵפֹ֔ד אַבְנֵ֥י זִכָּרֹ֖ן לִבְנֵ֣י יִשְׂרָאֵ֑ל וְנָשָׂא֩ אַהֲרֹ֨ן אֶת־שְׁמוֹתָ֜ם לִפְנֵ֧י יְהוָ֛ה עַל־שְׁתֵּ֥י כְתֵפָ֖יו לְזִכָּרֹֽן:

You shall take two **'abnê šōham** ('šōham stones') and you shall engrave upon them the names of the sons of Israel, six of their names on the

TABLE 5.2. Precious Stones of Exodus 28:17–21; 39:6, 10–14

Biblical Name of Stone	**Identification**	**Mohs Hardness Scale**
sappîr	lapis lazuli	3–5.5
nōpek	turquoise	5–6
yāšəpē	agate or jasper	7
šōham	amethyst or sardonyx variety of agate	7
ʾōdem	carnelian	6–7
piṭdā	submetallic variety of hematite	5–6.5
šəbô	banded agate	7
ʾaḥlāmā	red jasper	7
bāreqet	serpentinite or green jasper	3–6; 7
lešem	amazonite	6–6.5
taršîš	amber or specularite variety of hematite	2–2.5; 5–6
yāhălōm	milky quartz or sapphirine chalcedony	7; 9

one *ʾ**eben*** and the remaining six names on the second ***ʾeben***, according to their birth. Like the engraving of signets, the work of a craftsman of ***ʾeben***, so you shall engrave the two ***ʾăbānîm*** with the names of the sons of Israel; you shall make them enclosed with gold filigree settings. You shall place the two ***ʾăbānîm*** on the shoulders of the ephod as ***ʾabnê zikkārōn*** ('stones of remembrance') for the sons of Israel. Aaron shall carry the names before YHWH on his two shoulders for remembrance.

According to this passage, the engraving was to be done on two *šōham* stones, which may be amethyst stones or the sardonyx variety of agate stones, both 7 on the Mohs scale (Harrell, Hoffmeier, and Williams 2017, 45). Later in the passage (Exod 28:17–21; see also 39:6, 10–14), we read of eleven other precious stones that are to be engraved with the names of the twelve sons of Jacob. The stones are given in table 5.2 according their ranked hardness (Harrell, Hoffmeier, and Williams 2017, 45).[39]

The task of engraving a stone is achieved by following a simple principle: the medium used to engrave must be harder than the material being engraved. Table 5.2 shows that most of the stones given in the Exodus passage, assuming that their identification is correct, fall in the range of 5–7 on the Mohs hardness scale. We cannot know with certainty which medium would have been used to

39. It must be noted, however, that the identification of these stones is debated. Shipp's research on these gemstones has led him to certain identifications that differ from those in Harrell, Hoffmeier, and Williams (2017); e.g., Shipp identifies *piṭdā* as peridot, whereas Harrell, Hoffmeier, and Williams contend that *piṭdā* refers to hematite. I thank R. Mark Shipp for sharing his work with me, which is yet to be published.

FIGURE 5.6. Engraved weights from Syria-Palestine. Istanbul Archaeology Museums. Photo: © Todd Bolen /BiblePlaces.com.

inscribe stones like those ascribed to the ephod in this passage. Nevertheless, as discussed earlier (see 5.1.2.3), we may suggest flint (7 on the Mohs scale) or emery (6–9 on the Mohs scale) as possible media because these are relatively hard stones.

5.3.2.2. The Term ʾeben *and Engraved Weights*

In addition to referring to precious stones, the lexeme *ʾeben* can also designate stones that were used as weights and measures in ancient Israel. In his study of such weights, Kletter (1998, 93–107) points out that passages in the Bible employ *ʾeben* to speak of weights and measures in a literal sense (e.g., Deut 25:13) or in a figurative sense (e.g., Prov 11:1). In other passages, specific weights are mentioned by the name of the weight, such as *gērā* 'gerah' or *šeqel* 'shekel' (e.g., Exod 30:13; Jer 32:9–10). By 1998, about 430 inscribed weights dating to Iron Age II had been discovered in the land of Israel (Kletter 1998, 43, 150–252; see figure 5.6).[40] A significant majority of these weights were found in Judah as well as the Negev, the Shephelah, Samaria, and the Galilee (Kletter 1998, 49, 54). The weights include five types: *šql* 'shekel', *bqʿ* 'beqaʿ', *nṣp* 'neṣep', *pym* 'payim', and the *gērā* (Dobbs-Allsopp et al. 2005, 623). Many weights have the name of the particular weight inscribed on them, while others are inscribed with symbols and numbers designating particular weight measures (Kletter 1998, 150). The bulk of the weights are made of limestone while others are made of clay, metal, or other stone (Dobbs-Allsopp et al. 2005, 623). It would have been a relatively simple process to inscribe the weights made of limestone as this is a soft stone (3 on the Mohs scale).

The engraving of stone and bronze weights may be compared to the engraving of precious stones, briefly discussed above. Such weights have been found

40. Kletter (1998, 253–264) lists another 193 uninscribed weights in addition to the 434 inscribed weights (Kletter 1998, 43).

in Eshtemoaʿ, Gibeon, Samaria, Gezer, Ashkelon, and on the Ophel in Jerusalem (Aḥituv 2008, 243–48, 333, 349–50). Engraved precious stones differ in function from engraved weights, but the process of engraving these artifacts was probably similar. In both cases, metal tools, perhaps with hard stone tips, were utilized to incise words upon small-sized rock surfaces.

We have thus far discussed the engraving of weights and precious stones in ancient Israel. We should note that the process of engraving weights and especially precious stones is, of course, comparable to the engraving of seals and signets from ancient Israel and its vicinity (Avigad 1997; Hestrin and Dayagi-Mendels 1979); we may also compare this process to the engraving of cylinder seals and agates from Mesopotamia (Moorey 1999, 74–77, 99–100, 103–6).[41] Below, we will examine the Hebrew lexemes that denote ancient Hebrew seals and signet rings (i.e, *ḥôtām/ḥōtām*, *ḥōtemet*, *ṭabbaʿat*).

5.3.3. *The Terms* ḥôtām/ḥōtām *and* ḥōtemet

5.3.3.1. *Etymology and Biblical Usage*

The terms *ḥôtām/ḥōtām* and *ḥōtemet*, a feminine form derived from *ḥôtām/ḥōtām*, originate from the Egyptian term *ḫtm* 'seal' (Muchiki 1999, 246–47; Lambdin 1953, 151). In Egyptian, *ḫtm* is attested since the Old Kingdom (2663–2160 BCE; *WÄS* 3:350). Muchiki (1999, 259–63) points out that there is no difficulty in deriving the Hebrew consonants of *ḥōtām* (*ḥ, t, m*) from the consonants of Egyptian *ḫtm*. Furthermore, Lambdin (1953, 151) notes that the Hebrew lexeme has undergone the Canaanite shift, which suggests that the term was borrowed into Canaanite quite early, when the Canaanite shift was still operative; the borrowing must have occurred prior to the fourteenth–fifteenth centuries BCE because by then the *ā* > *ō* shift had already taken place (Lambdin and Huehnergard 2000, 7; Mankowski 2000, 159–60). Besides occurring in the Bible, the term *ḥōtām/ḥôtām* also occurs on a few West Semitic seals (Avigad 1997, 268, 302, 316), thereby confirming its meaning: 'seal'.

In the Bible, the masculine form *ḥôtām/ḥōtām* occurs fourteen times (Gen 38:18; Exod 28:11, 21, 36; 39:6, 14, 30; 1 Kgs 21:8; Jer 22:24; Hag 2:23; Job 38:14; 41:7; Song 8:6 [2x]), while the feminine *ḥōtemet* occurs only once (Gen 38:25). The masculine lexeme also probably occurs three times in the Dead Sea Scrolls (*DSSC* 1:257), although in one case a *khet* is restored while in another case a *mem* is restored and a *tav* is uncertain (4Q274 3ii3; 4Q365 12biii13; PAM 43.686 37,1; *DSSR* 1:316, 778; 2:1120); a passive participle of the verbal root also occurs

41. See 5.1.1.2 and 5.1.2.3 for further discussion of engraved stone seals from ancient Israel and the tools used to engrave them.

once in 4QMysteries[b] (4Q300 1aii-b, 2; *DSSR* 2:204). In all cases in the Bible, the masculine and feminine forms carry the meaning 'seal, signet' (GMD 333; *DCH* 3:180; *HALOT* 1:300). As mentioned earlier, Exod 28 and 39 discuss the engraving of precious stones in a manner similar to that of engraving seals. For instance, Exod 28:9 reads: וְלָקַחְתָּ֗ אֶת־שְׁתֵּ֖י אַבְנֵי־שֹׁ֑הַם וּפִתַּחְתָּ֣ עֲלֵיהֶ֔ם שְׁמֹ֖ות בְּנֵ֥י יִשְׂרָאֵֽל 'You shall take two *šōham*-stones and you shall engrave upon them the names of the sons of Israel'. And Exod 28:11 reads: מַעֲשֵׂ֣ה חָרַשׁ֮ אֶבֶן֒ פִּתּוּחֵ֣י **חֹתָ֗ם** תְּפַתַּח֙ אֶת־ שְׁתֵּ֣י הָאֲבָנִ֔ים עַל־שְׁמֹ֖ת בְּנֵ֣י יִשְׂרָאֵ֑ל מֻסַבֹּ֛ת מִשְׁבְּצֹ֥ות זָהָ֖ב תַּעֲשֶׂ֥ה אֹתָֽם 'Like the engraving of a *ḥōtām*, the work of a craftsman of stone, so you shall engrave the two stones with the names of the sons of Israel; you shall make them enclosed with gold filigree settings'.

While Exod 28 and 39 clearly refer to the engraving of seals, 1 Kgs 21:8 aptly depicts the act of stamping letters with the king's seal; the verbal root denoting the process of stamping is derived from *ḥōtām* (> *ḥ-t-m*). The verse reads: וַתִּכְתֹּ֤ב סְפָרִים֙ בְּשֵׁ֣ם אַחְאָ֔ב וַתַּחְתֹּ֖ם **בְּחֹתָמֹ֑ו** וַתִּשְׁלַ֣ח הַסְּפָרִ֗ים אֶל־הַזְּקֵנִ֤ים וְאֶל־הַֽחֹרִים֙ אֲשֶׁ֣ר בְּעִירֹ֔ו הַיֹּשְׁבִ֖ים אֶת־נָבֹֽות 'So she wrote letters in the name of Ahab, and she sealed (them) [*wattaḥtōm*] with *ḥōtāmô* ['his seal'], and she sent the letters to the elders and to the leaders who were in his city, dwelling with Naboth'. In at least one case, Jer 22:24, *ḥōtām/ḥôtām* refers specifically to a signet worn on a hand: חַי־אָ֗נִי '"As I נְאֻם־יְהוָה֒ כִּ֣י אִם־יִהְיֶ֞ה כָּנְיָ֤הוּ בֶן־יְהֹֽויָקִים֙ מֶ֣לֶךְ יְהוּדָ֔ה **חֹותָ֖ם** עַל־יַ֣ד יְמִינִ֑י כִּ֥י מִשָּׁ֖ם אֶתְּקֶֽנְךָּ live," declares YHWH, "For even if Coniah, son of Jehoiakim king of Judah, is a *ḥôtām* ['signet'] on my right hand, even from there I will tear you off"'.

Both the masculine *ḥōtām/ḥôtām* and feminine *ḥōtemet* may refer to a seal in Gen 38. Genesis 38:18 reads: וַיֹּ֗אמֶר מָ֣ה הָֽעֵרָבֹון֮ אֲשֶׁ֣ר אֶתֶּן־לָךְ֒ וַתֹּ֗אמֶר **חֹתָֽמְךָ֙** וּפְתִילֶ֔ךָ וּמַטְּךָ֖ אֲשֶׁ֣ר בְּיָדֶ֑ךָ וַיִּתֶּן־לָּ֛הּ וַיָּבֹ֥א אֵלֶ֖יהָ וַתַּ֥הַר לֹֽו 'And he said, "What pledge shall I give you?" And she said, "Your seal, and your lace, and your staff which is in your hand." So, he gave (them) to her and he went in to her and she conceived by him'. And verse 25 reads: הִ֣וא מוּצֵ֗את וְהִ֨יא שָׁלְחָ֤ה אֶל־חָמִ֙יהָ֙ לֵאמֹ֔ר לְאִישׁ֙ אֲשֶׁר־אֵ֣לֶּה לֹּ֔ו אָנֹכִ֖י הָרָ֑ה וַתֹּ֙אמֶר֙ הַכֶּר־נָ֔א לְמִ֞י **הַחֹתֶ֧מֶת** וְהַפְּתִילִ֛ים וְהַמַּטֶּ֖ה הָאֵֽלֶּה 'When she was brought out, she sent (word) to her father-in-law saying, "By the man whose these (items) are, I have conceived." And she said, "Identify whose these are, the *ḥōtemet*, and the cords, and the staff"'. It is also possible that both terms in these passages refer specifically to a signet. Alternatively, these two cases may refer to a cylinder seal (Seevers and Korhonen 2016, 2).

As is clear from the biblical passages mentioned above, the lexemes *ḥôtām/ ḥōtām* and *ḥōtemet* can denote seals and signets.

5.3.3.2. Translation of ḥôtām/ḥōtām and ḥōtemet in the Septuagint

In the Septuagint, *ḥôtām/ḥōtām* and *ḥōtemet* are primarily rendered with the lexeme σφραγίς 'seal, signet' (LSJ 1742; Muraoka 2009, 666). Ten times *ḥôtām/*

ḥōtām is translated as σφραγίς (Exod 28:11, 21, 36; 39:6, 14, 30 [36:13, 21, 37 LXX]; 1 Kgs 21:8 [20:8 LXX]; Hag 2:23; Song 8:6 [2x]), and *ḥôtām*/*ḥōtām* in Jer 22:24 is rendered with a form related to σφραγίς (i.e., ἀποσφράγισμα 'impression of seal, seal'; LSJ 221; Muraoka 2009, 85), although a variant reading has σφραγίς as do Aquila, Symmachus, and Theodotion, according to Origen (Ziegler 1957, 260). In Gen 38:18 and 38:25, both *ḥôtām*/*ḥōtām* and *ḥōtemet* are translated as δακτύλιος 'ring, signet' (LSJ 367; Muraoka 2009, 139). Another time, in Job 41:7, *ḥôtām*/*ḥōtām* is rendered in a paraphrastic manner as σμιρίτης λίθος 'emery stone' (LSJ 1049, 1620; Muraoka 2009, 431, 628), although Aquila's version of the passage has σφραγίς (Ziegler 1982, 404). In one case there is no corresponding Greek word to *ḥōtām* (Job 38:14). In sum, the translation of *ḥôtām*/*ḥōtām* and *ḥōtemet* in the Septuagint and its revisions points to these terms as designating seals and signets.

5.3.4. *The Term* ṭabbaʿat

5.3.4.1. Etymology and Biblical Usage

The lexeme *ṭabbaʿat* 'ring, signet' (GMD 416; *DCH* 3:342; *HALOT* 1:369) etymologically derives from Egyptian *ḏbʿ.t* 'seal, signet ring' (Muchiki 1999, 247; Lambdin 1953, 151; *WÄS* 5:566). In Egyptian, *ḏbʿ.t* is attested already in the Old Kingdom (2663–2160 BCE) (Muchiki 1999, 247; *WÄS* 5:566). In regard to the loan vector, there is no dilemma in deriving the Semitic consonants of *ṭabbaʿat* from Egyptian *ḏbʿ.t*. Both Egyptian *b* and *ʿ* entered Semitic as *b* and *ʿ*. Egyptian *ḏ,* however, usually entered Canaanite as *ṣ,* whereas Egyptian *d* entered Canaanite as *ṭ* (Muchiki 1999, 259–65). For this reason, the lexeme was probably borrowed into Canaanite sometime in the late third millenium BCE, after the shift of Egyptian *ḏ* > *d* had occurred, but before the Egyptian feminine suffix *-t* had fallen out, given that the latter is preserved in the Hebrew lexeme *ṭabbaʿat* (Muchiki 1999, 247; Allen 2013, 49, 61; Lambdin 1953, 151; Noonan 2019, 109–10).

The term *ṭabbaʿat* occurs a total of fifty times in the Hebrew Bible. It also occurs four times in the Dead Sea Scrolls, including two quotations of Exodus in 4QReworked Pentateuch[c] (11Q19 XXXIV, 6; 4Q365 12a-bii13; 13, 1; *DSSR* 1:666, 776, 778; *DSSC* 1:280). In the majority of cases in the Bible (40x), the lexeme refers to the rings of the tabernacle and the ephod (e.g., Exod 25:14; 28:26). Of the remaining ten instances of the lexeme, three designate jewelry (Exod 35:22; Num 31:50; Isa 3:21) and seven refer to a royal signet ring (Gen 41:42; Esth 3:10, 12; 8:2, 8 [2x], 10). In four of the latter seven cases, the lexeme is used alongside the verbal root *ḥ-t-m* 'to seal' in a context that concerns the sealing of documents with a royal seal (Esth 3:12; 8:8, 10). For instance, Esth

8:8 reads: וְאַתֶּם כִּתְבוּ עַל־הַיְּהוּדִים כַּטּוֹב בְּעֵינֵיכֶם בְּשֵׁם הַמֶּלֶךְ **וְחִתְמוּ בְּטַבַּעַת** הַמֶּלֶךְ כִּי־כְתָב אֲשֶׁר־נִכְתָּב בְּשֵׁם־הַמֶּלֶךְ **וְנַחְתּוֹם בְּטַבַּעַת** הַמֶּלֶךְ אֵין לְהָשִׁיב 'And you may write about the Jews as you see fit, in the name of the king, and seal [***wəḥitmû***] with the ***ṭabbaʿat*** of the king; for an edict that has been written in the name of the king and which has been sealed [***wənaḥtôm***] with the king's ***ṭabbaʿat*** cannot be revoked'.

5.3.4.2. Translation of ṭabbaʿat *in the Septuagint*

The Septuagint's translation of *ṭabbaʿat* supports the idea that it refers to signet rings. In the majority of cases, *ṭabbaʿat* is translated as δακτύλιος 'ring, signet' (LSJ 367; Muraoka 2009, 139). This is the rendering for thirty-one occurrences of *ṭabbaʿat* in the Hebrew text (e.g., Gen 41:42; Exod 25:12; Esth 3:10; Muraoka 2010, 213); in one case (Exod 26:24), the term is rendered as σύμβλησις 'place at which two things are joined' (LSJ 1675; Muraoka 2009, 646). In twelve cases (e.g., Exod 28:23–28; 36:29, 34; 37:27; 38:5, 7), the Septuagint does not include the relevant verses that are extant in the Masoretic Text, but Theodotion translates most of those cases of *ṭabbaʿat* as δακτύλιος 'ring, signet' (Muraoka 2010, 213; Hatch and Redpath 1998, 284). In some cases, however, the Septuagint text does not include a translation for the corresponding passages in the Masoretic Text (e.g., Esth 3:12).

Based on the use of *ṭabbaʿat* in the Bible, and based on the Septuagint's translation of the term, we may conclude that the lexeme designates rings in a general sense, as well as specifically royal signet rings used to seal documents.

5.3.5. Bullas and Jar Handles

Job 38:14 contains a reference to wet clay being impressed with a seal. The passage is somewhat opaque but seems to be comparing the transformation of wet clay when it is stamped by a seal with a symbolic transformation of the earth when evildoers are removed from it. The passage reads: תִּתְהַפֵּךְ **כְּחֹמֶר חוֹתָם** וְיִתְיַצְּבוּ כְּמוֹ לְבוּשׁ 'It changes like ***ḥōmer ḥôtām*** [clay of a seal], and they shall stand like a garment'. In this passage, the construct phrase *ḥōmer ḥôtām* 'clay of a seal' designates wet clay that is impressed with a seal. As discussed above, *ḥōmer* refers to workable clay utilized in construction projects, and it is used here also to signify workable clay, albeit a much smaller amount. And, while this passage refers to a wet lump of clay impressed with a seal, the Bible does not contain a passage that refers to dry lumps of stamped clay, whether bullae or jar handles. It nevertheless seems reasonable to suggest that the stamp upon a dry bulla or jar handle was designated by the term *ḥōtām*. After all, while the signet ring or seal utilized to imprint clay is designated by the term *ḥōtām*, it is the dried clay that actually comprises the impression of the seal. As mentioned above, a few West Semitic seals are indeed engraved with the lexeme *ḥōtām*, which would have appeared on clay jars and bullae stamped with such seals. The term *ḥōtām*, then, probably designates the actual seal as well as the seal impression, and *ḥōmer* designates the material (i.e., wet clay) impressed with seals, but it is not clear if there is a separate lexeme that specifically designates dried clay lumps (i.e., bullae).

5.3.6. Definitions of Terms Designating Seals

Having analyzed the ancient Hebrew words that designate seals, I suggest the following definitions for these terms.

***ʾeben*:** A term that carries the general meaning ‘rock, stone’ but also designates plaster-covered stones and probably also stelae with writing inscribed directly upon them (see 3.1.3.1–3.1.3.2 and 3.1.5). The term also denotes precious stones and weights that were used in ancient Israel.

***ḥōtām* and *ḥotemet*:** Both terms denote stamp seals and perhaps cylinder seals; *ḥōtām* also denotes signet rings. The term *ḥōtām* perhaps also refers to impressions of seals on clay.

***ṭabbaʿat*:** A term that carries the general meaning ‘ring’ and also specifically designates signet rings.

CHAPTER 6

Egypt's Influence on Canaan and Ancient Israel

6.1. Egypt's Contact with Canaan and Ancient Israel

Due to the geographical proximity of Egypt to Canaan and ancient Israel, contact between these neighboring regions was inevitable. Indeed, there is evidence of ties between the two cultures already in the Predynastic Period (5000–3050 BCE), especially in the mid- to late fourth millennium BCE (Mumford 2014, 70–71); contact increases in the Early Dynastic Period (3050–2663 BCE), particularly during the First Dynasty (3050–2813 BCE) (Mumford 2014, 71–72). Egyptian pottery from Early Bronze Age I and II levels has been found in southern Canaan, in Transjordan, and even as far north as Megiddo and Byblos (Mumford 2014, 70–72; Braun 2002), and Levantine pottery has been discovered in Egyptian tombs of the First Dynasty (Mumford 2014, 70–72; Braun 2009, 27–28). Egyptian annals from this period speak of smiting Asiatics (Hoffmeier 2004, 128–30; Redford 1992, 33), and art historical depictions of Asiatics have been found in Egypt, suggesting that foreigners settled in Egypt even in the Predynastic and Early Dynastic Periods (Bietak 2007, 417; Wilkinson 2002). Furthermore, serekhs of Narmer as well as the names of First Dynasty monarchs have been found in southern Canaan, confirming the presence of Egyptians in the region (Braun 2009; Hoffmeier 2004, 129).

During the Old Kingdom (2663–2160 BCE), the number of Egyptian artifacts in Canaan diminishes, but they are nevertheless present (Mumford 2014, 72). In Egypt, however, the same period exhibits a peak in Canaanite artifacts, which suggests that interaction between the two regions existed (Mumford 2014, 72; Sowada 2009, 245–55). During this period, Egypt's main interest in the Levant was economic, but Egypt also employed periodic military coercion when its interests were threatened (Hoffmeier 2004, 129). Strong trade connections between Egypt and Byblos existed already in the First Dynasty and also during the Old Kingdom, particularly because Egypt imported Byblian timber, cedar oil, and resin, as well as wine and perhaps olive oil (Genz 2014, 303–4; Sowada 2009, 128–41; Redford 1992, 38).

Beginning with the First Intermediate Period (2160–2066 BCE) and continuing through the Middle Kingdom (2066–1650 BCE), there was continual interaction between Egypt and its neighbor to the northeast (Mumford 2014, 72–72). The contact consisted of military confrontations as well as trade activities (Mumford 2014, 72–73). Commerce also continued between Egypt and the northern Levantine coast (Cohen-Weinberger and Goren 2004, 80–84). Furthermore, we learn from Egyptian sources that Asiatics had penetrated in great numbers into the Delta, especially during the eighteenth and seventeenth centuries BCE (Bietak 2007, 420–22; D. Ben-Tor 2004, 28; Redford 1992, 66–68, 101–2). The many scarabs discovered in Canaan of the Middle Bronze Age reflect the influence that Egypt had upon the Canaanite culture; moreover, D. Ben-Tor (2011; 2003, 244–46) argues that the presence of scarabs in Canaan points to the high population of Asiatics in the Delta, who would have introduced the use of such scarabs to their kin in Canaan. By the beginning of the Second Intermediate Period (1650–1549 BCE), foreigners in the Delta—specifically the Hyksos—had managed to take over Egypt and establish their own kingdom, which was in place during the Fifteenth–Seventeenth Dynasties (1650–1549 BCE) (D. Ben-Tor 2004, 31–32; Redford 1992, 101–11). Soon, however, foreign rule over Egypt ended, and the New Kingdom began (1549–1069 BCE).

Contact between Egypt and the Levant was at its height during the Eighteenth and Nineteenth Dynasties (1549–1187 BCE) of the New Kingdom; during this period Egypt gained control over Canaan and converted it into an Egyptian vassal state (Killebrew 2005, 81–83; Hoffmeier 2004, 134). Ancient records speak of at least two dozen Egyptian expeditions into Canaan during the Eighteenth Dynasty (1549–1298 BCE) (Killebrew 2005, 55), and Egyptian campaigns into Canaan continued into the Nineteenth and Twentieth Dynasties (1298–1069 BCE) (Killebrew 2005, 57). Thutmose III (1479–25 BCE) experienced a major victory over Canaanite armies at Megiddo in 1457 BCE, and Egypt's rule over Canaan would remain in place until the reign of Ramesses III (1185–53 BCE) (Panitz-Cohen 2014, 542; Hoffmeier 2004, 134). During this time of Canaan's subservience to Egypt, administrative and military garrisons were set up by the Egyptians in strategic Canaanite locations such as Deir el-Balah, Beth Shean, Jaffa, Gaza, Tel Mor, Lachish, Aphek, and Tel Sherʿa (Panitz-Cohen 2014, 548; Gilboa 2014, 628; Killebrew 2004, 309). Indeed, the presence of Egyptians is confirmed by the many finds of Egyptian-style pottery at various Canaanite sites, including Beth Shean, Tell es-Saʿidiyeh, Aphek, Tell el-Farʿah (South), and Deir el-Balah (Killebrew 2004; 2005, 67–80, 341; Mullins 2006). Furthermore, Egypt's influence is seen in the Egyptian-style architecture of various structures in Canaan (Killebrew 2005, 58–64; Panitz-Cohen 2014, 548). Egypt's impact is also evident in the many Egyptian artifacts discovered in Canaan; artifacts such as pendants and amulets, scarab seals, and anthropoid coffins have been discovered in various sites (Killebrew 2005, 64; Gilboa 2014, 628–30; D. Ben-Tor 2011; Brandl 2004; Martin 2004). Moreover, hieratic and hieroglyphic inscriptions on bowls and ostraca that date to this period have been found in Canaan (Killebrew 2005, 67); victory stelae and statues have also been discovered at northern sites such as Tell es-Shihab, Tell Nebi Mend, Tyre, and Beth Shean (Killebrew 2005, 55–56).[1]

In the Late Bronze Age, the interaction between Egypt and Canaan touched not only on politics and commerce but also on culture. Canaanite governors sent their children to the Egyptian court to be educated in Egyptian ways (Hoffmeier 2004, 135, 138; Redford 1992, 198), and diplomatic marriages between Egypt and Canaan were common (Hoffmeier 2004, 138). Canaanite gods were introduced into Egyptian religion (Sparks 2004, 40–41; Redford 1992, 231–33), and Asiatic literature was even translated into Egyptian (Redford 1992, 233–36). Bunimovitz (2019, 274) stresses that, during the Late Bronze Age, the Levant marked the coming together of two so-called high cultures, that of Egypt and that of Canaan. The lively interaction between the two cultures is especially reflected in the large number of Egyptian loanwords in Hebrew and other Northwest Semitic languages as well as the high number of Hebrew and Semitic loanwords in Egyptian.[2]

Contact between Egypt and Syria-Palestine continued into the time of the Israelite monarchy and even until the destruction of Jerusalem and beyond. In the Bible, we read that Solomon married the pharaoh's daughter (1 Kgs 9:16); we also read of Jeroboam's flight to Egypt (1 Kgs 11:40), and of the invasion of Palestine in the tenth century BCE by Sheshonq I (1 Kgs 14:25–26). A number of other military encounters between Egypt and ancient Israel are mentioned

1. Parker and Arico (2015) persuasively argue that the Moabite inscription from Kerak is actually an Egyptian stela that was appropriated and inscribed by a Moabite king. Although the historical circumstances of how this Egyptian statue would have ended up in Kerak is not known, the art-historical evidence for it being Egyptian is compelling, and this further points to the interaction between ancient Egypt and southern Canaan and Transjordan. Additionally, the Elibaal and Abibaal inscriptions (dating to the tenth–early ninth centuries BCE according to Rollston 2008, 59–62)—which appear on Egyptian stelae of Osorkon I and Sheshonq I, respectively—serve as further evidence of the contact between Egypt and the Levantine coast, specifically, the interaction that existed between the Twenty-Second Dynasty (948–743 BCE) of Egypt and the coastal cities of Byblos and Tyre.

2. The collection of Egyptian loanwords in Northwest Semitic language by Muchiki (1999, 322) can be categorized into the following semantic groups: mineral terminology, botanical terminology, tools and utensils, measures, textiles and cloths, architecture, and nautical terminology. Also, in his study of foreign words in Hebrew, including words borrowed from Egyptian, Noonan (2019, 268) adds the following categories: food and drink, metals and metallurgy, and vessels. Hoch (1994, 462–73) collects 380 words that entered from Semitic into Egyptian during the New Kingdom and the Third Intermediate Period (1064–656 BCE). He arranges the words according to specific categories, including military terms, topography, food and beverages, household objects, vessels, body and medicine, agriculture and animal husbandry, architecture, tools and equipment, raw materials, civilian occupations, political terms, flora and fauna, crafts, minerals, religion and cult, ointments and fragrance, music, weights and measures.

(2 Kgs 17:4; 23:28–37). The biblical text also states that, after the destruction of Jerusalem in 586 BCE, the Judean military commanders took Jeremiah the prophet, along with other Judeans, and descended to Egypt in search of refuge (Jer 43). The fact that the biblical text depicts interaction between Israel and Egypt at various points in history suggests that contact existed between the two regions. Indeed, Egyptian pottery from Iron Age I and II has been found in Israel (Evian 2011), and Levantine pottery of the late Iron Age has been found in Egypt (Maeir 2002).

In sum, the testimony of archeological finds, Egyptian records, and the biblical text indicates that the culture of ancient Egypt and that of Canaan and ancient Israel had ties that spanned from the Predynastic period (5000–3050 BCE) of Egypt until after the destruction of the Judean kingdom. In such an atmosphere of correspondence, the exchange of concepts, goods, and technologies is expected. It is no surprise, then, that ancient Israelite writing technology resembles that of its neighbor to the southwest.

6.2. The Influence of Egypt and Mesopotamia on Writing Technology in Canaan and Ancient Israel

It would be incorrect to say that the writing technology of Canaan and ancient Israel derives entirely from Egypt. After all, certain elements of writing in Canaan and Israel are not a result of Egyptian influence. As briefly mentioned in the opening of this study, cuneiform artifacts from as early as the Middle Bronze Age have been unearthed in Canaan. Indeed, about ninety cuneiform artifacts (e.g., royal stelae, administrative letters, education texts, seals) from the Middle Bronze Age to the Iron Age II–III have been discovered at sites such as Hazor, Taanach, Megiddo, and Aphek (Horowitz, Oshima, and Sanders 2018, 4–7; Cohen 2019, 248–52, 254). To this group of artifacts we may add about one hundred tablets that were discovered at Amarna but were produced at Canaanite sites including Gezer, Ashkelon, Jerusalem, and Megiddo, among others (Vita 2015, 59–102; Cohen 2019, 252). The Amarna tablets as well as cuneiform artifacts discovered at Canaanite sites clearly indicate a non-Egyptian influence upon the scribal culture of Canaan (Demsky 1990, 157–58; Horowitz, Oshima, and Sanders 2018; Cohen 2019). Moreover, such finds confirm that cuneiform scribal centers existed in various Canaanite cities even before the use of ostraca, papyrus, and ink took root in Canaan and Israel (Demsky 1990, 158; Carr 2005, 56–61).[3]

3. Here I should also mention the cuneiform alphabet, which was used in Ugarit (i.e., the Ugaritic alphabet) as well as in other parts of Canaan, Syria, and even in Cyprus (i.e., the reduced

Canaan's utilization of cuneiform as a writing system clearly indicates an influence from Mesopotamia, not Egypt. Also, Israel's tradition of monumental stela inscriptions does not necessarily derive from Egypt's writing practices. It is difficult to say whether Israel's use of royal stela inscriptions was a result of Egypt's influence upon Canaan, or whether this lapidary form of writing should be connected to the greater ancient Near Eastern practice of erecting such stelae. As mentioned above, such stelae were set up by the Egyptians in Canaan and elsewhere (e.g., Merneptah stela of Thebes) during the Late Bronze Age. It is therefore possible that Israel's practice of erecting inscribed stelae is a tradition that was established in Canaan when it was ruled by Egypt. On the other hand, it is noteworthy that of the few stelae fragments found in Israel, most date to Iron Age II, when Egypt was no longer ruling over Syria-Palestine. At this time, Assyria was on the rise and would eventually conquer the Levant (Schneider 2014, 98–104). An essential part of Assyrian domination was the use of royal stela inscriptions in conquered territories as a form of propaganda and intimidation (Schneider 2014, 98–99; Machinist 1983, 731); indeed, Assyrian stelae stood in Samaria and Ashdod (Machinist 1983, 731). Furthermore, the fragments of such stelae from ancient Israel as well as the stelae discovered in the Levant at large (i.e., Mesha stela; Tell Fakhariyah statue) resemble Mesopotamian stelae in shape, rock composition, and content.[4] Thus, while Canaan may have been initially exposed to monumental stelae by the Egyptians, this form of writing came to be used by the Israelites only during the Assyrian expansion, which was characterized by the use of such stelae; for this reason, Israel's own utilization of such royal stela inscriptions is probably a result of Mesopotamian rather than Egyptian influence.

It is also not entirely clear whether Israel's use of writing boards—assuming this practice existed in Israel—derives from Egyptian writing tradition or from Mesopotamian writing practices. Writing boards were indeed utilized in Egypt as early as the Old Kingdom (2663–2160 BCE), and a number of such boards survive from the New Kingdom (1549–1069 BCE) (Hagen 2013, 83–85). When Egyptian writing practices were introduced into Canaan during the New Kingdom, writing boards were presumably introduced as well, but we have no evidence of their use at that time in Canaan. On the other hand, writing boards were

cuneiform alphabet) (Dietrich and Loretz 1988, 145–294; Horowitz, Oshima, and Sanders 2018, 157–67). The connection between the cuneiform of Mesopotamia and the cuneiform alphabet of Canaan is obvious: these writing systems both utilize wedge-shaped signs, although the former is a syllabic system while the latter is a consonantal alphabet. Nevertheless, although the cuneiform alphabet resembles Akkadian cuneiform signs, Cross (1989, 84) points out that "it was developed under the inspiration of the Old Canaanite pictographic alphabet." The existence of the reduced cuneiform alphabet in Canaan thus points to the influence of the Mesopotamian writing tradition as well as that of Egypt upon Canaan's writing practices.

4. See 3.1.1–3.1.2 for discussion of lapidary inscriptions in the ancient Near East.

also used in Mesopotamia and the ancient Mediterranean, including Ugarit.[5] Furthermore, the fact that writing boards were designated in Akkadian and in Hebrew by cognate lexemes (i.e., *lē̓u*, *lēḫu* and *lûah*; *daltu* and *delet*) suggests that there may have been a common scribal tradition of using boards, or that boards were perhaps adopted by the Israelites from Mesopotamian scribal culture (Hicks 1983, 57). Alternatively, it may be that Egypt introduced wooden writing boards covered with gesso, while Mesopotamia introduced writing boards covered with wax, because the former were common in Egypt and the latter in Mesopotamia.

If the writing technology of ancient Israel does not entirely derive from Egypt, what, then, is Egypt's influence upon Israel's writing tradition? First and foremost, it is Egypt's writing system that inspired the invention of the Proto-Sinaitic alphabet (Hamilton 2014, 32–34; 2006, 2–21; Darnell et al. 2005), which developed into the Old Phoenician script; this alphabet was probably adopted by the Israelites.[6] While the Phoenician script may have served as an intermediary between the Proto-Sinaitic alphabet and the Hebrew script, the origin of both is ultimately in ancient Egypt; Hamilton (2014, 30; 2006, 2–21) traces almost all of the alphabetic graphemes to Egyptian hieroglyphic or hieratic prototypes. Consequently, Egypt's influence upon Israelite writing culture is foundational; without the Egyptian writing system, there would be no Hebrew alphabet.

The influence of Egyptian writing culture is evident not only in Israel's alphabetic script, but also in the materials and tools utilized to write this alphabet. Use of the ostracon as a writing surface was extremely common in ancient Egypt;

5. See 4.2.4.7 for a fuller discussion of writing boards.

6. There is debate as to the origin of the alphabet used by the Israelites. According to the traditional view, the Proto-Sinaitic alphabet developed into the Old Phoenician alphabet, which was borrowed by the Hebrews and the Aramaeans in Iron Age I (Albright 1969, 5–6; Naveh 1970, 277; Cross 2003a, 341), and by the ninth and eighth centuries BCE, the Hebrew and Aramaic scripts had begun to differentiate themselves from the Old Phoenician script (Naveh 1987, 53–57; Rollston 2010, 44; 2014, 72–76; Vanderhooft 2017, 443). There are, however, scholars who question whether or not the Old Phoenician alphabet served as an intermediary between the Proto-Sinaitic alphabet and the Hebrew and Aramaic scripts, arguing instead for a continuity between the Proto-Sinaitic alphabet and the script of Canaan/Israel during Iron Age I and IIA (McCarter 2008, 47–56; Hamilton 2014, 30, 42–50). But those who argue against the traditional view have not countered the main argument in support of the traditional view: that the Hebrew script, like the Phoenician script, has only twenty-two letters. Presumably, if Hebrew script were indeed a direct descendant of the Proto-Sinaitic script, Hebrew script would have preserved more graphemes to represent consonants that were clearly distinguished in the spoken language. It is clear that *š* and *ś* were distinguished during the First Temple Period (Khan 2013, 50–51; Faber 1981, 244); also, based on the Septuagint's transliteration of Hebrew names, it is also apparent that *ḥ* was distinguished from *ḫ* while ʿ was distinguished from *ġ*. One would expect to see different graphemes for these phonemes in the Hebrew alphabet, but this is not the case. The Phoenician language, on the other hand, has only twenty-two phonemes, so it is understandable why its script has the same number of alphabetic characters. The similarity in the number of consonants in the Phoenician and Hebrew scripts suggests that the latter derives from the former.

for instance, Deir el-Medina has yielded 17,000–20,000 finds that consist of potsherds and limestone flakes (Hagen 2011, 1, note 1).[7] These finds are either incised or written upon with black or red ink (Hagen 2011, 1–42). The corpus of Proto-Sinaitic inscriptions is also comprised of incised sandstone (Sass 1988, 10, 169–73), and the two Wadi el-Ḥol inscriptions are incised on a mountain face (Darnell et al. 2005). While the Proto-Sinaitic inscriptions were all incised upon sandstone, Old Canaanite inscriptions were either incised on limestone flakes or potsherds or written upon potsherds with ink (Hamilton 2014, 35; Sass 1988, 174–79), presumably with a rush pen. In total, around twenty inscribed potsherds or limestone flakes dating to the second millennium have been discovered, and another twenty or so inscriptions consist of bronze arrowheads incised with the Old Canaanite alphabet (Sass 1988, 51–52, 174–79; Cross 2003a; Finkelstein and Sass 2013; Hamilton 2014). Both the Canaanite alphabet (which derives from Egyptian signs) as well as the material on which this alphabet was written (i.e., ostraca and limestone flakes) thus speak to the influence of Egyptian writing tradition upon the writing practices of Canaan.

Writing on ostraca with ink became a very common form of communication in ancient Israel, as is confirmed by the finds of inscribed ostraca from Samaria, Arad, and Lachish. Papyrus also seems to have been frequently used for drafting official documents. And, while the use of ostraca, papyrus, rush and reed pens, and ink had become part and parcel of scribal culture in Iron Age II Israel, Schniedewind (2013, 36, 58–60) points out that this technology was adopted by Canaan from Egypt.[8] This is confirmed by the fact that the Hebrew terms designating these and other scribal materials are loanwords from Egyptian; the relevant terms are *gōmeʾ* ‘papyrus’, *dəyô* ‘ink’, and *qeset* (*hassōpēr*) ‘(scribal) palette’ (Schniedewind 2013, 36, 58–60).[9] In addition to these three lexemes, we should also mention the terms *ḥôtām* ‘seal’, *ḥôtemet* ‘seal, signet’, and *ṭabbaʿat* ‘signet ring’, all of which derive from Egyptian (Muchiki 1999, 246–47; Lambdin 1953, 151; Schniedewind 2013, 59) and have to do with a specific element of writing—that is, stamp seals. Most of these lexemes were probably

7. See 4.2.5.1, for a fuller discussion of inscribed pottery from Egypt, Israel, and Greece.

8. Discussing the finds of Lachish during the Late Bronze Age, Goldwasser (1991) writes about a fragmentary hieratic sherd that seems to mention an Egyptian scribe, which further points to the scribal influence Egypt had upon Canaan.

9. The Hebrew words *ʾāḥû* ‘sedges, reeds’, *sûp* ‘reeds, marsh, papyrus’, and *ʿārôt* ‘reeds, papyrus’ are also loanwords from Egyptian, yet they are not used in the Bible in connection with manufacturable papyrus. Nevertheless, it is possible that *sûp* and *ʿārôt* entered Canaanite at the same time that *gōmeʾ* came into Canaanite. In essence, a set of three Egyptian terms designating reeds and papyrus would have penetrated into Canaanite at a similar time; one lexeme designated manufacturable papyrus material (*gōmeʾ*), and two terms denoted the wild reed or its habitat (*sûp* and *ʿārôt*). The lexeme *ʾāḥû*, however, probably entered Canaanite during the Old Kingdom (Lambdin 1953, 146; see also 2.2.1 for discussion of *ʾāḥû*).

introduced into Canaanite society during the New Kingdom (1549–1069 BCE), a period when Syria-Palestine was ruled by Egypt (Schniedewind 2013, 29, 32, 34, 36, 56–60). Scholars argue that it was also during this period that Canaanite scribes adopted hieratic numerals, which appear in various Hebrew inscriptions (N. S. Fox 2000, 250–68; Carr 2005, 85–88; Wimmer 2008; Schniedewind 2013, 58).

Only a limited number of the writing-related lexemes in Hebrew derive from Egyptian, but these designate the essential materials of ancient Israel's writing technology: papyrus, ink, palette (Schniedewind 2013, 36). One may object that the words *ḥereś* and *ʿēṭ*, which refer to perhaps the most frequently used items by an Israelite scribe, were not borrowed from Egyptian.[10] But only those terms that refer to items foreign to Syria-Palestine needed to be borrowed. Accordingly, Egyptian terms for papyrus, ink, and a scribal palette were adopted, while the native Hebrew lexeme designating potsherds simply came to signify inscribed ostraca, in addition to pottery vessels and sherds.[11] The Egyptian word for a rush or reed pen was also not borrowed because Hebrew already had a word (*ʿēṭ*) that carries the general meaning 'pen; writing instrument' and denotes an iron pen used for engraving (*ʿēṭ barzēl*) as well as a rush and reed pen (*ʿēṭ sōpēr/sōpərîm*) utilized to write on ostraca and papyrus. It is noteworthy, though, that, while *ʿēṭ* was not borrowed from Egyptian, the lexeme needed to be modified by *sōpēr/sōpərîm* to specify the rush and reed pen; this specification demonstrates that *ʿēṭ* did not itself refer to a rush or reed pen but acquired this meaning, presumably when such pens became common in Canaan and ancient Israel. Hebrew also did not need to borrow words designating lapidary inscriptions because it already possessed terms indicating stone surfaces.

In sum, the writing technology of Canaan and Israel reflects the impact of two ancient Near Eastern cultures, those of Mesopotamia and Egypt. And while the source of Israel's presumed use of writing boards is not clear, its lapidary inscriptions probably indicate a sharing of scribal practices between Israel and its Mesopotamian and Syrian neighbors. This form of writing was impressive, but it was clearly not the common day-to-day manner of communication used in the ancient Near East in general or in ancient Israel in particular. Rather, Israel's usual form of correspondence (inscribed ostraca), as well as its form of legal documentation or literary composition (writing on papyrus and possibly leather), bespeaks Egyptian influence. Moreover, although cuneiform

10. Potsherds were designated by the term *nḏr* in Egyptian (also *blḏ*⁽ʾ⁾ in Demotic; Gestermann 1984, 701–2), and a rush pen was denoted by the lexeme *ʿr* (*WÄS* 1:208).

11. The papyrus plant was not inherently foreign to Canaan and ancient Israel because it did grow near the Sea of Galilee and Lake Huleh (Lewis 1974, 6). However, the manufacturable use of the plant for writing material was indeed a foreign technology adopted by the Canaanites from the Egyptians.

was employed by Canaan for international communication in the lingua franca (Akkadian), cuneiform was primarily used in the Middle and Late Bronze Ages. With time, cuneiform impressed on clay—a quintessentially Mesopotamian medium of communication—would be replaced in Canaan by Egyptian writing practices (Schniedewind 2013, 60).

The replacement of the Mesopotamian-inspired cuneiform writing system by an Egyptian-inspired alphabetic system on the part of Canaanites seems to have occurred as a result of Egypt's presence within Canaan during the New Kingdom (1549–1069 BCE). Canaan was a vassal of Egypt during this period, and Canaanites were thoroughly exposed to Egyptian culture, including Egypt's education tradition and scribal practices.[12] As is well known, it is common for a vassal state to adopt cultural aspects of the country by which the vassal state is ruled. The Canaanites' adoption of Egyptian writing practices is thus a direct result of Egypt's physical, military, and cultural presence within the territory of Canaan during the New Kingdom. This was the period when papyrus, ink, and rush and reed pens were introduced into Canaan by the Egyptians. The emergence of the Israelites within Canaan reinforced the use of the alphabetic writing tradition in ancient Israel because it was this writing system that was utilized to write ancient Israel's national language, Hebrew. The use of the alphabetic script—as well as the writing surfaces and tools that were associated with it—came to define Israelite scribal culture in Iron Age II. In sum, ancient Israel's writing technology, as a development of Canaanite writing practices, was essentially Egyptian in nature.

12. Various scholars discuss topics concerning the education, literacy, and scribal practices of ancient Egypt. J. J. Janssen (1992, 81–82, 84, 87, 90) stresses the high percentage of literacy among males at Deir el-Medina. He argues that about 40 percent of the male population of Deir el-Medina was fully literate, and the remainder of the male population was at least "semi-literate"; that is, they were able to comprehend the meaning of simple written messages but could not produce such a text (J. J. Janssen 1992, 81–82). R. M. Janssen and J. J. Janssen (1990, 67–89) discuss what comprised a regular day for a schoolboy in ancient Egypt in their book entitled *Growing up in Ancient Egypt*. McDowell (2000) considers questions of the status of scribal teachers and students in Deir el-Medina. She concludes that, while teachers were usually of a high rank, students were of both of high and lower ranks in the social stratigraphy of Deir el-Medina; the method of learning on the part of students consisted of copying and memorizing literary texts (McDowell 2000, 230). Hagen (2013) discusses writing boards and the function they served in the education curriculum of ancient Egypt. The significant work by Brunner (1991) presents a historical sketch of education in ancient Egypt, discussing the organization of schooling as well as the curriculum used.

CHAPTER 7

Conclusion

IN EXAMINING THE BIBLICAL HEBREW TERMS that refer to writing surfaces and instruments, this study has sought to incorporate a discussion of the biblical texts that use the relevant lexical items as well as the archeological and art historical evidence for them. In chapter 2, I argued that, while a number of terms denoted reeds and their habitats, it was the word *gōmeʾ*, an Egyptian loanword, that referred to manufacturable papyrus material. Additionally, this chapter showed that three other terms specifying wild reeds or sedges (i.e., *ʾāḥû*, *sûp*, *ʿārôt*) were also borrowed from Egyptian, which, of course, points to the interaction that Canaan and Israel had with Egypt. The discussion in chapter 3 focused on words indicating stone and plaster surfaces; in this chapter, I suggested that the terms *ʾeben* and *maṣṣēbā*/*maṣṣebet* may have denoted inscribed stelae. Chapter 4 looked at a variety of terms specifying common writing materials such as vellum (*ʿôr*), scrolls (*məgillā*; *gillāyôn*), stone and wooden tablets (*delet*; *lûaḥ*), and ostraca (*ḥereś*), as well as uncommon writing surfaces such as a wooden staff (*maṭṭe*), a stick (*ʿēṣ*), and a golden rosette (*ṣîṣ zāhāb ṭāhôr*). In chapter 5, the discussion shifted to examining writing instruments and glyptics. It was shown in this chapter that the words *dəyô* 'ink', *qeset* 'scribal palette', *ḥōtām*/*ḥotemet* 'seal, signet ring', and *ṭabbaʿat* 'ring, signet ring'—like the lexeme *gōmeʾ* and other words indicating reeds and sedges—are Egyptian loanwords.

After examining the various materials utilized as writing surfaces in ancient Israel (chapters 2–4) as well as the writing implements used to execute the writing (chapter 5), I considered in chapter 6 the issue of the origin of Israel's writing technology, seeking to set this technology within the context of other writing practices in the ancient Near East. The argument put forth in this chapter is that perhaps the most common form of writing in Canaan and Israel—writing on ostraca and papyrus using ink and rush or reed pens—was a technology borrowed from Egypt. This claim is buttressed by the fact that the terms denoting these and other writing materials are words loaned from Egyptian. Moreover, as pointed out in chapter 6, the interaction that existed between Egypt and Canaan/Israel from Egypt's Predynastic Period and especially during the second half of the second millennium BCE facilitated the sharing of various goods and cultural elements between these two regions. It was in this environment of communication that the Egyptians introduced their writing practices into Canaan, and the writing technology of the Israelites derives from that of the Canaanites. Ancient Israel's writing customs thus ultimately originate with Egyptian writing practices.

The scope of the current study was limited to ancient Hebrew words indicating writing surfaces as well as scribal instruments and glyptics. Other writing-related lexemes need to be examined in order to gain a fuller understanding of the semantic field of writing in Biblical Hebrew. For instance, words designating various types of writing (e.g., *kətāb*, *miktāb*, *pittûaḥ*), documents and records (e.g., *ʾiggeret*, *sēper*, *dibrê hayyāmîm*, *mityaḥăśîm*), and words denoting scribes (e.g., *sōpēr*, *ṭipsār*) have not been considered in this study. Additionally, Hebrew verbal roots specifying distinct kinds of writing processes require a semantic study of their own (e.g., *k-t-b*, *s-p-r*, *p-t-ḥ*). In addition to these sets of lexemes and roots that are in need of further research, there is also a significant sociohistorical question that necessitates more discussion: specifically, what was the influence of the Aramaic-speaking scribal culture upon that of ancient Israel? This question needs to be addressed inasmuch as many writing-related terms—especially those referring to types of writing, documents, records, and scribes—appear to be loanwords from Aramaic (e.g., *kətāb*, *ʾiggeret*, *ṭipsār*). These issues will have to be considered in future studies.

WORKS CITED

Abraham, Kathleen, and Michael Sokoloff. 2011. "Aramaic Loanwords in Akkadian–A Reassessment of the Proposals." *Archiv für Orientforschung* 52:22–76.

Adams, Matthew J. 2013. "Area J. Part III: The Main Sector of Area J." Pages 47–118 in vol. 1 of *Megiddo V: The 2004–2008 Seasons*. Edited by Israel Finkelstein, David Ussishkin, Eric H. Cline, Matthew J. Adams, Eran Arie, Norma Franklin, and Mario A. S. Martin. 3 vols. SMNIA 31. Winona Lake, IN: Eisenbrauns.

Adams, Matthew J., and James M. Bos. 2013. "Area J. Part IV: Sub-Area Upper J." Pages 119–42 in vol. 1 of *Megiddo V: The 2004–2008 Seasons*. Edited by Israel Finkelstein, David Ussishkin, Eric H. Cline, Matthew J. Adams, Eran Arie, Norma Franklin, and Mario A. S. Martin. 3 vols. SMNIA 31. Winona Lake, IN: Eisenbrauns.

Aharoni, Yohanan. 1974. "The Horned Altar of Beer-sheba." *BA* 37, no. 1:2–6.

Aḥituv, Shmuel. 2008. *Echoes from the Past: Hebrew and Cognate Inscriptions from the Biblical Period*. Jerusalem: Carta.

Aḥituv, Shmuel, Esther Eshel, and Ze'ev Meshel. 2012. "The Inscriptions." Pages 73–142 in *Kuntillet ʿAjrud (Ḥorvat Teman): An Iron Age II Religious Site on the Judah–Sinai Border*. Edited by Ze'ev Meshel and Liora Freud. Translated by John H. Tresman. Jerusalem: Israel Exploration Society.

Albrektson, Bertil. 1963. *Studies in the Text and Theology of the Book of Lamentations with a Critical Edition of the Peshitta Text*. Studia Theologica Lundensia 21. Lund: CWK Gleerup.

Albright, William F. 1934. *The Vocalization of the Egyptian Syllabic Orthography*. American Oriental Series 5. New Haven, CT: American Oriental Society.

———. 1969. *The Proto-Sinaitic Inscriptions and Their Decipherment*. Harvard Theological Studies 22. Cambridge, MA: Harvard University Press, 1966. Repr., Cambridge, MA: Harvard University Press.

Allen, James P. 2013. *The Ancient Egyptian Language: An Historical Study*. New York: Cambridge University Press.

Ambos, Claus, and Ingrid Krauskopf. 2010. "The Curved Staff in the Ancient Near East as a Predecessor of the Etruscan Lituus." Pages 127–53 in *Material Aspects of Etruscan Religion: Proceedings of the International Colloquium, Leiden, May 29–30, 2008*. Edited by L. Bouke van der Meer. Babesch Supplements 16. Leuven: Peeters.

Ameri, Marta, Sarah Kielt Costello, Gregg M. Jamison, and Sarah Jarmer Scott. 2018. "Introduction: Small Windows, Wide Views." Pages 1–10 in *Seals and Sealing in the Ancient World: Case Studies from the Near East, Egypt, the Aegean, and South Asia*. Edited by Marta Ameri, Sarah Kielt Costello, Gregg M. Jamison, and Sarah Jarmer Scott. Cambridge: Cambridge University Press.

Andrews, Ethan A., ed. 1958. *Harpers' Latin Dictionary: A New Latin Dictionary*. New York: Harper and Brothers; Oxford: Clarendon.

Arie, Eran, and Assaf Nativ. 2013. "Area K. Part II: Level K-6." Pages 165–77 in vol. 1 of *Megiddo V: The 2004–2008 Seasons*. Edited by Israel Finkelstein, David Ussishkin, Eric H. Cline, Matthew J. Adams, Eran Arie, Norma Franklin, and Mario A. S. Martin. 3 vols. SMNIA 31. Winona Lake, IN: Eisenbrauns.

Ashton, June. 2008. *Scribal Habits in the Ancient Near East, c. 3000 BCE to the Emergence of the Codex*. Mandelbaum Studies in Judaica 13. Sydney: Mandelbaum.

Aston, Barbara G., James A. Harrell, and Ian Shaw. 2000. "Stone." Pages 5–77 in *Ancient Egyptian Materials and Technology*. Edited by Paul T. Nicholson and Ian Shaw. Cambridge: Cambridge University Press.

Aufrecht, Walter E. 1989. *A Corpus of Ammonite Inscriptions*. Ancient Near Eastern Texts and Studies 4. Lewiston, NY: Edwin Mellen.

Avigad, Naḥman. 1997. *Corpus of West Semitic Stamp Seals*. Revised and enlarged by Benjamin Sass. Jerusalem: Israel Exploration Society.

Avrin, Leila. 1991. *Scribes, Script, and Books: The Book Arts form Antiquity to the Renaissance*. Chicago: American Library Association.

Baines, John. 2007. *Visual and Written Culture in Ancient Egypt*. Oxford: Oxford University Press.

Baker, Henry W. 1962. "Notes on the Opening of the Copper Scrolls from Qumrân." Pages 203–10 in *Discoveries in the Judaean Desert of Jordan III: Les 'Petites Grottes' de Qumrân*. Edited by Maurice Baillet, Józef T. Milik, and Roland de Vaux. Oxford: Clarendon.

Bar-Adon, Pesaḥ 1975. "An Early Hebrew Inscription in a Judean Desert Cave." *IEJ* 25, no. 4:226–32.

Bar-Ilan, Meir. 2000. "Writing Materials." Pages 996–97 in vol. 2 of *Encyclopedia of the Dead Sea Scrolls*. Edited by Lawrence H. Schiffman and James C. VanderKam. 2 vols. New York: Oxford University Press.

Barkay, Gabriel. 1992. "The Priestly Benediction on Silver Plaques from Ketef Hinnom in Jerusalem." *TA* 19:139–92.

Barkay, Gabriel, Marilyn J. Lundberg, Andrew G. Vaughn, and Bruce Zuckerman. 2004. "The Amulets from Ketef Hinnom: A New Edition and Evaluation." *BASOR* 334:41–71.

Barkay, Gabriel, and David Ussishkin. 2004. "Area S: The Iron Age Strata." Pages 411–503 in vol. 2 of *The Renewed Archaeological Excavations at Lachish (1973–1994)*. Edited by David Ussishkin. 5 vols. SMNIA 22. Tel Aviv: Emery and Claire Publications in Archeology of the Institute of Archaeology, Tel Aviv.

Barthélemy, Dominique. 1992. *Ézéchiel, Daniel, et les 12 Prophètes*. Vol. 3 of *Critique Textuelle de l'Ancien Testament*. OBO 50, no. 3. Fribourg: Éditions Universitaires; Göttingen: Vandenhoeck & Ruprecht.

Ben-Tor, Amnon. 1978. *Cylinder Seals of Third Millennium Palestine*. Bulletin of the American School of Oriental Research Supplements 22. Cambridge, MA: American Schools of Oriental Research.

Ben-Tor, Daphna. 2003. "Egyptian-Levantine Relations and Chronology in the Middle Bronze Age: Scarab Research." Pages 239–48 in *The Synchronisation of Civilizations in the Eastern Mediterranean in the Second Millennium B.C. II: Proceedings of the SCIEM 2000–Euroconference Haindorf, 2nd of May–7th of May 2001*. Edited by Manfried Beitak. Österreichische Akademie der Wissenschaften. Denkschriften der Gesamtakademie 29. Vienna: Österreichischen Akademie der Wissenschaften.

———. 2004. "Second Intermediate Scarabs from Egypt and Palestine: Historical and Chronological Implications." Pages 27–41 in *Scarabs of the Second Millennium BC from Egypt, Nubia, Crete, and the Levant: Chronological and Historical Implications. Papers of a Symposium, Vienna, 10th–13th of January 2002*. Edited by Manfred Bietak and Ernst Czerny. Österreichische Akademie der Wissenschaften. Denkschriften der Gesamtakademie 35. Vienna: Österreichischen Akademie der Wissenschaften.

———. 2007. *Scarabs, Chronology, and Interconnections: Egypt and Palestine in the Second Intermediate Period*. OBO 27. Series Archaeologica. Fribourg: Academic Press; Göttingen: Vandenhoeck & Ruprecht.

———. 2011. "Egyptian-Canaanite Relations in the Middle and Late Bronze Ages as Reflected by Scarabs." Pages 23–43 in *Egypt, Canaan, and Israel: History, Imperialism, Ideology, and Literature: Proceedings of a Conference at the University of Haifa, 3–7 May 2009*. Edited by Shay Bar, Dan'el Kahn, and J. J. Shirley. CHANE 52. Leiden: Brill.

———. 2018. "The Administrative Use of Scarabs During the Middle Kingdom." Pages 289–301 in *Seals and Sealing in the Ancient World: Case Studies from the Near East, Egypt, the Aegean, and South Asia*. Edited by Marta Ameri, Sarah Kielt Costello, Gregg M. Jamison, and Sarah Jarmer Scott. Cambridge: Cambridge University Press.

Biella, Joan Copeland. 1982. *Dictionary of Old South Arabic: Sabaean Dialect*. HSS 25. Chico, CA: Scholars Press.

Bierbrier, Morris L., ed. 1986. *Papyrus: Structure and Usage*. British Museum Occasional Paper 60. London: British Museum.

Bietak, Manfred. 2007. "Egypt and the Levant." Pages 417–48 in *The Egyptian World*. Edited by Toby Wilkinson. London: Routledge.

Bietak, Manfred, and Ernst Czerny, eds. 2004. *Scarabs of the Second Millennium BC from Egypt, Nubia, Crete, and the Levant: Chronological and Historical Implications. Papers of a Symposium, Vienna, 10th–13th of January 2002*. Österreichische Akademie der Wissenschaften. Denkschriften der Gesamtakademie 35. Vienna: Verlag der Österreichischen Akademie der Wissenschaften.

Biran, Avraham, and Joseph Naveh. 1993. "An Aramaic Stele Fragment from Tel Dan." *IEJ* 43, nos. 2–3:81–98.

Black, Jeremy A., Andrew George, and J. Nicholas Postgate, eds. 2007. *A Concise Dictionary of Akkadian*. Rev. ed. Santag Arbeiten und Untersuchungen zur Keilschriftkunde 5. Wiesbaden: Harrassowitz.

Black, Jeremy A., and William J. Tait. 2000. "Archives and Libraries in the Ancient Near East." Pages 2197–209 in vol. 4 of *Civilizations of the Ancient Near East*. Edited by Jack M. Sasson. 4 vols. Farmington Hills, MI: Scribner's Sons, 1995. Repr., Peabody, MA: Hendrickson.

Blau, Joshua. 1995. "A Misunderstood Medieval Translation of *śered* (Isaiah 44:13) and Its Impact on Modern Scholarship." Pages 689–95 in *Pomegranates and Golden*

Bells: Studies in Biblical, Jewish, and Near Eastern Ritual, Law, and Literature in Honor of Jacob Milgrom. Edited by David P. Wright, David N. Freedman, and Avi Hurvitz. Winona Lake, IN: Eisenbrauns.

Blenkinsopp, Joseph. 2000. *Isaiah*. AB 19. New York: Doubleday.

The Book of Ben Sira: Text, Concordance and an Analysis of the Vocabulary. 1973. Jerusalem: Academy of the Hebrew Language and the Shrine of the Book.

Bowman, Alan K., and Greg Woolf, eds. 1994. *Literacy and Power in the Ancient World*. Cambridge: Cambridge University Press.

Brandl, Baruch. 2004. "Scarabs and Plagues Bearing Royal Names of the Early 20th Egyptian Dynasty Excavated in Canaan—From Sethnakht to Ramses IV." Pages 57–71 in *Scarabs of the Second Millennium BC from Egypt, Nubia, Crete, and the Levant: Chronological and Historical Implications. Papers of a Symposium, Vienna, 10th–13th of January 2002*. Edited by Manfried Beitak and Ernst Czerny. Österreichische Akademie der Wissenschaften. Denkschriften der Gesamtakademie 35. Vienna: Verlag der Österreichischen Akademie der Wissenschaften.

Braun, Eliot. 2002. "Egypt's First Sojourn in Canaan." Pages 173–89 in *Egypt and the Levant: Interrelations from the 4th Through the Early 3rd Millennium BCE*. Edited by Edwin C. M. van den Brink and Thomas E. Levy. London: Leicester University Press.

———. 2009. "South Levantine Early Bronze Age Chronological Correlations with Egypt in Light of the Narmer Serekhs from Tel Erani and Arad: New Interpretations." *British Museum Studies in Ancient Egypt and Sudan* 13:25–48.

Breasted, James H. 1905. "The Report of Wenamon." *American Journal of Semitic Languages and Literatures* 21, no. 2:100–109.

Brenne, Stefan. 2001. *Ostrakismos und Prominenz in Athen: Attische Bürger des 5. Jhs. v. Chr. auf den Ostraka*. Tyche Supplement 3. Vienna: Holzhausens.

———. 2002. "Die Ostraka (487–ca. 416 v. Chr.) als Testimonien (T 1)." Pages 36–166 in *Ostrakismos-Testimonien I: Die Zeugnisse antiker Autoren, der Inschriften und Ostraka über das athenische Scherbengericht aus vorhellenistischer Zeit (487–322 v. Chr.)*. Historia 155. Edited by Peter Siewert. Stuttgart: Steiner.

Bron, François, and Andre Lemaire. 2009. "Nouvelle inscription sabéenne et le commerce en Transeuphratène." *Transeuphratène* 38:11–29.

Brooke, Alan E., Norman McLean, and Henry St. J. Thackeray. 1906–1940. *The Old Testament in Greek According to the Text of Codex Vaticanus, Supplemented from Other Uncial Manuscripts, with a Critical Apparatus of the Variants of the Chief Authorities for the Text of the Septuagint*. 4 vols. Cambridge: Cambridge University Press.

Brunner, Hellmut. 1991. *Altägyptische Erziehung*. 2nd ed. Wiesbaden: Harrassowitz.

Brysbaert, Ann. 2008. *The Power of Technology in the Bronze Age Eastern Mediterranean: The Case of the Painted Plaster*. Oakville, CT: Equinox.

Buchanan, Briggs. 1981. *Early Near Eastern Seals in the Yale Babylonian Collection*. Edited by Ulla Kasten. New Haven, CT: Yale University Press.

Bülow-Jacobsen, Adam. 2009. "Writing Materials in the Ancient World." Pages 3–29 in *The Oxford Handbook of Papyrology*. Edited by Roger S. Bagnall. Oxford: Oxford University Press.

Bunimovitz, Shlomo. 2019. "Late Bronze Age Egyptian Government in the Levant." Pages 265–79 in *The Social Archaeology of the Levant: From Prehistory to the Present*. Edited by Assaf Yasur-Landau, Eric H. Cline, and Yorke M. Rowan. Cambridge: Cambridge University Press.

Burlingame, Andrew. 2016. "Line Five of the Amman Citadel Inscriptions: History of Interpretation and a New Proposal." *BASOR* 376:63–82.

Byrne, Ryan. 2007. "The Refuge of Scribalism in Iron I Palestine." *BASOR* 345:1–31.

Carr, David M. 2005. *Writing on the Tablet of the Heart: Origins of Scripture and Literature*. Oxford: Oxford University Press.

Caminos, Ricardo. 1954. *Late Egyptian Miscellanies*. London: Oxford University Press.

Campbell, Edward F. 2002. *Schechem III: The Stratigraphy and Architecture of Shechem/Tell Balâṭah*. 2 vols. American Schools of Oriental Research Archaeological Reports 6. Boston: American Schools of Oriental Research.

Casson, Lionel. 1986. *Ships and Seamanship in the Ancient World*. Princeton, NJ: Princeton University Press, 1971. Repr., Princeton, NJ: Princeton University Press.

Černý, Jaroslav. 1952. *Paper and Books in Ancient Egypt*. Chicago: Ares.

Cline, Eric H., and Inbal Samet. 2013. "Area L." Pages 275–85 in vol. 1 of *Megiddo V: The 2004–2008 Seasons*. Edited by Israel Finkelstein, David Ussishkin, Eric H. Cline, Matthew J. Adams, Eran Arie, Norma Franklin, and Mario A. S. Martin. 3 vols. SMNIA 31. Winona Lake, IN: Eisenbrauns.

Cohen, Chaim. 2016. "The Hapax Legomenon דיו (Ink) in the Context of 'ואני כתב על הספר בדיו' (Jeremiah 36:18): A 'False Friend' in Modern Hebrew Due to the Masoretes' Misunderstanding of the Preposition בדי Meaning 'To' or 'For'." *Shnaton: An Annual for Biblical and Ancient Near Eastern Studies* 24, no. 1:77–101.

Cohen, Yoram. 2009. *The Scribes and Scholars of the City of Emar in the Late Bronze Age*. HSS 59. Winona Lake, IN: Eisenbrauns.

———. 2019. "Cuneiform Writing in Bronze Age Canaan." Pages 245–64 in *The Social Archaeology of the Levant: From Prehistory to the Present*. Edited by Assaf Yasur-Landau, Eric H. Cline, and Yorke M. Rowan. Cambridge: Cambridge University Press.

Cohen-Weinberger, Anat, and Yuval Goren. 2004. "Levantine-Egyptian Interactions During the 12th to the 15th Dynasties Based on the Petrography of the Canaanite Pottery from Tell el-Dab'a." *AeL* 14:69–100.

Collon, Dominique. 2001. *Catalogue of the Western Asiatic Seals in the British Museum: Cylinder Seals V: Neo-Assyrian and Neo-Babylonian Periods*. London: British Museum.

———. 2005. *First Impressions: Cylinder Seals in the Ancient Near East*. Rev. ed. London: British Museum.

Conder, Claude. 1881. "The Ancient Hebrew Inscription in the Pool of Siloam, II." *Palestine Exploration Fund Quarterly Statement* 13:285–87.

Crenshaw, James L. 1998. *Education in Ancient Israel: Across the Deadening Silence*. Anchor Bible Reference Library. New York: Doubleday.

Cross, Frank M., Jr. 1989. "The Invention and Development of the Alphabet." Pages 77–90 in *The Origins of Writing*. Edited by Wayne M. Senner. Lincoln: University of Nebraska Press.

———. 2003a. "Early Alphabetic Scripts." Pages 95–123 in *Symposia Celebrating the Seventy-Fifth Anniversary of the Founding of the American Schools of Oriental Research (1900–1975): Archaeology and Early Israelite History*. Edited by Frank M. Cross. Cambridge, MA: American Schools of Oriental Research, 1979. Repr., pages 330–43 in *Leaves from an Epigrapher's Notebook: Collected Papers in Hebrew and West Semitic Palaeography and Epigraphy*. HSS 51. Winona Lake, IN: Eisenbrauns.

———. 2003b. *Leaves from an Epigrapher's Notebook: Collected Papers in Hebrew and West Semitic Palaeography and Epigraphy*. HSS 51. Winona Lake, IN: Eisenbrauns.

Darnell, John C., F. W. Dobbs-Allsopp, Marilyn J. Lundberg, Peter K. McCarter, Bruce Zuckerman, and Colleen Manassa. 2005. *Two Early Alphabetic Inscriptions from the Wadi el-Ḥôl: New Evidence for the Origin of the Alphabet from the Western Desert of Egypt*. Annual of the American Schools of Oriental Research 59. Boston: American Schools of Oriental Research.

Davies, Graham I. 1995. "Were There Schools in Ancient Israel?" Pages 199–211 in *Wisdom in Ancient Israel: Essays in Honour of J. A. Emerton*. Edited by John Day, Robert P. Gordon, and Hugh G. M. Williamson. Cambridge: Cambridge University Press.

Davies, Philip R. 1998. *Scribes and Schools: The Canonization of the Hebrew Scriptures*. Library of Ancient Israel. Louisville, KY: Westminster John Knox.

Davies, Philip R., and Thomas Römer, eds. 2013. *Writing the Bible: Scribes, Scribalism, and Script*. Durham: Acumen.

Demsky, Aharon. 1990. "The Education of Canaanite Scribes in the Mesopotamian Cuneiform Tradition." Pages 157–70 in *Bar Ilan Studies in Assyriology Dedicated to Pinḥas Artzi*. Edited by Jacob Klein and Aaron Skaist. Ramat Gan: Bar Ilan University Press.

———. 2007. "Writing." Pages 235–41 in vol. 21 of *Encyclopedia Judaica*. Edited by Fred Skolnik. 2nd ed. 22 vols. Jerusalem: Keter.

———. 2012. ידיעת ספר בישראל בעת העתיקה. ספריית האנציקלופדיה המקראית. Jerusalem: Bialik Institute.

Demsky, Aharon, and Meir Bar-Ilan. 2004. "Writing in Ancient Israel and Early Judaism." Pages 1–38 in *Mikra: Text, Translation, Reading, and Interpretation of the Hebrew Bible in Ancient Judaism and Early Christianity*. Edited by Martin J. Mulder and Harry Sysling. Peabody, MA: Hendrickson.

Dever, Wiliam G., and H. Darrell Lance. 1986. *Gezer IV: The 1969–71 Seasons in Field VI, the "Acropolis"*. 2 vols. Annual of the Nelson Glueck School of Biblical Archaeology. Jerusalem: Keter.

Dietrich, Manfried, and Oswald Loretz. 1988. *Die Keilalphabete: Die phönizisch-kanaanäischen und altarabischen Alphabete in Ugarit*. Abhandlungen zur Literatur Alt-Syrien-Palästinas. Münster: Ugarit.

Dion, Paul E., and P. M. Michèle Daviau. 2000. "An Inscribed Incense Altar of Iron Age II at Ḫirbet el-Mudēyine (Jordan)." *Zeitschrift des Deutschen Palästina-Vereins* 116, no 1:1–13.

Diringer, David. 1953. *The Hand-Produced Book*. London: Hutchinson's Scientific and Technical Publications.

Dobbs-Allsopp, F. W., J. J. M. Roberts, Choon L. Seow, and Richard E. Whitaker. 2005. *Hebrew Inscriptions: Texts from the Biblical Period of the Monarchy with Concordance*. New Haven, CT: Yale University Press.

Dougherty, Raymond P. 1928. "Writing upon Parchment and Papyrus Among the Babylonians and the Assyrians." *JAOS* 48:109–35.

Doumet, Claude. 1992. *Sceaux et cylindres orientaux: La collection Chiha*. OBO 9. Series Archaeologica. Fribourg: Academic Press; Göttingen: Vandenhoeck & Ruprecht.

Drewes, Abraham J., Thomas F. G. Higham, Michael C. A. Macdonald, and Christopher B. Ramsey. 2013. "Some Absolute Dates for the Development of the Ancient

South Arabian Minuscule Script." *Arabian Archaeology and Epigraphy* 24:196–207.

Drewes, Abraham J., and Jacques Ryckmans. 2016. *Les inscriptions sudarabes sur bois dans la collection de l'Oosters Instituut conservée dans la bibliothèque universitaire de Leiden*. Edited by Peter Stein and Harry Stroomer. Wiesbaden: Harrassowitz.

Driver, Godfrey R. 1976. *Semitic Writing: From Pictograph to Alphabet*. Edited by S. A. Hopkins. Rev. ed. London: Oxford University Press.

Drower, Ethel S., and Rudolf Macuch. 1963. *A Mandaic Dictionary*. Oxford: Clarendon.

Dušek, Jan. 2007. *Les manuscrits araméens du Wadi Daliyeh et la Samarie vers 450–332 av. J.-C.* CHANE 30. Leiden: Brill.

———. 2019. "Dating the Aramaic Stele Sefire I." *AS* 17:1–14.

Edelman, Diana. 2013. "The 'Seeing God' Motif and Yahweh as a God of Justice." Pages 197–224 in *Loi et justice dans la littérature du proche-orient ancien*. Edited by Oliver Artus. Beihefte zur Zeitschrift für Altorientalische und Biblische Rechtsgeschichte 20. Wiesbaden: Harrassowitz.

Ellison, John L. 2002. "A Paleographic Study of the Alphabetic Cuneiform Texts from Ras Shamra/Ugarit." PhD diss., Harvard University.

Eshel, Hanan. 2000. "Two Epigraphic Notes." *Zeitschrift für Althebraistik* 13:181–87.

Evian, Shirly Ben-Dor. 2011. "Egypt and the Levant in the Iron Age I–IIA: The Ceramic Evidence." *TA* 38:94–119.

Faber, Alice. 1981. "Phonetic Reconstruction." *Glossa* 15, no. 2:233–62.

Fernández Marcos, Natalio. 2000. *The Septuagint in Context: Introduction to the Greek Version of the Bible*. Translated by Wilfred G. E. Watson. Leiden: Brill.

Fichter, Eitan, and Sang-Yeup Chang. 2014. "Area C–Square Supervisors' Reports: The Stratigraphy of Square DD9." Pages 451–52 in *Khirbet Qeiyafa Vol. 2: Excavation Report 2009–2013, Stratigraphy and Architecture (Areas B, C, D, E)*. Edited by Yosef Garfinkel, Saar Ganor, and Michael G. Hasel, and Martin G. Klingbeil. Collegedale, TN: Institute of Archaeology, Southern Adventist University; Jerusalem: Israel Exploration Society; Jerusalem: Institute of Archaeology, the Hebrew University.

Field, Fridericus. 1875. *Origenis Hexaplorum Quae Supersunt: Sive Veterum Interpretum Graecorum in Totum Vetus Testamentum Fragmenta*. 2 vols. Oxford: Clarendon.

Finkelstein, Israel. 2013. "Area M: Part III: Another Interpretation of the Remains–The Nordburg and Chamber F." Pages 228–46 in vol. 1 of *Megiddo V: The 2004–2008 Seasons*. Edited by Israel Finkelstein, David Ussishkin, Eric H. Cline, Matthew J. Adams, Eran Arie, Norma Franklin, and Mario A. S. Martin. 3 vols. SMNIA 31. Winona Lake, IN: Eisenbrauns.

Finkelstein, Israel, and Benjamin Sass. 2013. "The West Semitic Alphabetic Inscriptions, Late Bronze II to Iron IIA: Archeological Context, Distribution and Chronology." *Hebrew Bible and Ancient Israel* 2, no. 2:149–220.

Fischer, Henry G. 1978. "Notes on Sticks and Staves in Ancient Egypt." *Metropolitan Museum Journal* 13:5–32.

Fitzmyer, Joseph A. 1966. "The Phoenician Inscription from Pyrgi." *JAOS* 86, no. 3:285–97.

Forsdyke, Sara. 2005. *Exile, Ostracism, and Democracy: The Politics of Expulsion in Ancient Greece*. Princeton, NJ: Princeton University Press.

Fox, Joshua. 2003. *Semitic Noun Patterns*. HSS 52. Winona Lake, IN: Eisenbrauns.

Fox, Nili S. 2000. *In the Service of the King: Officialdom in Ancient Israel and Judah.* Cincinnati, OH: Hebrew Union College Press.

Frachtenberg, F., and J. Yellin. 1992. "Preliminary Study of Flint Sources in Israel by Neutron Activation Analysis." Pages 149–52 in *Ancient Stones: Quarrying, Trade and Provenance: Interdisciplinary Studies on Stones and Stone Technology in Europe and Near East from the Prehistoric to the Early Christian Period.* Edited by Marc Waelkens, Norman Herz, and Luc Moens. Acta Archaeologica Lovaniensia 4. Leuven: Peeters.

Franken, Henk J., and Moawiyah M. Ibrahim. 1977–78. "Two Seasons of Excavations at Tel Deir 'Alla, 1976–78." *Annual of the Department of Antiquities of Jordan* 22:57–79.

Franklin, Norma. 2013a. "Area M: Part I: The Excavation." Pages 178–214 in vol. 1 of *Megiddo V: The 2004–2008 Seasons*. Edited by Israel Finkelstein, David Ussishkin, Eric H. Cline, Matthew J. Adams, Eran Arie, Norma Franklin, and Mario A. S. Martin. SMNIA 31. Winona Lake, IN: Eisenbrauns.

———. 2013b. "Area P." Pages 286–91 in vol. 1 of *Megiddo V: The 2004–2008 Seasons.* Edited by Israel Finkelstein, David Ussishkin, Eric H. Cline, Matthew J. Adams, Eran Arie, Norma Franklin, and Mario A. S. Martin. 3 vols. SMNIA 31. Winona Lake, IN: Eisenbrauns.

Freikman, Michael. 2014. "Area C–Square Supervisors' Reports: Stratigraphy of Squares KK14." Pages 485–86 in *Khirbet Qeiyafa Vol. 2: Excavation Report 2009–2013, Stratigraphy and Architecture (Areas B, C, D, E)*. Edited by Yosef Garfinkel, Saar Ganor, Michael G. Hasel, and Martin G. Klingbeil. Jerusalem: Israel Exploration Society.

Friedrich, Johannes, Annelies Kammenhuber, and Inge Hoffman. 1984–2017. *Hethitisches Wörterbuch*. 5 vols. Heidelberg: C. Winter.

Friedrich, Johannes, and Wolfgang Röllig. 1999. *Phönizisch-Punische Grammatik.* 3rd ed. Analecta Orientalia 55. Rome: Pontifical Biblical Institute.

Friesem, David, and Ruth Shahack-Gross. 2013. "Area J, Part V: Analysis of Sediments from the Level J-4 Temple Floor." Pages 143–52 in vol. 1 of *Megiddo V: The 2004–2008 Seasons*. Edited by Israel Finkelstein, David Ussishkin, Eric H. Cline, Matthew J. Adams, Eran Arie, Norma Franklin, and Mario A. S. Martin. 3 vols. SMNIA 31. Winona Lake, IN: Eisenbrauns.

Gale, Rowena, Peter Gasson, Nigel Hepper, and Geoffrey Killen. 2000. "Wood." Pages 334–71 in *Ancient Egyptian Materials and Technology*. Edited by Paul T. Nicholson and Ian Shaw. Cambridge: Cambridge University Press.

Galling, Kurt. 1971. "Tafel, Buch und Blatt." Pages 207–23 in *Near Eastern Studies in Honor of William Foxwell Albright*. Edited by Hans Goedicke. Baltimore: Johns Hopkins University Press.

Genz, Hermann. 2014. "The Northern Levant (Lebanon) During the Early Bronze Age." Pages 292–306 in *The Oxford Handbook of the Archaeology of the Levant*. Edited by Margreet L. Steiner and Ann E. Killebrew. Oxford: Oxford University Press.

Gestermann, Luise. 1984. "Schreibmaterial." Pages 700–703 in vol. 5 of *Lexikon der Ägyptologie*. Edited by Wolfgang Helck, Eberhard Otto, and Wolfhart Westendorf. 7 vols. Wiesbaden: Harrassowitz.

Gilbert, Allan S. 2000. "The Flora and Fauna of the Ancient Near East." Pages 153–74 in *Ancient Egyptian Materials and Technology*. Edited by Paul T. Nicholson and Ian Shaw. Cambridge: Cambridge University Press.

Gilboa, Ayelet. 2014. "The Southern Levant (Cisjordan) During the Iron Age I Period." Pages 624–48 in *The Oxford Handbook of the Archaeology of the Levant*. Edited by Margreet L. Steiner and Ann E. Killebrew. Oxford: Oxford University Press.

Gilibert, Alessandra. 2011. *Syro-Hittite Monumental Art and the Archaeology of Performance: The Stone Reliefs of Carchemish and Zincirli in the Earlier First Millennium BCE.* Topoi Berlin Studies of the Ancient World 2. Berlin: de Gruyter.

Gill, Dan. 1996. "The Geology of the City of David and Its Ancient Subterranean Waterworks." *Qedem* 41:1–28.

Gitin, Seymour, Trude Dothan, and Joseph Naveh. 1997. "A Royal Dedicatory Inscription from Ekron." *IEJ* 47, nos. 1–2:1–16.

Goldwasser, Orly. 1991. "An Egyptian Scribe from Lachish and the Hieratic Traditions of the Hebrew Kingdoms." *TA* 18:248–53.

———. 2016. "From the Iconic to the Linear—The Egyptian Scribes of Lachish and the Modification of the Early Alphabet in the Late Bronze Age." Pages 118–60 in *Alphabets, Texts, and Artifacts in the Ancient Near East: Studies Presented to Benjamin Sass*. Edited by Israel Finkelstein, Christian Robin, and Thomas Römer. Paris: Van Dieren.

Golka, Friedemann W. 1993. *The Leopard's Spots: Biblical and African Wisdom in Proverbs*. Edinburgh: T&T Clark.

Graesser, Carl F. 1972. "Standing Stones in Ancient Palestine." *BA* 35, no. 2:33–63.

Graham, M. Patrick. 1989. "The Discovery and Reconstruction of the Mesha Inscription." Pages 41–92 in *Studies in the Mesha Inscription and Moab*. Edited by Andrew Dearman. Atlanta, GA: Scholars Press.

Greenberg, Moshe. 1983. *Ezekiel 1–20*. AB 22A. New York: Doubleday.

———. 1997. *Ezekiel 21–37*. AB 22B. New York: Doubleday.

Gunter, Ann C. 2000. "Materials, Technology, and Techniques in Artistic Production." Pages 1539–51 in vol. 3 of *Civilizations of the Ancient Near East*. Edited by Jack M. Sasson. 4 vols. Farmington Hills, MI: Scribner's Sons, 1995. Repr., Peabody, MA: Hendrickson.

Hackett, Jo Ann. 1984. *The Balaam Text from Deir ʿAlla*. Harvard Semitic Monographs 31. Chico, CA: Scholars Press.

———. 2008. "Phoenician and Punic." Pages 82–102 in *The Ancient Languages of Syria-Palestine and Arabia*. Edited by Roger D. Woodard. Cambridge: Cambridge University Press.

Hackett, Jo Ann, and Walter E. Aufrecht, eds. 2014. *"An Eye for Form": Epigraphic Essays in Honor of Frank Moore Cross*. Winona Lake, IN: Eisenbrauns.

Hagen, Fredrik. 2006. "Literature, Transmission, and the Late Egyptian Miscellanies." Pages 84–99 in *Current Research in Egyptology 2004: Proceedings of the Fifth Annual Symposium Which Took Place at the University of Durham, January 2004*. Edited by Raphael J. Dann. Oxford: Oxbow; Exeter: Short Run.

———. 2007. "Ostraca, Literature and Teaching at Deir el-Medina." Pages 38–51 in *Current Research in Egyptology 2005: Proceedings of the Sixth Annual Symposium Which Took Place at the University of Cambridge, 6–8 January 2005*. Edited by Rachel Mairs and Alice Stevenson. Oxford: Oxbow; Exeter: Short Run.

———. 2011. *New Kingdom Ostraca from the Fitzwilliam Museum, Cambridge*. Leiden: Brill.

———. 2013. "An Eighteenth Dynasty Writing Board Ashmolean (1948.91) and the Hymn to the Nile." *Journal of the American Research Center in Egypt* 49:73–91.

Hamilton, Gordon J. 2006. *The Origins of the West Semitic Alphabet in Egyptian Scripts*. Catholic Biblical Quarterly Monograph Series 40. Washington, DC: Catholic Biblical Association of America.

———. 2014. "Reconceptualizing the Periods of Early Alphabetic Scripts." Pages 30–55 in *"An Eye for Form": Epigraphic Essays in Honor of Frank Moore Cross*. Edited by Jo Ann Hackett and Walter E. Aufrecht. Winona Lake, IN: Eisenbrauns.

Haran, Menachem. 1980–81. "מלאכת הסופר בתקופת המקרא–מגילות הספרים ואביזרי הכתיבה." *Tarbiz* 50: 65–87.

———. 1982. "Book-Scrolls in Israel in Pre-Exilic Times." *JJS* 33, no. 1–2: 161–73.

———. 1983. "Book-Scrolls at the Beginning of the Second Temple Period: The Transition from Papyrus to Skins." *Hebrew Union College Annual* 54:111–22.

Harl, Marguerite, Cécile Dogniez, Laurence Brottier, Michel Casevitz, and Pierre Sandevoir. 1999. *Les douze prophètes 4–9: Joël, Abdiou, Jonas, Naoum, Ambakoum, Sophonie*. La bible d'Alexandrie 23. Paris: Cerf.

Harrell, James E., James K. Hoffmeier, and Kenton F. Williams. 2017. "Hebrew Gemstones in the Old Testament: A Lexical, Geological, and Archaeological Analysis." *Bulletin for Biblical Research* 27, no. 1:1–52.

Harris, William V. 1991. *Ancient Literacy*. Cambridge, MA: Harvard University Press.

Hasel, Michael G. 2014. "Area D." Pages 227–308 in *Khirbet Qeiyafa Vol. 2: Excavation Report 2009–2013, Stratigraphy and Architecture (Areas B, C, D, E)*. Edited by Yosef Garfinkel, Saar Ganor, Michael G. Hasel, and Martin G. Klingbeil. Jerusalem: Israel Exploration Society.

Hatch, Edwin, and Henry Redpath. 1998. *A Concordance to the Septuagint and the Other Greek Versions of the Old Testament (Including the Apocryphal Books)*. 2nd ed. Grand Rapids, MI: Baker.

Hayes, William C. 1968. *From the Earliest Times to the End of the Middle Kingdom*. Vol. 1 of *The Scepter of Egypt: A Background for the Study of the Egyptian Antiquities in The Metropolitan Museum of Art*. New York: Harper and Brothers, 1953. Repr., New York: Metropolitan Museum of Art.

———. 1990. *The Hyksos Period and the New Kingdom (1675–1080 B.C.)*. Vol. 2 of *The Scepter of Egypt: A Background for the Study of the Egyptian Antiquities in The Metropolitan Museum of Art*. Rev. ed. Lunedburg, VT: Meriden-Steinhour.

Heimpel, Wolfgang. 2009. *Workers and Construction Work at Garšana*. Cornell University Studies in Assyriology and Sumerology 5. Bethesda, MD: CDL.

Hess, Richard S. 2002. "Literacy in Iron Age Israel." Pages 82–102 in *Windows into Old Testament History: Evidence, Argument, and the Crisis of "Biblical Israel"*. Edited by Gordon J. Wenham, David W. Baker, and V. Philips Long. Grand Rapids, MI: Eerdmans.

———. 2006. "Writing About Writing: Abecedaries and Evidence for Literacy in Ancient Israel." *VT* 56, no. 3:342–46.

Hestrin, Ruth, and Michal Dayagi-Mendels. 1979. *Inscribed Seals: First Temple Period Hebrew, Ammonite, Moabite, Phoenician and Aramaic From the Collections of the Israel Museum and the Israel Department of Antiquities and Museums*. Jerusalem: Israel Museum.

Heurgon, Jacques. 1966. "The Inscriptions of Pyrgi." *Journal of Roman Studies* 56, nos. 1–2:1–15.

Hezser, Catherine. 2001. *Jewish Literacy in Roman Palestine*. Texts and Studies in Ancient Judaism 81. Tübingen: Mohr Siebeck.

Hicks, R. Lansing. 1983. "*Delet* and *Megillāh*: A Fresh Approach to Jeremiah XXXVI." *VT* 33, no. 1:46–66.
Hoch, James E. 1994. *Semitic Words in Egyptian Texts of the New Kingdom and Third Intermediate Period*. Princeton, NJ: Princeton University Press.
Hoffmeier, James K. 2004. "Aspects of Egyptian Foreign Policy in the 18th Dynasty in Western Asia and Nubia." Pages 121–41 in *Egypt, Israel, and the Ancient Mediterranean World: Studies in Honor of Donald B. Redford*. Edited by Gary N. Knoppers and Antoine Hirsch. Leiden: Brill.
Hoftijzer, Jacob. 1976. "General Remarks on the Plaster Texts." Pages 268–82 in *Aramaic Texts from Deir ʿAlla*. Edited by Jacob Hoftijzer and Gerrit van der Kooij. Leiden: Brill.
Hoftijzer, Jacob, and Gerrit van der Kooij, eds. 1976. *Aramaic Texts from Deir ʿAlla*. Leiden: Brill.
Holmes, Robert, and James Parsons. 1798–1827. *Vetus Testamentum Graecum cum Variis Lectionibus*. 5 vols. Oxford: Clarendon.
Hornkohl, Aaron D. 2013. "Biblical Hebrew: Periodization." Pages 315–25 in vol. 1 of *Encyclopedia of Hebrew Language and Linguistics*. Edited by Geoffrey Khan. 4 vols. Leiden: Brill.
———. 2014. *Ancient Hebrew Periodization and the Language of the Book of Jeremiah: The Case for a Sixth-Century Date of Composition*. Leiden: Brill.
Hornung, Erik, and Elisabeth Staehelin, eds. 1976. *Skarabäen und andere Siegelamulette aus Basler Sammlungen*. Mainz: von Zabern.
Horowitz, Wayne, Takayoshi Oshima, and Seth Sanders. 2018. *Cuneiform in Canaan: The Next Generation*. 2nd ed. University Park, PA: Eisenbrauns.
Huehnergard, John. 2002. "Introduction to the Comparative Study of the Semitic Languages: Course Outline." Unpublished manuscript.
———. 2008. *Ugaritic Vocabulary in Syllabic Transcription*. Rev. ed. HSS 32. Winona Lake, IN: Eisenbrauns.
———. 2011. *A Grammar of Akkadian*. 3rd ed. HSS 45. Winona Lake, IN: Eisenbrauns.
Hurvitz, Avi. 1996. "לתולדות צמיחתו של הביטוי 'מגלת־ספר'—פרק בהתפתחות מינוח הכתיבה בתקופת המקרא." Pages 37*–46* in *Text, Temples, and Traditions: A Tribute to Menahem Haran*. Edited by Michael V. Fox, Victor A. Hurowitz, Avi Hurvitz, Michael L. Klein, Baruch J. Schwartz, and Nili Shupak. Winona Lake, IN: Eisenbrauns.
———. 1997. "The Historical Quest for 'Ancient Israel' and the Linguistic Evidence of the Hebrew Bible: Some Methodological Observations." *VT* 47, no. 3:301–15.
———. 2003. "Hebrew and Aramaic in the Biblical Period: The Problem of 'Aramaisms' in Linguistic Research on the Hebrew Bible." Pages 24–37 in *Biblical Hebrew: Studies in Chronology and Typology*. Edited by Ian Young. London: T&T Clark.
———. 2013. "Biblical Hebrew, Late." Pages 329–38 in vol. 1 of *Encyclopedia of Hebrew Language and Linguistics*. Edited by Geoffrey Khan. 4 vols. Leiden: Brill.
———. 2014. *A Concise Lexicon of Late Biblical Hebrew: Linguistic Innovations in the Writings of the Second Temple Period*. Leiden: Brill.
Hyatt, J. Philip. 1943. "The Writing of an Old Testament Book." *BA* 6, no. 4:71–80.
Ikram, Salima. 2010. *Ancient Egypt: An Introduction*. New York: Cambridge University Press.
Jamieson-Drake, David W. 1991. *Scribes and Schools in Monarchic Judah: A Socio-Archeological Approach*. Social World of Biblical Antiquity 9. Sheffield: Journal for the Study of the Old Testament.

Janssen, Jac. J. 1992. "Literacy and Letters at Deir el-Medina." Pages 81–94 in *Village Voices: Proceedings of the Symposium "Texts from Deir el-Medina and Their Interpretation," Leiden, May 31–June 1, 1991*. Edited by Robert J. Demarée and Arno Egberts. Centre of Non-Western Studies Publications 13. Leiden: Centre of Non-Western Studies, Leiden University.

Janssen, Rosalind M., and Jac. J. Janssen. 1990. *Growing up in Ancient Egypt*. London: Rubicon.

Jastrow, Marcus. 1926. *A Dictionary of the Targumim, the Talmud Babli and Yerushalmi, and the Midrashic Literature*. 2 vols. New York: Choreb.

Jenner, K. D. 2011a. "*ēṭ*–stylus, graver." Online: http://www.otw-site.eu/en/kli-database/ (כלי Database: Utensils in the Hebrew Bible website).

———. 2011b. "*ḥereṭ*–burin, stylus." Online: http://www.otw-site.eu/en/kli-database/ (כלי Database: Utensils in the Hebrew Bible website).

———. 2011c. "*qeset*–inkpot (?), writing-case (?)." Online: http://www.otw-site.eu/en/kli-database/ (כלי Database: Utensils in the Hebrew Bible website).

———. 2011d "*śered*–scriber, scratch awl." Online: http://www.otw-site.eu/en/kli-database/ (כלי Database: Utensils in the Hebrew Bible website).

———. 2011e. "*ṣippōren*–nail, tip of angle-tint tool." Online: http://www.otw-site.eu/en/kli-database/ (כלי Database: Utensils in the Hebrew Bible website).

Johnson, William A., and Holt N. Parker, eds. 2009. *Ancient Literacies: The Culture of Reading in Greece and Rome*. New York: Oxford University Press.

Johnstone, Thomas M. 1987. *Mehri Lexicon and English-Mehri Word-List*. London: School of Oriental and African Studies, University of London.

Kang, Hoo-Goo. 2014. "Area C–Square Supervisors' Reports: Stratigraphy of Square EE10." Pages 456–57 in *Khirbet Qeiyafa Vol. 2: Excavation Report 2009–2013, Stratigraphy and Architecture (Areas B, C, D, E)*. Edited by Yosef Garfinkel, Saar Ganor, Michael G. Hasel, and Martin G. Klingbeil. Jerusalem: Israel Exploration Society.

Keimer, Kyle H. 2014. "Iron Age Stone Quarries." Pages 333–45 in *Khirbet Qeiyafa Vol. 2: Excavation Report 2009–2013, Stratigraphy and Architecture (Areas B, C, D, E)*. Edited by Yosef Garfinkel, Saar Ganor, Michael G. Hasel, and Martin G. Klingbeil. Jerusalem: Israel Exploration Society.

Keimer, Ludwig. 1927. "Flechtwerk aus Halfagras im alten und neuen Ägypten." *Orientalistische Literaturzeitung* 30:145–54.

Keinan, Adi. 2013. "Area J, Part II: Sub-Area Lower J." Pages 28–46 in vol. 1 of *Megiddo V: The 2004–2008 Seasons*. Edited by Israel Finkelstein, David Ussishkin, Eric H. Cline, Matthew J. Adams, Eran Arie, Norma Franklin, and Mario A. S. Martin. 3 vols. SMNIA 31. Winona Lake, IN: Eisenbrauns.

Kemp, Barry. 2000. "Soil (Including Mud-Brick Architecture)." Pages 78–103 in *Ancient Egyptian Materials and Technology*. Edited by Paul T. Nicholson and Ian Shaw. Cambridge: Cambridge University Press.

Khan, Geoffrey. 2013. *A Short Introduction to the Tiberian Masoretic Bible and Its Reading Tradition*. 2nd ed. Piscataway, NJ: Gorgias.

Killebrew, Ann E. 2004. "New Kingdom Egyptian-Style and Egyptian Pottery in Canaan: Implications for Egyptian Rule in Canaan During the 19th and Early 20th Dynasties." Pages 309–43 in *Egypt, Israel, and the Ancient Mediterranean World: Studies in Honor of Donald B. Redford*. Edited by Gary N. Knoppers and Antoine Hirsch. Leiden: Brill.

———. 2005. *Biblical Peoples and Ethnicity: An Archaeological Study of Egyptians, Canaanites, Philistines, and Early Israel, 1300–1100 B.C.E.* Atlanta, GA: Society of Biblical Literature.

King, Philip J., and Lawrence E. Stager. 2001. *Life in Biblical Israel.* Louisville, KY: Westminster John Knox.

Kletter, Raz. 1998. *Economic Keystones: The Weight System of the Kingdom of Judah.* Journal for the Study of the Old Testament Supplement 276. Sheffield: Sheffield University Press.

Koller, Aaron J. 2012. *The Semantic Field of Cutting Tools in Biblical Hebrew: The Interface of Philological, Semantic, and Archeological Evidence.* Catholic Biblical Quarterly Monograph Series 49. Washington, DC: Catholic Biblical Association of America.

Lambdin, Thomas O. 1953. "Egyptian Loan Words in the Old Testament." *JAOS* 73, no. 3:145–55.

Lambdin, Thomas O., and John Huehnergard. 2000. "The Historical Grammar of Classical Hebrew: An Outline." Unpublished manuscript.

Lane, Edward William. 1968. *An Arabic-English Lexicon.* 8 vols. London: William and Norgate, 1863–93. Repr., Beirut: Librairie du Liban.

Lang, Mabel L. 1990. *Ostraka: The Athenian Agora.* Results of the Excavations Conducted by the American School of Classical Studies 25. Princeton, NJ: American School of Classical Studies at Athens.

LaRocca-Pitts, Elizabeth. 2001. *"Of Wood and Stone": The Significance of Israelite Cultic Items in the Bible and Its Early Interpreters.* Harvard Semitic Monographs 61. Winona Lake, IN: Eisenbrauns.

Leach, Bridget, and John Tait. 2000. "Papyrus." Pages 227–53 in *Ancient Egyptian Materials and Technology.* Edited by Paul T. Nicholson and Ian Shaw. Cambridge: Cambridge University Press.

Lee, Lorna, and Stephen Quirke. 2000. "Painting Materials." Pages 104–20 in *Ancient Egyptian Materials and Technology.* Edited by Paul T. Nicholson and Ian Shaw. Cambridge: Cambridge University Press.

Lemaire, André. 1981. *Les écoles et la formation de la Bible dans l'ancien Israël.* OBO 39. Fribourg: Éditions Universitaires; Göttingen: Vandenhoeck & Ruprecht.

———. 1984. "Sagesse et écoles." *VT* 34, no. 3:270–81.

———. 1992. "Writing and Writing Materials." Pages 999–1008 in vol. 6 of *The Anchor Bible Dictionary.* Edited by David N. Freedman. 6 vols. New York: Doubleday.

———. 2001. "Schools and Literacy in Ancient Israel and Early Judaism." Pages 207–17 in *The Blackwell Companion to the Hebrew Bible.* Edited by Leo G. Perdue. Oxford: Blackwell.

———. 2015. "Levantine Literacy ca. 1000–750 BCE." Pages 11–45 in *Contextualizing Israel's Sacred Writings: Ancient Literacy, Orality, and Literary Production.* Edited by Brian B. Schmidt. Atlanta, GA: Society of Biblical Literature.

———. 2017. "Alphabetic Writing in the Mediterranean World: Transmission and Appropriation." Pages 103–15 in *Cultural Contact and Appropriation in the Axial-Age Mediterranean World.* Edited by Baruch Halpern and Kenneth S. Sacks. CHANE 86. Leiden: Brill.

Leslau, Wolf. 1958. *Ethiopic and South Arabic Contributions to the Hebrew Lexicon.* University of California Publications in Semitic Philology 20. Berkeley: University of California Press.

———. 1987. *Comparative Dictionary of Geʿez*. Wiesbaden: Harrassowitz.
Levine, Baruch A. 2000. *Numbers 21–36: A New Translation with Introduction and Commentary*. AB 4A. New York: Doubleday.
Levy, Jacob. 1867–68. *Chaldäisches Wörterbuch über die Targumim und einen Grossen Teil des rabbinischen Schrifttums*. 2 vols. Leipzig: Baumgartner.
Lewis, Naphtali. 1974. *Papyrus in Classical Antiquity*. Oxford: Clarendon.
Loprieno, Antonio. 1995. *Ancient Egyptian: A Linguistic Introduction*. Cambridge: Cambridge University Press.
Löw, Immanuel. 1967. *Die Flora der Juden*. 4 vols. Vienna: R. Löwit, 1924–34. Repr., Hildesheim: Olms.
Lucas, Alfred. 1962. *Ancient Egyptian Materials and Industries*. 4th ed. London: Arnold.
Lundbom, Jack R. 1999. *Jeremiah 1–20*. AB 21A. New York: Doubleday.
———. 2004a. *Jeremiah 21–36*. AB 21B. New York: Doubleday.
———. 2004b. *Jeremiah 37–52*. AB 21C. New York: Doubleday.
Machinist, Peter. 1983. "Assyria and Its Image in the First Isaiah." *JAOS* 103, no. 4:719–37.
Maeir, Aren M. 2002. "The Relations Between Egypt and the Southern Levant During the Late Iron Age: The Material Evidence from Egypt." *AeL* 12:235–46.
Mankowski, Paul V. 2000. *Akkadian Loanwords in Biblical Hebrew*. HSS 47. Winona Lake, IN: Eisenbrauns.
Manuelian, Peter der. 2000. "Furniture in Ancient Egypt." Pages 1623–34 in vol. 3 of *Civilizations of the Ancient Near East*. Edited by Jack M. Sasson. 4 vols. Farmington Hills, MI: Scribner's Sons, 1995. Repr., Peabody, MA: Hendrickson.
Maraqten, Mohammed. 1998. "Writing Materials in Pre-Islamic Arabia." *Journal of Semitic Studies* 43, no. 3:287–310.
Martin, Geoffrey Thorndike. 1971. *Egyptian Administrative and Private-Name Seals Principally of the Middle Kingdom and Second Intermediate Period*. Oxford: Griffith Institute.
Martin, Mario A. S. 2004. "Egyptian and Egyptianized Pottery in Late Bronze Age Canaan: Typology, Chronology, Ware Fabrics, and Manufacture Techniques: Pots and People?" *AeL* 14:265–84.
Masson, Emilia. 2007. "Greek and Semitic Languages: Early Contacts." Pages 733–37 in *A History of Ancient Greek: From the Beginnings to Late Antiquity*. Edited by A. F. Christidis. Cambridge: Cambridge University Press.
Mastnjak, Nathan. 2016. "Hebrew *ṭaḥaš* and the West Semitic Tent Tradition." *VT* 66:1–9.
Mazar, Amihai. 1992. *Archaeology of the Land of the Bible: 10,000–585 B.C.E.* New York: Doubleday.
Mazar, Benjamin, Michael Avi-Yonah, and Abraham Malamat, eds. 1958–61. *Views of the Biblical World*. 5 vols. Jerusalem: International.
McCarter, Peter K. 2008. "Paleographic Notes on the Tel Zayit Abecedary." Pages 45–59 in *Literate Culture and Tenth-Century Canaan: The Tel Zayit Abecedary in Context*. Edited by Ron Tappy and Peter K. McCarter. Winona Lake, IN: Eisenbrauns.
McDowell, Andrea G. 1996. "Student Exercises from Deir el-Medina: The Dates." Pages 601–8 in vol. 2 of *Studies in Honor of William Kelly Simpson*. Edited by Peter der Manuelian. 2 vols. Boston: Museum of Fine Arts.

———. 1999. *Village Life in Ancient Egypt: Laundry Lists and Love Songs*. New York: Oxford University Press.

———. 2000. "Teachers and Students at Deir el-Medina." Pages 217–33 in *Deir el-Medina in the Third Millenium AD: A Tribute to Jac. J. Janssen*. Edited by Robert Demarée and Arno Egberts. Leiden: Nederlands Instituut voor het Nabije Oosten.

McLean, Bradley H. 2002. *An Introduction to Greek Epigraphy of the Hellenistic and Roman Periods from Alexander the Great down to the Reign of Constantine (323 B.C.–A.D. 337)*. Ann Arbor: University of Michigan Press.

Meehl, Mark W., Trude Dothan, and Seymour Gitin. 2006. *Tel Miqne-Ekron Excavations, 1995–1996: Field INE East Slope, Iron Age I (Early Philistine Period)*. Tel Miqne-Ekron Final Field Report Series 8. Jerusalem: W. F. Albright Institute of Archaeological Research and Institute of Archaeology, Hebrew University of Jerusalem.

Mehra, V. R., and J. Voskuil. 1976. "Conservation and Analysis: Conservation of the Deir ʿAlla Inscription." Pages 18–21 in *Aramaic Texts from Deir ʿAlla*. Edited by J. Hoftijzer and G. van der Kooij. Leiden: Brill.

Meiggs, Russell, and David Lewis. 1988. *A Selection of Greek Historical Inscriptions to the End of the Fifth Century B.C.* Rev. ed. Oxford: Clarendon.

Merino, Luis Díez. 1982. *Targum de Salmos: Edición Príncipe del Ms. Villa-Amil n. 5 de Alfonso de Zamora*. Madrid: Consejo Superior de Investigaciones Cientificas, Instituto "Francisco Suárez".

Meshel, Ze'ev. 1978. "Kuntillet ʿAjrud: An Israelite Religious Center in Northern Sinai." *Expedition* 20:50–54.

Meshel, Ze'ev, and Avner Goren. 2012. "Architecture, Plan, and Phases." Pages 11–59 in *Kuntillet ʿAjrud (Ḥorvat Teman): An Iron Age II Religious Site on the Judah-Sinai Border*. Edited by Ze'ev Meshel and Liora Freud. Translated by John H. Tresman. Jerusalem: Israel Exploration Society.

Millard, Alan R. 1997. "Writing." Pages 1286–95 in vol. 4 of *The New International Dictionary of Old Testament Theology and Exegesis*. Edited by Willem A. VanGemeren. 5 vols. Grand Rapids, MI: Zondervan.

Miroschedji, Pierre de. 1997. "La glyptique palestinienne du Bronze Ancien." Pages 187–227 in *De Chypre à la Bactriane, les sceaux du Proche-Orient ancien: Actes du colloque international organisé au Musée du Louvre par le Service Culturel, le 18 Mars 1995*. Paris: Documentation Française.

Mitchell, T. C., and Ann Searight. 2008. *Catalogue of the Western Asiatic Seals in the British Museum: Stamp Seals III: Impressions of Stamp Seals on Cuneiform Tablets, Clay Bullae, and Jar Handles*. Leiden: Brill.

Moore, James D. 2011. "Writing Religion: A Comparative Study of Ancient Israelite Scribes, their Writing Materials and their Methods Used in the Writing of the Hebrew Prophecies." MA thesis, Brandeis University.

Moorey, Peter R. S. 1999. *Ancient Mesopotamian Materials and Industries: The Archaeological Evidence*. Oxford: Clarendon, 1994. Repr., Winona Lake, IN: Eisenbrauns.

Morag, Shelomo. 1971. "המסורת הטברנית של לשון המקרא: הומוגניות והטרוגניות." *Pəraqîm* 2:104–55.

———. 1972. Review of Max Wagner, *Die Lexicalischen und Grammatikalischen Aramaismen im Alttestamentlichen Hebräisch. JAOS* 92, no. 2:298–300.

Morgan, Teresa. 1998. *Literate Education in the Hellenistic and Roman Worlds*. Cambridge Classical Studies. Cambridge: Cambridge University Press.

Mosk, J. A. 1976. "Analysis of the Ink." Pages 21–22 in *Aramaic Texts from Deir 'Alla*. Edited by Jacob Hoftijzer and Gerrit van der Kooij. Leiden: Brill.

Muchiki, Yoshiyuki. 1999. *Egyptian Proper Names and Loanwords in North-West Semitic*. Society of Biblical Literature Dissertation Series 173. Atlanta, GA: Society of Biblical Literature.

Mullins, Robert A. 2006. "A Corpus of Eighteenth Dynasty Egyptian-Style Pottery from Tel Beth-Shean." Pages 247–62 in vol. 1 of *"I Will Speak the Riddles of Ancient Times": Archaeological and Historical Studies in Honor of Amihai Mazar on the Occasion of His Sixtieth Birthday*. Edited by Aren M. Maeir and Pierre de Miroschedji. 2 vols. Winona Lake, IN: Eisenbrauns.

Mumford, Gregory D. 2014. "Egypt and the Levant." Pages 69–89 in *The Oxford Handbook of the Archaeology of the Levant*. Edited by Margreet L. Steiner and Ann E. Killebrew. Oxford: Oxford University Press.

Muraoka, Takamitsu. 2009. *A Greek-English Lexicon of the Septuagint*. Leuven: Peeters.

———. 2010. *A Greek-Hebrew/Aramaic Two-Way Index to the Septuagint*. Leuven: Peeters.

Na'aman, Nadav. 2011. "A New Appraisal of the Silver Amulets from Ketef Hinnom." *IEJ* 61, no. 2:184–95.

———. 2015. "Literacy in the Negev in the Late Monarchical Period." Pages 47–70 in *Contextualizing Israel's Sacred Writings: Ancient Literacy, Orality, and Literary Production*. Edited by Brian B. Schmidt. Atlanta, GA: Society of Biblical Literature.

Najjar, Mohammed. 1999. "'Ammonite' Monumental Architecture." Pages 103–12 in *Ancient Ammon*. Edited by Burton MacDonald and Randall W. Younker. Studies in the History and Culture of the Ancient Near East 17. Leiden: Brill.

Naveh, Joseph. 1970. "The Scripts in Palestine and Transjordan in the Iron Age." Pages 277–83 in *Near Eastern Archaeology in the Twentieth Century: Essays in Honor of Nelson Glueck*. Edited by James A. Sanders. Garden City, NY: Doubleday.

———. 1987. *Early History of the Alphabet: An Introduction to West Semitic Epigraphy and Palaeography*. 2nd ed. Jerusalem: Magnes.

———. 2009. "Semitic Epigraphy and the Antiquity of the Greek Alphabet." *Kadmos* 30 (1991): 143–52. Repr. pages 105*–14* in *Studies in West-Semitic Epigraphy: Selected Papers*. Jerusalem: Magnes.

Nemet-Nejat, Karen Rhea. 1993. "A Mirror Belonging to the Lady of Uruk." Pages 163–69 in *The Tablet and The Scroll: Near Eastern Studies in Honor of William W Hallo*. Edited by Mark E. Cohen, Daniel C. Snell, and David B. Weisberg. Bethesda, MD: CDL.

Neufeld, Ephraim. 1951. *The Hittite Laws*. London: Luzac.

Nicholson, Paul T., and Ian Shaw, eds. 2000. *Ancient Egyptian Materials and Technology*. Cambridge: Cambridge University Press.

Niditch, Susan. 1996. *Oral World and Written Word: Ancient Israelite Literature*. Louisville, KY: Westminster John Knox.

Noonan, Benjamin J. 2012. "Hide or Hue? Defining Hebrew *taḥaš*." *Biblica* 93, no. 4: 580–89.

———. 2019. *Non-Semitic Loanwords in the Hebrew Bible: A Lexicon of Language Contact*. Linguistic Studies in Ancient West Semitic 14. University Park, PA: Eisenbrauns.

Ornan, Tallay, and Laura A. Peri. 2017. "Cylinder Seals." Pages 475–513 in *Hazor VII: The 1990–2012 Excavations: The Bronze Age*. Edited by Amnon Ben-Tor, Sharon Zuckerman, Shlomit Bechar, Débora Sandhaus, and Tzipi Kuper-Blau. Jerusalem: Israel Exploration Society and Institute of Archaeology, Hebrew University of Jerusalem.

Panitz-Cohen, Nava. 2014. "The Southern Levant (Cisjordan) During the Late Bronze Age." Pages 541–60 in *The Oxford Handbook of the Archaeology of the Levant*. Edited by Margreet L. Steiner and Ann E. Killebrew. Oxford: Oxford University Press.

Payton, Robert. 1991. "The Ulu Burun Writing-Board Set." *AnSt* 41:99–106.

Pearce, Laurie E. 2000. "The Scribes and Scholars of Ancient Mesopotamia." Pages 2265–78 in vol. 4 of *Civilizations of the Ancient Near East*. Edited by Jack M. Sasson. 4 vols. Peabody, MA: Hendrickson, 1995. Repr., Peabody, MA: Hendrickson.

Pechuro, Alexander. 2013. "Area M, Part II: An Architectural Study of Chamber F." Pages 215–27 in vol. 1 of *Megiddo V: The 2004–2008 Seasons*. Edited by Israel Finkelstein, David Ussishkin, Eric H. Cline, Matthew J. Adams, Eran Arie, Norma Franklin, and Mario A. S. Martin. 3 vols. SMNIA 31. Winona Lake, IN: Eisenbrauns.

Peri, Arina-Laura. 2010. "Minor Artifacts from a Major Abode: Preliminary Notes on the Mitannian Common-Style Cylinder Seals from Area H at Hazor, with a Special Emphasis on their Archaeological Context." Pages 525–26 in *Islamic Session. Poster Session*. Vol. 3 of *Proceedings of the 6th International Congress on the Archaeology of the Ancient Near East, May 5th–10th 2009, "Sapienza"–Università di Roma: The Ceremonial Precinct of Canaanite Hazor*. Edited by Paolo Matthiae, Frances Pinnock, Lorenzo Nigro, and Nicholò Marchetti. Wiesbaden: Harrassowitz.

Piacentini, Patrizia. 2001. "Scribes." Pages 187–92 in vol. 3 of *Oxford Encyclopedia of Ancient Egypt*. Edited by D. B. Redford. 3 vols. Oxford: Oxford University Press.

———. 2002. *Les premières dynasties: Les nécropoles memphites*. Vol. 1 of *Les scribes dans la société égyptienne de l'Ancien Empire*. Études et mémoires d'Égyptologie 5. Paris: Cybele.

Petrie, William M. Flinders. 1896. *Six Temples at Thebes, 1896*. London: Quaritch.

Pittman, Holly. 2018. "Administrative Role of Seal Imagery in the Early Bronze Age: Mesopotamian and Iranian Traders on the Plateau." Pages 13–35 in *Seals and Sealing in the Ancient World: Case Studies from the Near East, Egypt, the Aegean, and South Asia*. Edited by Marta Ameri, Sarah Kielt Costello, Gregg M. Jamison, and Sarah Jarmer Scott. Cambridge: Cambridge University Press.

Pope, Marvin H. 1965. *Job*. AB 15. New York: Doubleday.

Porten, Bezalel, J. Joel Farber, Cary J. Martin, Günther Vittmann, Leslie S. B. MacCoull, and Sarah Clackson. 2011. *The Elephantine Papyri in English: Three Millennia of Cross-Cultural Continuity and Change*. 2nd ed. Atlanta, GA: Society of Biblical Literature.

Posener, Georges. 1940. *Princes et pays d'Asie et de Nubie: Textes hiératiques sur des figurines d'envoûtement du Moyen Empire*. Brussels: Fondation égyptologique Reine Élisabeth.

Postgate, J. Nicholas. 1980. "Palm-Trees, Reeds and Rushes in Iraq, Ancient and Modern." Pages 99–109 in *L'Archéologie de l'Iraq du début de l'époque néolithique à 333 avant notre ère: Perspectives et limites de l'interprétation anthropologique des documents. Paris 13–15 Juin 1978*. Edited by Marie-Thérèse Barrelet. Colloques internationaux du Centre National de la Recherche Scientifique 580. Paris: Centre National de la Recherche Scientifique.

Prince, J. Dyneley. 1904. "The Code of Hammurabi." *American Journal of Theology* 8, no. 3:601–609.

Pritchard, James B. 1974. *The Ancient Near East in Pictures Relating to the Old Testament*. 2nd ed. Princeton, NJ: Princeton University Press.

Propp, William. 1990. "The Meaning of *Tāpel* in Ezekiel." *Zeitschrift für die alttestamentliche Wissenschaft* 102, no. 3:404–8.

———. 2006. *Exodus 19–40: A New Translation with Introduction and Commentary*. AB 2A. New York: Doubleday.

Quick, Laura. 2014. "Recent Research on Ancient Israelite Education: A Bibliographic Essay." *Currents in Biblical Research* 14, no. 1:9–33.

Rabin, Chaim. 1963. "Hittite Words in Hebrew." *Orientalia* 32:113–39.

Rahlfs, Alfred, and Robert Hanhart. 2006. *Septuaginta: Id est Vetus Testamentum Graece iuxta LXX Interpretes*. Stuttgart: Deutsche Bibelgesellschaft.

Redford, Donald B. 1992. *Egypt, Canaan, and Israel in Ancient Times*. Princeton, NJ: Princeton University Press.

———. 2000. "Ancient Egyptian Literature: An Overview." Pages 2223–41 in vol. 4 of *Civilizations of the Ancient Near East*. Edited by Jack M. Sasson. 4 vols. Peabody, MA: Hendrickson, 1995. Repr., Peabody, MA: Hendrickson.

Reed, William L., and Fred W. Winnett. 1963. "A Fragment of an Early Moabite Inscription from Kerak." *BASOR* 172:1–9.

Reich, Ronny. 1992. "Building Materials and Architectural Elements in Ancient Israel." Pages 1–16 in *The Architecture of Ancient Israel from the Prehistoric to the Persian Periods*. Edited by Aharon Kempinski and Ronny Reich. Jerusalem: Israel Exploration Society.

Reich, Ronny, Eli Shukron, and Omri Lernau. 2007. "Recent Discoveries in the City of David, Jerusalem." *IEJ* 57, no. 2:153–69.

Renz, Johannes, and Wolfgang Röllig. 1995–2003. *Handbuch der althebräischen Epigraphik*. 3 vols. Darmstadt: Wissenschaftliche Buchgesellschaft.

Richelle, Matthieu. 2016. "Elusive Scrolls: Could Any Hebrew Literature Have Been Written Prior to the Eighth Century BCE?" *VT* 66:1–39.

Richter, Sandra L. 2007. "The Place of the Name in Deuteronomy." *VT* 57, no. 3:342–66.

Rico, Christophe, and Claudia Attucci, eds. 2015. *Origins of the Alphabet: Proceedings of the First Polis Institute Interdisciplinary Conference*. Cambridge: Cambridge Scholars.

Rollston, Christopher A. 2006. "Scribal Education in Ancient Israel: The Old Epigraphic Evidence." *BASOR* 344:47–74.

———. 2008. "The Dating of the Early Royal Byblian Phoenician Inscriptions: A Response to Benjamin Sass." *Maarav* 15, no. 2:57–93.

———. 2010. *Writing and Literacy in the World of Ancient Israel: Epigraphic Evidence from the Iron Age*. Atlanta, GA: Society of Biblical Literature.

———. 2014. "The Iron Age Phoenician Script." Pages 72–99 in *"An Eye for Form": Epigraphic Essays in Honor of Frank Moore Cross*. Edited by Jo Ann Hackett and Walter E. Aufrecht. Winona Lake, IN: Eisenbrauns.

———. 2015. "Scribal Curriculum During the First Temple Period: Epigraphic Hebrew and Biblical Evidence." Pages 71–101 in *Contextualizing Israel's Sacred Writings:*

Ancient Literacy, Orality, and Literary Production. Edited by Brian B. Schmidt. Atlanta, GA: Society of Biblical Literature.

Roskop, Angela R. 2011. *The Wilderness Itineraries: Genre, Geography, and the Growth of Torah*. Winona, Lake, IN: Eisenbrauns.

Salters, Robin B. 2010. *A Critical and Exegetical Commentary on Lamentations*. International Critical Commentary 21A. London: T&T Clark.

Sanders, Seth. 2009. *The Invention of Hebrew*. Urbana, IL: University of Illinois Press.

Sass, Benjamin. 1988. *The Genesis of the Alphabet and Its Development in the Second Millennium B.C.E.* Ägypten und Altes Testament 13. Wiesbaden: Harrasowitz.

———. 1993. "The Pre-Exilic Hebrew Seals: Iconism vs. Aniconism." Pages 194–256 in *Studies in The Iconography of Northwest Semitic Inscribed Seals: Proceedings of a Symposium Held in Fribourg on April 17–20, 1991*. Edited by Banjaim Sass and Christoph Uehlinger. OBO 125. Fribourg: University Press; Göttingen: Vandenhoeck & Ruprecht.

———. 2005. *The Alphabet at the Turn of the Millennium: The West Semitic Alphabet ca. 1150–850 BCE. The Antiquity of the Arabian, Greek, and Phrygian Alphabets*. Tel Aviv: Journal of the Institute of Archaeology of Tel Aviv University Occasional Publications 4. Tel Aviv: Emery and Claire Yass Publications in Archaeology.

Sax, Margaret, J. McNabb, and Nigel D. Meeks. 1998. "Methods of Engraving Mesopotamian Cylinder Seals: Experimental Confirmation." *Archaeometry* 40, no. 1:1–21.

Sayce, Archibald H. 1881. "The Ancient Hebrew Inscription Discovered at the Pool of Siloam in Jerusalem." *Palestine Exploration Fund Quarterly Statement* 13:141–54.

Schmidt, Brian B., ed. 2015. *Contextualizing Israel's Sacred Writing: Ancient Literacy, Orality, and Literary Production*. Atlanta, GA: Society of Biblical Literature.

Schneider, Tammi J. 2014. "Mesopotamia (Assyrians and Babylonians) and the Levant." Pages 98–106 in *The Oxford Handbook of the Archaeology of the Levant*. Edited by Margreet L. Steiner and Ann E. Killebrew. Oxford: Oxford University Press.

Schniedewind, William M. 2004. *How the Bible Became a Book: The Textualization of Ancient Israel*. Cambridge: Cambridge University Press.

———. 2013. *A Social History of Hebrew: Its Origins Through the Rabbinic Period*. New Haven, CT: Yale University Press.

———. 2014. "Understanding Scribal Education in Ancient Israel: A View from Kuntillet ʿAjrud." *Maarav* 21, nos. 1–2:271–93.

———. 2017. "Education in Ancient Israel and Judah into the Persian Period." Pages 11–28 in *Second Temple Jewish Paideia in Context*. Edited by Jason M. Zurawski and Gabrielle Boccaccini. Beihefte zur Zeitschrift für die neutestamentliche Wissenschaft 228. Berlin: de Gruyter.

———. 2019. *The Finger of the Scribe: How Scribes Learned to Write the Bible*. New York: Oxford University Press.

Seevers, Boyd, and Rachel Korhonen. 2016. "Seals in Ancient Israel and the Near East: Their Manufacture, Use, and Apparent Paradox of Pagan Symbolism." *Near East Archaeological Society Bulletin* 61:1–17.

Shiloh, Yigal, and Aharon Horowitz. 1975. "Ashlar Quarries of the Iron Age in the Hill Country of Israel." *BASOR* 217:37–48.

Shimron, Aryeh E. 2004. "Studies in Pottery, Petrography, Geology, Environment, and Technology, Section I: Selected Plaster and Glassy Samples." Pages 2620–55 in vol. 5 of *The Renewed Archaeological Excavations at Lachish* (1973–1994). Edited by David Ussishkin. 5 vols. SMNIA 22. Tel Aviv: Emery and Claire Publications in Archeology of the Institute of Archaeology, Tel Aviv.

Smith, Stuart Tyson. 2018. "Middle and New Kingdom Sealing Practice in Egypt and Nubia: A Comparison." Pages 302–24 in *Seals and Sealing in the Ancient World: Case Studies from the Near East, Egypt, the Aegean, and South Asia*. Edited by Marta Ameri, Sarah Kielt Costello, Gregg M. Jamison, and Sarah Jarmer Scott. Cambridge: Cambridge University Press.

Sokoloff, Michael. 2002. *A Dictionary of Jewish Babylonian Aramaic of the Talmudic and Geonic Periods*. Baltimore: Johns Hopkins University Press; Ramat Gan: Bar Ilan University Press.

———. 2003. *A Dictionary of Jewish Palestinian Aramaic of the Byzantine Period*. 2nd ed. Ramat Gan: Bar Ilan University Press; Baltimore: Johns Hopkins University Press.

———. 2009. *A Syriac Lexicon: A Translation from the Latin, Correction, Expansion, and Update of C. Brockelmann's Lexicon Syriacum*. Winona Lake, IN: Eisenbrauns; Piscataway, NJ: Gorgias.

Sowada, Karin. 2009. *Egypt in the Eastern Mediterranean During the Old Kingdom: An Archaeological Perspective*. Fribourg: Academic; Göttingen: Vandenhoeck & Ruprecht.

Sparks, Rachael. 2004. "Canaan in Egypt: Archaeological Evidence for a Social Phenomenon." Pages 27–56 in *Egypt, the Aegean and the Near East, 1650–1150 BC*. Vol. 2 of *Invention and Innovation: The Social Context of Technological Change*. Edited by Janine Bourriau and J. Phillips. Oxford: Oxbow.

Sperber, Alexander, ed. 2004. *The Bible in Aramaic Based on Old Manuscripts and Printed Texts*. 3 vols. 3rd ed. Leiden: Brill.

Stager, Lawrence E. 1980. "The Rite of Child Sacrifice at Carthage." Pages 1–11 in *New Light on Ancient Carthage: Papers of a Symposium Sponsored by the Kelsey Museum of Archaeology, the University of Michigan, Marking the Fiftieth Anniversary of the Museum*. Edited by John G. Pedley. Ann Arbor: University of Michigan Press.

Stager, Lawrence E., J. David Schloen, Daniel M. Master, Michael D. Press, and Adam Aja. 2008. "The South Tell: The Grid 38 Excavation Area." Pages 251–98 in *Ashkelon 1: Introduction and Overview (1985–2006)*. Edited by Lawrence E. Stager, J. David Schloen, and Daniel M. Master. Winona Lake, IN: Eisenbrauns.

Stec, David M. 1994. *The Text of the Targum of Job: An Introduction and Critical Edition*. Arbeiten zur Geschichte des Antiken Judentums und des Urchristentums 20. Leiden: Brill.

Stein, Peter. 2005. "The Ancient South Arabian Minuscule Inscriptions on Wood: A New Genre of Pre-Islamic Epigraphy." *Jaarbericht van het vooraziatisch-egyptisch Genootschap "Ex Oriente Lux"* 39:181–91.

Steiner, Richard. 1987. "Lulav versus **lu/law*: A Note on the Conditioning of **aw > ū* in Hebrew and Aramaic." *JAOS* 107, no. 1:121–22.

Stol, Marten. 1980–83. "Leder(industrie)." Pages 527–43 in vol. 6 of *Reallexikon der Assyriologie und vorderasiatischen Archäologie*. Edited by Dietz Otto Edzard. Berlin: de Gruyter.

Symington, Dorit. 1991. "Late Bronze Age Writing-Boards and Their Uses: Textual Evidence for Anatolia and Syria." *AnSt* 41:111–23.

Tait, William J. 1988. "Rush and Reed: The Pens of Egyptian and Greek Scribes." Pages 477–81 in vol. 2 of *Proceedings of the XVIII International Congress of Papyrology, Athens, 25–31 May 1986*. Edited by Basil G. Mandilaras. 2 vols. Athens: Greek Papyrological Society.

Tawil, Hayim ben Yosef. 2009. *An Akkadian Lexical Companion for Biblical Hebrew: Etymological-Semantic and Idiomatic Equivalents with Supplement on Biblical Aramaic*. Jersey City, NJ: Ktav.

Taylor, Jonathan. 2011. "Tablets as Artefacts, Scribes as Artisans." Pages 5–31 in *The Oxford Handbook of Cuneiform Culture*. Edited by Karen Radner and Eleanor Robson. Oxford: Oxford University Press.

Teissier, Béatrice. 1984. *Ancient Near Eastern Cylinder Seals from the Marcopoli Collection*. Berkeley: University of California Press.

———. 1997. "Seals and Communication in Middle Bronze Age Palestine." Pages 229–38 in *De Chypre à la Bactriane, les sceaux du Proche-Orient Ancien. Actes du Colloque International Organisé au Musée du Louvre par le Service Culturel, le 18 Mars 1995*. Paris: La Documentation Française.

ter Haar Romeny, Bas, and Wido Th. van Peursen. 1972–2019. *The Old Testament in Syriac According to the Peshiṭta Version*. Leiden: Brill.

Thomas, Rosalind. 1992. *Literacy and Orality in Ancient Greece*. Cambridge: Cambridge University Press.

Thompson, Amanda. 2014. "Area C–Square Supervisors' Reports: The Stratigraphy of Squares FF8 and FF9." Pages 459–60 in *Khirbet Qeiyafa Vol. 2: Excavation Report 2009–2013, Stratigraphy and Architecture (Areas B, C, D, E)*. Edited by Yosef Garfinkel, Saar Ganor, Michael G. Hasel, and Martin G. Klingbeil. Jerusalem: Israel Society and Khirbet Qeiyafa Expedition.

Tov, Emanuel. 2004. *Scribal Practices and Approaches Reflected in the Texts Found in the Judean Desert*. Studies on the Texts of the Desert of Judah 54. Leiden: Brill.

———. 2012. *Textual Criticism of the Hebrew Bible*. 3rd ed. Minneapolis, MN: Fortress.

Tufnell, Olga. 1984. *Scarab Seals and Their Contribution to History in the Early Second Millennium B.C.* Vol. 2 of *Studies on Scarab Seals*. Warminster: Aris and Phillips.

Ussishkin, David. 1993. *The Village of Silwan: The Necropolis from the Period of the Judean Kingdom*. Jerusalem: Israel Exploration Society.

———. 2004a. "Area P: The Late Bronze Strata." Pages 188–214 in vol. 1 of *The Renewed Archaeological Excavations at Lachish (1973–1994)*. Edited by David Ussishkin. 5 vols. SMNIA 22. Tel Aviv: Emery and Claire Publications in Archeology of the Institute of Archaeology, Tel Aviv.

———. 2004b. "Area P: The Middle Bronze Age Palace." Pages 140–87 in vol. 1 of *The Renewed Archaeological Excavations at Lachish (1973–1994)*. Edited by David Ussishkin. 5 vols. SMNIA 22. Tel Aviv: Emery and Claire Publications in Archeology of the Institute of Archaeology, Tel Aviv.

van de Mieroop, Marc. 1987. *Crafts in the Early Isin Period: A Study of the Isin Craft Archive from the Reigns of Išbi-Erra and Šū-Ilīšu*. Orientalia Lovaniensia Analecta 24. Leuven: Orientaliste.

Vanderhooft, David S. 2017. "The Final Phase of the Common 'Proto-Semitic' Alphabet in the Southern Levant: A Rejoinder to Sass and Finkelstein." Pages 441–50 in *Rethinking Israel: Studies in the History and Archaeology of Ancient Israel in*

Honor of Israel Finkelstein. Edited by Oded Lipschits, Yuval Gadot, and Matthew J. Adams. Winona Lake, IN: Eisenbrauns.

van der Kooij, Gerrit. 1976a. "The Plaster and Other Materials Used." Pages 23–28 in *Aramaic Texts from Deir ʿAlla*. Edited by Jacob Hoftijzer and Gerrit van der Kooij. Leiden: Brill.

———. 1976b. "The Writing Instrument." Pages 31–41 in *Aramaic Texts from Deir ʿAlla*. Edited by Jacob Hoftijzer and Gerrit van der Kooij. Leiden: Brill.

———. 1986. "Early North-West Semitic Script Traditions: An Archeological Study of the Linear Alphabetic Scripts up to c. 500 B.C., Ink and Argillary." PhD diss., Rijksuniversiteit te Leiden.

van der Toorn, Karel. 2007. *Scribal Culture and the Making of the Hebrew Bible*. Cambridge, MA: Harvard University Press.

van Driel-Murray, Carol. 2000. "Leatherwork and Skin Productions." Pages 299–319 in *Ancient Egyptian Materials and Technology*. Edited by Paul T. Nicholson and Ian Shaw. Cambridge: Cambridge University Press.

van Egmond, W. S., and Wilfred H. van Soldt, eds. 2012. *Theory and Practice of Knowledge Transfer: Studies in School Education in the Ancient Near East and Beyond: Papers Read at a Symposium in Leiden, 17–19 December 2008*. Leiden: Nederlands Instituut voor het Nabije Oosten.

van Heel, Koenrad D., and Ben Haring, eds. 2003. *Writing in a Workman's Village: Scribal Practice in Ramesside Deir el-Medina*. Egyptologische Uitgaven 16. Leiden: Brill.

Vaughn, Andrew G. 1999. *Theology, History, and Archaeology in the Chronicler's Account of Hezekiah*. Atlanta, GA: Scholars Press.

Veldhuis, Niek. 1997. *Elementary Education at Nippur: The Lists of Trees and Wooden Objects*. Groningen: Styx.

Vernus, Pascal. 2002. "The Scripts of Ancient Egypt." Pages 45–63 in *A History of Writing*. Edited by Anne-Marie Christin. Paris: Flammarion.

Visicato, Giuseppe. 2000. *The Power and the Writing: The Early Scribes of Mesopotamia*. Bethesda, MD: CDL.

Vita, Juan-Pablo. 2015. *Canaanite Scribes in the Amarna Letters*. Alter Orient und Altes Testament 406. Münster: Ugarit-Verlag.

Waal, Willemijn. 2018. "On the 'Phoenician Letters': The Case for an Early Transmission of the Greek Alphabet from an Archaeological, Epigraphic, and Linguistic Perspective." *Aegean Studies* 1:83–125.

Wagner, Max. 1966. *Die lexicalischen und grammatikalischen Aramaismen im alttestamentlichen Hebräisch*. Beihefte zur Zeitschrift für die alttestamentliche Wissenschaft 96. Berlin: Töpelmann.

Ward, William A. 1974. "The Semitic Biconsonantal Root *sp* and the Common Origin of Egyptian *čwf* and Hebrew *sûp*: 'Marsh(-Plant).'" *VT* 24, no. 3:339–49.

———. 1978. *Pre-12th Dynasty Scarab Amulets*. Vol. 1 of *Studies on the Scarab Seals*. Warminster: Aris and Phillips.

Warnock, Peter, and Michael Pendleton. 1991. "The Wood of the Ulu Burun Diptych." *AnSt* 41:107–10.

Weber, Robert and Roger Gryson, ed. 2007. *Biblia Sacra Iuxta Vulgatam Versionem*. 5th ed. Stuttgart: Deutsche Bibelgesellschaft.

Wegner, Josef. 2018. "The Evolution of Ancient Egyptian Seals and Sealing Systems." Pages 229–57 in *Seals and Sealing in the Ancient World: Case Studies from the*

Near East, Egypt, the Aegean, and South Asia. Edited by Marta Ameri, Sarah Kielt Costello, Gregg M. Jamison, and Sarah Jarmer Scott. Cambridge: Cambridge University Press.

Wehr, Hans. 1976. *A Dictionary of Modern Written Arabic*. Edited and translated by J. Milton Cowan. 3rd ed. Ithaca, NY: Spoken Languages Services.

Wendrich, Willemina Z. 2000. "Basketry." Pages 254–67 in *Ancient Egyptian Materials and Technology*. Edited by Paul T. Nicholson and Ian Shaw. Cambridge: Cambridge University Press.

Wente, Edward. 2000. "The Scribes of Ancient Egypt." Pages 2211–21 in vol. 4 of *Civilizations of the Ancient Near East*. Edited by Jack M. Sasson. 4 vols. Farmington Hills, MI: Scribner's Sons, 1995. Repr., Peabody, MA: Hendrickson.

Wevers, John W., ed. 1974. *Genesis*. Septuaginta. Vetus Testamentum Graecum Auctoriatate Academie Scientiarum Gottingensis Editum 1. Göttingen: Vandenhoeck & Ruprecht.

Wevers, John W. and Udo Quast, ed. 1977. *Deuteronomium*. Septuaginta: Vetus Testamentum Graecum Auctoriatate Academie Scientiarum Gottingensis Editum 3, no. 2. Göttingen: Vandenhoeck & Ruprecht.

———. 1986. *Exodus*. Septuaginta: Vetus Testamentum Graecum Auctoriatate Academie Scientiarum Gottingensis Editum 2, no. 1. Göttingen: Vandenhoeck & Ruprecht.

———. 1991. *Leviticus*. Septuaginta: Vetus Testamentum Graecum Auctoriatate Academie Scientiarum Gottingensis Editum 2, no. 1. Göttingen: Vandenhoeck & Ruprecht.

Whisenant, Jessica. 2015. "Let the Stones Speak! Document Production by Iron Age West Semitic Scribal Institutions and the Question of Biblical Sources." Pages 133–60 in *Contextualizing Israel's Sacred Writings: Ancient Literacy, Orality, and Literary Production*. Edited by Brian B. Schmidt. Atlanta, GA: Society of Biblical Literature.

Whitt, William D. 2000. "The Story of the Semitic Alphabet." Pages 2379–97 in vol. 4 of *Civilizations of the Ancient Near East*. Edited by Jack M. Sasson. 4 vols. Farmington Hills, MI: Scribner's Sons, 1995. Repr., Peabody, MA: Hendrickson.

Wieringen, Archibald L. H. M. van 2011a. "*gillāyôn*." Online: http://www.otw-site.eu/en/kli-database/ (כלי Database: Utensils in the Hebrew Bible website).

———. 2011b. "*lûaḥ*." Pages 1–6. Accessed 15 May 2015. Online: http://www.otw-site.eu/en/kli-database/ (כלי Database: Utensils in the Hebrew Bible website).

Wiese, André B. 1996. *Die Anfänge der ägyptischen Stempelsiegel-Amulette: Eine typologische und religoinsgeschiechtliche Unteruchung zu den "Knopfsiegel" und verwandten Objekten der 6. bis frühen 12 Dynastie*. OBO 12. Series Archaeologica. Fribourg: Academic Press; Göttingen: Vandenhoeck & Ruprecht.

Wiggerman, Frans A. M. 1985–86. "The Staff of Ninšubura: Studies in Babylonian Demonology, II." *Jaarbericht van het Vooraziatisch-Egyptisch Gezelschap Ex Oriente Lux* 29:3–34.

Wilkinson, Toby. 2002. "Reality versus Ideology: The Evidence for 'Asiatics' in Predynastic and Early Dynastic Egypt." Pages 514–20 in *Egypt and the Levant: Interrelations from the 4th Through the Early 3d Millennium BCE*. Edited by Edwin C. M. van den Brink and Thomas E. Levy. London: Leicester University Press.

Wimmer, Stefan. 2008. *Palästinisches Hieratisch: Die Zahl und Sonderzeichen in der althebräischen Schrift*. Ägypten und Altes Testament 75. Wiesbaden: Harrasowitz.

Wiseman, Donald J. 1955. "Assyrian Writing-Boards." *Iraq* 17, no. 1:3–13.
Wright, George R. H. 1985. *Ancient Building in South Syria and Palestine*. 2 vols. Leiden: Brill.
Younger, John G. 2018. "Aegean Bronze Age Seal Stones and Finger Rings: Chronology and Functions." Pages 334–54 in *Seals and Sealing in the Ancient World: Case Studies from the Near East, Egypt, the Aegean, and South Asia*. Edited by Marta Ameri, Sarah Kielt Costello, Gregg M. Jamison, and Sarah Jarmer Scott. Cambridge: Cambridge University Press.
Ziegler, Joseph. 1939. *Isaias*. Septuaginta: Vetus Testamentum Graecum Auctoriatate Academie Scientiarum Gottingensis Editum 14. Göttingen: Vandenhoeck & Ruprecht.
———. 1943. *Duodecim prophetae*. Septuaginta: Vetus Testamentum Graecum Auctoriatate Academie Scientiarum Gottingensis Editum 13. Göttingen: Vandenhoeck & Ruprecht.
———. 1952. *Ezechiel*. Septuaginta: Vetus Testamentum Graecum Auctoriatate Academie Scientiarum Gottingensis Editum 12, no. 1. Göttingen: Vandenhoeck & Ruprecht.
———. 1957. *Ieremias, Baruch, Threni, Epistula Ieremiae*. Septuaginta: Vetus Testamentum Graecum Auctoriatate Academie Scientiarum Gottingensis Editum 15. Göttingen: Vandenhoeck & Ruprecht.
——— 1982. *Iob*. Septuaginta: Vetus Testamentum Graecum Auctoriatate Academie Scientiarum Gottingensis Editum 12, no. 1. Göttingen: Vandenhoeck & Ruprecht.
Zohary, Michael. 1982. *Plants of the Bible*. Cambridge: Cambridge University Press.

ANCIENT SOURCES INDEX

Hebrew Bible and Apocrypha

Genesis
- 1:10 25n29
- 1:11 119, 120n55
- 1:29 119
- 2:7 64
- 2:12 51
- 3:14 64
- 3:19 64
- 3:21 86, 87
- 6:14 119
- 9:21 99n32
- 11:3 69
- 13:16 64, 64n24
- 18:4 120
- 18:27 64
- 19:6 95, 96n24
- 21:14–15 86n3
- 21: 19 86n3
- 22:3 119
- 26:15 64
- 28:14 64n24
- 28:18 50n5, 51, 52
- 28:22 50n5, 51
- 31:13 50n5, 51
- 31:45 50n5
- 31:51–52 50n5
- 35:7 99n32
- 35:14 49, 50n5, 51
- 35:20 50n5, 51
- 37:29 143n28
- 38:18 116, 116n49, 155, 156, 157
- 38:25 155, 157
- 41:2 13, 13n9, 14
- 41:5 28, 29, 29n37
- 41:18 13, 14, 15
- 41:22 28, 29, 29n37
- 41:42 157, 158
- 49:24 51n7

Exodus
- 1:14 69
- 2:3 34, 35, 41, 42, 43
- 2:5 34, 35
- 4:2 116n49
- 4:4 116n49
- 4:8 23
- 4:17 116n49
- 4:20 116n49
- 7:9–10 116n49
- 7:12 116n49
- 7:15 116n49
- 7:17 116n49
- 7:19 23, 24, 25n28
- 7:19–20 116n49
- 8:1 23, 24, 25n28, 116n49
- 8:12–13 64n24, 116n49
- 9:23 116n49
- 10:13 116n49
- 10:19 35
- 12:14 98
- 13:18 35
- 14:16 116n49
- 15:3–4 35
- 15:4 35
- 15:16 51

Exodus (cont'd)
15:22 35
17:5 116n49
17:6 54, 56
17:9 116n49
20:25 49, 52, 152
22:26 87, 87n4
23:24 50n5
23:31 35
24:4 50n5, 52n8, 120n56
24:12 49, 102n36, 103n37, 109
25:5 119
25:12 158
25:14 157
25:31 29
25:31–33 28n35
25:35–36 28n35
26:14 86
26:24 158
27:8 105, 105n39, 109, 110
28:9 156
28:9–12 51, 125, 132n11, 152–53
28:11 51, 155, 156, 157
28:17 51
28:17–21 125, 153
28:21 51, 155, 157
28:23–28 158
28:26 157
28:36 50, 122, 123, 155, 157
28:36–38 116, 122, 123
30:13 154
30:23 27, 28
31:6 117
31:18 49, 102n36, 103n37, 109
32:4 133, 134
32:15 103, 109
32:15–16 102n36
32:19 102n36, 103
33:22 53
34:1 49, 102n36, 103, 103n37
34:4 49, 102n36, 103, 103n37
34:13 50n5
34:28–29 102n36
34:29 87, 103
35:22 157
36:19 86
36:29, 34 158
37:27 158
37:17–19 28n35
37:21–22 28n35
38:5 158
38:7 105, 105n39, 109, 110, 158
39:6 51, 155, 157
39:14 51, 155, 157
39:30 122, 123, 155, 157
39:30–31 122
39:34 86
40:42 52

Leviticus
6:21 113, 114
8:9 122, 122n60, 123
8:17 86, 87
11:33 113
13:4 86
13:53 86
14 64, 73, 75
14:4 119
14:5 113
14:33–54 57, 73–74, 78
14:36b–48 77
14:40 49
14:42–43 71, 77
14:43 77
14:48 71
14:50 113
15:12 113
17:13 64
18:6 99
19:36 51
24:11 116n49
26:1 49, 50n5
26:26 116n49

Numbers
5:17 113
6:5 143, 144
6:24–26 123
8:7 143
11:5 20n16
11:15 20, 22
14:25 35
17 118
17:16–26 116–18
17:17 120n56
17:17–18 116n49

17:23 122
18:2 120n56
19:5 86
19:69 64n24
20:8 54, 55
20:10–11 54
21:4 35
23:9 56n12
23:10 64
31:50 157
33:10 35
33:11 35

Deuteronomy
1:1 35
1:40 35
2:1 35
3:5 96n24
4:13 49, 102n36, 103n37
5:22 49, 102n36, 103n37
7:5 50n5
8:15 54
9:9–11 49, 102n36, 103n37
9:15 102n36, 103
9:17 102n36, 103
9:21 64n24
10:1 49, 103, 103n37
10:1–5 102n36
10:3 49, 10, 103n37
11:4 35
12:1–3 51
12:3 50n5, 51
16:22 50n5
19:5 119
21:12 130, 131
25:13 51, 154
27:1–3a 49–50
27:1–4, 8 79
27:1–12 49, 50, 51, 57, 79, 79n35, 80
27:2 78, 81
27:4 78, 81, 81n37
28:28 98n27
32:4 56
32:13 55
32:31 54

Joshua
2:10 35
4:3–9 49
4:20–21 49
4:23 35
6:26 96n24
7:6 64
8:30–35 49, 50, 79n35
8:34 91
10:1 130n9
10:2 130n9
10:18 49
15:6 49
15:48 130n9, 131n10
18:17 49
24:6 35
24:26–27 49

Judges
4:21 148
6:20–21 54
10:1 131n10
10:2 131n10
11:6 35
11:16 35
13:19 56
15:8 53, 55n10
19:22 95

1 Samuel
2:2 54, 56n13
2:27 99n32
3:15 95
6:14 119
14:27 116, 116n49, 118n50
14:43 116n49, 118n50
17:40 49, 152
17:51 143, 144
22:8 99
24:5–6 143n28

2 Samuel
2:31 148
7:17 98, 98n27
13:6 53
13:31 143n28
14:26 51n7
18:18 50, 52
20:8 143
21:19 119

2 Samuel (cont'd)
22:2–3 54
22:3 56n13
22:32 54, 56n13
22:43 66
22:47 54, 56n13
23:23 56n13

1 Kings
1:9 51
5:31 52
5:31–32 49
6:7 148
6:18 120
6:29 23
6:32 120, 122
6:35 120, 122
6:36 52
7:9 52, 53, 148
7:11–12 52
7:36 105, 105n39, 109, 110
8:9 49, 102n36, 103n37
9:16 162
9:26 35
10:11 152
11:40 162
13:3 143n28
13:5 143n28
14:15 27, 29
14:23 50n5
15:25–26 162
17:10 119, 120n55
18:5 20
18:33–34 120
19:11 54
21:8 155, 156, 157

2 Kings
1:8 86
3:2 50n5
3:16 18
5:23 133n13
6:6 119
7:23 99
10:26–27 50n5, 51
12:10 96n24
12:13 49
17:4 163
17:6 99
17:10 50n5
18:4 50n5
18:21 27, 28, 29
19:26 20n16, 22
22:6 49
23:14 50n5
23:28–37 163

1 Chronicles
2:3 148
5:10 102n36
22:2 52, 148
22:15 49
22:28 71
24:24 134n9
26:13 91
29:2 152
29:4 75, 77, 78

2 Chronicles
33:14 23
2:6 50
2:13 50
3:7 50
14:2 50n5
25:12 55n10
31:1 50n5

Ezra
2:1 99
6:2 90, 90n9, 92

Nehemiah
3:34 64
3:35 49
9:9 35
9:15 54
13:1 91

Esther
1:18 98
2:6 99n32
3:10 157, 158
3:12 157, 158
8:2 157
8:8 157, 158
8:10 157

Job
1:22 72, 78n34
2:8 113, 114
3:10 95n22
4:19 64n24, 69
4:22 66
5:6 64
6:6 71, 76, 77n33
7:5 87n4
8:11 13, 14, 15, 16, 41, 43, 60
8:11–12 21
8:12 15–16, 20, 20n16, 21, 22
8:17 51n7
9:25–26 16
9:26 16
10:9 69
13:4 72, 78
13:12 69
14:2 122
14:8 64n24
14:17 72, 78
14:18 54
17:6 72n31
17:16 64
18:4 56n12
18:13 87n4
19:23–24 54
19:24 54, 56, 124, 125, 125n2, 126, 128, 129
20:28 99
24:12 72, 78n34
27:16 69
28:2 64
29:6 56n12
30:19 69
31:22 28, 29, 29n37
33:6 69
33:16 99
38:8 95n22
38:10 95n22
38:14 69, 155, 157, 158
38:38 64n24
40:15 20n16
40:21 15, 16, 27, 28, 60
40:26 25, 26
40:31 86
41:6 95n22
41:7 155, 157
41:12 25, 26
41:20 51n7
41:22 66, 113, 114

Psalms
10:8 20n17
18:3 55n11, 56n13
18:3–4 54
18:32 56
18:43 66
19:15 56n13
22:16 64, 113, 114
22:30 64
23:4 120n56
31:3 54
31:4 56n11
37:2 20, 20n16, 21
40:3 62, 63, 66, 70, 83, 91n13
40:8 90n9, 91, 92, 92n14, 93n17
42:10 54, 56n11
45:2 29, 124, 126, 128, 129
52:4 143
68:31 27, 28
69:3 61n21, 62, 63, 83
69:15 66
71:3 54, 55n11
78:16 54
78:20 54
78:23 95n22
78:35 56n13
89:27 56n13
90:5 20n16, 22, 22n20
94:22 56n13
103:15 20n16, 122
104:14 20n16
105:16 116n49, 118n50
105:41 54
106:7 35
106:9 35
106:22 35
107:35 23, 24
110:2 116, 116n49
114:8 23, 24, 24n28
119:25 64n24
119:69 72, 78
129:6 20n16
136:13 35
136:15 35

Psalms (cont'd)
147:8 20n16, 22n21

Proverbs
3:3 105, 109, 110
7:3 105, 109
8:26 64n24
8:34 96n25
11:1 51, 154
11:13 99
11:30 120
16:24 91
18:2 99n32
20:19 99
26:23 113, 114
27:5 99n32
27:25 20, 20n16, 22, 99

Ecclesiastes
1:11 23
12:4 95n22

Song of Songs
4:14 28
2:14 54
8:9 95, 105, 105n39, 109, 110
8:6 155, 157

Isaiah
2:10 53
2:19 53, 64
2:21 53, 55
3:16–26 101, 102
3:18–23 101
3:21 157
3:22 133n13
3:23 97, 98, 98–99, 101, 115
5:6 130, 131, 131n10
6:13 50
7:20 143
7:23 130, 131, 131n10
7:24 130, 131n10
7:25 130, 131n10
8:1 97, 98, 98n30, 99, 100, 102, 115, 120n56, 133, 134, 135, 147
8:14 54
9:3 116n49
9:9 52
9:13 25, 26
9:17 130, 131
10:5 116n49
10:6 69, 70
10:10 56n13
10:15 116n49
10:17 131n10
10:24 116n49
10:26 116n49
14:5 116, 116n49, 118n50
14:23 23, 24
15:6 20, 20n16, 21
16:11 113, 114, 114n47
18:1–2 41
18:2 41, 42, 43
19:6 27, 28, 30, 34, 35
19:6–7 17–18
19:7 17
19:15 25, 26, 26n31
19:18 50n5
19:19 52
19:19–20 51
22:16 54
24:11 99
25:12 64n24
26:4 56n13
26:5 64n24
27:4 130, 131n10
28:1 122
28:27 116n49
29:4 64n24
29:16 68
30:8 105, 106, 106n40, 109, 110, 121
30:14 18, 19, 113, 114
30:29 56
30:32 116n49
32:2 54
32:13 130, 131n10
33:12 78, 80, 81
34:13 20n16, 21n19
35:7 20, 20n16, 21, 21n19, 23, 24, 25n28, 27, 41, 43
36:6 27
37:27 20n16, 22
40:6–7 21, 22n23, 122
40:6–8 20n16, 22n20
40:7 22n20
40:8 21
41:7 148
41:12 25

41:18 23, 24, 25n28
41:25 66, 67, 68
42:3 27
42:15 23, 24, 25n28
43:24 27, 28, 29, 29n37
44:4 20, 21, 22, 22n22
44:9–20 135
44:12 135, 148
44:13 135, 136, 136n15
44:18 71
45:9 68, 113, 114, 114n45
46:6 28, 29, 29n37
48:21 54, 56
51:1 54, 148
57:20 62, 66, 70, 84
58:5 25, 26
61:5 98n28
64:7 68, 69

Jeremiah
6:20 28, 29, 29n37
8:8 124, 126, 127, 128, 129, 137
10:4 148
10:11 90n8
13:19 99n32
13:23 86
14:3 18
14:4 98n28
17:1 54, 55, 105, 106, 109, 110, 124, 125, 126
128, 129, 130, 131, 147
17:18 98
18:4 68, 70
18:6 68
19:1 113, 114
22:24 155, 156, 157
23:13 72, 78n34
23:29 148
29:4 99
31:17 118n50
32:9–10 154
36 90, 92, 95, 126, 127, 137
36:2 90n9, 91, 92, 92n14, 93n16, 93n17
36:4 90n9, 91, 92n14, 92n16, 93n17
36:6 90n9, 91, 92n16
36:10 146
36:12 146
36:14 90n9, 91, 93n16, 93n17
36:18 136, 137
36:20–21 90n9, 91, 146
36:23 88n7, 90, 90n9, 91, 95, 96, 96n24
97, 115, 143, 143n28, 144, 146
36:25 91, 92n16
36:26 126, 146
36:27 91
36:27–29 90n9
36:28 91, 92n16
36:28–29 92
36:32 90n9, 92, 93n16
38:6 66, 67, 70
38:22 60, 61, 83
43 163
43:13 50n5, 51, 52n8
43:18 LXX 137
47:6 143, 144
48:17 116
48:31 113, 114, 114n47
48:36 113, 114, 114n47
49:10 99
49:16 53
49:21 35, 36
50:16 92n15
50:23 148
51:1–58 24
51:11 24
51:32 24, 24n27, 25n28
52:27 99

Lamentations
2:14 71, 76–77, 77n33
3:9 52
4:2 113

Ezekiel
2:9 90n9, 91, 92, 92n14, 93n17
2:9–3:3 92
3:1 93n17
3:1–3 90n9, 92
3:9 130, 131
4:16 116, 116n49, 118n50
5:1 143
5:16 116n49, 118n50, 118n50
7:10–11 116n49
7:11 116
9:2 142
9:2–3 139, 142
9:2–4 139

Ezekiel (cont'd)
9:11 139, 142
13:9–15 57, 75–76, 78
13:10 77n33
13:10–11 77, 78
13:10–12 71
13:11 71
13:12 71, 77
13:14–15 71, 77
13:15 77n33
14:13 116n49, 118n50
19:11–12 116n49
19:12 116
19:14
21:8–10 143
21:35 143, 144
22:28 71, 77, 77n33, 78
23:34 113, 114, 114n46
24:7–8 55n10
26:2 95n22
26:4 55n10
26:11 50n5, 52n8
26:14 55n10
27:5 105, 105n39, 109, 110
27:19 28
29:6 27
37 121
37:6 86
37:15–20 116, 119, 120, 120n56, 121, 122
39:23 99
40:3 28, 28n34
40:5–8 28n34
40:42 52
41:8 28n34
41:23, 24 96n24
42:16–19 28n34
47:11 15, 16, 18, 19, 60

Daniel
12:2 64

Hosea
3:4 50n5, 52n8
4:12 118n52, 120, 120n57
8:5 98, 98n27
10:1–2 50n5
10:5 99

Joel
3:1 98n27

Amos
2:1 78, 80, 81
3:7 99
4:6 98n27
5:11 52

Obadiah
3 53–54

Jonah
2:6 34, 35, 36

Micah
5:12 50n5
6:9 116n49
7:10 66

Nahum
2:8 99n32
3:14 66, 69, 70

Habakkuk
2:2 105, 106, 106n40, 109, 110, 121
2:11 119
3:9 116, 118n50
3:13 17n14
3:14 116n49

Zechariah
3:9 49, 50, 51
5:1 92, 93n16
5:1–2 90n9, 92
5:4 51, 119
7:12 130, 131
9:3 66
10:1 91
10:5 66, 67
12:4 98n27

1 Maccabees
8:22 97
14:18 97
14:26 97
14:48 97

3 Maccabees
4:20 29

Septuagint (LXX)
Exodus
36:13 51, 157
36:21 51, 157
36:37 157
36:37 122–23

1 Kings
6:1 52
7:21–22 109
7:46 53
7:48–49 52
20:8 157

Psalms
17:3 55n11
21:16 114
22:4 120n56
30:4 56n11
36:2 21
39:3 63, 70
39:8 92n14, 93n17
41:10 56n11
44:2 29, 128–29
68:3 63
70:3 55n11
89:5 22, 22n20
102:15 122
104:16 118n50
106:35 24
113:8 24
118:25 64n24
118:69 78
146:8 22n21

Jeremiah
27:16 92n15
28:32 24–25
29:6 144
30:15 36
31:31, 43 114
31:31 114n47
31:36 114n47
38:17 118n50
43 92
43:2, 4 92, 92n14, 93n17
43:2, 4, 6, 14, 32 93n16
43:4, 6, 25, 28 92n16
43:14 93n17
43:14, 20–21, 25, 27–29 92–93n16
43:18 137
43:23 92, 96, 96n24, 144
45:6 70
45:22 61
50:13 52n8

Dead Sea Scrolls
1QHodayot[a]
V, 21 64
X, 14 62
X, 15 66
XI, 19 95
XI, 33 62
XII, 24 71
XIV, 18 122
XV, 1 53
XV, 5 28, 60, 61
XVI, 6 119
XVI, 16 62
XVI, 23 53
XVI, 26 130
XVI, 34 28

1QPesher to Habakkuk
V, 1 53
VI, 15 102

1QRule of Benedictions (1QSb)
V, 27 66

1QWar Scroll (1QM)
XI, 10 30
XII, 3 133, 134

4QIsaiah[p] (pap4QIsa[p]) 93n18

4QSeptuagint Leviticus[b]
(4QpapLXXLev[b]) 93n18

4QSeptuagint Numbers
(4QLXXNum) 93n18

4QReworked Pentateuch[a] (4QBibPar = 4QRP[a])
7–8, 8 52

4QVision of Samuel (4QVisSam)
5, 1 63, 66

4QIsaiah Pesher[b] (4QpIsa[b])
I, 3 130

4QNahum Pesher (4QpNah)
5, 3 66

4QPsalms Pesher[a] (4QpPs[a])
1–10iv26 124

Catena A (4QCatena A = 4QMidrEschat[b]?)
1–4, 12 102

4QSapiental Work
1–2ii10 20
1–2ii10–11 22

4QHalakhah B
1, 4 90n10

4QDamascus Document[a] (4QD[a])
16a, 3 28

4QDamascus Document[e] (4QD[e])
6iv21 18

4QDamascus Document[f] (4QD[f])
2, 10 86
5i5 71

4QPurification Rules A (4QTohorot A)
3ii3 155
3ii10 113

4QPurification Rules B[a] (Tohorot B[a])
3 113

4QMysteries[a] (4QMyst[a])
65, 2 78

4QMysteries[b] (4QMyst[b])
1aii-b, 2 156

4QReworked Pentateuch[b] (4QRP[b])
20a–c, 2 30
26bii+e, 5, 8 102

4QReworked Pentateuch[c] (4QRP[c])
12biii13 155
12a-bii13; 13, 1 157

4Qapocryphon Pentateuch A (4QapocrPent A)
2, 5 50
10ii5 130

4Qapocryphon Joseph[b] (4QapocrJoseph[b])
12, 2 122

4Qapocryphon Pentateuch B (4QapocrPent B)
2ii8 53

4QNon-Canonical Psalms B
1, 4 23
24a+b, 7 53

4QParaphrase of Kings (4Qpap paraKings et al.)
25, 4 133, 134

4QSapiental Hymn
1ii8 15

4QWays of Righteousness[b]
8, 2 90

4QSapiental Text (Instruction- like Composition B)
1, 3 71

4Q491 4QWar Scroll[a] (4QM[a])
18, 5 30

4QFestivals Prayer[c] (4QpapPrFêtes[c])
1–2, 3 66

Unclassified Fragments
5Q20 1, 1 113n44

6QKings (6QpapKgs) 93n18

6QDaniel (6QpapDan) 93n18

4QSeptuagint Exodus (7QLXXExod) 93n18

11Q19 Temple Scroll[a] (11QT[a])
II, 6 50
III, 7 52
IX, 9 28
XIX, 14–15 116
XXVI, 8 86
XXXIV, 6 157
XXXVI, 11 95
XLVII, 17 86
XLIX, 8 113
L, 18 113
LI, 4 130
LI, 20 50
LII, 2 50
LXIII, 12 130
LXIV, 8 119

11Q21 Temple Scroll[c]? (11QT[c]?)
2, 2 28

CD Damascus Document (Cairo Geniza)
VI, 13 94–95
VIII, 12 71
X, 5 116
X, 10–12 19
X, 12 18, 53
XI, 9 71
XI, 19 119
XII, 16 64
XIX, 25 71

Unclassified Fragment
PAM 43.675 1, 2 50
PAM 43.686 37,1 155

Extra-Biblical Works

Ostraca
Arad letter 24 112
Lachish letter 4 96–97

Ben Sira
6, 3 119
6, 21 49
8, 3 119
14, 18 119
27, 6 119
32, 23 116
38, 5 119
40, 4 122
40, 15 53
41, 3 53
41, 5 72
42, 4 49
43, 15 49
43, 19 122
45, 6 116
45, 11 49
45, 12 122
45, 25 116
46, 5 49
48, 2 116
49, 13 95
50, 9 49
50, 10 119

Classical Works

Eusebius
Praep. ev. 10.5.4 97

Jerome
Epist. XXX.5 97

SUBJECT INDEX

Abusir Papyri, 11
Accordance Bible Software, 6
Akkadian, 1, 3, 14n10, 15, 16, 23, 23n25, 27, 32n43, 43, 49, 53n9, 60, 60n18, 61, 62, 64–69, 72, 73, 83, 85, 86, 89, 90, 94, 97, 102, 107, 118, 130, 164n3, 165, 168
Alalakh, 59
Alexandria, 57, 93
alphabet, 1, 3, 10, 165, 168
  cuneiform, 163–64n3
  Hebrew, 97, 146, 165, 165n6
  Old Phoenician, 165, 165n6
  origin of, 2n1, 165, 165n6
  Proto-Sinaitic, 165, 165n6
  Ugaritic, 163n3
  West Semitic, 10
altar(s), 46, 51, 52, 52n8, 54–55, 106, 125, 129, 131, 140, 143n28, 147
Amarna archive, 1, 163
Amman citadel inscription, 48n1, 97n26, 104–5
Ammon, 47, 48, 112
Amon, temple of, 10
Amos, book of, 80
Anatolia, 59, 101n34
Aphek, 1, 161, 163
Apollo Delphinios, temple of, 46
Aquila, 15, 16, 19, 22n20, 25n28, 29n37, 36, 36n46, 43, 52, 62, 70, 78, 78n34, 92, 100, 109, 114n47, 120n57, 128, 131, 131n10, 136, 142, 157
Arabic, 15, 16, 18, 19, 20, 24n27, 27, 51, 53, 60, 60n18, 61, 64, 66n26, 67, 68, 69, 71, 72, 72n31, 73, 78, 79, 86n3, 90n11, 98n28, 99–100, 102, 112, 112n43, 124, 130, 133n13, 135, 136, 136n15
Arad, 60n16, 111–12, 166
Aramaic, 13, 13n9, 19, 23, 23nn25–26, 31–32, 37, 43, 51, 53, 60, 61, 61n21, 72, 72nn30–31, 73, 78, 89–90, 94, 99, 102, 102n35, 115, 118, 128–30, 136, 140, 141nn25–26, 170
  Christian Palestinian, 60
  from Elephantine, 12
  Galilean, 94
  influence on Hebrew, 89–90
  Jewish, 78
  Old, 13n9, 51
  Palmyrene, 51
  script, 165n6
  seals, 151n37
  Targumic, 13n9
  from Wadi ed-Daliyeh, 12
archaeology, 5
Arslan Tash, 58
Ashkelon, 59n15, 155, 163
Assyria, 10, 111, 164
awls, 136

basalt, 46–48, 147
Beer Sheba, 55
Ben Sira, 5, 20, 49, 53, 72, 95, 116, 119, 122
Beth Shean, 81, 161–62

Beth Shemesh, 1, 119
bullae, 12, 127, 149, 151, 151n37, 158–59
Byblos, 10–11, 41, 160, 162n1

Canaan, 1–2, 111–12, 149, 151, 169–70
scarabs in, 161
Egyptian artifacts in, 161–62
Egyptian control of, 41, 160–68
Canaanite language, 41, 89, 155
Amarna, 31, 37
dialects, 1
lexemes and loanwords, 5, 14–15, 14n10, 31, 33–34, 41, 137–38, 141, 157, 166n9
Old, 111, 166
Carthage, 59
City of David, 12, 48n1, 127, 151
coffins, 7, 162
Copper Scrolls, 94n21, 123, 123n61
Coptic, 30, 30n41
covenant, tablets of the, 102–5, 103n38, 109
cuneiform, 1, 4, 103, 107, 163–64, 167–68

Dan, Tel, altar from, 54
Dead Sea Scrolls, 5, 12, 18, 18n15, 27, 28, 30, 49, 50, 52, 53, 62n22, 64, 66, 71, 86, 88, 90, 91, 93, 93n18, 94, 96, 102, 113, 116, 119, 122, 123n61, 133, 134, 139, 155, 157
Deir ʿAlla inscription, 33, 59, 80–82, 116, 127, 139
Deir el-Balah, 161
Deir el-Medina, 110, 111, 166, 168n12
Delta, 59
presence of Asiatics in, 161
as source of papyrus, 9, 35
dialect(s)
Aramaic, 23n25
Canaanite, 1
Egyptian, 40–41
Dialogue of a Man with His Ba, 11
diptych. *See* writing board
Djoser, 45
Dreros, 46

Edom, 80, 112
Egypt
awls, 136
contacts with Canaan/Israel, 2, 139, 149–51, 160–69
dynasties: First, 11, 136, 160; Third, 58; Fourth, 11, 87, 127, 128, 140, 141; Fifth, 11, 13, 128; Twelfth, 11, 87, 118n51; Eighteenth, 13, 58, 87, 107, 128, 144, 161; Nineteenth, 11, 87; Twentieth, 37, 161; Twenty-First, 10, 11; Twenty-Second, 162n1
periods: Predynastic, 57, 149, 160, 163, 169; Early Dynastic, 160; Old Kingdom, 11, 14, 17, 40, 85, 107, 139, 149, 155, 157, 160, 164, 166n9; First Intermediate, 161; Middle Kingdom, 11, 33, 136, 149, 161; Second Intermediate, 161; New Kingdom, 2, 8, 11, 13, 30, 33, 34, 107, 111, 138, 138n20, 141, 150, 161, 162n2, 164, 167, 168; Third Intermediate Period, 33, 162n1
influence on writing in Canaan and Israel, 3, 163–68
ink in, 138–39
palettes, 141–42
papyrus use in, 8–12
pens from, 126–28
plaster use in, 57–58
religion, 162
scribal knives, 144–45
scribes in, 13, 107, 128, 168n12
staves from, 118
tombs, 11, 13, 45, 57, 85, 118n51, 128, 142, 147, 160
writing case from, 140
writing system, 8, 165
Ekron, 48n1, 59n15
Elephantine, 12, 128
Ethiopic, 18, 67, 69, 72n31, 102, 119
Eusebius, 22n22, 97, 114, 114n47, 128, 131n10
Exodus, book of, 34, 36, 122, 153, 157

Fakhariyah, Tell, statue, 164
First Temple Period, 4, 89, 94, 165n6

Garshana archive, 11, 58, 58n14
Gaza, 121n59, 161
Gebelein, 11
Geʿez, 18, 49, 60n19, 66n26, 99, 130

Gezer, 1, 59n15, 111, 155, 163
Gezer calendar, 48n1, 54, 104, 125, 148
glyptics. *See* seals
Great Isaiah Scroll, 88–89
Greece/Greek, 4, 46, 59, 87n5, 111, 147, 150, 166n7
gypsum. *See* plaster

Hammurabi, code of, 45–46, 103n38
Hattusha, 59
Hazor, 1, 111, 163
Hebrew Bible, 1, 3, 6, 14n11, 20, 34, 60, 62n22, 71, 87, 113, 116, 157
Hebrew
  Biblical, 2, 5, 13, 14, 36, 66, 69, 73, 86, 99, 144, 169, 170
  Classical, 90n8
  Late, 63, 90n8, 91, 94, 115
  Mishnaic, 000
  Standard, 94, 115
  Rabbinic, 101
  Transitional, 90n8
Hebrew script, 2n1, 165, 165n6
Hezekiah, 47
hieratic
  inscriptions, 162
  numerals, 167
hieroglyphs, hieroglyphics, Egyptian, 45, 107n41, 162
Hittite language, 32n43, 112–13. *See also* Neo-Hittite
Hittite law tablets, 103–4
Hyksos, 161

Ibn Janah, 24n27
ink, 127n5, 136–37, 137n18, 138–42, 145, 163, 167–68
  inkwell, 142n27
  on ostraca, 2, 111–12, 166, 169
  on papyrus, 2, 12, 169
  and pen, 126–27, 127n5, 129, 134, 140, 142, 148, 166, 169
  on plaster, 3, 60n16, 81–82
  on scrolls, 127
  on stone, 48n2
inscriptions, monumental. *See* stone, inscriptions
Isaiah, book of, 36, 80, 105–6

Jaffa, 161
Jehoiakim, 90, 95–96, 156
Jeremiah, book of, 3, 61, 67, 89–90, 90n8, 91–92, 95, 105, 126, 131
Jeremiah (prophet), 163
Jeroboam, 162
Jerome, 26n31, 92, 97, 109, 131n10, 142
Jerusalem, 47–48, 95n22, 123, 140, 155, 162–63
  fall of, 111, 163
  seal impressions from, 151
  siege of, 89
  temple of, 24
Jewish texts, medieval, 136n15
Jonah, book of, 36
Josephus, 29n37
Joshua, 50, 79n5, 119
Judah, 54, 61, 76, 89, 90, 91, 99, 106, 113, 119–20, 121n59, 125, 129, 131, 146, 154, 156

Ketef Hinnom inscriptions, 94n21, 123, 125
Khaemhet, tomb of, 142
Khirbet Qeiyafa, 59n15
Khorsabad, 58, 107
Kidron Valley, 47
knife, scribal, 3, 95, 143–46
Knossos, 59
Kuntillet ʿAjrud inscriptions, 59, 59n15, 82, 82n38, 83, 127, 139

Lachish, 1, 11, 59n15
  letter 4, 96–97, 111, 139, 161, 166, 166n8
  ostraca, 139
Lake Huleh, 10, 167n11
Late Egyptian, 30n41, 33, 37, 40, 41
leather. *See* skins, animal
limestone, 48
  inscriptions, 46, 47–48, 47n1, 54–55, 104, 147
  flakes with writing, 111, 166
  plaster (quicklime), 50, 57–60, 59n15, 66, 78–80, 80n36, 81–84
  seals, 132, 151
  tablet, 104, 125
  weights, 154
literacy, 2, 146n30, 168n12

Mari, 58
Masada Scroll, 20
Masoretic Text, 7, 22n20, 42, 88, 89, 158
Mediterranean, ancient/eastern, 000
Megiddo, 1, 48, 59, 59n15, 142, 160–61, 163
Melos, 59
menorah, 28–29
Merneptah stela, 45, 164
Mesha stone, 46–47, 47n1, 164
Mesopotamia, 2, 4–5, 7, 10–11, 13, 27, 28n36, 45, 58–59, 85, 87, 95, 101n34, 102n34, 107, 110, 127–28, 132, 149, 150, 155
  influence on writing in Canaan and Israel, 163–68
  eye stones, 50n4
metal, 123–23. *See also* scrolls; writing boards
Miletus, 59
Milkom, 104
Minaic dialect, 121
mirrors, 101–2, 101n34, 115
Moabite inscripton, 47n1, 162n1
Mohs hardness scale, 48, 48n2, 131–32, 151, 153–54
Moses, 24, 34, 41, 49, 54, 79, 79n35, 86, 91, 103, 103n38, 109, 116, 117
mudbricks, 59, 59n15
Mycenae, 59

Narmer, 160
Neo-Hittite, 108
Neolithic Period, 112
Nile River, 9, 13, 13n8, 14, 17–18, 34, 35, 41, 44, 57
Nimrud, 96, 107
Northwest Semitic, 3, 31–32, 34n44, 37–38, 40, 65, 162, 162n2

Old Greek translation, 5–6
Old Phoenician script, 165
Old South Arabian, 52, 121, 121n59
Ophel, 47n1, 155
Origen, 29n37, 109, 128, 142, 157
Osorkon I, 162n1
ostraca, 2, 3, 89, 110–15, 125–27, 127n5, 129, 139, 162, 163, 166, 167, 169

palette(s), 38, 124, 127–28, 139–43, 145, 166, 167, 169
palimpsest, 12, 104
papyrus, 8–44
  conversion to writing material, 9
  evidence for use in ancient world, 11–13
  plant, 8–10, 13n8, 14–18, 26–30, 34–37, 41–43, 167n11. *See also* reed(s)
  terms for, 13–44
  use in Egypt, 8–10
  use outside of Egypt, 10–11
Papyrus Lansing, 38n47
parchment, 4, 99, 99n31, 100, 102, 134
pen(s), 3, 4, 11, 17, 29–30, 48, 54, 106, 124–29, 132, 134, 137–42, 145, 146n30, 148, 166–69
Persian Period, 4, 93
Peshitta, 5, 5n3, 6n3, 17, 18, 29, 61, 62, 77n32, 96, 101, 101n33, 129, 134, 136, 137, 142, 144
Philistia, 47, 112
Phoenician, 31–32, 37, 40n50, 51, 94, 97, 141n26, 151n37, 165n6
  alphabet, 165n6
  inscription, 111, 123
  script, 165, 165n6
plaster
  in Egypt, 57–58
  clay, 45, 57–60, 80, 81, 83
  gypsum, 39, 57–58, 60, 80–81, 80n36, 82n38, 83, 84
  in ancient Mediterranean, 59–60
  in Mesopotamia, 58–59
  mud. *See* plaster, clay
  quicklime, 50, 57–60, 59n15, 66, 78–80, 80n36, 81–84
  whitewash, 45, 57–60, 75–80, 83, 84
Pliny the Elder, 9
potsherds. *See* ostraca
pottery, 71, 83, 112–15, 126, 160–61, 163, 166n7, 167. *See also* ostraca
Predynastic Period, 57, 149, 160, 163, 169
Prophecy of Neferti, 11
Proverbs, book of, 105
Ptolemaic Period, 8, 11, 58, 83, 126

Qatna, 59
quicklime. *See* plaster

Qumran, 3, 88–89, 93–94, 94n21, 96, 97
Copper Scrolls from, 123n61
inkwells found at, 142n27
leather scrolls, 88

Rameses II, 87
Rameses III, 142
Red Sea, 36, 57
reed(s), 8–17, 20–30, 34–37, 41, 43–44, 62, 140, 166n9, 169. *See also* papyrus
religion
Egyptian, 162
Levantine, 51
rosette of gold, 122–23

Saadya Gaon, 136n15
Samaria, 47, 48, 48n1, 111, 120, 164
ostraca, 111, 166
weights, 154–55
sarcophagi, 147
Saul, 144n28
scarabs, 149–51, 161. *See also* seals, scarab
scribal instruments. *See* relevant entries
scribes, 2, 7, 170, 121n59, 126, 135, 137, 143, 146–48, 163, 167, 170
Egyptian, 13, 107, 128
Mesopotamian, 87, 108, 128
Syrian, 142
training, 146–47
scrolls, 89–90, 94, 94n21, 99, 101n33, 115, 126, 169. *See also* Qumran
copper, 123n61
leather, 87, 87n5, 88, 90, 90n11, 94, 139
metal, 94n21
papyrus, 11, 13, 42, 90, 90n11, 93, 94
"Sea of Reeds," 30, 35
Sea of Galilee, 10, 167n11
seals, 149–52, 155–59. *See also* bullae, signet rings
cylinder, 149, 150, 155, 156, 159
on jar handles, 151, 151n36, 152, 158
scarab, 149–51, 161
stamp, 66n26, 149, 156, 158, 159, 166
seal impressions, 149, 151, 158–59
Sefire I, stele of, 13n9
Semitics, comparative, 5, 67
Shechem, 1, 59n15, 60n16
Sheshonq I, 162, 162n1
signet rings, 150, 151, 155–59, 166, 169
Siloam inscription, 47, 47n1, 54
skins (animal), 85–89. *See also* vellum
Slavic, 73n31
Solomon, 162
South Arabia, 118, 121, 121n59
Southwest Palace of Nineveh, 13, 108
staffs, 38, 39, 116–18, 120n56, 156, 169
as writing surface, 116–18, 120–22
staves, as writing surface, 116–18, 120n54
stela(e), 47–51, 53, 54, 56, 81, 104, 142, 147, 148, 159, 162, 162n1, 163–64, 169. *See also* stone inscriptions
stone
inscriptions, 45–47, 147–48
precious, 148–56, 159
as monumental writing surface, 45–56, 79, 79n35, 147–48, 167, 169. *See also* limestone, flakes
Story of Two Brothers, 11
stylus, 4, 11, 100, 124n1, 133n12, 134, 135n14
Sukkôt, 31
Symmachus, 15, 16, 22n20, 22n22, 24, 25n28, 29n37, 36, 42, 43, 52, 62, 70, 77, 78, 78n34, 92, 100, 109–10, 114, 114n47, 120n57, 128, 131, 157
Syria-Palestine. *See* Canaan, Israel, Levant
Syriac, 20, 20n18, 27, 30, 64, 79, 98, 102, 130, 133
Peshitta, 101, 101n33
Syro-Hexapla, 6, 15, 22n20, 22n21, 24n28, 29, 43, 52, 77, 77n33, 78, 78n34, 92, 109, 114n47, 120n57, 128, 137, 142

Taanach, 1, 163
tablets, 1, 4, 89, 97, 102–3, 115, 163
stone, 49, 102–6, 109–10, 127, 148. *See also* covenant
wooden, 105, 109–10, 115, 169. *See also* writing boards
Targums, 5, 5n3, 129
Job, 129
Jonathan, 18, 23n26, 61, 62, 77n32, 78, 92n14, 26, 101n33, 129, 131, 135, 136, 137, 142, 144

Onkelos, 92n14, 101, 120n56, 134
Psalms, 92n14, 129
Tel Dan stele, 46, 47n1
Tell el-Far'ah (South), 161
Thebes, 10, 41, 45, 59, 107, 118, 164
Theodotion, 15, 16, 22n20, 22n22, 24n31, 29n37, 36, 42, 62, 70, 78n34, 92, 100, 109–10, 114n47, 128, 131, 142, 157, 158
Theophrastus, 42n52
Third Intermediate Period, 33, 162n2
Ti, tomb of, 13, 128
Til Barsib, 58
trade connections, 121n59, 160–61
Transjordan, 5, 47n1, 60, 80–83, 160, 162n1
Tell el-Dab'a, 59
Tell es-Sa'idiyeh, 161
Tell es-Shihab, 162
Tel Mor, 161
Tell Nebi Mend, 162
Tell Sakka, 59
Tel Sher'a, 161
Thebes, 59
Tyre, 162, 162n1

Ugarit, 4, 109, 163n3, 165
Ugaritic, 14n10, 27, 37, 49, 53, 64, 67–69, 71, 86, 89, 94, 100, 102, 116, 141n26, 143, 163n3

vellum, 85, 89, 115, 127, 169

Wadi ed-Daliyeh, 12
Wadi Murabba'at, 12
weights, 51, 56, 124, 125, 149, 152–55, 159, 162n2
Wenamun, Report of, 10–11, 41
wooden stick, as writing surface, 118–22, 120, 120nn56–57, 169
writing boards, 97, 105–9
in Egypt, 107
Etruscan, 107–8
ivory, 96, 107–8, 126
metal, 97, 102, 105, 109–10
in ancient Near East, 106–9
origin of tradition, 164–65
Uluburun, 96, 107
wax-covered, 106–7, 106n40, 109–10, 165
wooden, 13, 96–97, 105–8, 106n40, 109–10, 115, 165
writing surfaces. *See* metal; ostraca; papyrus; plaster; scrolls; skins; stone; tablets; wooden sticks; writing boards
writing system
alphabetic, 1, 10, 164n3, 168
cuneiform, 164, 164n3, 168
Egyptian, 8, 165

Yemen, 121

Zincirli, 108, 142

CPSIA information can be obtained
at www.ICGtesting.com
Printed in the USA
BVHW030920211220
594984BV00015B/6

9 781646 020621